Astrofuturism

A cartoon by Charles Addams, 1946. Reprinted, by permission, from *The New Yorker 75th Anniversary Cartoon Collection*, ed. Bob Mankoff (New York: Pocket Books, 1999), 25.

Astrofuturism

Science, Race, and Visions of Utopia in Space

DE WITT DOUGLAS KILGORE

PENN

University of Pennsylvania Press
Philadelphia

10   9   8   7   6   5   4   3   2   1

Published by
University of Pennsylvania Press
Philadelphia, Pennsylvania 19104-4011

Library of Congress Cataloging-in-Publication Data

Kilgore, De Witt Douglas.
     Astrofuturism : science, race, and visions of utopia in space / De Witt Douglas Kilgore.
         p. cm.
     Includes bibliographical references (p.) and index.
     ISBN 0-8122-3719-6 (cloth : alk. paper)—ISBN 0-8122-1847-7 (pbk. : alk. paper)
     1. Science fiction, American—History and criticism. 2. Literature and science—United States.
3. Life on other planets in literature. 4. Space and time in literature. 5. Astronautics in literature.
6. Utopias in literature. 7. Future in literature. 8. Race in literature. I. Title.

PS374.S35K43 2003
813'.08762093299—dc21
                                                                                        2002043045

To the memory of Cecil Douglass Bell, my grandfather

Contents

I am captivated more by dreams of the future than by the history of the past.

—Thomas Jefferson

Dreams are not so different from deeds as some may think. All the deeds of men are only dreams at first. And in the end, their deeds dissolve into dreams.

—Theodor Herzl

Introduction:
The Wonderful Dream

I have a dream that one day this nation will rise up and live out the true meaning of its creed: "We hold these truths to be self-evident: that all men are created equal."

—Martin Luther King, Jr. (1963)

Dreams and Realities in the Space Age

This book is an investigation of the ideals and conflicts evident in America's dream of its future, as represented in the intellectual, aesthetic, scientific, and political tradition of astrofuturism. Devoted to breaking the limits placed on humanity by the surface of this planet, astrofuturism forecasts an escape from terrestrial history. Its roots lie in the nineteenth-century Euro-American preoccupation with imperial expansion and utopian speculation, which it recasts in the elsewhere and else*when* of outer space. Astrofuturism imagines the good or perfect society not simply spatially but in what might be called, to use Einstein's term, "spacetime." This speculative tradition has developed as a part of U.S. intellectual and popular culture since the Second World War. Not surprisingly, the future it imagines is an extension of the nation's expansion to continental and global power in the nineteenth and twentieth centuries. The idea of a space frontier serves contemporary America as the west served the nation in its past: it is the terrain onto which a manifest destiny is projected, a new frontier invalidating the 1893 closure of the western terrestrial frontier. But it is also the space of utopian desire. Astrofuturist speculation on space-based exploration, exploitation, and colonization is capacious enough to contain imperialist, capitalist ambitions and utopian, socialist hopes. Visions of an American conquest of space go hand in hand with thought experiments seeking some barely glimpsed alternative to the economic and po-litical problems that dominated the twentieth century. Astrofuturism posits the space frontier as a site of renewal, a place where we can resolve the domestic and global battles that have paralyzed our progress on earth. It thus mirrors and codifies the tensions that characterize America's dream of its future.

By astrofuturism, I mean the tradition of speculative fiction and science writing inaugurated by scientists and science popularizers during the space race of the 1950s. Although it draws upon a rich history of science-fiction, astro-futurism as a narrative genre is distinguished by its close connections to engineering projects funded by the government and the military. The first gen-eration of astrofuturist writers—including Wernher von Braun, Willy Ley, and Robert A. Heinlein—began as a band of science-fiction and rocket enthusiasts, backyard experimenters dreaming of the ideal spaces that they would conquer.[1] They were followed by successive generations that inherited their passion, if not their politics. Contemporary astrofuturists fall along a political spectrum that ranges from Jerry Pournelle on the right, offering readers a neocolonial, space-based Empire of Man that escapes the democratization of mid-twentieth-century America, to Vonda N. McIntyre and Kim Stanley Robinson on the left, whose struggles to articulate the conventions of imperial exploration with a left-egalitarian politics have resulted in genre-bending thought experiments.

Astrofuturist writing appears as both fiction and popular science. Its dra-matic conventions include: characters that embody the future of humanity; the historical, political, literary, and scientific knowledges that those characters represent; the environments they craft, explore, or occupy; and the machines/instruments they create, control, and deploy. These conventions are shared by the expository and fictional aspects of the intellectual tradition. In its fictive guise as a subgenre within hard science fiction, astrofuturism is as concerned with education as it is with entertainment.[2] It is a self-consciously didactic lit-erature unapologetically aiming to produce readers who understand the me-chanics of science and technology, are able to defend their rationale, and take pleasure in their dramatization in particular exotic contexts. Astrofuturist nov-els regularly include what Kim Stanley Robinson calls "expository lumps" im-parting the knowledge necessary to understand why and how the world of the future might differ from our present.[3] In their guise as science writers, astro-futurists often include miniature fictions illustrating lectures on rocketry, celes-tial mechanics, soil composition, terraformation techniques, and so on—concepts that might otherwise be too dry or complex for pleasurable consumption. The space-born societies that futurists imagine are not physical anomalies or satiric fantasies. They are not catalyzed by the romantic, scientifically uninformed speculations of a Lucian of Samosata or a Cyrano de Bergerac. Rather, they are grounded in the astronomy, mathematics, biology, and engineering that evolved from the terrestrial explorations of the nineteenth century. Advocating the benefits of new knowledge and new tools, astrofuturist narratives make that knowledge accessible, even familiar. They transform the expensive and complex machines and habitats of the space frontier into familiar tools and mundane, lived spaces. The science fiction and popular science from which the space future emerges are invitations to worlds (real and imagined) that are ordinarily inaccessible. Most importantly, the space future is presented not as an impossible Arcadia, but as a feasible movement into new territories that conform to established and predictable physical laws.

While I consider astrofuturism primarily an American phenomenon anchored by the nation's mid-century commitment to the space race, its roots and membership are international. Its early form emerged among the groups of amateur enthusiasts in Germany, Great Britain, and the United States who laid the groundwork for the rocket technology that became a dominant factor in international relations. Although many of those early experimenters were involved in the arms race prompted by Germany in the 1930s, their initial imperative was the seemingly impractical dream of the "conquest of space." This dream brought together groups of people separated by barriers of language, nation, and political difference. It brought some of their number a form of American absolution for their wartime links to the Nazi party. It influenced and justified American global ambitions for a few crucial decades in the cold war era. And it gave many Americans a new faith in a national destiny at a time when the popular culture was awash with nostalgic images of the lost western frontier of dime novels and Buffalo Bill's Wild West show.[4] The future imagined by the scientists and writers who built and promoted the space program offered an endless frontier that would redeem the past and transform the present.

The astrofuturists I follow are distinguished by the ease with which they move between prosaic and expositive accounts of their singular objective: spaceflight. That objective demands a progressive, evolutionist account of physical reality and social history; correspondingly, the political hopes fostered by astrofuturism are classically liberal in orientation. The futures proposed under its banner generally advocate individual freedom, equality, and rationality as primary social and political goods. The space frontier represents for astrofuturists the landscape in which the human condition can improve. From this perspective, the existing order, which limits human activity and aspiration to the Earth, is a conservatism that cannot help but preserve the status quo. Although it is possible to reduce the work of any particular author to his or her political affiliations, their faith in the political and environmental potential of the space frontier links them as astrofuturists and distinguishes them from the resolutely earthbound concerns of their non-astrofuturist political allies.

However disparate their political agendas, all astrofuturists are unreconciled to the moment of their production, the world as it exists now. Their futures can be treated, according to Peggy Deamer's characterization of utopian thought, as "not a guide to the future but a protest of the present."[5] Whether their dis-ease is caused by irritation with the welfare state (Pournelle), discontent with what architectural critics and urban sociologists call "the malling of America" (O'Neill), exasperation with the limits-to-growth thesis (Bova), a rejection of the direction and methods of late capitalism (Robinson), or a desire to intervene against institutional arrangements around race and gender (McIntyre), their political and technical solution to discontent is the human expansion into space. This prospect provides astrofuturism's fundamental rationale and shapes its character as an expression of contemporary American thought. Whatever the particular political persuasion of a futurist, astrofuturist fictions inevitably present new societies that result from advances in knowledge most readily evident in technoscientific achievements. Indeed, advances in science and technology are the catalysts that prompt social and political experimentation. This characteristic alerts us to the genre's affiliation with the technological utopianism that Howard Segal identifies as a persistent feature of American thought.[6]

As a reflection on the legacy of American imperialism and utopianism, astrofuturism provides a window into the way we construe the relationship between scientific knowledge, the uses of technology, the entertainments we find attractive, and the political arrangements we proclaim desirable. Astrofuturism is speculation about the progress and final aims of technological and political power. It calls for the creation of technosciences, which will perfect humanity's control over itself and the natural world. This impulse has produced a strand of futurist thought that seeks an eternal extension of contemporary political and economic arrangements, albeit stripped of unpleasant resonances and rendered innocent. However, astrofuturism also carries within it an idealism, a liberal or utopian commitment that seeks alternatives and solutions to the problems and conflicts characterizing contemporary American life. It can imagine space frontiers predicated on experimental arrangements and the production of relationships uncommon or unknown in the old world. Astrofuturist speculation is deeply implicated in debates on race, class, and gender: inequities and conflicts thought to represent the chief impediments to the perfection of demo-cratic society. The astrofuturist version of the good society is double-edged. It can, in the hands of Vonda N. McIntyre or Kim Stanley Robinson, challenge the hierarchies described by traditional definitions of difference, or it may, as with writers such as Heinlein and Pournelle, reinforce those hierarchies in the name of space-born technocratic elites. In all instances, the intellectual tradi-tion described by astrofuturism insists that moving beyond the Earth's physical envelope will have a salutary effect on human development and prosperity.

Voyaging Around the Future

The study of astrofuturism as a social movement and a mode of literary expres-sion is necessarily the study of the culture of a science and its associated tech-nologies. The scientists, engineers, and writers examined here are public apologists for the value of science. They have been instrumental in conceiving the exploration of space, providing the public explication of the sciences and technologies involved, and arguing for the political, economic, even moral benefits of space expansion. Their work as writers, spaceflight lobbyists and, in some cases, media celebrities is an important conduit between professional sci-ence and the public; astrofuturism is, therefore, one of the ways in which sci-ence is done outside the fora of classrooms, laboratories, and corporations. In its practice, the connections between technoscience and the general culture are made visible.

This study is positioned against the conceit that science and technology have little to do with political, economic, or social issues. On the contrary, the professional activities of astrofuturists—science-fiction and popular science writing, participation in spaceflight advocacy and colonization groups, lectur-ing before general audiences at institutions such as the Massachusetts Institute of Technology (MIT) and the California Institute of Technology (Caltech), ap-pearing on radio shows and television, serving as screenwriters or science con-sultants for motion pictures, and editing science-fiction magazines—are all ways of doing science and making technology.[7] Such activities are made possi-ble by the material connections between the laboratory, the field, the instru-ment, the paper, and the culture, to say nothing of the material conditions of the participants' lives. Through them, science becomes visible to the public and achieves its effects on our culture. The popularization of science as fiction or exposition connects science with the public and scientists with each other. The futurism with which this project is concerned often represents the speculative, marginal, even unrespectable edges of mainstream science; it is here that science becomes glamorous. Here fields, ideas, machines, jargons, contents, and aims are introduced and made meaningful to those not privy to the daily conversations of practitioners. If nothing else, science-fiction and popular science authors respect the amateur status of their readers, and through imaginative mediation allow access to otherwise arcane knowledges and dialogues. Their transgeneric interventions help make the space future reasonable to the reader. In turn, the scientific message inevitably is influenced by the political, economic, and social concerns of its intended audience.

Astrofuturism's literary experiments are supported by a substantial social and political phenomenon, institutionalized in what William Sims Bainbridge has called the pro-space movement.[8] The German *Verein für Raumschiffarht* (Society for Space Travel), the American Interplanetary Society, and the British Interplanetary Society organized the efforts of science-fiction writers and early rocket pioneers as early as the 1920s and 1930s.[9] Since the Second World War, numerous other groups have been founded by scientists, engineers, and amateur enthusiasts, either in support of or to dissent from the national space program. A short list of these organizations includes Wernher von Braun's government- and-industry-oriented National Space Institute, founded in 1974; the L-5 Society, founded in 1975, and the Space Studies Institute, founded in 1977, both supporting Gerard K. O'Neill's space colony proposals; the Planetary Society, founded by Carl Sagan and Bruce Murray in 1980; and the Mars Society, organized in 1998 to promote aerospace engineer Robert Zubrin's plans for the exploration and colonization of Mars. Consisting primarily of academics, students, aerospace professionals, and interested amateur scientists, these organizations exhibit many of the characteristics of professional associations: annual conferences, papers, poster sessions, workshops, plenary sessions, book exhibits, Web sites, journals, newsletters, and so forth. Their primary purpose, however, is to function as citizens' advocacy groups, which represent and organize public opinion. In addition, they are conduits through which professional and amateur scientists, science-fiction and science writers, and other interested parties exchange information and opinions. These organizations, along with allied groups of science-fiction aficionados, constitute the web of relations that makes astrofuturism a movement of people who participate in an ongoing conversation based upon a shared intellectual and technical history.

For much of the twentieth century, scholars of rocketry and the spaceflight movement relied on the work of historians who recorded the development of missile technology and space science as it happened: Erik Bergaust, Eugene M. Emme, Frederick I. Ordway III, and Martin Caidin all served as journalists of the spaceflight movement and the space programs it fostered. However, their record is confined to descriptions celebrating great feats of engineering by the heroes of rocketry. At best, their work makes the spaceflight initiatives of the 1950s and 1960s legible within the complex technical and political histories of the west. They produced textbook examples of the mobilization narratives necessary to any large-scale social project. At worst, their accounts are limited to hagiographies of the founders of modern liquid-fueled rocketry. Their work must be seen as a complement to the astrofuturists's own efforts, rather than as independent scholarly review.

In recent years, several excellent studies have created that independent analysis. Walter A. McDougall's *". . . the Heavens and the Earth": A Political History of the Space Age* delineates the political terrain of the cold war space effort. Howard E. McCurdy's *Space and the American Imagination* critiques the effect of popular spaceflight tropes and their effect on government policy. Dale Carter's *The Final Frontier: The Rise and Fall of the American Rocket State* links the emergence of the "Rocket State" to the totalitarian and genocidal technical forms of Germany's Third Reich and traces a corresponding influence on American culture in the postwar era.[10] Although the rapid growth and vibrancy of this scholarly field suggests a ready audience, the intellectual and literary history of space futurism remains as yet unexplored. To date, scholars have not attempted detailed analysis of the narratives produced by the spaceflight movement, save as documents supplementing the primacy of its engineering project. For McDougall, science fiction is only a distant backdrop to the political drama of the space age; it is evidence of popular interest in the harnessing of space science to superpower conflict. McCurdy limits his insightful treatment of space-focused science fiction and science writing to their utility as NASA propaganda, measuring their success by government policies that fueled the space race, despite the availability of simpler and more economic means of accomplishing international goals. In Carter's study, the ideology that produced rocketry is emblematic of the "incipient totalitarianism" that led to the ovens of Nazi Germany.

In this scholarly constellation, the scientists and writers who make up my futurism are distant figures moved by odd impulses that seem inexplicable, opportunistic, or sinister. My approach is to bring these figures center stage and to ask sometimes difficult questions about the political solutions they propose in all sincerity as they pursue their goals. I am interested to discover what influential spaceflight advocates require of a national destiny. Hence, I examine the positively intended side of their ideology: the nature of their optimism and their desire for the future. The scientific romances of Kurd Lasswitz and H. G.

Wells, the Weimar futurism of Fritz Lang's *Die Frau im Mond*, the speculative scenarios produced by Wernher von Braun and Walt Disney in the 1950s, Arthur C. Clarke's ambivalent engagements with the British empire, Gerard K. O'Neill's "humanization of space" in the 1970s, Ben Bova's response to the issues raised by the antiwar and civil rights movements, and the revisionist fictions of McIntyre and Robinson in the 1990s all provide us with ample data to consider the multivalence of a discourse as it emerges from and responds to the moments of its production.

In the cultural studies of popular science, Constance Penley and Henry Jenkins have pioneered research on the uses of media-based science fictions.[11] While they attend to fans and I attend to writers, I share their insistence that in this area of cultural production, the line between producers and consumers is often porous. Astrofuturism roughly follows the communicative and interventionist model laid out for media fandom by Jenkins in *Textual Poachers: Media Fans and Participatory Culture*. Astrofuturist writers are both writers and readers of science fiction and popular science; the field is an interactive medium that sustains its effects through a continuous process of "poaching" and revision, call and response.[12]

For models of the study of the popular literature and culture of science, I turn to the work of cultural anthropologists Sharon Traweek and Emily Martin, and to the seminal essays of historian of science and cultural critic Donna J. Haraway.[13] These scholars meticulously uncover the historically specific web of relations that links machines and ideas, politics and people. I aim for a similar delineation of the milieu from whence came the literary ventures and prospace activism of my scientists, engineers, and writers. I maintain that science must engage familiar aesthetic conventions and legitimating narratives to make its knowledge attractive to the lay public. In the case of astrofuturism, this means noting the debt owed by the genre to utopian literature and boys' adventure literature, as well as attending to the political and economic benefits promised by space exploration. Hence, I engage an aesthetics of exploration and discovery formed long before the space race and chart its profound influence on the production, representation, and reception of subsequent physical and geographic knowledge.

Thematically, if astrofuturism is to be considered a school of thought that presents space exploration and colonization as viable alternatives to our terrestrial order, then it is fair to consider its relationship to the problems it hopes to solve. In the decades following the Second World War, the predominantly white and male ranks of astrofuturists confronted a great crisis for which race became the most potent signifier. In response to criticisms inspired by the civil rights movement and the new left, their space frontiers promised to extend the reach of the human species and to heal its historic wounds. The space future thereby carries both the imperatives of an imperial past and the democratic hopes of its erstwhile subjects. For my purposes, questions regarding racial justice serve to pry open the workings of the dramatic and expositive syntheses between people, machines, and landscapes; exploratory and colonization movements; ever expanding physical knowledge and technological power. Within the professions of science and engineering, racial markers have determined who studies and who must be studied, who designs and who labors. I take it as a given that the legitimating narratives of exploration, colonization, resource extraction, and utopian speculation are influenced by social practices and ideals of knowledge production and application. In the study of popular science and science fiction, however, and despite its ubiquitous influence, race is virtually an undiscovered country. Making due allowance for studies on the work of African American writers of science fiction—principally Samuel R. Delany and Octavia E. Butler—research on the political and social future of racialized beings in the genre has been sparse. To date, the only full-length studies that take up the issue have both emerged from scholarship on race, racism, and ethnicity in *Star Trek*.[14]

For the most part, the critical conversation on race-based inequities has been restricted to considering the issue as one of the social problems the genre leaves behind as a relic of a past that has been transcended. In their survey, for example, Scholes and Rabkin congratulate liberal science-fiction authors who point out the triviality of the differences magnified by racial stereotyping. They praise authors who go beyond liberalism to "render the matter of race comparatively unimportant."[15] They do not consider that a future responsible to our past may not be able to declare race irrelevant, but might have to imagine how to allow it to be lived differently. Nor do they consider that differently racialized beings may not wish to be declared irrelevant and assimilated into a singular human or posthuman norm.[16] Race plays a small role in the vast canvas Brian W. Aldiss undertakes in his history of science fiction *Trillion Year Spree*, entering significantly only as the biographical spice that makes Butler's address of racism and sexism satisfying.[17] Interestingly, Aldiss does not mention race in Delany's case, other than to note that Butler was his "protégé" (427). He chooses instead to emphasize the author's status as a major stylist and an important critic of the genre (291–93). Although he avoids reducing Delany's significance to the biological and political accidents of race, Aldiss's emphasis leaves open the question of how we should approach the thematization of race in Delany's fiction.[18] Finally, these studies do not address the overwhelming recurrence of racialized characters and reliance upon racial difference for plot devices in the narratives produced by white authors.

The first edition of Peter Nicholls's *The Science Fiction Encyclopedia* (1979) offers the most provocative early guide to the significance of race as a trope in science fiction. Under the heading "Politics," Nicholls remarks, "An interesting and not uncommon theme in mainstream political science fiction is racial prejudice and racial conflict, especially conflict between black and white."[19] The ensuing paragraphs describe books by authors whose connection to the genre is marginal. However, by grouping together science-fiction authors with mainstream black and white writers, Nicholls implies that the discourse of race is part of a shared repertoire of political signifiers. It is a collectively authored category necessary to thoughts or narratives about the future, even within those scenarios in which race plays no obvious role. The disappearance of race from any realistic political future would constitute a fantastic alienation from contemporary life, and would indicate something about the political desires and commitments of the author of such a scenario.

Science fiction and popular science have been produced and consumed primarily by Euro-American males; given the gender and racial barriers institutionalized around science and technology in the twentieth century, this demographic narrowness should not surprise us.[20] It is therefore easy to assume that somehow these genres are innocent of engagement with the problematics of either gender or race. Yet race and gender recur in astrofuturist novels as either threats or promises, never as something unremarkable or unremarked upon. When I discuss the ideal space pioneers created by a Robert A. Heinlein or a Jerry Pournelle—characters who are by and large white, male, and middle class—I engage a specific idealization of an identity peculiar to American culture. Since that idealization is based on a series of exclusions, it is as raced and gendered as the "Africanist" identity (to use Toni Morrison's term), which is among its primary foils.[21] While the technophilic, masculine, and white space future hero anchors astrofuturism's representation of the good or perfectible society, authors commonly appeal to a space frontier that is pioneered "for all mankind" and populated by a racially and ethnically diverse constituency of both sexes. Hence, characters who are companions to space-future heroes are central to my history and critique. Their ubiquity suggests that race, my dominant trope of alterity, should not be considered marginal to the astrofuturist project; rather, racial difference is a wellspring of its agenda. If the wonderful dream of the space frontier is the American dream writ large, then it is appropriate to ask the same questions of it that we have asked of its terrestrial counterpart.

Thus, I read astrofuturism as part of, rather than apart from, the political and social struggles that have marked the American landscape during this past half century. Through its renewal of the geographic tradition of imperialism and utopianism in an imagined and actual space frontier, astrofuturism extends the nineteenth-century notion that conquest and empire are the logical modus operandi of any progressive civilization. It thus represents twentieth-century American culture's attempts to deny the possibility of limits to its physical and metaphysical reach. But the genre also represents an extension of the desire to escape the logic of empire and find some space beyond the reach of old powers and obsolete identities. The hopeful rhetoric, which, in part, fueled European American expansion into the west (as well as Asian, African, and Latin American immigration to that continental frontier), finds its renewal in the twentieth-century reconstruction of frontier in the endless spaces that lie beyond terrestrial constraints.

Who Can Open the Doors?

In her 1997 study *Modest_Witness@Second_Millenium.FemaleMan_Meets_ OncoMouse*, Donna J. Haraway writes, "I will critically analyze, or 'deconstruct,' only that which I love and only that in which I am deeply implicated."[22] Among some contemporary historians and critics of culture, choosing to study material that has been important in one's own formation has become a necessary strategy. It serves, perhaps, the same function as the apologias of historians of previous generations who begged the reader's indulgence for their inability to present a complete account of their subject. However, declaring personal interest is not now done in a spirit of apology, but in recognition of the partial, incomplete, and always interested nature of any history or interpretation. Haraway's notion of vulnerability is a gesture toward responsible scholarship, not a disavowal of serious intellectual effort. The scholar, she implies, has a responsibility not to stand above her subject in an arrogant display of omniscience, but to engage it on its own ground.[23]

An instance of such a scholarly method is provided by *Textual Poachers*, Henry Jenkins's valuable study of media fandom. Jenkins emphasizes the importance of exploring a culture from within rather than from without. He acknowledges that it was not "academic curiosity" that led him into his course of study, but his "fannish enthusiasm" for the narratives and the communities within his subset of media culture (5). In other words, Jenkins's work is motivated by his desire to understand why media culture has the power to move him and so many others. His study, while "not overtly autobiographical . . . is nevertheless deeply personal" (5). As such, it enables him to stake out a dual position as both a scholar who brings a wealth of disciplinary training to his project and as a participant who has access to otherwise unavailable knowledges and understandings (6).

Haraway and Jenkins represent a cultural studies methodology that eschews condescending to popular culture or to the people who produce and consume it. Their approach is controversial, for the scholar who uses it is encouraged not to hide his own taste preferences or political commitments. The resulting scholarship has to drop the veil of scientific objectivity and account for its own investments. The scholar must leave the safety of a grand tradition and expose himself to often nasty debates about the kinds of questions a discipline asks, the ideas it considers valuable, and the people it deems worthy of attention. To be sure, this is not new. It is not history but nostalgia that assumes that politics and special pleadings have only recently become a part of the academic's stock in trade.

During the years I have worked on this study, I have often been asked a question that still catches me by surprise: Why do you work on science and science fiction? Behind this question lies a tangle of assumptions about the academy, its relation to popular culture, and my place within both. While answering, I find myself having to fight the increasingly boring canon war by declaring the importance of studying popular culture. I am also required to defend the right of African American scholars to range farther afield than our own backyards. Let me, however, restate this question in a more interesting way. Given my history, my multiple-subject positions within the United States as a Midwestern, middle-class, college-educated, African American male, what does it mean for me to be vulnerable to a genre produced primarily by and for affluent white men? And what light does that vulnerability shed on the intellectual and cultural trends I study?

In 1983, prompted by the imminent arrival of 1984, the *Village Voice* devoted a special issue to the future. Since the most fearful claims of the Orwellian vision have to do with the abuse of science and technology, most articles in this special issue attend to the problems raised by contemporary technoculture. The issue includes an essay by Thulani Davis, "The Future May Be Bleak, But It's Not Black," in which she examines the role of science fiction's fantastic narratives in shaping political expectations. Davis argues that science fiction and its futurism are expressions of an American popular culture dominated by the willful blindness of white racism. As an important discourse about the future, she argues, the genre has failed to imagine any that contain a complex, affirmative portrait of the black community. She points out that all too often the futures that "sci-fi" presents assume that African peoples are "missing and presumed extinct."[24] When they do appear, it is as isolated individuals, "affirmative action representatives," whose only function is to provide a liberal gloss on an otherwise white world:

They are usually men, and always folks with no family, old school buddies, hometowns, or Harlems. They do not play the dozens, probably for lack of someone to play them with. They talk like Richard Pryor does when he imitates a white man being asked for his driver's license by the police. They never have dates, or listen to James Brown or even Miles Davis . . . but then the music of the future is the worst anyway. They have good jobs and probably worked their way up through the system. But they have it hard. (18–19)

Davis is disturbed by the political logic of futurist narrative, not only because it guarantees the near invisibility of African peoples, but also because it does not expect blacks to have any influence over their own or human destiny. This logic is clearest in plots that assume that "blacks will either be freed by someone else or not survive" (17). Where, she asks, are futures that contain blacks who are part of communities and who are central to the management of their world? She concludes that such futures are not found in science fiction, the primary concern of which is to extend Anglo-American hegemony ad nauseam.

Even a superficial review of science fiction substantiates the basic tenor of Davis's view. As an expression of twentieth-century American culture, science fiction is marked by the racial logic of its surrounding society. Davis's analysis of the racial and gender aspects of futurist narrative in science fiction, however, is influenced by her self-declared status as an outsider to the genre. She is not unaware of that position, and even uses it to strengthen her argument: "I have always disliked sci-fi because in all its forms it seemed overwhelmingly adolescent, white, and male. For middle-class luxuries in my teens I preferred love stories, collecting records, buying makeup, and imagining myself as an adult in the world I knew. That hasn't changed much" (17). Because she is not vulnerable enough to the genre to have actually read much of it, Davis has little firsthand knowledge. Most of her anecdotes of the way African Americans are represented in science fiction are drawn from Hollywood movies and from fan informants. For Davis, the popular culture of the future is an alien, hostile, and "trivial" expression of someone else's culture (18).

Davis follows a tradition of cultural criticism that regards popular culture, particularly mass-produced culture, as detrimental to the best traditions of Western civilization. Her position is strikingly similar to that of pioneering

critics of modern popular culture such as F. R. Leavis, T. S. Eliot, George Orwell, Richard Hoggart, and Dwight Macdonald. These critics regarded the creation and extension of mass-produced culture in the twentieth century as a
threat to the high and folk cultures, which they believed represented the core of
civilization. Consequently, they recommended a cultivated contempt for the
commercially produced materials and narratives of popular culture, as well as
for its producers and consumers. The conservative elitist Eliot, the radical populist George Orwell, the social democrat Richard Hoggart, and the American
socialist Dwight Macdonald all found in American popular culture a common
foe.[25] Eliot and Leavis defended the high culture, which they believed to be the
best of the Western tradition. Hoggart and Orwell sought to preserve what they
thought was the "authentic" culture of the working class and the folk. And
Macdonald attacked the "spreading ooze" of middlebrow culture, which he regarded as the unfortunate legacy of the breakdown of the barrier between high
and folk art.[26] They all shared the presumption that mass culture represents a
corruption of otherwise pure cultural essences. For these critics, the mass-
produced materials of popular culture, which they recognized as the extension
of the communications and transportation technologies that matured in the
early twentieth century, posed a threat to the parts of the general culture that
they wished to defend.

There are marked differences between Davis's project and that of earlier
mass-culture critics. Her predecessors, whatever their political affiliation, were
repelled by the popular youth culture of the 1950s, which they considered "infantile" and "mindless."[27] During the 1960s and 1970s, however, the oppositional political culture of the young was also heavily mediated by commercial
forces. Coming of age in that context, Davis took popular products not as a
threat to the future, but as the tools with which she could make her future.[28] In
admitting that she consumed the "middle-class luxuries" of romances, records,
and makeup, Davis allows that she was formed by the forces that drove earlier
cultural critics to distraction. For her, being "an adult in the world I knew"
means a willing participation in the popular culture sustained by consumer
capitalism. It also means defending the value of African American cultural
expression in music and literature.[29] Unlike the mass-culture critics, therefore, she is not attacking popular culture; rather, she is ennobling one popular
subculture while dismissing another.

Despite these differences, Davis's project overlaps with that of the mass-
culture critics, because she shares their belief in authentic, original, and unas-
similated cultures and cultural differences. Davis's alienation from science
fiction makes it easy for her to condemn its futurism as inevitably hostile to the

cultural and political ambitions of African Americans. Regarding the genre as a simple projection of a racist and sexist culture, she would oppose it with another simple projection: a white future will be replaced by a black one. The solution that she proposes is predictable: the elevation, on the one hand, of a high black culture represented by writers and musicians such as Amiri Baraka and Sun Ra and, on the other, of an organically vibrant folk culture represented by the youth of "the South Bronx and the Lower East Side" (19). From these elements, she hopes, will arise representations that celebrate African American culture and identity. This strategy is, for Davis, the only antidote to the threat represented by the white futures of science fiction.

Although I am sympathetic to her aims, I suggest that Davis's analysis becomes a blunt instrument that does not allow her to consider legitimate African American cultural production within science fiction. Nor does it allow her to appreciate the complex role that race plays in the futurism of all science fiction. Consider the short passage she devotes to Samuel R. Delany, the prominent African American science-fiction writer and critic:

Samuel R. Delaney [sic], our premier sci-fi writer, takes the most complicated sci-fi voyages. For a long time he seemed to be the only published black sci-fi writer. . . . Delaney's people are black in fact, if not so much culturally. His utopias, if you want to call them that, allow for the same kinds of diversity you find in Piercy's. Gays are like blacks, tribal and free. But I found the folks in Babel-17 and Dhalgren something like the people in The Terrible Twos. . . . Living in the future seems to deprive black characters of the unmistakable "soul" that seems so obvious in the endless inventiveness among kids in the South Bronx or the Lower East Side. (19)[30]

"Unmistakable soul" distinguishes genuine black identity and culture. Delany is faulted for not respecting the boundaries between "black" and "white": his gays (presumably all white) are too much like his blacks, and his blacks simply are not black enough. Moreover, it is not only Delany's black characters who lack "soul"; Delany himself is soul-less—he is not black enough.

Davis raises questions that go to the heart of what is at stake in my study of astrofuturism as an intellectual discourse, a genre, and an industry. It does not matter whether she is correct in her assessment of science fiction and its corner of the popular-culture industry. She articulates the reasons behind the suspicion I (or Delany, for that matter) encounter from those who wonder why I am vulnerable to the futurism of popular science and science fiction, why I take pleasure from it as a fan, and why I pursue it as something worthy of serious study. For although Davis's knowledge of science fiction is limited, her assessment of its limitations is not entirely incorrect. Euro-American men have been the dominant, and certainly most visible players in the production of space futures. Wernher von Braun and Willy Ley brought the knowledge and practices of German futurism and engineering with them to the United States in the 1930s and 1940s. Robert A. Heinlein and Arthur C. Clarke produced fictions that worked the conquest of space into existing Anglo-American narratives of conquest and colonization. The popular science texts of Gerard K. O'Neill, Freeman Dyson, and Carl Sagan offered the exploration of space as an enterprise necessary to the intellectual and cultural survival of the human species. Politically and professionally, these men have been enfranchised to speak about and to the future on behalf of the rest of us. Is astrofuturism then a phenomenon that takes the temperature of a narrow ideological range, strictly limited by a "boys' own" sensibility? By speaking from their own particular position within white European and American culture, are these writers talking only to themselves, imagining an expansion of their privileges literally over and above the rest of us? It is only fair to ask what, if anything, is at stake in astrofuturism for those of us who are not included in the elite band of "universal" humanity. But using authorial characteristics to limit narrative meanings does not help explain why marginalized people have long been fans and consumers of science fiction and popular science. Nor does it allow us to consider why, despite obvious obstacles, they are becoming more visible as its producers.[31]

My intellectual and social history differs from those represented by Thulani Davis and the mass-culture critics who preceded her. From my point of view, science fiction is not an alien subculture. Nor is it intrinsically hostile to my interests, at least, no more than any other aspect of American culture. Moreover, I believe that the genre is more than, as Davis terms it, "an adventure we escape to," the venue for endless iterations of nationalist—whether Anglo- or African American—utopia (17). The genre has been an important part of my acculturation, for it gave me, when a child, a language of aspiration. As a result, it has been as important an influence in my life as the love stories that Davis cites in her own list of vulnerabilities. From that very particular and interested point of view, I believe that African Americans must participate in and contest those parts of American culture to which we are not supposed to belong. It is of critical importance to problematize the cultural essentialism, which would have us believe that some scholarly projects and aspects of the general culture are proper to black people and others are not. It is important to question why well-intentioned as well as contemptuous blacks and whites define blackness as a box into which we must crawl. Why is it not instead a metaphor for a powerful and transformative presence of alterity that both belongs in and questions every part of American culture, even and perhaps especially in those areas mistakenly thought to be free of race?

We are often hasty to dismiss the power of mainstream projects to move us. At its most constructive, this impulse allows us to attend to marginalized ventures. But while valorizing the avant-garde, we overlook the liberatory potential of less-than-revolutionary gestures: the importance of affiliations, career paths, and life choices offering skills and resources that are withheld from particular segments of our society as a matter of custom or law. The hurdles to a better future for members of disenfranchised groups are not simply a matter of test scores and "innate" abilities. They are also bound up in the dreams to which we have access, the promises they hold for the future, and the social orders that either block the dreamer or provide the resources necessary for the realization of her aspirations. The "conquest of space" and its promise of a bright future was a crucial component of the American dream in the mid-twentieth century, the period of Davis's and Delany's childhoods. Spaceflight was imagined as an open door to freedom for those brave and smart enough to step through it. Space itself was a new frontier offering opportunities denied or no longer available on earth. Hence, while the space program of the 1950s and 1960s was as segregated and antidemocratic as any other institution of American life, many white women, poor white men, and members of racial minorities dreamed of sharing in its ambitions and its rewards.

Consider the example of Homer H. Hickam, Jr., a writer and former NASA aerospace engineer. In 1998, Hickam published *Rocket Boys*, an autobiography recounting his late 1950s childhood in Coalwood, a town in the coal-mining counties of West Virginia. Early in the following year, *October Sky*, a film based on Hickam's book, was released to modest but enthusiastic success.[32] His memoir of that place and time is an effective portrait of a community living out the contradictions in our political economy. Coalwood is not Mayberry. It is a company town dedicated to "extracting the millions of tons of rich bituminous coal that lay beneath it."[33] The town mirrors a nation segregated along the lines of race and class and stabilized by gender inequities. Authority is structured hierarchically, with a handful of white businessmen atop a pyramid ordered by class, ethnicity, education, gender, and race. At issue is who labors and how that labor is organized. Hickam's memoir recounts the coming of age of a lower-middle-class child destined for the blue-collar work of the mines who instead became a NASA engineer. His story is the stuff of American dreams, and it coincides with the birth of the space age. As our young hero watches the first *Sputnik* move across the night sky of Coalwood, he sees himself as part of a larger world for the first time. The year is 1957; the cold war is hot.

Many feared that *Sputnik* extended the reach of Soviet power, for it represented the ability of the Soviet Union to span the distance between the Eastern Bloc and the free world of the West with decisive force. But Hickam is not interested in understanding the beginning of the space age as a political historian or public policy analyst. He is concerned with how this moment, defined by the presence and promise of liquid-fueled rocketry, influenced the lives and destinies of an ordinary group of people far removed from the centers of power. His emphasis uncovers the common motivations that made spaceflight so much a part of the intellectual and social landscapes of mid-century America that it had the power to restructure a community's sense of itself. Hickam's memoir gives pride of place to images and emotions of transcendence. Sonny's (Hickam's boyhood nickname) *Sputnik* is neither the emblem of John F. Kennedy's missile gap nor a symbol of Communist aggression. It is an open door, a way out, an ensign of hope. Representing as it does the dream of spaceflight, the satellite offers a material transcendence that can be achieved with the tools of this world.

Hickam's meticulous rendering of Coalwood society circa 1957 documents how struggles between classes generally are played out in a minor and nonrevolutionary key. He signals this with his opening words:

Until I began to build and launch rockets, I didn't know my hometown was at war with itself over its children and that my parents were locked in a kind of bloodless combat over how my brother and I would live our lives. . . . And I didn't know that the enthalpy decrease in a converging passage could be transformed into jet kinetic energy if a divergent passage was added. The other boys discovered their own truths when we built our rockets, but those were mine. (1)

His community's ambivalent response to end of its "industrial symphony" carried over into the education of its children. The ideals of a liberal public education have often been the chink in the armor of a system that tracks people into predetermined stations. Hickam's account makes it clear that given the expectations indicated by the distribution of resources in West Virginia, the under-resourced primary and secondary education available in McDowell County should not have produced an aerospace engineer, much less children with big dreams. The ordinary business of the Coalwood school system, to produce disciplined coal miners or sports stars, is made clear when Sonny and his three friends ask for a calculus class.[34] Their math teacher, Mr. Hartsfield, lays out the obstacles:

"This is Big Creek High School. Maybe if this was Welch High, the county superinten-
dent would approve such a class, but not here. We're a football and a coal miner's
school, and that's all we've ever been."
    We were outraged. "That's not fair!"
    Mr. Hartsfield looked up sharply. "Who ever told you boys life was fair?" he de-
manded. (257)

Despite such obstacles, Sonny finds many teachers willing to promise him
the benefits of education. Hickam recalls, "when I wasn't outside playing, I
spent hours happily reading. I loved to read, probably the result of the unique
education I received from the Coalwood School teachers known as the 'Great
Six,' a corruption of the phrase 'grades one through six.' . . . It seemed very important to these teachers that I read" (12). His great discovery as a reader occurs when he is allowed to use the junior high school library. There he finds
Jules Verne:

I fell in love with his books, filled as they were with not only great adventures but scientists and engineers who considered the acquisition of knowledge to be the greatest
pursuit of mankind. When I finished all the Verne books in the library, I became the first
in line for any book that arrived written by modern science-fiction writers such as Heinlein, Asimov, van Vogt, Clarke and Bradbury. I liked them all unless they branched out
into fantasy. I didn't care to read about heroes who could read minds or walk through
walls or do magic. The heroes I liked had courage and knew more real stuff than those
who opposed them. (13)

Sonny's imagination is fired by literary images of open, adventurous inquiry, in
a world structured by physics rather than custom or commerce. The key value
of the authors he cites lies in what they teach him about how the world works.
In addition to knowledge about the properties of the physical world, they provide the outlines of an ethical framework for action in the world. Sonny's use
of the school library lays the foundation for his aspirations. As a child, he does
not know that his dreams at once mirror national ideals and expose national
contradictions.
    Sonny knows that he cannot play football and he will not go down into the
mines, and so needs an exit from the narrow social and economic options available in Coalwood. And through him and the rest of the rocket boys, the dream
of spaceflight gives Coalwood a "non-productive," creative outlet other than
sports. The citizens who support the rocket boys' efforts to launch their home-
built, scale-model, solid ("rocket candy") and liquid-fueled ("zincoshine")
rockets find an outlet for their skills and aspirations, the value of which cannot
be limited to the demands of the mine. As a result, Coalwood, at the time of

Hickam's memoir a political and industrial backwater, grasps an opportunity to demonstrate that football players and coal are not the limits of its productive capacity. Both film and text celebrate the ordinary heroism of individual and collective refusals to accept the status quo. Ubiquitous acts of resistance, at times undertaken despite considerable personal risk or economic cost, indicate some of the very terrestrial stakes of Hickam's personal and professional involvement in spaceflight.

The title of Hickam's autobiography, *Rocket Boys,* tells us that Homer's childhood is set in an America organized around particular social and political segregations. There are no girls in the rocket boys' club. Blacks work, study, and even play with whites, but live and pray in another part of town. They are not considered part of the official Coalwood community.[35] The story that Hickam tells is of a life that begins constrained by race, gender, class, and a dying industry. It is important to recognize that the potential for change is located in a teenager's vision at a time when the social order was awakening to the dangers posed by youngsters who did not want to live the lives of their parents. The struggle over the children of Coalwood is a struggle about how the future might be lived. Unconstrained as they often are by the conventions that confine adult life, the liminal space that children inhabit can be used to question established routines and relationships. Their open futures encourage hope, which may find root even in the most unpromising soil. To understand this, we must take seriously moments when individual members of Coalwood's social order reach across the customary boundaries to help Sonny and his colleagues.

The initial and most significant support for the rocket boys' experiments comes not from the white men who direct the mine, the church, the government, and the schools. These men, whose numbers include Sonny's father, recognize the rocket boys' efforts only grudgingly, and generally only to condemn or forbid. The rocket boys find their most ardent champions in people far removed from the levers of power. Elsie Hickam, Sonny's mother, is the driving force behind her son's ambition; from her he inherits the vision and drive necessary to leave Coalwood. She is joined by the group of primary-school teachers that Coalwood calls the Great Six. Miss Frieda Riley, their science teacher, prompts the rocket boys to compete in science fairs and to develop the intellectual discipline essential to their project. The Reverend "Little" Richard and Junior, both African American men, provide spiritual guidance, strategic public support, and the material supplies necessary for the project.[36] And Messrs. Dubonnet and Bykovski, white union leader and immigrant European Jew, respectively, encourage Sonny's efforts as an alternative to life in the mines. Through their guidance, Sonny gains the strength and the wherewithal to pursue his goal of working with Dr. Wernher von Braun. And through Sonny's interactions with these people, the adult Hickam presents the political and social parameters of Coalwood.

In *Rocket Boys* and *October Sky*, spaceflight is a joint project undertaken by the entire community of Coalwood. In turn, the town and its people stand metonymically for the nation. The film emphasizes this connection in its penultimate sequence, in which the boys shoot off their final rocket. As it follows that rocket toward space, the camera moves from the crowd at the launch pad to other uplifted faces all over the town. The bedridden Miss Riley, the miners at the coal tipple, and the manager of the company store are shown looking up at the sky at the same moment, watching the rocket rise from the hills. The scene then cuts three decades forward to Cape Canaveral and a much bigger crowd watching a space-shuttle launch. The juxtaposition suggests that Hickam's dream has been fulfilled and the nation is drawn together by his great technological project.

People marginalized by Coalwood's structures dissent from the town's orthodoxies to help the boys not because they want to produce another engineer for von Braun's machine. They are not duped by a system larger than Coalwood. They are people who recognize the affinities and obligations that obtain even under regimes of rigid unfairness and ritual cruelty. They work with what they have and, in so doing, reject a present that has no outside and no end.

We should take seriously the liberal promise that some people saw in the technical project of space frontier: that through our joint efforts and very material means, we could make a better world. But there remains the problem of the relationship of this hope to everyday life. For most of the people of Coalwood, life did not change. Despite its symbolic inclusion in the success of the rocket boys, the community as a whole does not share in their eventual affluence and prominence. Instead, the town is sold off by its company, the mine is closed, and most of the townsfolk disperse. The rocket boys who are the hope of the community are not able to save it. Certainly Hickam's escape was purchased at a cost, borne by the people who are left behind while the individual ascends into an imperium of good fortune. Optimistic and critical readings of *Rocket Boys* are equally true. Since life is lived in that duality, it would be cynical to deny how creatively people make do with what they have, particularly as they rearticulate pedagogical narratives of the status quo into subversive vehicles of their utopian longings.

Paradoxically, even as it was disciplined by the political imperatives of the cold war, the spaceflight movement provided a cornucopia of subversive rhetorical tools. Nowhere is this paradox more apparent than in the first serious effort at televised science fiction, *Star Trek*. Grounded in popular fictions of Anglo-American expansion and dominance, *Star Trek* made room in that tradition for liberal political hopes.[37] Within the context of the cold war space race, *Star Trek* created a strategic and popular fantasy of pluralism contained by a meritocratic disciplinary order. In so doing, the series responded to the civil rights movement and the counterculture while maintaining a future that salvaged national institutions and priorities.[38] But growing up African American in the 1960s and 1970s meant watching for African and Asian faces on television and movie screens. A short list would include Keye Luke of *Kung Fu*; Eddie "Rochester" Anderson of the *Jack Benny Program*; Victor Sen Yung of *Bonanza*; Sammy Davis, Jr., putting in a guest appearance in the otherwise white *Wild Wild West*; Eartha Kitt, as "Catwoman" in *Batman*; Diahann Carroll of *Julia*; Sabu in the often replayed *Thief of Baghdad* (1940); Lloyd Haynes of *Room 222*; Bill Cosby of *The Bill Cosby Show* and *I-Spy*; and Clarence Williams III of the *Mod Squad*. However, George Takei and Nichelle Nichols, the actors who played in the first *Star Trek* series from 1966 through 1969, were something different. They were the future.

In 1997, I attended a performance at East West Players (EWP), the nation's oldest Asian American theater company, in Los Angeles. The moment was marked by the impending move of the EWP from its original, humble quarters to a new facility in Little Tokyo, a space signaling material, artistic, and political success. At that final performance in the old building, Filipino-American actor and comedian Alec Mapa paused during his one-man show, "I Remember Mapa," to acknowledge the presence of George Takei in the audience. As he excitedly waved and shouted, "Hi, Mr. Sulu," the predominantly, but not exclusively, Asian American audience burst into loud and long applause, while Takei grinned and looked mildly embarrassed. The obvious emotion of the audience and my own feelings catalyzed by the moment allow us to peer deeper into the web of associations that describe what is at stake in this project.

George Takei has built a solid reputation in Los Angeles as a politician, community activist, and writer. His visibility within the general American culture, however, is due to his work as a motion picture and television actor, particularly as the actor who created the character Lt. Hikaru Sulu on *Star Trek*. Takei was at ground zero of the attempt to liberalize the representation of racial minorities in theater, film, and television in the 1960s and 1970s.[39] He became part of Gene Roddenberry's then unique vision that racial minorities would be part of any American future in space. Roddenberry's original vision was radical for television not because he was willing to imagine nonwhites as more than second-class citizens in a future America; the gradualist political commonsense of the time was willing to allow for that distant future. The creator of this "Wagon Train to the Stars" was innovative because he was willing to represent racial minorities and women as key participants on the command deck of "man's" exploration of space in the here and now of network television.[40] Within the rigidly segregated expressive and visual cultures of the mid-1960s, his gesture was understood as pushing the envelope, a significant revision of dominant meanings of race and gender.

In "*Star Trek* in the 1960s: Liberal Humanism and the Production of Race," Daniel Bernardi argues that the show's token representations of people of color ultimately served to justify the continuing supremacy of whites. He notes that the most prominent minority characters on the show, Sulu and Uhura (the latter played by Nichelle Nichols), spent very little time on center stage in the first series. Moreover, their moments in the spotlight only underscored the political and narrative trouble occasioned by their presence.[41] In essence, the characters functioned only as tokens of integration underwriting a future that remained "dominantly white" (213). Bernardi's argument makes sense if we restrict our analysis to the written and visual evidence left by the show's producers. But Takei and Nichols were not simply passive puppets of Roddenberry's vision, meekly acting out the roles assigned to them. To read them thus is to rely on a top-down explanation for social change and artistic accomplishment that does not take into account the interventions of those whom we might consider the subjects of any orchestrated ideology.

To support his argument, Bernardi notes that Sulu was first conceived as a fully assimilated individual whose Asian ancestry would not disturb the assumption of a "Euro-American melting pot of humanity's future." Sulu is "white-identified" and culturally alienated from his background as a Japanese American (217). Bernardi uses Sulu's one moment of narrative centrality as the uninhibited swordsman of "The Naked Time" (which first aired 29 September 1966) to underscore the show's effacement of the character's particularity. But the story that Takei tells of that moment is quite different. He recounts that he had the opportunity to influence Sulu's representation when the scriptwriter for "The Naked Time" asked him if he was good at "samurai swordsmanship." Takei immediately responded:

Samurai sword fighting is too obvious. It's too ethnically consistent. Sulu is a multi-interested twenty-third-century man, and his sense of heritage should be much broader than just ethnic. His sense of his culture should be of the greater human heritage. I'm a twentieth-century Japanese-American, and although I saw samurai movies as a kid, I actually grew up with more swashbucklers and westerns. I think it'd be more interesting to see a fencing foil in Sulu's hand.[42]

Ever concerned with the way Asian Americans have been represented in film and television, Takei's first instinct was to break with obvious cultural stereotyping. In other words, conscious as he was of the racial politics that reduced the range of cultural references available to Asian artists, Takei intervened to break with viewer expectations of where Sulu must belong in the twenty-third century. In doing so, Takei emphasized a *Japanese American* identity formed by a wider range of reference than some transhistorical notion of medieval Japan. In such instances and in his performance, Takei not only played Sulu but also authored him.[43]

We in Mapa's audience applauded Takei not because we viewed him as the dupe of a white supremacist "conquest of space" dedicated to limiting his political options. We recognized him because he made the wonderful dream account for its promises through the fact of his enduring and creative presence. My applause was informed by the value of Takei's strategic interventions as a working actor and community activist. He has helped to resignify the meaning of race in popular media. Takei's own assessment of his life and career, *To the Stars: The Autobiography of George Takei, Star Trek's Mr. Sulu,* is at once a celebrity advertisement, an exploration of personal and public memory, and a serious meditation on the kinds of dreams that a member of a racial minority could have in the years following the Second World War. Starting his career as an actor in the late 1950s and 1960s, Takei found himself facing social prescriptions that had nothing to do with his talents and everything to do with the politics of race. By the time he was selected to play "Astrophysicist Sulu" in *Star Trek*'s second pilot, "Where No Man Has Gone Before," the actor understood quite well what it meant to make one's way through a discriminatory and often cruel profession.[44]

Takei begins his autobiography with his childhood memories of his family's relocation to and internment at the Rohwer Relocation Center in Arkansas (13). Young Takei began sensible life in the land of his birth as No. 12832–C, a subject of one of the most shameful home-front episodes of Second World War: the imprisonment of Japanese and Japanese American families, the expropriation of their property, and the administration of loyalty oaths, all without concrete evidence of wrong-doing or access to legal remedy. This beginning roots Takei's future in a calamity that was unavoidably political and personal. It was as a political prisoner in the camps at Rohwer, Alabama, and Tula Lake, California, that young Takei was confronted with the contradictions inherent in the practice of American ideals of freedom and justice for all.[45]

Takei's account balances the terrors and humiliations of internment with the protection provided by his parents' care and the childhood adventures offered by the strange, exotic locations of the camps. The behavior and actions of his parents during that time became Takei's moral foundation. Takekuma Norman Takei, his father, served as a block manager at both Rohwer and Tula Lake (27–28). The senior Takei's love for his family was coupled with a broad and active sympathy for his fellow internees. Fumiko Emily Nakamura Takei, George's mother, practiced a "fierce determination" to care for her family. She defied government restrictions on what she could retain of their personal property and renounced her American citizenship in an effort to keep the family together (24–26, 57).[46] These individuals exhibited the kind of necessary heroism that ordinary people all too often had to practice during the upheavals and trials of the twentieth century.[47] Takei's account makes clear that their example set high standards of private behavior and public action for their son.

Takei's experience allows us to furrow the apparent imperial and racist topsoil of astrofuturism in order to uncover why it might appeal to people of color and other disenfranchised peoples in contemporary culture. *To the Stars* argues that in performing Mr. Sulu, Takei always carried with him a sure sense of who he is, where he comes from, and to whom he owes his allegiance. And that sense of himself has meant a life dedicated to creating a better future in America with all the tools available to him. A record of his public service and activism includes work with the Los Angeles city council; a decade on the Board of Directors of the Southern California Rapid Transit District; cochairship of the EWP's New Theatre Campaign Committee, during which time the committee raised $1.6 million for EWP's move to Little Tokyo; chairmanship of the Japanese American National Museum; and continuing, unapologetic advocacy for increasing and appropriate minority representation in the television and film industries.[48]

Takei does not separate his political life from his work as an actor. During the years of his association with *Star Trek*, he worked hard to widen the range and weight of Sulu's presence in its fictional universe. His concern with the character derives both from his desire to enhance his career as an actor and from a feeling of responsibility for what the character represents as a symbol of political hope. In *To the Stars*, he discusses his campaign to force *Star Trek's* producers to promote Lt. Sulu from sidekick and second-banana to a captaincy. Takei undertook this campaign with a sense of mission that may seem, from the outside, out of proportion to its worth as a gesture. However, when in *Star Trek VI: The Undiscovered Country* (1991), *Captain* Sulu of the U.S.S *Excelsior* raised a cup of tea to his lips and sat back with an air of satisfaction, I understood the emotion that made several of my fellow audience members burst into applause. Takei's goal was not to prove that he or his character could compete in "a white man's world," but to create a future in which the politics described by that phrase no longer exist. The culmination of Takei's campaign was a powerful gesture of ownership, heralding a future that is held in common, not just one safe for Asian American starship skippers. As Captain Sulu, Takei recasts our conception of who owns narratives of our future, whose history will be represented there.

Takei's backstage maneuvering to grant Sulu his moment and the force of his brief gesture as captain of the Excelsior is informed by the history he recounts in *To the Stars*. As a chronicler of Japanese American reaction to white racism during the Second World War, Takei acknowledges radical, moderate, and "accommodationist" stances as legitimate responses to an intolerable situation that had to be endured. His esteem for his parents' decision to answer "no-no" to the Loyalty Test does not diminish his regard for those who answered "yes-yes" as "the substance of American citizenship—most vitally, freedom and justice—was torn away from us" (43). It would be easy to condemn the actions of those who answered "yes-yes" as a servile accommodation to "a country that had humiliated them, stripped them of property and dignity, and placed them behind barbed wire" (43). But such judgements, Takei might argue, are the luxury of those who have little to lose. Writing of the men who joined the American war effort, he writes, "But the young Japanese American GIs were fighting literally to get their moms out from behind American barbed wire fences. They were in combat to assert, under the most incredible of circumstances, their faith in the fundamental ideals of a country that had itself betrayed those ideals" (57). It is clear that Takei sees their "crazy trust" in their country's ideals as a kind of political heroism, the demonstration of a fidelity to democratic values. The feelings expressed here might be condemned as overly sentimental if the circumstances were not so tragic. In the Second World War, Japanese American soldiers stood roughly in the same position as African American soldiers and sailors, fighting a war on two fronts for a free and just nation that was neither.[49]

The lesson George Takei offers is directly applicable to my concerns. What he finds in the record of the Japanese Americans who served in the 442nd Regimental Combat Team (an all Asian American regiment) are the resources with which to redefine America and its dream: "In their determination . . . they jolted America into a reappraisal of their citizenship and the very notion of patriotism. . . . Through their heroism, these Japanese American GIs revitalized the ideals of this country and brought added dimension to the definition of American citizenship" (57–58). Takei is not justifying a passive and servile devotion to a trenchantly racist white republic. Rather, his history represents a practical utopianism that is not content merely to argue and dream, but must act to change the world by all available means.[50]

The obstinate insistence that America keep its promises may not be revolutionary, but it is a central resource in the repertoire of the everyday activist. By working within the ordinary practices of a culture industry driven by the logic of late twentieth-century capitalism, Takei provides a good model for the kind of activism possible in these times. The respect shown to Takei by Mapa and his audience is more complex than simple infatuation with television celebrity. It has to do with how he represents the future through Sulu and with the energetic citizenship he demonstrates in his offstage life. That informal acclaim was followed a year later by "HERO: A Tribute to George Takei," mounted by the EWP in their new theater.[51] Takei is their hero in part because of the significance of Captain Sulu as a symbol of minority aspiration. EWP honors Takei's courage and persistence in taking responsibility for Sulu as a cultural icon, his activism in Asian American theater, and his support of Asian American actors in the culture industry.

Takei's autobiography emphasizes the connection between the author and the space-future vision of *Star Trek*. The jacket of the first cloth edition sports a photograph of Takei in costume as Sulu on the front cover and another of Takei as himself on the back. The title, *To the Stars,* coupled with Sulu's upward gaze, signals the autobiography's central theme of aspiration, connecting it to the unbounded horizons that are the core of *Star Trek*'s popular appeal. The identification between the actor and his role is completed by the subtitle that links their names, *The Autobiography of George Takei, Star Trek's Mr. Sulu.* To dismiss this juxtaposition as a simple extension of the commercialism that makes *Star Trek* a mainstream commodity is to overlook Takei's appropriation of *Star Trek*'s promises to stake his own claim to America's future. That astro-futurist dream allows him to bring the story of his family and his community to the fore and to argue that his presence in a future imagined from within the mainstream of culture has been paid for by Japanese Americans many times over. To give up the liberatory resources of space future narratives is to betray the struggles that made possible his place in American culture.

Finally, the importance of staking a claim to the present and to the future, even within the realm of popular culture, is emphasized in Nichelle Nichols's account of her early years as *Star Trek*'s Lt. Uhura. During the run of the original series, the actress became disenchanted with her character's minimal role and with the off-camera racial harassment to which she was subjected.[52] She mentioned her dissatisfaction and her decision to leave the show in a conversation with Martin Luther King, Jr. Dr. King dissuaded her, assuring the actress that her visibility as a competent black woman on a starship of the future made an important and necessary statement.[53] Despite her on- and off-camera problems with the racial politics of the show, Nichelle Nichols went on to become an important emissary for the national space program when it belatedly opened its mission to white women and racial minorities.[54] One result of her pioneering persistence is the respect shown to her by Dr. Mae C. Jemison, who served as science mission specialist during a 1992 flight of the space shuttle *Endeavor*. Jemison, who became the first African American woman in space during that voyage, credits her career choice to the role model Nichols provided as Lt. Uhura.[55] She invited Nichols to her launch and while in orbit flouted NASA protocol to open her mission communications with Uhura's tag line, "Hailing frequencies open."[56] In so doing, she honored Nichols's contribution to her own astronautic ambitions. Although Jemison resigned from NASA shortly after her historic flight, her resignation implies a dissatisfaction with the agency and not with the dream of spaceflight.[57] Penley notes that Jemison went on to appear in a *Star Trek: The Next Generation* episode and that she periodically appears with Nichols and Whoopi Goldberg, who played the alien bar-owner and confessor Guinan, at *Star Trek* conventions (150).[58]

Hickam, Takei, Nichols, and Jemison all demonstrate a way of making do: encountering stories of aspiration, success, and national belonging that were never intended to include them, each reorients their meaning around her own centrality. Thus, a legitimizing narrative of individual merit is transformed into a tale of collective, cooperative effort, leaving us questioning the exclusions of a meritocratic hierarchy that separates individuals from families and communities. And the story of a freedom-loving people threatened by ubiquitous enemies is turned into a tale of a frightened, petty, tyrannical majority that has had the great fortune of encountering successive waves of obstinate minorities who dare to claim its promise of liberty and justice for all.

This way of reading, of troping intended meanings for unintended purposes, is particularly well suited for astrofuturism. On the one hand, disciplined as it was by the political demands of the cold war, astrofuturism is the product of elite, white, male scientists, intellectuals, politicians, industrialists, and soldiers. On the other, even while it imagines ways to extend the dominance of its producers, it also invites speculation about alternatives. It thus recalls its origins in the nonelite, marginal dreams of the early spaceflight movement, keeping the faith long after spaceflight has ceased to be awarded prominence in the national agenda. In the tension between its two valences, readers find a treasury of rhetorical resources available for troping. Its multivalence is one of the reasons why the line between the consumers and producers of astrofuturist narratives is unusually porous, with consumers regularly seizing the reigns of production.

This book is an intervention into an aspect of American culture in which I feel very much at home. In the chapters that follow, I will examine the work of Wernher von Braun, Willy Ley, Robert Heinlein, Arthur C. Clarke, Gentry Lee, Gerard O'Neill, and Ben Bova—names that together constitute the dominant tradition of American astrofuturism. The trajectory described by these figures takes us from the astrofuturist consensus of the cold war space race to the doubts raised by the social movements that snowballed, one into another, from the 1950s to the 1980s. Now the dominant tradition is beset on all sides by dissenters and radical experimenters who have troped its conventions, capturing it for social projects that insist on the liberatory potential of space futures. Although the exciting thought experiments of Vonda N. McIntyre, Allen Steele, and Octavia E. Butler perhaps answer the questions I raise in this study, I want to interrogate mainstream astrofuturism to see how it answers undeniable evidence of its complicity in the injustices of this world and attempts to rescue its goals for new political realities. To readers who wonder at my unwavering focus on the extrapolations of privileged white men, I can only say that I believe it is worth acknowledging the hold that the dominant culture has on those it excludes, grasping the tools it inadvertently (and sometimes deliberately) provides to those of us who use its vocabularies of aspiration as we voice our dissent from the restrictions placed on its promises.

My evaluation of astrofuturism has required turning a cold eye (or cultivating a proper hatred, to use Gramsci's phrase) to the claims made by the technoscientific literature to which I am most vulnerable. At stake for me in this project is the shape of the future: whether or not we can imagine, in any meaningful way, a future that both reflects and influences the complex realities of a complex world. Astrofuturism had a tremendous impact on the twentieth century. It made the technosocial project of human expansion into cislunar space, both crewed and robotic, imaginable and possible. During the 1950s and 1960s, through its most articulate proselytizers, it supplied the cultural meanings and the technological schemes, which drove the space race of the cold war. In the 1970s and 1980s, it became a part of the political debates over whether science and technology are part of the problem or part of the solution to poverty, racism, the limits to growth, and war. In contemporary culture, astrofuturism continues to influence the vocabulary we use to evaluate and direct the impact of technoscience. Its public-interest groups constitute a political and imaginative movement that continues to seek influence with the government and the public. In recent years, for example, the Planetary Society, a citizen's organization founded by Carl Sagan and Bruce Murray in 1979, has been lobbying for a return to space with the human exploration of Mars.[59] During both the Reagan and Bush administrations, this and other spaceflight organizations gained influence in Washington. One of the high points of their advocacy occurred in 1990 when President George H. W. Bush lent rhetorical support to the idea of landing Americans on the red planet in the early twenty-first century.[60] This statement of intent was followed only by the outlines of a policy, not by standing commitments. However, it seems to have served as the catalyst for regenerating astro-futurist speculations about the "new world" that the first human settlers of Mars might create. Thus, a flurry of "conquest of Mars" novels have appeared in the past few years, including Norman Spinrad's *Russian Spring*, Allen Steele's *The Labyrinth of Night*, Ben Bova's *Mars*, and Kim Stanley Robinson's *Red Mars*.[61] These books, set in the near future, continue to engage the ideas and politics that I have examined in this chapter; the political drama of Bova's novel, for instance, is supplied by the politics of race and nation through the half-Navaho geologist who is part of the first crew to land on Mars.

As a discursive practice within contemporary American culture, astro-futurism continues to shape our perception of the present and our expectations of the future. As I have argued, it serves as a common language that connects social actors of diverse political and economic backgrounds and sympathies. It has also served as a forum for a complex dialogue about our common cultural inheritance. With or without the critical intervention of African Americans and other historically disenfranchised peoples, books are being written, attitudes and expectations are being shaped, policies are being decided, and resources are being allocated. If the future is to be also black and other than bleak, it is imperative that scholars such as myself understand the conditions, not of our own choosing, under which we make our history.

1. Knocking on Heaven's Door: David Lasser and the First Conquest of Space

A generation that grew up space-minded from their childhood could create, from that new prospective, a sense of community of mankind, sharing a common destiny on this little earth. With this new enlarged viewpoint, future generations might hopefully revolt against those who would try to confine them into narrow, airtight prisons of intolerance, to further their reckless and selfish ambitions.

—David Lasser, 1982[1]

As a mature technocultural project, astrofuturism came of age in the years after the Second World War, not least because of that war's technological innovations. But by the time it gained respectability in those postwar years, astrofuturism was at least twenty years old. Its authors and engineers had been part of amateur rocket societies formed during the late 1920s and early 1930s in Germany, France, Great Britain, the Soviet Union, and the United States. Of those groups that arose from the literary and technological ferment of early rocketry, the *Verein für Raumschiffahrt* (Society for Space Travel; henceforth referred to as the VfR), the British Interplanetary Society (BIS), and the American Interplanetary (Rocket) Society (AIS and ARS) were most influential on postwar astrofuturism. After the end of the war, many of their key innovators and proselytizers found themselves on American soil, becoming the scientists and engineers who developed the technology of spaceflight and the American space program of the 1960s. They also became the popular science and science-fiction writers who presented the spaceflight project to audiences enthralled by its potential. In the books and articles they wrote and in the movies and television programs that they made or inspired, astrofuturists sought to convince the public and the government that the conquest of space was the next great goal of American civilization. Hence, their narratives were designed to explicate the social and political importance of a future dominated by the space frontier. As a result, a spaceflight movement, which had aspired to the openness and liberality of international science, began to serve the parochial interests of a burgeoning superpower. In this chapter, I will explore the genesis of first-generation astrofuturism in the rocket societies of Germany, England, and America. We will follow the early enthusiasm and careers of David Lasser, Wernher von Braun, and Willy Ley, rocket-society members who played a vital role in the astrofuturism of the postwar years. Their disparate political allegiances and hopes for a future in space will set the stage for the conflicts in astrofuturism that will be examined in subsequent chapters.

In spring 1930, as the Great Depression was beginning, several science-fiction writers and editors met in a New York apartment to form the American Interplanetary Society, the first group in this country devoted to the promotion of space travel. Members delineated their goals as the "promotion of interest in and experimentation toward interplanetary expeditions and travel, . . . the stimulation by expenditure of funds and otherwise of American scientists toward a solution of the problems which at present bar the way toward travel among the planets, and the raising of funds for research and experimentation."[2] Although three of its founding members were educated in the sciences, the AIS's interest in spaceflight sprang not from the laboratory and the workbench, but from its participation in the early culture of science fiction. For instance, many members were drawn together through their work for *Wonder Stories*, one of the magazines important to the shaping of the new literature.[3] They approached the question of interplanetary flight from what another founding member, G. Edward Pendray, would later call a "theoretical" perspective. That is, in its inaugural years the society dedicated itself to the creation of a space-minded public that could understand and accept its vision of a new technological frontier. Beryl Williams and Samuel Epstein write that "They were drawn together by the dream they all shared—the vision of sending vehicles up into space. But if they were visionary about space ships, they were more realistic in their approach to one of the aims they established for their new society: the promotion of interest in interplanetary expeditions. Promotion of interest is something writers know a great deal about. It wasn't long before the Society's first publicity venture was under way."[4] The charter members of the American Interplanetary Society were initially more interested in providing the inspirational narratives they believed necessary to make spaceflight plausible than in devel-

oping the new rocket technology. To that end, they championed an exotic technological utopianism that addressed familiar histories and ordinary hopes.

The utopian legacy of astrofuturism is ably represented by David Lasser,
founder of the AIS. Lasser was not only one of the first science-fiction editors,
but also unique in that his principle training was in engineering. Born in Baltimore in 1902 to Russian Jewish immigrants, Lasser grew up in Newark, New
Jersey.[5] Lasser's parents, Leonard and Lena Joffe Lasser, were sent to America
shortly after their wedding in 1885. The pogroms that followed the 1881 assassination of Czar Alexander II prompted them to join the first wave of Russian
Jewish emigration to the United States. Lena Joffe was the daughter of a rab-
binical family and "a leader in Jewish welfare work in Newark for many years
as a founder of the Hebrew Maternity Aid Society and a member of the Volunteer League of Beth Israel Hospital."[6] Following her example of active participation in community affairs, Lasser threw himself into the great events and
political movements of his time. In 1918, one month before his fifteenth birthday (20 March), he lied about his age and enlisted in the U.S. Army. Like many
others of his generation, Lasser understood the European contest as a final "war
to make the world safe for democracy."[7] He arrived in France just in time to be
gassed at the Western Front during the American-led Meuse-Argonne Offensive, the last major battle of the war.[8] Sergeant Lasser sat out the following
Armistice in a hospital and was discharged in February of the following year.[9]

To continue an education disrupted by family poverty and war, Lasser
took advantage of his status as a disabled veteran to win a college scholarship
from the U.S. government (31). He graduated from the Massachusetts Institute
of Technology in 1924 with a bachelor of science in engineering management.
For the young Lasser, the engineering profession offered the prospect of "an interesting, useful, and profitable career" (46). In the years following graduation,
he held a series of positions in engineering, insurance, and technical writing,
which provided little scope for his imagination and even less for the exercise of
his political ideals. His last in this series of "dead end jobs" was as a technical
writer with New York Edison; after two years in that position, he was dismissed
for protesting the harm caused by a profit-motivated layoff (31). In the decades
that followed, he would often sacrifice his own comfort for the sake of social
and economic justice.

In 1929, Lasser applied for an editorial position with Hugo Gernsback's
Stellar Publishing, a move that ensured his influence at the dawn of American
science fiction. Despite his lack of experience, he was hired on the strength of
his MIT degree to edit two of Gernsback's early science-fiction magazines, *Air
Wonder Stories* and *Science Wonder Stories*. As an editor, he worked closely

with his authors, offering constructive editorial intervention aimed at improving the prose and science of writers who were often novices in both fields. For example, in a 1932 letter to Jack Williamson, he wrote: "I might say that our policy is aimed more at the realistic than at the fantastic in science fiction. We find that our readers have wearied a little of unbelievable monsters, unbelievable situations and feats of the imagination that could never become reality. We want imagination used, but we want the author to back it up with a convincing background, so that the reader will find that these things could be true."[10] The new genre was imagined by this pioneering generation to be the fusing link between science and literature. Its ideal reader would read "scientifiction," but work as a professional or amateur scientist. Lasser and his colleagues were intent on producing a literature that would participate in furthering scientific knowledge and shaping technological advances.

Working with a board of "associate science editors" and through such magazine columns as "Science News of the Month" and "Science Questions and Answers," Lasser was well positioned to interpret science for writers and readers.[11] During the period in which *Wonder Stories* was owned and managed by Gernsback and his editors, the promotion of science fiction was also the promotion of science and engineering. In this atmosphere, it seems that Lasser saw little distinction between encouraging fiction writers to produce speculative narratives that made physical sense, on the one hand and, on the other, reading science and researching engineering principles. At a time when scientific exploration and heroic invention were the stuff of newsreels and popular cinema, the connection between science and social adventure was commonplace.[12] Since many of the stories he edited for *Air Wonder Stories* invoked spaceflight, following the examples of Jules Verne and H. G. Wells, Lasser became intrigued by the technical and social opportunities offered by interplanetary voyages.

Most of the stories submitted to *Wonder Stories* relied on improbable or fantastic means to get their protagonists into space. While some of the strategies proposed could have passed muster elsewhere on the strength of literary precedent, Lasser's commitment to the Gernsbackian ideal of science fiction as popular science made him sensitive to the speculative infelicities of his writers. More importantly, his training as an engineer prompted him to seek out reasonable solutions to the spaceflight dream. What he found convinced him that the rocket was the technology that would make space travel possible and inevitable. His research led him to the theories and research agendas of Clark University physics professor Robert H. Goddard, the German experimenters of the *Verein für Raumschiffahrt*, and other rocket pioneers. The science-fiction editor described his discovery of the modern rocket as "a clap of lightning . . .

here was the instrument that could conquer space."[13] The rocket opened up a prospect that launched Lasser on a new crusade; in its service, he recruited disciples and wrote the first English-language popularization of the new science, *The Conquest of Space*.

In the early 1930s, Lasser's enthusiastic advocacy of space travel as credible science was remarkable. As an editor of *Wonder Stories*, he could simply have channeled his visionary energy into writing space stories for the magazine or encouraging others to do the same. He did, in fact, collaborate with a fellow AIS founding member, writer and psychiatrist David H. Keller, on a story called "The Time Projector," in which they imagined a machine that could predict the future.[14] In an interview with Eric Lief Davin, Lasser remarked, "I felt at the time that science fiction could—and *should*—become an important field of literature. As science took over more and more of our lives, the *meaning* of science, the future of science, how science would affect our lives, would become extremely important. And there were cases where science fiction stories stimulated inventions and scientific development" (51–52).

In 1930, Lasser became president of the American Interplanetary Society, one of the first and most successful readers' groups inspired by science fiction. For Hugo Gernsback, the society was an extension of his activities as a publisher, because it helped stimulate a large and active readership for *Wonder Stories* and the popular science magazine *Science and Invention* (1913–31). Hence, he offered to defray the society's costs and encouraged members of other readers' clubs, such as the Scienceers, to join the AIS.[15] However, members of the group wanted to do more than provide unpaid public-relations services for Gernsback's magazines. In fact, the statements they published explaining their organizational goals make no direct mention of any ties to Gernsback's publishing ventures.

This divergence of interest is evident in the notifying statement that the AIS published as a letter to the editor in the June 1930 issue of *Wonder Stories*. Its author, C. P. Mason, identifies himself not an associate editor of the magazine, but as the new society's secretary.[16] Mason describes the AIS as "a group of mature, scientifically-trained men who believe that through forming a strong national society for the encouragement of interplanetary experiments, etc., a great public interest can be aroused in the matter, and the day when the first flight is made may be brought closer by perhaps many years" (78). By highlighting the maturity and scientific background of society members, Mason prompts recognition of the interplanetary project as a venture rising above the fictional soil in which it germinated. The "sole purpose" of the AIS, he writes, "is the promotion of interplanetary travel." Its constitutional goals include the mutual enlightenment of its members bearing on the astronomical, physical and other problems pertinent to man's ultimate conquest of space; the stimulation, by expenditure of funds and otherwise, of American scientists toward a solution of the problems which at present bar the way toward travel among the planets; the collection, correlation and dissemination of facts, information, articles, books, pamphlets and other literature bearing on interplanetary travel and subjects relating thereto . . . the raising of funds for research, experimentation, and such other activities as the Society may from time to time deem necessary or valuable in connection with the general aim of hastening the day when interplanetary travel shall become a reality. (78)[17]

While Mason's prose permits no explicit recognition of the connection between the new space science advocacy group and the magazine, the list of officers in his final paragraph includes Lasser, Fletcher Pratt, and G. Edward Pendray, all of whom were connected with Gernsback's interests. It comes as no surprise, therefore, that the editorial response from *Wonder Stories* is an "enthusiastic" endorsement of the group and its aims.

Finally, in addition to fostering a technological and narrative project, Lasser also used his position at *Wonder Stories* to shape the political content of the imagined future. In the early years of the Depression, his own imagination was fired by thoughts of democratic reform. Late in his life, Lasser remembered the years from 1929 to 1933 as a "horrible" time of national crisis that prompted him to undergo "a mental revolution."[18] As a liberal idealist educated in a curriculum that emphasized the importance of the engineer as an efficient manager of the social good, Lasser no doubt was disappointed that the president of those years, Herbert Hoover, performed so poorly. Hoover had been a world-class mining engineer, a public official who had helped organize the relief effort following World War I, and a secretary of commerce concerned about unemployment and internal improvements. This record made him a famous humanitarian and popularized the social benefits of engineering, but his failure to address the human distress caused by the depression prompted Lasser to look for solutions at the margins of mainstream politics. He searched socialism, technocracy, science fiction, and space travel for strategies that would relieve economic distress and create a better world.

Lasser's political quest was prompted also by the egregious political injustices of the 1920s. Like many others of his generation, he was outraged by the infamous trial of Nicola Sacco and Bartolomeo Vanzetti. Their execution in 1927 and the stock-market crash of 1929 convinced him that "we needed a political change. Not a revolutionary change, but a peaceful change to bring us up to what a lot of other countries were doing for their citizens."[19] He joined the

League for Industrial Democracy and attended lectures by Norman Thomas, the prominent pacifist and socialist politician.[20] He volunteered to work with jobless Italian workers at the settlement house in his neighborhood and, in what must have seemed a natural progression, organized a small group to represent the unemployed to a sympathetic Fiorello LaGuardia at City Hall. That group soon organized on a city-wide scale as the Workers Unemployed Union.[21]

As union president, Lasser's advocacy for the unemployed conferred a notoriety that inevitably caught the eye of his employer. As a consequence, Gernsback called his editor in and fired him with the words, "If you like working with the unemployed so much, I suggest you go and join them."[22] He did. Pat Jefferson notes that when freed to concentrate his full attention on the union, "Lasser began to hitchhike around the country organizing new groups, calling public attention to the issue, and pressing state and federal agencies to provide more generous funds."[23] By 1935, the union became the Workers Alliance of America (WAA), a national organization headquartered in Washington, D.C., with Lasser continuing as president. With this move, Lasser began his involvement in national politics as a public official under the New Deal and a combatant in the political battles that served as the prelude to the McCarthyist purges of the 1950s.

Lasser's concern with race begins with his family's political experiences and the working-class life that was their American reality. It matured through his settlement-house work and the analogous circumstances of first-generation immigrants and of other disenfranchised Americans. His work in unemployment and labor movements included creating coalitions across racial boundaries. Early in his tenure as president, the WAA was in contact with the National Negro Congress, an African American organization created in 1935 around a platform proposing cooperation between black activists across political and religious differences. Their common interest in addressing the problems of the unemployed and strengthening the ability of workers to bargain with government and business suggests a natural affinity.

Lasser's political and scientific commitments are evident in his first book, *The Conquest of Space* (1931). Structurally, the book is a restless mix of science popularization and fiction. His zeal for the conquest of space accounts for the didacticism of its technological explication, but he also tells a story that communicates a passionate investment in space travel. Therefore, *The Conquest of Space* is a textbook for the space age, a manifesto that could serve as both blueprint and bible for humanity's advance into space. Lasser's investment in space travel's utopian potential is informed by his background as the child of immigrants and his commitment to a politically active scientism. As the terrestrial land of freedom and opportunity was for his parents, space could be for his children.

To reassure readers of the scientific viability of his proposal, Lasser recruited physicist Harold H. Sheldon to write an introduction for the book. Sheldon is prominently identified on the title page as "Chairman of the Department of Physics, Washington Square College, New York University." The physicist carefully defends the new science of rocketry being developed by experimenters in America, France, and Germany, and establishes the obvious historical analogy with the recently proven (and therefore prestigious) technology of heavier-than-air flight. In addition, he offers cautious vindication of Lasser's interest in space travel and warns against the kind of unthinking skepticism indulged by those who "have never given the rocket any serious thought or studied the rocket even superficially."[24] More importantly, he endorses Lasser as an informed writer who "has written like a scientist off his guard for the moment" and can therefore display the enthusiasm the scientist must disavow to offset public misunderstanding or suspicion (4). To recommend *The Conquest of Space*, Sheldon offers a variation on the most common sentiment in science popularization: "In writing the book Mr. Lasser has displayed a fine sense of balance. He has not introduced enough technical matter to discourage the poorly equipped nor has he left out so much as to disappoint the scientist" (3). The result, according to Sheldon, is the first coherent statement of the new science of rocketry in America and, by extension, the rest of the English-speaking world.

In *The Conquest of Space*, Lasser articulates the utilitarian, technological, and moral reasoning that would become the norm in astrofuturism over the following generations. First, he presents spaceflight as the necessary extension of human endeavor in both science and literature. Space exploration, he contends, will add new discoveries to our knowledge of nature and create an indefinite extension of every other field of knowledge (249–50). Second, he introduces the rocket as the vehicle that makes space travel not only possible but likely, and he speculates about inventions that may accompany its development. Third, in an innovative move, he provides the moral and political rationale for undertaking the "peaceful" conquest of space (216): "We cannot but feel now that this journey has served its purpose in the breaking down of racial jealousies. All nations have united in a communion of joy. All the earth's people share in the glory—and the names of the men who form our party have already become internationalized—so minutely does the world know us" (137). Lasser identifies national and racial antagonism as the central impediment to a glorious global unity. The conquest of space will increase civilized knowledge and unite the human race. The global communion at the focus of Lasser's political hopes produces an image of transcendence that could both excuse international rivalry and offer maneuvering room to the disenfranchised. Four decades passed before his ecstatic rhetoric finally emerged as a commonplace of 1969 Moon landing. Lasser established the ethical promise that became a core convention of astrofuturist science fiction, long before its popularity in the 1950s and 1960s.

As is the case with the generations of astrofuturists who would reiterate and revise this early apologia, the democratic progressivism of Lasser's space-flight vision is based on a particular reading of human nature and history. Space travel holds the promise of a future golden age in part because it will redeem the history of Euro-American civilization by extending and justifying the adventures of oceanic explorers such as Columbus and Cook. Lasser argues that the technological conquest of the Atlantic produced a new, cosmopolitan race: "we . . . acquired . . . a planetary instead of a provincial outlook—the whole earth is our home" (15). The trajectory of this history gives clear direction to the next stage of our evolution: "It is but a single step from this to the acquisition of an interplanetary mind, and extension of our concept to include the solar system" (15). As an interplanetary species humanity eventually will rule the empire of matter and itself, but it must first unite in a grand project that will knit all its races into one communion (206, 251). This is an evolution that seeks to avoid the violent potential in revolutions driven by race, class, and national conflict. Like the ocean-going ship and the steam-driven locomotive before it, the rocket will open new vistas for political experimentation and civilizational advance, and thus be the catalyst for our next evolutionary leap.

To emphasize the close coincidence of technological, intellectual, and moral advance, Lasser inaugurates a form of space-travel writing that bridges the disciplinary divide between fiction and nonfiction. His *Conquest* is divided into three parts: "The Rocket" introduces the cultural and technical history of spaceflight and rocketry; "The Flight into Space" is a space future narrative, a fictional account of the first trip to the Moon; and "New Worlds" describes technical barriers to spaceflight and speculates on the dangers and rewards of the project. The first trip to the Moon is an ancient mode of Western satiric and utopian literature; indeed, Lasser's immediate literary models are provided by Jules Verne, the underappreciated satirist, and H. G. Wells, the modern utopian.[25] However, unlike his predecessors, Lasser's intent is not satiric and he eschews the compensatory aspect of the utopian tradition. Instead, he presents space travel as a variety of political reform realizable in this world. Because he hopes to popularize a science that could change human relationships,

his introduction to modern rocketry and the mechanics of space travel emphasizes their probable emotional and social effects.

Lasser's seminal text functions also as a primer for science-fiction writers
and astrofuturists. His quest to raise the literary and scientific standards of science fiction prompted him to attempt two tasks: establish a literary tradition
and respectable predecessors for space travel narratives, and infuse the best discoveries of contemporary science and technology into that tradition. Hence, the
first two chapters of the book, "The Meaning of Space Flight" and "Space
Flight In Literature," present space travel as a well-established motif in Western literature. Lasser argues that without the literary inventions of Daniel De-
foe, Cyrano de Bergerac, John Wilkins, and Bishop Godwin interplanetary
travel would never have become a reasoned or even reasonable notion, let
alone science. He notes that "it was Verne, truly, who prepared the public mind
for the scientific proposals of Goddard, Oberth and Pelterie that were to come
five decades later" (28).

Thus, although in this proto-astrofuturism the rocket and other technologies of spaceflight authorize the literary imagination, literature in turn makes
that science culturally viable. At the height of its influence, rocketry and the
space programs associated with it became instruments for the projection of
crude national ambitions. But thirty years before its involvement in cold war
realpolitik, Lasser imagined space travel as an international venture directed by
an International Interplanetary Commission headquartered in the Swiss Alps.
The significance of this cooperation is established by a journalist who speaks to
a worldwide audience:

It is now apparent how wise and far-seeing were the great nations when they agreed to
abandon the race to reach the moon, and pooled their knowledge, skill and resources.
For what had threatened to become a new source of national pride and jealousy had
been turned into a joint endeavor, in which each nation could feel its contribution.
Races unable to settle amicably their political and social differences had received from
their scientists a striking lesson in international cooperation. (114)

Here spaceflight offers political hope, because it borrows the ideal of scientific
cooperation for its project. As Lasser imagined them, the first astronauts would
not be a corps of "right stuff" military flight test pilots but a group of eighteen
people, including the spaceship crew and "ten scientific experts" (118). The
scientists would be on hand to "decide their program for the exploration and
study of the moon when we land" (136). In Lasser's future, the great reward of
space exploration is the extension of human knowledge instead of national
prestige.[26]

Lasser is writing against the space-adventure tradition represented by the prominent German science fictionist Kurd Lasswitz and his intellectual heirs, in whose hands the conquest of space will reinforce the racial hierarchy "discovered" during the European age of exploration. Lasswitz imagines the challenge of convincing extraterrestrial races that white Europeans not only are superior among human breeds but also that they are the equal of any kind of extraterrestrial race.[27] Taking a different tack, Lasser sees in space travel the trigger for what Doris Lessing would later call a "sense of we-feeling."[28] His narrator reports that "we cannot but feel now that this journey has served its purpose in breaking down of racial jealousies. All nations have united in a communion of joy."[29]

As the world enjoys a moment of ecstatic communality, the astronauts also find their perspective altered. The sight of the turning earth suspended in space generates an understanding that transcends the limits of quotidian life: "A great spiritual tranquillity fills us—a humbleness and a yearning for the continuance of this immense peace. Our being seems spread through the eternity that we can see. We realize now the full meaning of Einstein's 'cosmic religion.' Cities, empires, states; dreams and ambitions; conflict and confusion are infinitely remote, part of the dream-world of that slowly turning globe" (138). By referring to Einstein's 1930 article on "Religion and Science," Lasser evokes a sensibility that links democratic socialism with a progressive scientific positivism. In that piece for the *New York Times Magazine*, Einstein wrote "that the cosmic religious feeling is the strongest and noblest motive for scientific research." That feeling arises from thoughts and actions dedicated to "the satisfaction of deeply felt [human] needs and the assuagement of pain."[30] For Lasser, space travel is a practical means to cosmic religion, a way out of political and cultural conflict. As an extension of scientific exploration, the conquest of space will illuminate the provinciality of nationalist ambitions and the racial divisions they require. For Lasser, the space frontier offers humanity the same release from religious and racial oppression purchased by his Russian Jewish parents when they emigrated to the United States in 1885.

Lasser eventually left the literary genre he helped develop to pursue his social commitments elsewhere. In 1969, he wrote to Arthur C. Clarke, "As the impact of large scale unemployment, visible to me every day in downtown New York, became more powerful, I decided that solving our domestic earthly problems had to come first."[31] But his subsequent career as a labor activist, government administrator, and union official did little to alter his commitment to the dream of space travel. Three years after the publication of *The Conquest of Space*, the American Interplanetary Society's quest for respectability prompted its transformation into the American Rocket Society. The visionary science-fiction writers who were the core of its membership in its early years were replaced by stolid engineers. While G. Edward Pendray argued that the move in no way represented a neglect of the ultimate goal, the organization renamed itself to "attract able members repelled by the present name."[32] Lasser seems to have accepted this change as the cost of keeping the society "alive and vigorous." However, he retained his commitment to the dream that motivated its founding even as he began work as Workers Alliance of America president in Washington, D.C. In a letter to Pendray, Lasser expresses his regret that while "circumstances made it impossible for me to continue" as a member of the rocket society, "I still hope to fly on an honest to goodness rocket ship before I die."[33]

Lasser inaugurated an American spaceflight movement that attracted kindred souls and encompassed a large variety of conflicting interests. However, it was difficult to persuade the public that liquid-fueled rocketry should be developed as a instrument in the conquest of space. As the president of the AIS and the author of its popularizing manifesto, Lasser understood the value of retaining the most senior and distinguished American expert of the new science, Robert H. Goddard. The science-fiction editor held Goddard in great esteem as the reigning American experimenter in the field of rocketry; indeed, *Conquest of Space* would become the first sympathetic and well-informed popular presentation of Goddard's work to a general, English-speaking public. Shortly after founding the AIS, Lasser offered an honorary membership to the physicist and asked him to serve as a member of the group's Advisory Committee.[34] Goddard accepted the honor but declined the editor's invitations to contribute as either consultant or lecturer.[35] Goddard's early unwillingness to accept more than a token relationship with the AIS frustrated its leadership, but in later years Lasser admitted that it was a reluctance both cautious and pragmatic. While his work as a physicist had been inspired by an early dream of space travel to Mars, as a professional scientist Goddard was well aware of the cost that public advocacy of the dream could levy in the early years of the twentieth century. Privately, he felt otherwise.

In his accounts of the passions that underlay Goddard's work, Carl Sagan recounts the "magic moment" the physicist experienced when he climbed a cherry tree at age seventeen: "While idly looking down at the ground around him, [he] experienced a kind of epiphanal vision of a vehicle that would transport human beings to the planet Mars. He resolved to devote himself to the task."[36] As was the case with other spaceflight visionaries, Goddard's inspiration was literary as well as physical; for he read Wells, Verne, and the astronomer Percival Lowell.[37] His 1898 reading of Wells's *The War of the Worlds* may have helped spark the cherry tree vision; he would indicate as much in a gracious letter to the author in 1932.[38] In any case, both dream and fiction remained with him while he made a career as a practical, suitably restrained physics professor. He dreamed of earth-orbiting space stations and of creating a probe that would search for life on Mars, but spoke only of those earthly rewards expected by his world. Goddard's interest in finding funds for his research and his desire for privacy clashed with the public's eagerness to treat any unorthodox proposal as an opportunity for carnival. An early 1920s brush with newspaper sensationalism taught him that proposing space travel as a reasonable application for the rocket created popular amusement and collegial condescension. Within the scientific and cultural context of the 1920s, Goddard was aware that his private goals and blueprints would either bemuse or dissuade the institutions and individuals that could afford to back expensive, speculative research.

By the time Lasser became interested in the rocket as an instrument of political reform, Goddard had been confirmed in a policy of public caution completely at odds with the sensibilities of the fledgling cultures of science fiction and spaceflight enthusiasm. Lasser's attempts to involve Goddard in his projects predated his creation of the AIS by some months. Goddard's desire to find stable and well-heeled backing for his research set the stage for their first encounter. In 1929, at Lasser's request, the Stellar Publishing Corporation's Hugo Gernsback contacted the physicist and offered him an "interesting proposition."[39] The cash-strapped Gernsback offered the physicist stock in his magazine as payment for working as an associate science editor for *Wonder Stories*. As a reviewing editor, the publisher argued, the professor could help "open thresholds in all the sciences particularly in space flight" to the reading public.[40] It was at that meeting that Goddard met David Lasser, who, no doubt, championed his employer's proposal and the benefits of an active collaboration. The physicist may have seen what the magazine stood to gain from the arrangement but saw no help in it for his own work. Lasser's follow-up letter nine months later reintroducing himself as AIS president, "the managing editor of the Gernsback Publications—*Science and Air Wonder Stories*," and "an enthusiast on the possibilities of space flying" drew a cool response.[41]

The exchange between Lasser and Goddard exposes the tensions between science and fiction that have always attended the astrofuturist pursuit of the wonderful dream. The serious tone, which Lasser maintained in *The Conquest of Space*, could not mask the enthusiastic, utopian, and, as a consequence, radical nature of his society's initial platform. Privately Goddard agreed that "the interplanetary application is really physically possible."[42] And Tom Crouch notes that Goddard was also no snob about science fiction. Not only did he revere Wells, but as an undergraduate he "bombarded English professors with science-fiction stories and themes."[43] However, he preferred a gradualist approach to managing news of the new science that endeavored neither to amuse nor to shock the public or, more importantly, his patrons. As late as 1945, Goddard remarked that "The subject of projection from the earth, and especially a mention of the moon, must still be avoided in dignified scientific and engineering circles."[44] Whatever interest he may have had in joining the Gernsback partisans' technophilic crusade evaporated when a Guggenheim grant for aeronautical research solved his fund-raising dilemma. Upon winning that grant, the rocket pioneer's unwillingness to break with the culture of private scholarship that nurtured his research came into conflict with Lasser's interest in highlighting the significance of his work to the spaceflight movement.

Goddard, however, was not completely shy of publicity. In cooperation with the prominent public relations firm of Ivy P. Lee and Associates, he sought to control the public reception of rocketry. As the AIS sought his aid in legitimizing their agenda, Goddard pursued public credit by offering his experiments as boon to the development of meteorology, aviation, and astronomy. The sober language of the Lee office press release heralding Guggenheim's support made no mention of extending the rocket's capabilities into the fantastic realm of outer space.[45] In the time between the initial announcement of Goddard's Guggenheim and the account that Lasser published in the New York *Herald Tribune* three days later, a brief exchange between Goddard and Lee account manager Harcourt Parrish illustrates the physicist's interest in deflecting the kind of conclusions Lasser was willing to draw in public fora. Parrish informed Goddard that

Mr. David Lasser of the Interplanetary Society called me this morning for more information. He asked about interplanetary communication and the propulsion of airplanes by jets. He said the *New York Herald Tribune* had commissioned him to write an article for next Sunday's edition, and I am quite sure that in this article we will have wild dreams about interplanetary communication, although I called his attention especially to the fact that no mention of such possibilities was made in the news article sent out by this office.[46]

Though the goal of Goddard and his associates was to avoid all mention of spaceflight in connection with the Guggenheim grant, they found that it was, in fact, impossible to completely control popular interest in the idea. The *Herald*

Tribune placed the Lasser article on the front page of its Sunday science section. Beneath a fairly pedestrian drawing of the rocket and its engineers, the story recounts much of the information provided by Lee and company. However, Lasser's final paragraph promises that the rocket offers a prospect more exciting than the worthy dullness affected by Goddard's mediated statement:[47]

With the serious problem of the perfection of the rocket to be settled, and with rewards enough in exploration of the neighborhood [of] our atmosphere to content them, the Goddard committee is not attempting to prophesy the ultimate development of the rocket. The recent statements of Colonel Charles A. Lindbergh, however, that future long distance flying will be made at high altitudes, and the statements of German experimenters that long distance flights can be made at high altitudes by rocket-driven planes at what seems phenomenal speeds lend a reasonable promise of a new and revolutionary, method of transportation. . . . As to the truth of this, of course, only the future can tell. But meanwhile rocket travel by plane, as well as the remoter vision of travel to other planets, has indeed been given new life and impetus by the Guggenheim award.[48]

This is precisely the kind of statement that Goddard had hoped to avoid. He seems to have realized, however, that such inferences were unavoidable. In a note written on the day following the *Tribune* article, Goddard commiserates with Parrish, praising the science emphasis of the official statement, and remarking that "the problem is an especially difficult one to handle, for the reason that the interplanetary application is really physically possible."[49]

From the 1920s through the 1940s, the ultimate goal of the early rocket pioneers, spaceflight, could not be taken seriously outside of the small, conjoined literary and engineering community that nurtured the idea. However seriously this minority viewed their own dreams and experiments the public could only see it as either light entertainment or disorderly escapism. Long after his activities in science fiction and the spaceflight movement had ended, Lasser was to encounter the rough side of these opinions.

Following his separation from the technocratic circle that included *Wonder Stories* and the American Interplanetary Society, Lasser moved on to devote his full attention to his settlement house–inspired work. By 1936, he was in Washington, D.C., as national president of the Workers Alliance of America. As the depression wore on and when in 1939 World War II began, Lasser's brand of anticommunist socialism evolved into a New Deal liberalism, straining relations with his more radical peers. By 1940, Lasser had resigned from the WAA, leaving its revolutionary faction in charge. With other anti-Red Alliance members he founded a new organization called the American Security Union, whose "purpose was to secure training of the long-term unemployed to enable them to compete for the new jobs that were opening up."[50] The union also embraced the liberal capitalism of Roosevelt's New Deal, which many socialists saw as the pragmatic resolution of politics and patriotism. Lasser developed a productive relationship with the Roosevelt White House and established strong institutional ties between his union and the Works Projects Administration (WPA).[51] Those relationships resulted in an invitation to serve as consultant to the WPA job training program, which his advocacy had helped found.[52] Lasser's rise in the Roosevelt administration put him in the way of politicians who had been distressed by his effectiveness as head of the WAA and resented his popularity with New Deal functionaries. He soon found himself facing the political consequences of his determined advocacy for spaceflight and for the economically disenfranchised.

Congressional approval of Lasser's consultancy became hostage to conservative contempt for the WPA and to the anticommunism that simmered beneath wartime alliances. The WAA's reputation among conservatives as a "communist front" made Lasser vulnerable to attack from the right, despite his very public repudiation of revolutionary communism. As part of its war against organizations and individuals deemed politically subversive, the Department of Justice, through the Federal Bureau of Investigation, collected a great deal of information on both the WAA and its founding president.[53] As a result, Lasser's name came to the attention of Representative Martin Dies, a Democrat from Texas (1931–44) and chairman of the Special House Committee for the Investigation of Un-American Activities and Propaganda.[54]

It is not clear whether Lasser was the subject of an extensive investigation by the Dies committee; however, the information that reached Representative Dies was enough to prompt punitive action. During the House debate on WPA appropriations for 1942–43, Dies vilified the social activist's intellectual and political commitments:

Here is the case of David Lasser, about whom this House has heard so much before. A few years ago, one of the largest and most influential front organizations of the Communist Party in this country was the Workers' Alliance. At the height of its influence—and I may add its mischief—the Workers' Alliance was headed by David Lasser. In 1940 Lasser broke with the Communists too and denounced the Workers' Alliance. But in addition to his past affiliation with and leadership of communist front organizations, Lasser was also connected with technocracy. He was, in fact, editor of a technocracy magazine. Furthermore, as illustrative of marked tendency toward one form of mental aberration or another, Lasser was president of the Interplanetary Travel Association. Today David Lasser is Senior Labor Economist of the War Production Board at a salary of $4600.[55]

In later years, Lasser, who witnessed the scene from the House gallery, was not to forget the laughter elicited by the powerful and opportunistic legislator. Communism, technocracy, interplanetary travel, the New Deal: Dies's anti-Roosevelt sympathizers followed this chain of equivalences and drew the conclusions he intended. The extraordinary result of his defamation was the passage of the appropriations bill with the proviso "that no money could be expended by the WPA to pay the wages of one David Lasser."[56] While Lasser's political affiliation with communists may have been the immediate cause of this episode, his early attraction to the political hopes represented by space travel and technocracy tipped the scales against him in debate. The political atmosphere of the 1940s and 1950s discouraged any visible link between Lasser's liberal progressivism and the military-industrial complex that would make his conquest of space possible. Official and popular interest in the possibility of spaceflight would emerge from the unique object lessons that the German rocket team would deliver in war and peace. Their willingness to appeal to nationalist ambitions sold the dream in a way that the idealistic New Dealer could not.

As the space age dawned and the space race proceeded, Lasser, now Economics and Research Director for the International Union of Electrical, Radio and Machine Workers, gained prestige as labor's own space pioneer.[57] He was positioned to define what spaceflight could mean for labor and the democratic left. At a meeting of Americans for Democratic Action, a body of reform liberals, seven months after the launch of the first *Sputnik* in October 1957, Lasser presented his "views on the meaning of the Space Age." His talk allowed him to introduce the early idealism of the space travel movement into the political conversations of the cold war. Presaging the professional and political agendas that space scientists such as Carl Sagan would follow in the 1980s, Lasser argued that the conquest of space should be an international venture that supersedes national divisions. And, like Sagan, he was particularly interested in sharing that conquest with the Soviet Union in pursuit of the twin goals of "a liberalization of their regime" and the embrace of a new era in the evolution of "our race": "Perhaps, where we have failed to find the basis for cooperation from the ground up we may do so from space down. We may so establish the idea of the common heritage and common destiny that we share, that we can in time overcome the things that separate us."[58] This vision of a common human destiny remained stable throughout Lasser's political career. His postwar pronouncements differ from those of the 1930s only in the sense of urgency lent by the specter of nuclear superpowers toying with mutually assured destruction. His hope of a new destiny in space is matched by an apocalyptic fear of what might happen without a conquest of space: "[We] must find new and better ways to meet our international problems. Above all, we must continue to demonstrate over and over again that on this shrinking planet we must choose between a tremendous destiny and mutual destruction."[59]

2. An Empire in Space: Europe and America as Science Fact

"Always the goal."

—Michael Flynn[1]

In the closing days of the Second World War, German rocket engineers and their technologies became one of the most coveted spoils of a defeated Third Reich. Led by Wernher von Braun and General Doctor Walter Dornberger, these were the rocket scientists and technicians who had designed and built the infamous flying bomb, the V-2 (*Vergeltungswaffen Zwei*, or Retaliatory Weapon Two).[2] Shortly after the Allied victory, the German rocket team was shipped to the United States, where it was required to continue its wartime experiments. The arrival of the Germans on American soil was the necessary catalyst for postwar astrofuturism. Their presence brought together three national spaceflight movements—American, British, and German—that had been sundered by the war (significantly excluding that of the Soviet Union), enabling the collaboration that made the space age technically feasible in the West. Under the auspices of U.S. Army Ordinance at the White Sands Proving Ground in New Mexico, the German rocket team mated a V-2 with a small missile called the WAC Corporal and launched the result. On 24 February 1949, the rocket code-named "Bumper" reached a height of 250 miles in six and a half minutes. At that point, "the missile for all practical purposes was outside the earth's atmosphere."[3] The barrier to space had been broken.[4] Thus the United States followed Germany in realizing the twenty-year-old dream of the rocket societies, and the official imagination endorsed the space frontier as an achievable reality.

The rocket team had come to the United States under a War Department program called "Project Paperclip." While many

Americans thought that the Paperclip scientists should have been tried as war criminals, a few men in the Army and the War Department believed that the knowledge and expertise of these men were too valuable to waste. The terror that the "flying bomb" had created in London and its suburbs convinced them that this new technology could be an important factor in determining the postwar balance of power. Pragmatism overcame the moral scruples even of those who knew the conditions under which the V-2 had been produced. In his work on the compromises that the Allies made at the end of the war in the race to profit from German wartime research, Tom Bower notes that the conquering nations were fully aware that the Mittelbau, the underground rocket factory at Nordhausen, which was the first modern mass production facility for ballistic missiles, was supported by a concentration camp system and the most brutal kind of slave labor. The system increased production tremendously but at the cost of thousands of lives:

At least twenty thousand men would die there before the end of the war. Working without power drills or mechanical excavators, the slaves were constantly threatened and beaten while they dug, hammered and heaved their pickaxes. Since there was scarcely any food or water and no sanitation or medical facilities, life expectancy rarely exceeded six months. During their daily tour through the tunnels, the Peenemunde scientists felt the extreme humidity, the chill gusts of air, the dusty atmosphere, and intense depression. Despite the constant arrival of new labor the number of workers never increased. On average, one hundred men a day died of exhaustion, starvation, and disease, or were murdered by the SS guards, either on a whim or as punishment. . . . Replacements supplied by the SS from other concentration camps arrived on demand from [Arthur] Rudolph or Werner [sic] von Braun. Neither scientist was directly responsible for these conditions, but they accepted the situation created by the SS without demur.[5]

This record of rocket team complicity in Nazi war crimes was adroitly covered up by the U.S. Army and the War Department to avoid the public outcry that would have resulted from its broadcast.[6]

Despite the rhetoric of freedom, wealth, and equality that marked the space future vision both in its beginnings during the Weimar Republic and in its reformulation on American soil, the technology and organization required for movement into space were allied to what Dale Carter has called the "Oven State": the totalitarian technocracy of Nazi Germany, an ideology that found its most vivid expression in the extermination camps of Dachau and Auschwitz.[7] In Carter's view, the Oven State was replaced after the war by the "Rocket State," which created an "incipient totalitarianism" in the Western democracies. Walter McDougall makes much the same point in his description of the reluctance with which President Eisenhower took the steps necessary to address the Soviet challenge in space after *Sputnik*. Eisenhower believed that if a space race began between the United States and the Soviet Union, American institutions and policy would be forced into a technocratic mode. Under such a system, he feared, American values of democracy, individualism, and free trade would be compromised by the large-scale institutions necessary to facilitate the conquest of space. McDougal writes, "Ike cried forth the economic, political, even spiritual dangers posed by the growth of a military industrial complex" and a "scientific-technological elite."[8]

Eisenhower's "technocratic nightmare" could not have been more different in spirit and intent from the political hopes expressed by the German rocketeers who helped shape an American astrofuturism. They believed the military-industrial complex, which allowed for the creation of space-capable missiles, the largest and most complex of humanity's machines, would open up new terrains for scientific exploration and material exploitation. It would wage a peaceful war against the limits imposed by the natural world through the creation of spacecraft, space stations, lunar mining colonies, and outposts on distant planets. The result would be a conquest of space generating the same economic, political, and moral benefits that accrued from earlier terrestrial conquests. These hopes were informed by a historical and ideological faith, common to Europeans and Americans, that the blessings of civilization followed the course of empire. Arthur C. Clarke represented majority opinion in astrofuturism when he declared, shortly after the war, that "Interplanetary travel is now the only form of 'conquest and empire' compatible with civilization."[9] On the American ground this has meant that even ardent anti-imperialists, such as Carl Sagan, came to believe in space exploration as a logical and desirable consequence of the Western history of contact with new frontiers.[10]

In essence, whether the space future is defined as an imperial adventure or a peaceful exploration, astrofuturists across the political spectrum have promoted the belief that only by escaping its terrestrial cradle will the American experiment realize its full potential. The conquest of the space frontier will renew virtues they believe are essential to the American character, specifically those allowing for the expansion of individual freedom. Hence the rhetorical and ideological appeal of first-generation astrofuturists would have been in full accord with the values that Eisenhower wished to defend. Thus the astrofuturists ignored the irony inherent in their formulation of space futures: in order to achieve the benefits that they expected from the space frontier—more wealth, freedom, and democracy for the individual—the world would have to be organized and its masses mobilized as never before. Megalithic concentrations of power encompassing control of both the public and private sectors would be necessary to concentrate the resources needed to make a lunar colony, establish a human presence on Mars, and mine the asteroids. The controllers of this necessarily global initiative would be a technocratic elite who would function as custodians of the common good. It is not surprising that that elite would resemble the astrofuturists.

In the 1950s and 1960s, the technocrats of the space future were identified largely as the German émigrés who, by then, held senior positions in the American space program. The rocket team's rehabilitation as assimilated and valued American citizens was accomplished with astonishing speed. As the cold war with the Soviet Union proceeded, their value to national security could not be ignored by government strategists. However, it was not the demands of foreign policy that convinced the general public of their useful and essentially American character. Rather, it was the rocket team's connection with the optimistic social and political rhetoric of space future advocacy. Astrofuturism, through popular science and science fiction, transformed some members of the rocket team into celebrities, iconic exemplars of science and the future in the landscape of American culture.

Wernher von Braun was the most prominent representative of the German rocket team in the United States. As an amateur rocketeer in the late 1920s, a civilian employee of the German Army in the 1930s and early 1940s, an SS officer, a prisoner of war and later employee of the U.S. Army, and finally the head of rocket development for NASA, von Braun was part of an international community whose members believed the new technology to be a means to a noble end: freeing humanity from its earthly cradle. Appointed the director of the George C. Marshall Space Flight Center in Huntsville, Alabama, when NASA established the facility in 1960, von Braun continued as the managing engineer of the team that developed the Saturn V carrier rocket and made possible the Apollo lunar voyages. Despite his wartime background (or, perhaps, because of it), he became a genuine American hero by the end of the 1950s. He earned his initial celebrity in popular culture as a prominent champion of the new rocket technology and of its application in spaceflight. In a series of books and articles published during the early and mid-1950s, he helped legitimize the spaceflight movement for a broad audience. Never afraid of new technologies, von Braun helped produce the first television documentary on the idea of spaceflight. The "Man in Space" series on Walt Disney's then new prime-time show, *Disneyland*, introduced America to a fantastic notion in the most prosaic and commercial of fora. In a move that must have seemed slightly risky, Disney asked von Braun to present the series to its audience. Fortunately, the engi-

Figure 1. Wernher von Braun signs autographs at the Gulf South State Fair in Picayune, Mississippi, October 1963. NASA Image Exchange, Stannis Space Center Image No. 63–484. Courtesy of NASA.

neer proved to be an able and enthusiastic host. As a result, he became part of the pioneering generation of American television personalities.[11]

Disney fostered what Fredric Jameson has called the "common-sense" notion of what science fiction does as a genre.[12] Since the mid-twentieth century, practitioners and fans of science fiction have argued that the genre serves a useful social function as a literature of anticipation, a way of modeling the near and far future on paper. Through its models, the reasoning goes, we become accustomed to the future and are prepared to accept the changes that science and technology might cause in our social and political life. Whether or not one agrees with this logic, and Jameson does not, science fiction's self-definition as an anticipatory genre has been central to the claims of readers and writers who argue for its moral and social utility.[13] In any case, Walt Disney Productions, a motion-picture company whose international reputation was founded on the dissemination of delightful fantasies, provided the visual expertise necessary to make speculative science real in the minds of its viewers.

In contemporary astrofuturism, Wernher von Braun is a foundational but problematic progenitor. According to Carl Sagan, there can be no doubt regarding von Braun's significance: "Wernher von Braun played an absolutely essential role in the history of rocketry and the development of spaceflight—equally on the inspirational as on the technical side. . . . His Collier's articles and his popular books—especially the *Conquest of the Moon* and the *Conquest of Mars*—were influential in shaping my teenage view about the feasibility and nature of interplanetary flight. Much later, his 'Mars Project' fell into my hands, and I'm sure affected my later view of Martian exploration."[14] There is little doubt that von Braun's example also encouraged the planetary scientist in his secondary career as a science popularizer and celebrity. However, as an academic scientist with little patience for the military-industrial complex that fostered von Braun's working life, Sagan also found the engineer's smooth compliance with the militarism and racist ideology of Nazi Germany "deeply disturbing" (250). The moral that Sagan draws from von Braun's apparent complaisance under the Nazi regime is that it "is the responsibility of the scientist or engineer to hold back and even, if necessary, to refuse to participate in technological development—no matter how 'sweet'—when the auspices or objectives are sufficiently sinister" (250).[15] While Sagan spent a good portion of his public career working for the scientific exploration of space, he was no fan of von Braun's single-minded devotion to the dream. Despite von Braun's eminence, Sagan could not sanction his predecessor's "willing[ness] to use any argument and accept any sponsorship as long as it could get us into space" (251). Whether he served Germany's Third Reich or the United States and despite drastic changes in his moral and institutional instruments, von Braun's commitment to spaceflight never wavered.

In the Third Reich, government control and funding of rocket technology turned a group of idealistic backyard experimenters into the technical managers of a large-scale enterprise that could use slave labor as an efficient means of production. The central object of the research carried out at Peenemünde did not change with its transplantation to American soil: the rocket team's work for U.S. Army Ordinance was designed around the overt goal of carrying harm to the enemy. Von Braun was unable to escape completely the implications of this association. However, his biographers and rocket historians, for whom his contributions outweigh his shortcomings, consistently portray him as a man who regretted the use of the rocket in war. For von Braun and the other members of the German rocket team, the spaceflight dream represented the innocence of their youth, the cleansing of their wartime records, and the vindication of their promotion of the space future as a natural extension of the American dream.

The von Braun team's removal to the United States opened up opportunities unavailable in the German police state of the 1930s and 1940s. Von Braun found himself in command of the resources necessary to develop the rocket's space-going potential and free to campaign for spaceflight as its ultimate and most important use. In service to this goal he proved his natural gifts as a politician, embracing an American identity that masked but made good use of his privileged background as a scion of Germany's Junker aristocracy. Shortly after their arrival in America, his rocket team was established at the Army's base in Fort Bliss, New Mexico. Their first assignment was to assemble and test the V-2s that the American military had spirited away from Germany at the end of the war. At the White Sands Proving Ground near Fort Bliss, the German émigrés began their service as consultants to the newly named defense community in various phases of rocket technology and ordinance. The expatriated Germans also threw themselves into the task of becoming American citizens. No one did this with more zest than von Braun.[16] He seems to have made a conscious decision to change elements of his character, language, and political vision to make him acceptable in the American context. If he wanted to gain access to the U.S. government and to the American people, he could not play the role of a German aristocrat.[17]

The desert environment of White Sands was a fortuitous setting for this transformation and has provided an irresistible metaphor for rocket historians. It was during those years, they say, that von Braun refined the prewar spaceflight vision and realized the importance of presenting that vision to the common man: "After five years in the desert von Braun decided to go public in pressing for space exploration. One day, while walking among the sage brush with his associate Dr. Adolf K. Thiel, he suddenly turned to him and said with bluntness and facility in the idiom of his newly polished English, 'We can dream about rockets and the Moon until Hell freezes over. Unless the *people* understand it and the man who pays the bill is behind it, no dice. You worry about your damned calculations, and I'll talk to the people.' "[18] This account of von Braun's assumption of a public mission is deliberately mythic, evoking widely available stories of desert prophets and religious enlightenment. It implies that von Braun the Prussian aristocrat has been replaced by a hellfire and whiskey democrat. It is at variance, however, with Thiel's more pedestrian account: "One day, I showed the boss some recent calculations I had made about rockets to the Moon. Von Braun at first discussed the matter with great interest, but suddenly he said: 'You know what? Even if we continued our calculations until hell freezes over, we will not touch or move anybody. You may continue your theoretical studies, but I will talk to the people! I will go public now, because this is where we have to sow our seeds for space exploration!' "[19] Here the desert is replaced by an office, and the fiery rhetoric of a newly minted populist preacher is exchanged for the cooler tones of an intelligent politician.

Von Braun's desire to create a political and economic coalition around extraterrestrial conquest blinded him to every other consideration. As a result, the technology the engineer nurtured with his inspired management and the means by which he maintained the quality and coherence of his vision have left, in Sagan's assessment, a decidedly mixed legacy: "The modern rocket, which he pioneered, will prove to be either the means of mass annihilation through a global thermonuclear war or the means that will carry us to the planets and the stars. This dread ambiguity which faces us today, is central to the life of Wernher von Braun" (94). Sagan's caution is a refreshing corrective to those who would portray von Braun either as a misunderstood saint or an unapologetic sinner. Indeed, most studies represent him as either a hero or a villain in the war and the space race that followed. Writers dedicated to defending his reputation do so by producing an ahistorical figure that is more a force of destiny than a human being. Writers committed to producing an accurate history of the Nazi regime and the political compromises that followed tend to be fired by a determination to prosecute inadequately punished crimes against humanity.[20] The von Braun they give us is an amoral technocrat who opened a Pandora's box. Although the latter uncover the history suppressed by the heroic myth of the former, in their turn they often ignore the complexity of human moral experience and the precarious nature of circumstance.

Von Braun's most powerful contribution to the inspirational astrofuturism that fed the national interest in space during the 1950s and 1960s was as a politician. And as do many professional politicians, he practiced the arts of compromise and the possible. If he could not convince the majority that space is the terrain of manifest destiny, then he would appeal to the minority interest in the attractions of an ever-expanding capitalism; if the expansion of human rights displeased, then he allowed that an incipient totalitarianism could be accommodated; if an audience was unmoved by secular rationalism, then he would deploy the gospel of space. Carl Sagan's complaint that "there were many von Brauns" gives us some insight into the strategies of this natural politician.[21] At the heart of von Braun's charisma was his ability to allow his audiences to project onto him and through him their desires and fears as he pursued his own project. Tellingly, he defined his approach as "the art of letting someone else have your will" (94).

Von Braun's skill at framing the space frontier for a wide variety of interests and factions implies that there was no core to his own vision. In a sense this is true. Von Braun was not a utopian in the classic sense of proselytizing a blueprint for a better world some place else. His interest lay solely in the process and technique of getting there from here. However, this is not to say that we cannot identify the kind of social vision von Braun represented at mid-century. Consider, for instance, the image he projected through the medium that made him famous: television. In 1954, von Braun became a consulting "imagineer" for Walt Disney on a series of episodes for *Disneyland*, the network television show that helped transform the animation studio into a cultural superpower. In the midst of his busy schedule as director of rocket development for the Army Ballistic Missile Agency, von Braun took time to become part of a significant force in American cultural history. At this time, Disney was at the height of his career as a national impresario. His studio set standards for American animation; he was a pioneer in television and was on the verge of reviving the theme park as a form of mass entertainment. Disneyland combined education with amusement through a site plan organizing images paradigmatic to the national imagination: the small town (Main Street), the frontier (Frontierland), wild animal safaris (Adventureland), medieval romance (Fantasyland), and the future (Tomorrowland). As they planned both park and television series, the imagineers turned to von Braun and Willy Ley as the experts who were building the hardware that would make tomorrow a reality. The engineers were brought into the Tomorrowland project to teach their science to scriptwriters and artists.[22] The result was a three-part series, which placed an authoritatively

American stamp on the conquest of space: "Man in Space" (which first aired 9 March 1955), "Man and the Moon" (which first aired 28 December 1955), and "Mars and Beyond" (which first aired 4 December 1957).

These episodes present space travel not as the dream of some far distant future but as an imminent reality. Von Braun frames the scientific explanations of Heinz Haber and Ley, well-crafted models of space stations and craft, and animations illustrating the functions of his designs with the declaration, "If we were to start today on an organized, well supported space program, I believe a practical passenger rocket could be built and tested within ten years."[23] In "Man in Space," von Braun introduces his design for a four-stage moon rocket. In "Man and the Moon," the conquest of space proceeds with the presentation of "a realistic and believable trip to the moon in a rocket ship" (154). In this episode as well, von Braun reveals his classic space-station design, a key element in his early thoughts on how a lunar trip might be accomplished. The final episode, "Mars and Beyond," illustrates the next step, a trip to Mars using the mission profile argued for in *The Mars Project* and rocket team member Ernst Stuhlinger's ambitious plan for an "atomic electric space ship" (155).

The enthusiastic reception of the spaceflight dream in the early 1950s after so much indifference must be considered within the tenor of the times. At the dawn of what some historians have called "the American century," a time of tremendous national power and international influence, the space futurists found themselves speaking to a public as nervous about the national position as that which greeted the Weimar spaceflight movement.[24] The American victory in Europe and the Pacific brought a peace that seemed vulnerable to hot (Korea) and cold wars against communism, the insurgent civil rights movement, and the overwhelming burden of the atomic bomb.[25] The prospect that von Braun and his associates offered to the American public provided a fresh iteration of the frontier nostalgia that dominated popular culture in the 1950s. Disney writers dressed up the space future with the triumphant rhetoric of a "new frontier," thus reassuring their public that the great and good in America would survive and prosper. Steven Watts makes a strong case that the "Man in Space" series was understood by a good portion of its audience as a weapon in the cold war with the Soviet Union.[26] He argues that the series was "true to the imperatives of Cold War culture" and that its narratives "confidently assumed that *American* scientific expertise would lead the human caravan into outer space" (310, emphasis in original). But acceptance of that brave new world also meant embracing a future dominated by the large corporations and government agencies that Disney and von Braun so ably represented. For instance, the space future's materialization in Tomorrowland's rocket to the Moon ride was sponsored by Trans World Airlines (394). Following the example of the futuristic world's fairs of the 1930s, Disney and his German-American collaborators offered a future that marshaled familiar economic and political forces.[27]

Von Braun and his colleagues lavished a great deal of energy on the Disney project. One of Ray Spangenberg and Diane K. Moser's informants recalls that von Braun approached the effort in the same manner as if he were building an actual piece of hardware. The Disney collaboration gave him a bully pulpit from which to declaim his vision, and working on the programs functioned as a dress rehearsal for the real thing. The general impact of the "Man in Space" television series should not be underestimated. Indeed, the confluence of German-American science and spaceflight enthusiasm and the fantastic conventions of American cinema is a key turning point in postwar astrofuturism. The combination joined the technical avant-gardism, which carried Disney's apple-pie nostalgia to the exotic but hard-edged space-future vision of rocketry's pioneers. The most significant benefit for von Braun and his colleagues was access to the Disney stamp of unimpeachable Americanism. Henceforth, their patriotism was guaranteed by Walt Disney's standing as a highly visible anticommunist and his clandestine status as a "Special Agent in Charge contact" for the FBI.[28] Disney also provided an aesthetic of documentary filmmaking that mixed "education with entertainment," a genre fine-tuned by the studio's experience at producing celebratory narratives hailing the domestication of nature and the taming of natural forces.[29] It was a match made in heaven.

Mike Wright records that when the American Rocket Society held a 1955 regional meeting in southern California, its members screened "Man in Space" and toured Disneyland.[30] Randy Liebermann notes that after viewing its first broadcast Dwight D. Eisenhower called Disney, borrowed a copy, and kept it for two weeks to show it to Pentagon officials.[31] He further speculates that exposure to the piece may have convinced the Eisenhower administration to announce that America would participate in International Geophysical Year, 1957–58, by launching an earth satellite.[32] Disney also released a copy to the scientists and engineers of Pasadena's Jet Propulsion Laboratory. The success of the first episode convinced the studio to rebroadcast it twice in the following year and to release it as a theatrical film.

A result of the *Disneyland* episodes's success was von Braun's elevation to public celebrity as an ambassador for an American space program.[33] He and his work became central to Disney's animation of America's future in all the media at the studio's command—film, television, comic books, and amusement parks. The new technoscience of rocketry was at last able to bring its ambitions to a mass audience. To make its aims palatable for the broadest possible consumption, it domesticated them through the nostalgia for frontier prevalent in the 1950s and 1960s. Henceforth the notion of space as an American property would dominate mid-century discourses on the power of Western science to expand social and economic freedoms.

In the attractive mix of fact and fancy sold by Disney, von Braun held center stage as both scientific consultant and charismatic presenter. In this role, he took on the mantle of a particular kind of hero: young, handsome, outgoing, a leader, a scientific genius, a brilliant engineer. He embodies, with Disney's mediation, a boys' own image of an explorer who seeks new territory and tames it with his technology. This is not to say that von Braun pretended to be what he was not. Rather, the very masculine ideals and images that organized his own life also organized the way he could be perceived by a popular audience. In their 1995 biography, Spangenberg and Moser review his credentials as a pilot in gliders and advanced military aircraft (Stuka and Messerschmitt) and his exploits as one of rocketry's first flight test pilots.[34] In an earlier biographical sketch, Erik Bergaust draws attention to his enthusiasm for big game hunting and deep-sea diving. In a culture that celebrated the adventurous white masculinity exemplified by Theodore Roosevelt and Ernest Hemingway, von Braun easily fit into the mold of boy's idol.

Von Braun's American success must also be attributed to the positive value assigned to whiteness in the middle of the last century. Von Braun and his associates could be models for American youth because he was an educated and cultured European and was not racially other; to be blunt, he was German and not Japanese.[35] Moreover, his rapid assimilation of colloquial American English and his willingness to avoid any overt reliance on his aristocratic background made him an easily consumable public figure in a nation that tolerated and in some places required racial segregation. Whatever cultural refinements the German émigrés brought to their new hometown of Huntsville, Alabama (and there were many), there is no evidence to suggest that that they were fired by a determination to overturn several generations of white supremacist practice. As Europeans representing a cultivated heritage and as U.S. government employees of the Alabama Ballistic Missile Agency (ABMA), they fit neatly into the racial dynamic of Huntsville as members of its white elite.

Von Braun's position in Huntsville forced him to confront race under political circumstances drastically different from those that structured life in Germany. By the time he became Director of the George C. Marshall Space Flight Center (MSFC) in 1960, Alabama had experienced almost a decade of civil rights activity. The deep southern cities of Birmingham, Montgomery, and Selma had become the heart of the African American campaign for an end to racial segregation and race-based inequities. The political conditions under which von Braun worked underwent an almost overnight transformation from the presumption of white supremacy as ordinary culture to emergent conditions of racial equality. The civil rights movement was considered as an emergency by both white and black authorities, indeed by anyone who had an investment in the standing order of things. As they had done in Hitler's Germany, von Braun, his family, and colleagues lived, worked, and found their places in the standing order. However, the challenge of the civil rights movement also made it impossible to ignore the agency and critique of the disenfranchised.

In Stuhlinger and Ordway's account of that time, the civil disturbances around civil rights were also perceived as a challenge to Huntsville, Alabama's part of the newly minted space program (187). James E. Webb, then NASA Administrator, "implored von Braun to make every effort to hire qualified blacks into MSFC's labor force" (187). In response, the director moved to "avoid any trace of racism" in his operation and "desegregation proceeded smoothly in Huntsville" (187). In contrast to Governor George Wallace's famous stand in the schoolhouse door, Stuhlinger and Ordway point out that von Braun established an early "affirmative action initiative with local contractors," worked to create technical contracts with traditionally black Alabama A&M University, and gave a number of talks to local businessmen encouraging support for improvement of local "education, transportation and recreation" (188). Concluding their account of von Braun's civil rights record, his memoirists quote a congratulatory 1965 newspaper account praising the visionary as "one of the most outspoken and persistent spokesmen for moderation and racial reconciliation in the South" (188). With satisfaction they record that "civil rights leaders saw little reason to campaign in the city" (187).

In their haste to establish von Braun's benevolent social credentials, Stuhlinger and Ordway neglect the record of civil rights activity in Huntsville, including "lunch counter sit-ins, boycotts, picket lines" and a visit by Martin Luther King, Jr.[36] Nevertheless, if we take seriously von Braun's singular goal, his intervention into civil rights, prompted by federal interest in civil stability, makes sense. No doubt von Braun was sincere when he encouraged George Wallace to "shed the shackles of the past" during a 1965 encounter in Huntsville. But, characteristically, he did not tell Huntsville's elite that racial equality should be offered on constitutional or principled grounds. Rather, he argued that "Alabama's image is marred by civil rights incidents and statements." Since he was speaking to the chamber of commerce of a segregated Huntsville, it is safe to read this statement not as an indictment of white racism, but as a complaint against black objections to racism. Von Braun was concerned to make improvements that would allow the state to save face and contribute to the social peace required for a quiet and dependable work force.

Von Braun reached the pinnacle of his visibility when Soviet success with placing artificial satellites into planetary orbit threatened American prestige and self-interest.[37] The U.S. Navy's attempt to mount a quick response to the Soviet initiative through its rocket program resulted in an embarrassingly public failure when *Vanguard I* exploded on the launch pad in December 1957, to the delight and dismay of a national television audience. The reaction of the media was immediate and rancorous.[38] When Von Braun's team successfully answered *Sputnik* by launching *Explorer I* in 1958, they gave their adopted homeland the confidence it needed to initiate a superpower-dominated space race. The nation breathed a sigh of relief and von Braun was lionized by the national press. In February of that year, "Missileman Von Braun" joined other famous faces on the cover of *Time* magazine. The 17 February issue included an article that told von Braun's story, from his early experiments with the VfR to the triumph of *Explorer I*. One thing stands out in the resume provided by *Time*: von Braun's professional life was circumscribed by his work in the military—both German and American—developing weapons designed to deliver destruction at long range. Even so, the writer of the article contends, creating weapons was not what drove the scientist. Rather, he was motivated by was the heroic dream of conquering the space frontier:

[of] the legions of scientists, generals, admirals, engineers and administrators at work on missiles and man-made moons, German-born Wernher von Braun, 45, best personified man's accelerating drive to rise above the planet. Von Braun, in fact, has only one interest: the conquest of space, which he calls man's greatest venture. To pursue his lifelong dream, he has helped Adolph Hitler wage a vengeful new kind of war, has argued against bureaucracy in two languages and campaigned against official apathy and public disbelief on two continents through most of his adult years.[39]

Such accounts present spaceflight as a noble end in itself, and represent von Braun as a hero and martyr transcending the petty allegiances of this world in his devotion to the promise of the future.

Von Braun's celebrity helped domesticate the spaceflight agenda. It broadcast the wonderful dream in familiar cultural narratives through easily accessible views. By 1960, his fame was so great that Hollywood released a laudatory bio-pic called "I Aim at the Stars," with German actor Curt Jurgens in the star-ring role. NASA Administrator T. Keith Glennan attended a Congressional screening of the film and provides an intriguing glimpse of the engineer's response to his celebrity: "Von Braun was there and spoke briefly before the film was shown. He was his usual relaxed and seemingly good-natured self. He stated that it was a little difficult to be objective about a film of one's own life but that, given the usual discount for love interest and drama required by screen writers, he thought the film was a reasonably accurate portrayal."[40] Glennan and his wife found the film disingenuous at best. "Von Braun is made out to be an anti-Nazi and seems to epitomize the scientist's lack of responsibility for the end use of the products of his mind," Glennan wrote.[41] The Hollywood attempt to make von Braun fit the sanitized formula it used for great historical figures—conventions that exchange complex human realities for icons—was only partially successful. Even at the height of his fame, some American collaborators harbored doubts about the icons made of the man and his vision.

It was von Braun's good fortune to be the right man at the right time. His crusade took him far beyond the laboratories, lecture halls, and conferences familiar to most scientists and engineers, and gave him the energy to produce "a barrage of talks and articles on every aspect of astronautics that was to fascinate Rotarians, Kiwanians and, for a few critical years, senators and congressmen, as well as readers of the popular press."[42] His training as an ordinance engineer in Germany and in the United States authorized his public persona as a popularizer of science, technology, and the conquest of space during the 1950s. Here was a man who, unlike the legion of writers of pulp science fiction and cheaply produced Saturday morning serials, knew what he was talking about and had the backing of big science and government money. He was a man of great personal charm, and his passion in promoting the space future made him a very persuasive salesman. Frederick C. Durant III, science writer, spaceflight advocate, and von Braun intimate, recalls:

Over the years I have had the opportunity to introduce von Braun to numerous people of widely diverse backgrounds—editors, physicists, the military, Madison Avenue types and businessmen, large and small. Again and again, I have seen von Braun's personality work magic on opinionated individuals who had preconceived notions and erroneous impressions of von Braun himself, his projects and accomplishments. It is human nature I suppose, to suspect and to be a little envious of someone who had been a wartime enemy and who has had subsequent widespread publicity in a technology as yeasty as rockets and spaceflight. But over and over I've watched these opinions change, usually within a few minutes of a first meeting, as von Braun's personal warmth and engaging manner and obvious honesty are communicated as if by a sixth sense.[43]

Von Braun proved equally persuasive to politicians in the wake of the first *Sputnik*:

[T]estifying before Congress had become a relatively simple task for von Braun. He had considerable experience from his many contacts in the Pentagon, and his frequent visits to Capitol Hill to appear before this or that committee soon became routine. . . . Indeed, several congressmen welcomed the opportunity to question von Braun—simply because he mesmerized them with his overwhelming knowledge, wisdom and charm. "Listening to Dr. von Braun," the late Senator Alexander Wiley said, "is like listening to a radio science fiction spectacular in the old days."[44]

Of course, von Braun and other first-generation astrofuturists may have contested the senator's comparison; they were eager to present their future visions to the general public as factual science, not science fiction.[45] The comparison does emphasize, however, one of the most interesting characteristics of astrofuturism since 1945: the constant interchange that occurs between fact and fiction, fantasy and valid scientific speculation within the field. While the main thrust of astrofuturist work has been in the realm of popular science—explaining the space future to a lay audience as a feasible project for current science and technology—communicating that vision through the medium of journalistic articles, lectures, and documentaries allied it with science fiction. Because of their backgrounds in technoscience, astrofuturists have felt a close affinity with science fiction and have used the genre to communicate their speculations to a mass audience. In fact, many astrofuturists who have served as professional scientists and engineers, including von Braun and Carl Sagan, point to boyhood reading of science fiction as the initial motivation for pursuing technical educations and careers in science and engineering.[46] Von Braun's early enthusiasm for the spaceflight movement can be traced to his adolescent reading of Jules Verne, H. G. Wells, Garrett P. Serviss, and Kurd Lasswitz.[47]

As with any other field of literature, early exposure and continued affection led many of the astrofuturists to try their hand at writing science fiction. Some of the more successful accomplished the move from working in the aerospace industry to professional writing on the strength of their work. But whether or not an individual futurist became a successful writer, the early astrofuturists as a group had a tremendous impact on science fiction. The popular science essays and books that they produced supplied the basic information and technology for the work of such authors as Robert A. Heinlein and Lester del Rey. Before *Sputnik*, science fiction had become a critical outlet for the astrofuturist vision, in part because of its pedagogical function for a young audience. Von Braun knew that the scientific or technological imagination could not be explained adequately to the public simply by showing graphs, diagrams, and equations. Illustrating the future technical feasibility of a space station or a lunar voyage was not enough; such ventures had to be explained in a way that proved compelling within the social, political, and economic confines of the present. The scientific and technological platform of von Braun's astrofuturism required literary explication through a set of expository conventions that would explain it and place it within the existing culture. In short, the space future needed science fiction's characters, plots, narratives, and adventures to make it glamorous to the public.

During his time at Fort Bliss, von Braun's desire to reach the public prompted him to write a novel that described what a trip to Mars would be like sometime in the near (1948) future. Perhaps he was encouraged by the postwar boom in science fiction to believe that there might be a receptive market for his speculations if they were properly packaged as a standard science-fiction adventure.[48] As Frederick Ordway and Eric Bergaust tell the story, it was those years of enforced isolation and boredom in the New Mexican desert that stimulated the space adventure that von Braun called *Das Marsprojekt*. They write, "The high, thin clouds above the light sandy soil of the desert had turned his receptive imagination to thoughts of Mars. He formulated a plot and a story of seventy passengers and their journey to the red planet."[49] However, like many a first-time author, von Braun found the market more resistant to his offering than he would have liked: "von Braun, with all the pride of anticipation of a man who had written his first book, sent the manuscript of [*The*] *Mars Project* off to a publishing house in New York. After six weeks it came back with a polite no. 'It sounds too fantastic,' the reply said. Von Braun tried somewhere else, and again the answer was no."[50] *The Mars Project* was eventually published in 1952, but without the fantastic adventure von Braun had originally hoped would sell the book. His publisher decided that the novel's appendix was the most valuable part of the exercise; it contained the detailed equations, charts, graphs, and cost estimates that represented von Braun's early thoughts on what it would take to actually mount an interplanetary expedition to Mars. Significantly, the publishing house was German. Mainstream American publishers could see no market for a trip to Mars too exotic for science fact and too quotidian for formulaic adventure.[51]

In *The Mars Project*, von Braun emphasizes a theme that recurs time and again in American astrofuturism: a future in space is no dream but, with current science and technology, an immediate possibility. Through tables, graphs, and equations, von Braun describes and illustrates the elaborate infrastructure he thought necessary for a successful trip to another world. Unlike the cost-conscious scenarios of a later date, his imagined expedition of the late 1940s followed precedents set by earlier, terrestrial explorations. Invoking the memory of Columbus's New World voyages, von Braun imagined the first Mars trip as an immense project requiring an armada of ten ships with a crew of at least seventy astronauts. His justification for the commitment and expense required to undertake the voyage refers to the man he takes as a predecessor: "In 1492 Columbus knew less about the far Atlantic than we do about the heavens, yet he chose not to sail with a flotilla of less than three ships, and history tends to prove that he might never have returned to Spanish shores with his report of discoveries had he entrusted his fate to a single bottom. So it is with interplanetary exploration: it must be done on the grand scale."[52] The scale of von Braun's project is based on his assumption that the first journey to the red planet will lead inevitably to the establishment of a permanent human presence there with all of the development that implies. He also advocates the creation of a social and technological infrastructure that violate popular American stories of technoscientific progress accomplished through the efforts of backyard mechanics and visionary inventors. Von Braun realized that he had to convince the public to think beyond the democratically inflected "Yankee Tinkerer" notion supported by a great deal of science fiction and by the popular mythology surrounding inventor/industrialists such as Benjamin Franklin, Thomas Edison, and George Eastman. From his own experience in the development of rocketry, von Braun knew that the efforts of the "back-yard inventor, no matter how ingenious he might be" could not bring about the dawn of the Space Age. That goal "can only be achieved by the coordinated might of scientists, technicians, and organizers belonging to very nearly every branch of modern science and industry. Astronomers, physicians, mathematicians, engineers, physicists, chemists, and test pilots are essential; but no less so are economists, businessmen, diplomats, and a host of others" (10). Instead of the solitary man of genius who dominates popular fiction, a vast corps of people recruited from every walk of life must contribute to the conquest of space. American society would have to be reconfigured to meet the challenge offered by the space frontier.

Von Braun's articulate defense of the rocket state does not mean that he dismisses individual genius as irrelevant. On the contrary, that genius must be harnessed to create a dedicated elite whose training would fit it seamlessly into the managerial and technological machine required by the grand scale of interplanetary exploration (2). In *The Mars Project*, von Braun works hard "to explode once and for all the theory of the solitary space rocket and its little band of bold interplanetary adventurers" (1). Instead, his conquest of space is undertaken by a vast army of specialists "trained to co-operate unfailingly" (2). In other words, while von Braun respects his literary predecessors, he rearticulates their future vision in the light of his own experience. Reasoning from the immense complexity of the rocket and his own experience of the large organizations necessary to its development and manufacture, he implies that only a military-based society can marshal the resources, precision, and expertise necessary for a Martian expedition. For example, he reassures the reader that "the logistic requirements for a large, elaborate expedition to Mars are no greater than those for a minor military operation extending over a limited theater of war" (4). His assumption of the prominence of a military-style organization in the conquest of space was also a response to the continuing necessity of persuading the government officials who controlled America's purse strings. During one of his first meetings with T. Keith Glennan, NASA's first administrator, von Braun bluntly declared, "Look, all we want is a very rich and very benevolent uncle."[53] Thus, he wove issues of national security and the cold war into his delineation of the benefits of mounting a Mars expedition or building a space station.

In "Prelude to Space Travel," his contribution to the pioneering anthology *Across the Space Frontier*, von Braun provides further details of the endeavor he imagines. He argues that a space station must be built as a permanent base for manned space operations. Such a station would provide a staging ground for exploration and its personnel could make useful contributions to meteorology, astronomy, and ocean navigation. It would also serve as "a guardian of the peace."[54]

Technicians in this space station, using specially designed, powerful telescopes attached to large optical screens, radarscopes, and cameras, will keep under constant inspection every ocean, continent, country, and city. Even small towns will be clearly visible through optical instruments that will give the watchers in space the same vantage point enjoyed by a man in an observation plane only 4,000 feet off the ground.

Nothing will go unobserved. Within each 2–hour period, as the earth revolves inside the satellite's orbit, one-twelfth of the globe's territory will pass into the view of the space station's occupants; within each 24–hour period, the entire surface of the earth will have been visible. (12–15)

Despite this Orwellian description, von Braun does not mean to suggest that his space station will be the instrument of some dystopian oppression. On the contrary, he argues that in the proper hands, American hands, such surveillance will serve the interests of peace and freedom: "because of the telescopic eyes and cameras of the space station, it will be practically impossible for any nation to hide warlike preparations for any length of time" (15). This space station is the ultimate observation post, unassailable in its occupation of orbital and moral high ground. Here von Braun supplies the ideological building blocks on which the 1960s space race found its political justification.

Across the Space Frontier was published in 1952 during America's involvement in Korea, with its implications of a coming war with "red" China. International tensions kept the military agenda foremost in the minds of futurists who owed their living to the military-industrial complex.[55] It is no surprise, therefore, that von Braun offered his space station to those leading the postwar rush to impose an international order. Commanding the orbital high ground, it would be the ideal place for hitherto unheard of concentrations of military might. Making explicit its strategic importance, he wrote, "It can be converted into an extremely effective atomic-bomb carrier. Small winged rocket missiles with atomic war heads could be launched from the station in such a manner that they would strike their targets at supersonic speeds. By simultaneous radar tracking of both missile and target, these atomic-headed rockets could be accurately guided to any spot on the earth."[56] A detailed description of the tactical considerations of this conversion follow, and the passage closes with a discussion of why a fully armed space station would be virtually invulnerable to attack. Here von Braun caters to the needs of the early cold war and to the political desire for a dominance accomplished through sole ownership of a high technology. He concludes, "The important point is that the station could defend itself in case of attack and that it could prevent rival stations from being established. Therefore, whether in the hands of a single peace-loving nation, or in the hands of the United Nations, the space station would be a deterrent which might cause a successful outlawing of war."[57] In the right hands, the space station could be the all-powerful doomsday weapon that would force the end of humanity's favorite pastime. As H. Bruce Franklin points out in his invaluable study *War Stars,* the idea that a super-weapon might secure a lasting peace, the first condition of utopia, frequently recurs in the popular culture of techno-science.[58] In his astrofuturism, therefore, von Braun follows a venerable tradition in the technological imagination of the West.

Failure as a fiction writer did not diminish von Braun's desire to write and publish. Rather, it forced him to concentrate his energies on making the fantastic real within contemporary life. In an account of himself as a writer von Braun remarked, "After a day of excruciating meetings for the Redstone Project . . . it is such an enjoyable relaxation to transpose yourself to the lunar surface and simply charge ahead with a colorful description of all the exciting adventures that expect you [*sic*] there. . . . I mix me some martinis, put a Brandenburg concerto on the record player, and just write and write . . . until Maria [*his wife*] gets out of bed and reminds me that I must be in the office two hours from now."[59] The space future is an adventure to which von Braun could escape the pressures of creating the vehicles he hoped would make it possible. He presents his literary activity as a culturally expressive act dignified by professional activity and the consumption of middle-class luxuries. The astrofuturist places himself within a context of industrial activity and suburban domesticity, thereby offering his readers is a fair example of how astrofuturism could make sense during the 1950s and 1960s.

Astrofuturism's expository conventions were not, however, the creation of one man. Willy Ley, another German émigré, was the necessary mediator in the importation and integration of German spaceflight enthusiasm into what became an American vision of the space future. With the exception of those years when the National Socialists were in power in Germany, Ley's career was intimately intertwined with that of von Braun and the other members of the rocket team. He was a founding member of the *Verein für Raumschiffahrt* when it was established in 1927 and he served as its vice president from 1928 through 1933. During the society's early experiments, Ley helped devise some of the basic principles and methods that guided the development of liquid-fueled rocketry in Germany.[60] His greatest contribution to science, rocketry, and astrofuturism, however, was not as an experimenter, but as a writer.

While von Braun received the call to carry the gospel of the space future to the American public during his late 1940s exile at the White Sands Proving Ground, Ley found his commission much earlier. It is apparent from the slim biographical material that exists on his life that Ley provided much of the enthusiasm and energy required to bring together the early group of German space visionaries. For example, he is credited with introducing von Braun to Hermann Oberth, the Transylvanian educator who inspired rocketors on both sides of the Atlantic with his 1923 book *Die Rakete zu den Planetenräumen* (The Rocket into Planetary Space).[61] Moreover, Ley's rough facility with foreign languages allowed him to become astrofuturism's first international publicist.[62] During the late 1920s and early 1930s, he corresponded with all the major spaceflight and rocket societies in Europe, America, and the Soviet Union, keeping in touch with major practitioners of the art and serving as a clearinghouse for information. He also kept spaceflight enthusiasts on both sides of the Atlantic apprised of developments and progress in the German society. Ley's international correspondence complemented his freshly minted career as a science popularizer. In 1926, he wrote *Die Fahrt ins Weltall* (The Journey into the Universe), a popularization of Hermann Oberth's heavily technical book. The success of his first effort to make the subject comprehensible to a popular audience can be measured by Oberth's enthusiastic approval and by the strong reception the book received in the general literary market.[63]

Ley's career began in the early days of the rocket societies, when the groups were searching for funds and a sense of legitimacy in their nations. Although all the amateur spaceflight enthusiasts dreamed of the same goal, the conquest of space, tempers flared and bitter arguments occurred as each faction fought to establish its priority, the power to command resources, and the right to set the agenda both within and outside the rocket community. As Ley reported the impressive advances made by the VfR, for example, he was met with cries of "foul," "idea piracy," and "patent infringement" from some members of the American branch of rocket invention. In 1944, following the publication of Ley's *Rockets*, Robert H. Goddard, rocket pioneer and Professor of Physics at Clark University in Massachusetts, complained to Edmund Wilson of *The New Yorker* that Ley neglected American (that is, Goddard's own) contributions to liquid-fueled rocketry in his haste to promote German advances.[64] In correspondence with Pendray, Goddard indicated that his "patience was tried by the Ley book."[65] In response, Ley attempted to redress the balance in later editions of his rocket history, but argued that although Goddard's work was important, the early isolation of rocket experimenters by distance and language made duplication of effort and independent creation inevitable.[66]

It is interesting that the members of the VfR should have been so successful both in experimentation and in the publication of their work. Their success in both areas is attributable to the fact that of all the early amateur rocket societies, they were the most fortunate in terms of physical and economic resources. As Michael Neufeld has demonstrated, they were part of the intellectual and cultural ferment of a nation pursuing projects that could recover the prestige and stability lost in its 1918 defeat.[67] They survived longer than any other group of active experimenters outside the military-industrial complex that became crucial to the mature development of rocket technology. Their unblushing idealism and commitment to developing the technology exclusively for a space future also lasted longer than all but that of the British Interplanetary Society. By the early 1930s, the international rocket community watched developments at the Berlin *Raketenflugplatz* with excitement and envy. That success drew the interest of the German government, which had more earthbound reasons for being interested in rocket technology: when Colonel Becker and Captains Dornberger and Dorn of German Army Ordinance visited the VfR's test site in 1932, they were looking for a way around the Versailles conventions that limited the type and size of their long-range guns. The nascent technology of modern rocketry looked like a promising way of achieving that goal.

While the interest of the *Reichswehr* was attractive as a stable source of income, it also meant that the rocketeers had to play by military rules rather than by those of an amateur scientific club. That was made abundantly clear as first von Braun and then other vital experimenters were hired away by Army Ordinance. The Army then began a campaign to shut down German participation in the international spaceflight movement. VfR veteran Rolf Engel was arrested "for corresponding with prominent space pioneers in other countries."[68] Ley's own journalism and networking quickly got him in trouble with security-conscious Army authorities, who "ordered [him] to cease writing on rocketry for foreign publications."[69] The campaign proceeded with a Gestapo raid on the *Raketenflugplatz*, which Ley witnessed in October 1933.[70] Army maneuvering eventually resulted in a water bill that the rocket group could not pay and the final loss of their lease on the old ammunition dump that had been their home for three years.[71] Ley's connections with VfR innovators were severed as the *Reichswehr* ordinance program dropped a veil of secrecy.

By 1934, the VfR disbanded and the vigorous astronautical network that Ley had helped build dissolved.[72] In 1935, Ley wrote his overseas correspondents that he was in trouble with the authorities. And on the eve of the 1936 Olympic Games held in Berlin, Ley became a part of the migration of German intellectuals and political dissidents fleeing the rise of national socialism.[73] As the storm clouds of war gathered, spaceflight activity in Europe ground to a halt.[74] Ordway and Sharpe note that, "With Ley's departure from Germany, the flow of rocket society news virtually ceased—and hardly anyone noticed. This is not surprising, for outside of small amateur societies operating on shoestring budgets and occasional isolated dreamers and experimenters typified by America's Robert H. Goddard, interest in rocketry was virtually nil in the United States and the United Kingdom."[75] Spaceflight advocates who remained and continued their work in Nazi Germany were pressed into the practical business of making weapons.

After a short stay in London where, under the sponsorship of the British Interplanetary Society, he presented a series of lectures and articles on rocketry, Willy Ley arrived in New York. There he was given a warm welcome by representatives of the American Rocket Society and found that his work was easily transferable to the American context. In short order, he was ready to raise American public awareness of the latest in rocket technology and the spaceflight vision.[76] Not surprisingly, Ley took his ideas on the space future to the most receptive audiences America had to offer: the amateur rocket societies and the science-fiction community. In 1937, he began contributing popular science articles to *Astounding Science Fiction*, a magazine that was moving toward a hard science bias under the editorial direction of John W. Campbell.[77] By 1952, he became the science editor for *Galaxy Science Fiction*, a position he held until his death almost two decades later. While producing popular science articles and many books on natural history, he also dabbled in writing genre science fiction.[78] Because of his intimate connection with science fiction in America, Ley became an important link between European rocketry and its American counterpart. During the early 1950s, he reestablished contact with those of his old *Raketenflugplatz* colleagues who had been brought to America by the U.S. Army. By the middle of the decade, he was working with von Braun and others from both the German rocket team and the American scientific and science-fiction communities on a series of books that described an imminent conquest of space.[79]

By the mid-1950s, the conquest of the space frontier seemed to be an idea whose time had come. The derision and embarrassed dismissal the subject had encountered in earlier years evaporated as a growing number of writers and artists with solid science and engineering credentials came forward to promote it. In contrast to an earlier generation of writers who used space as a background for formulaic pulp adventures, many of these new writers, including von Braun, held positions of authority within the scientific and technical communities of their day. Although their faith in the importance of space and its relevance to a scientific agenda made them a definite minority within those communities, they could not easily be dismissed as crackpots. They were tied into a postwar military-industrial complex that was actively experimenting with the new rocket technology, doing research and development that had government sanction. The aerospace industry that emerged from this constellation of interests in the 1950s also realized the importance of selling the new technology to the public. The American people had to be convinced that the investment being made in rocket technology was the only sure way of guaranteeing a tranquil and prosperous future. The astrofuturist agenda, as a result, dovetailed nicely with the interests of the aerospace industry. As astrofuturists wooed the public with their wonderful space futures, they also demystified rocket technology and advertised the benign intent of the industries behind it. Their message was that crossing the space frontier was no fantasy for the far future; rather, it was a goal that could be accomplished in the near future. Their books and articles presented a conquest of space that would not threaten social and political constants. On the contrary, it would allow for an endless renewal of the democratic values and prosperity central to the American way of life.

Almost twenty years after David Lasser's pioneering effort, Willy Ley wrote his own version of *The Conquest of Space*, a book that sought to widen the audience for the spaceflight dream.[80] Published by the Viking Press in 1950, it gained wide notice in the spaceflight and science-fiction communities on both sides of the Atlantic. In a contemporary review of the book, Arthur C. Clarke describes it as "an outstanding example of co-operation between art and technology."[81] The synthesis that excited Clarke and his colleagues was a result of Ley's collaboration with Chesley Bonestell, the architect who would make space art a respectable discipline in the aerospace and science-fiction communities. Ley's technical authority coupled with Bonestell's hard-edged illustrations of the machines and landscapes of space exploration helped move astrofuturism from the fantastic to the real. By creating the atmosphere of technological verisimilitude essential to the project, Bonestell's illustrations and paintings supported Ley's history of technology, replaced the tin-pot space ships so familiar from the Flash Gordon science-fiction serials of the 1930s and the pulp iconography of spaceships produced by artists such as R. Frank Paul, and connected rocket flight and space travel to other transportation revolutions.

The Ley and Bonestell collaboration drew interest from the world beyond the science-fiction ghetto. While Lasser's *The Conquest of Space* was almost completely ignored, the later book met with widespread acclaim. The twenty-year gap between the two books helps explain the difference in popular reception. Produced in the 1930s, Lasser's *Conquest* appeared at a time when science fiction was in its infancy and rocketry was not dignified by government funding or corporate profits. By the early 1950s, all that was changing. Rocketry had become a strategic asset, a tool of international science and campaign fodder for politicians with presidential aspirations. Lester Del Rey writes that as a result of these changes, the American public began to accept science fiction as more than "that Flash Gordon stuff": "The atomic bomb was partly responsible for this; science fiction had accepted and written about atomic power when there was total ignorance of the subject elsewhere—partly caused by an imposed government secrecy, of course. As a result, a sort of grudging respect entered into mention of the field in newspapers and other magazines. For the first time, being a writer of science fiction carried a measure of respectability."[82]

In the popular mind the technological power represented by rocketry was conflated with that of the atomic bomb. The most recognizable technological icons of the 1950s and 1960s were that of the rocket and the atom, often placed in immediate juxtaposition. During the 1950s, the two became symbols not only of science fiction but of any forward-looking company hoping to identify itself with the future. They were used on the painted covers of science-fiction magazines and paperbacks, and became the trademarks of science-fiction publishers such as the John C. Winston Company.[83] Automobile manufacturers used the rocket as a design feature on their cars to suggest the idea that a look or an engine was produced by cutting-edge research and development. For example, O. B. Hardison, Jr., notes that "between 1950 and 1965 General Motors put tail fins on its cars to intimate that they were rockets."[84] In this atmosphere, Ley's *The Conquest of Space* with its Bonestell paintings and coffee-table presentation reached a popular audience hungry for information that would explain the technology of the rocket and its possible impact on American culture.

Ley's *The Conquest of Space* introduced its audience to what Michael A. G. Michaud calls the "classic agenda" for manned spaceflight: a technosocial plan that represents the core of the space future as it was imagined in the 1950s and 1960s. Michaud points out that the "classic agenda is positive and expansionist. To the advocates of spaceflight, humanity's outward expansion was not only desirable but obviously so."[85] It is around this agenda that the first-generation astrofuturists formed their technical and ideological consensus in the 1950s. *The Conquest of Space* set the epistemological framework for the astrofuturist project by weaving together the literary, scientific, and technological background to the spaceflight idea. It also used the narrative strategies of science fiction to present the reader with attractive social and cultural reasons for accepting its inevitability. Perhaps the most important aspect of the Ley text is his presentation of the space future as a natural extension of Western and, therefore, American culture. For Ley, the conquest of space is mandated by natural and historical law, ordained in the same fashion as the European conquest of the New World. Support for this teleology comes from his understanding of history as the advancement of Western science and technology.

To persuade the reader that the conquest of space is a logical consequence of humanity's fascination with the stars from ancient to modern times, Ley focuses attention on the development of the sciences, particularly that of astronomy. According to Ley's account, there have been two eras of astronomy up to the early 1900s. The first era covers "the time when Babylonian astronomer-priests looked up to the lights in the sky to see the abodes and possibly to learn the will of their gods to the time of Kepler's own teacher Tycho Brahe."[86] The second era proceeds from the invention of the telescope in the Netherlands (by Anton van Leeuwenhoek) and its use by astronomers from Galileo Galilei to the present. According to Ley, the telescope "gradually added a new discipline to astronomy, that of exploring and describing the surfaces of the heavenly bodies."[87] Ley's 1950 vision situates the beginning of the third era of astronomy in the first manned landing on "the shining island of Levania of which Kepler dreamed": the Moon.[88]

For Ley, an astronomical/historical era is distinguished by its technology.

He defines the first two eras of astronomy by the technology of sight: the un-
aided eye is superseded by the primitive telescopes of sixteenth-century Europe
and their ever more powerful and sophisticated descendents. Optical technology is still a part of Ley's postulated third era, but with the addition of
a transport technology powerful enough to escape Earth's gravity. Although
in his discussion of Kepler he acknowledges astronomy's theoretical side, he
believes that the discipline advances through practice, not theory. In other
words, progress occurs through advances in technology, not through abstract
reasoning. The spaceship, therefore, is the next logical step in the progress of
astronomy:

> It almost seems that each era of astronomy does best when it comes to solving the
> problems of the preceding era. The inaccuracies of naked-eye observation were easily
> corrected by the optical instruments of the second era. The questions posed by the
> telescope—mostly concerning the surface conditions of the planets—will be answered
> by the spaceship. If the third era also poses new problems and questions without an-
> swering them, it will be up to the scientists of the third era to find ways and means
> toward a fourth era.[89]

Using astronomy as both metaphor and guide, Ley presents the conquest
of space as a historical inevitability arising from the technological progress
forced by the needs of scientific observation. Thus science and technology are
placed in the service of a human need to control the material universe. Progress
in astronomy is not measured by an interest in abstract knowledge, but by the
increasing ability to provide the tools necessary for an inventory of the *weltall*.
Astronomy itself becomes a technoscientific tool that will allow us to explore
other worlds, just as it enabled the exploration of distant islands and continents
on our own. Projecting this instrumental view of astronomy into the future and
aided by a further forty more years of science fiction and technological speculation, it is easy to imagine what the fourth age of astronomy might be: the
direct manipulation of extraterrestrial bodies—asteroids, planets, and even
stars—for fun and profit.

Ley's historical scheme speaks to presuppositions of science fiction well
grounded in the Western scientific and technological imagination. In one of
his popularizations not dedicated to spaceflight, *Engineer's Dreams* (1954),
the science writer speculates about the possibility of mammoth terrestrial projects such as a tunnel between Britain and continental Europe, a central African
lake, moving icebergs to warmer climes as a source of fresh water, partially
draining the Mediterranean Sea to provide new land mass, and a range of
by now familiar alternatives for generating energy: geothermal, solar, oceanic

induction, and wind. The book's reigning presupposition is that there is no limit to humanity's ability to reshape nature to suit its own ends.[90] The grand scale of Ley's dreams echoes the great civil engineering endeavors that transformed the North American landscape in the nineteenth and early twentieth centuries, including the Brooklyn Bridge, the Hoover Dam, the Panama Canal, and the projects of the Tennessee Valley Authority. As his title indicates, he also invokes popular narratives of heroic engineers who tame nature for the public good.[91] In an atmosphere of public optimism about such work, it is not surprising that gigantic engineering projects—encapsulating the Sun to capture all its ambient energy, moving asteroids into Earth orbit for easy access to the minerals they contain, and "terraforming" other planets—have been commonplace in space futurist speculation since the 1920s.[92] Ley mobilizes this history to validate both the present in which he lives and the future he desires. His teleology comes vested in the robes of progress; it is, in effect, a technological manifest destiny. The classic agenda of manned spaceflight that he promoted was an extension of the technological triumphs and subsequent terrestrial expansion that marked the conquest of the American west in the nineteenth century and the nation's imperial adventures in the early twentieth.

At this point in the development of American astrofuturism, however, the space-future vision was recognized as desirable only by its immediate constituency, habitual readers of science fiction and boys' adventure literature. The evangelism of the pioneering astrofuturists demanded a wider audience, one that transcended the generic and social confines of that era's science-fiction community. The search for that audience led to the creation of a symposium at the Hayden Planetarium at the American Museum of Natural History in New York focusing exclusively on the topic of space travel. It was the brainchild of the ubiquitous Willy Ley, who, while in contact with Robert R. Coles, the chairman of the planetarium, mentioned "the annual astronautical congresses which were then just starting in Europe." Because of the distance involved, Americans had difficulty finding the time and money to attend the European conferences. While the home-grown American Rocket Society did hold annual meetings, sessions on space travel took up very little of its time. On the other hand, the European meetings "were devoted to nothing else." Ley proposed a conference at the planetarium that would redress the balance.[93] As it had done in the 1930s, the planetarium would provide a forum for a new generation of space travel visionaries.

Significantly, the organizers of the First Annual Symposium on Space Travel picked Columbus Day, 1951, for their first meeting, "partly for symbolic reasons." They had to restrict the size of that first gathering because of limited space, but the committee made sure they had a representative cross section of the constituencies the space futurists wanted to reach. The meeting led to interest by two of most powerful forces influencing public opinion in the 1950s: the upscale general interest magazine and motion pictures. Ley notes, "Those invited were representative of universities, other scientific institutions, of the armed forces stationed in New York, of city and state governments, and of publications."[94] Among those publications was *Collier's*, a mass-market magazine whose audience was the crucial middle-class, college-educated reader, also sought by *Life, Look,* and the *Saturday Evening Post.*[95]

Collier's interest in the proposals of von Braun, Ley, and company at the Hayden Planetarium resulted in the publication of a series of articles on the science and technology of space travel under the optimistic heading, "Man Will Conquer Space Soon."[96] These articles were published in an expanded form as *Across the Space Frontier* (1952), a hardbound book that served as a popular primer for an entire generation of space enthusiasts. The symposium and the books that followed it constituted the first postwar attempt to introduce the idea of space travel to the public as a serious possibility. It was also the first major exposure the American public had to the central figures of first-generation astrofuturism. *Across the Space Frontier* contained articles by Heinz Haber, a pioneer of space medicine as well as one of its initial popularizers; Fred Whipple, a Harvard astronomer who became a well known popularizer of his subject; Joseph Kaplan, one of the designers of the B-29; Wernher von Braun, discussing the design and use of space stations and spaceships; Willy Ley, with a more detailed explanation of the space station and its uses; and the pioneering space illustrators, Chesley Bonestell, Fred Freeman, and Rolf Klep. These men were introduced to the public as part of a community who took the space alternative seriously and had concrete, realizable proposals.

The impact of this volume was reinforced by the publication of a second book the following year called *Conquest of the Moon*. Its authors, von Braun, Whipple, and Ley, attempt a coherent, singular vision emphasizing that their speculations were not to be taken merely as science fiction, but as a technological reality based on factual science. "The ships the explorers will use for the long journey through space will bear little resemblance to those depicted by the science-fictionists," they wrote. "In fact their appearance is even more fantastic. But there is this difference: they work."[97] After collaborating on *Across the Space Frontier* and *Conquest of the Moon*, the von Braun/Ley team worked with Bonestell on *The Exploration of Mars*. In that text, they present a plan for reaching the red planet, a goal of American space visionaries since the fantastic speculations of Percival Lowell in the early years of the twentieth century.

By the mid-1950s, with the help of these books, American astrofuturism had reached a consensus on the likely nature of the space future, particularly as a technological and a cultural challenge. Organized around the idea of a "conquest of space," the astrofuturists understood that going beyond the earth's atmosphere, making the journey to the Moon, and planning the exploration of Mars were on par with the conquest of the New World. Many of them, including Willy Ley and Arthur C. Clarke, were interested in the history of the age of exploration—the five-century-long history of the European exploration and conquest of the terrestrial globe—and regularly invoked the names and achievements of Columbus, Cook, Lewis, and Clark to explain the significance and nature of the astrofuturist project. Thus the basis for advocating expansion into space grew from a popular history read from the point of view of explorers, missionaries, and colonizers. At the dawn of the space age, the astrofuturist consensus formed around progressive science and technology, territorial expansion, and a tacit acknowledgement of a social order that placed Europe and white America at the pinnacle of racial and national hierarchies.

The imperial ambitions and benevolent impulses, which motivated European conquest of the New World and the United States's expansion to its west and beyond, found new expression in the astrofuturist imagination. Hence utopian ideals of renewing a wealthy, benign, and egalitarian society on the space frontier cohabit with racist and nationalist impulses. Rather than presenting alternatives (as later futurists would demand), the space future of the 1950s and 1960s was to be a realm in which the contemporary status quo would find infinite room for expansion. The classic agenda for manned spaceflight was also an articulation of technological goals that the astrofuturists thought essential to the conquest of space. The agenda focused around the scenario that Ley did so much to popularize and that was identified as the intellectual property of the German rocket team. That basic scenario described the creation of a technological infrastructure composed of a rocket plane, a station in orbit around the Earth, rocket-powered vehicles to the planets, a voyage to the Moon and the establishment of a base there, an expedition to Mars, and the creation of a base and colony on that planet's surface. After these goals had been accomplished, the ultimate mission of the classic agenda was the conquest of the solar system and a hope for technological capability (most often thought of as nuclear) that would allow humanity to expand outward into extra-solar space.

The classic agenda of first-generation astrofuturists had a measurable impact on the lives of many American scientists, writers, and social activists. Second-generation futurists as different in background and political outlook as Carl Sagan, Ben Bova, and Jerry Pournelle have pointed toward the space literature and science fiction of the 1930s, 1940s, and 1950s as the catalyst for their interest in science and their involvement in the space program. Long after he became a leading figure in science fiction and space popularization, Arthur C. Clarke credited Lasser's *Conquest of Space* for giving him his start.[98] Carl Sagan echoes Clarke by crediting the science fiction of the 1930s for his career as a planetary scientist and spaceflight advocate: "Such ideas, when encountered young, can influence adult behavior. Many scientists deeply involved in the exploration of the solar system (myself among them) were first turned in that direction by science fiction. And the fact that some of the science fiction was not of the highest quality is irrelevant. Ten-year-olds do not read the scientific literature."[99] Sagan's explanation for the historical and continuing popularity of science fiction among young people is that "it is *they* who will live in the future" (171). For him, as for many other astrofuturists, science fiction helps provide those who listen with alternatives, blueprints for the ever-advancing future. Sagan also presents what may be considered the often unstated rationale for astrofuturism when he says, "It is my firm view that no society on earth today is well adapted to the earth of one or two hundred years from now (if we are wise enough or lucky enough to survive that long). We desperately need an exploration of alternative futures, both experimental and conceptual" (171).

What we have seen up to this point is most of what went into the creation of the astrofuturism in the years immediately before and after the Second World War. Many of the amateur rocket enthusiasts of the 1920s and 1930s went on to become the astrofuturists of the late 1940s and 1950s. The differences between the eras are akin to the difference between dream and reality. Before the war, the dream of interplanetary travel had belonged to satiric and utopian literature and was just moving into the realm of the West's growing mass culture. After the war and the advent of a very real and devastating rocket technology, the dream of space travel began to move out of its small portions of high and popular culture onto the political agenda of nations. No longer simply the province of literary scholars, adolescent boys, backyard engineers, and mass-market publishers, vast amounts of human, economic, and political capital were diverted into the technology that would make the space future possible.

By the end of the 1950s, astrofuturists had come far from their predecessors, the amateur enthusiasts who talked to one another through newsletters, pulp fiction, and fan conventions. They had become professional explainers to large audiences, writing and publishing popular science books, speculative essays, and science fiction, and working on television and Hollywood movies as well. All the major astrofuturists after the Second World War—Wernher von

Braun, Willy Ley, Arthur C. Clarke, Robert A. Heinlein, and Krafft Ehricke—share both a background in science and/or engineering and a willingness to work in many different fields of public communication to introduce their ideas to as broad an audience as possible. If nothing else, this first postwar generation of modern space futurists succeeded in making their science-fictional future real to the youngsters who were influenced by their work. Through their popular science and science-fiction, von Braun and Ley re-created the conversion and enlightenment experience that characterized their own youthful reading of Verne, Wells, Lasswitz, and Oberth. They created a unique blend of techno-scientific extrapolation and fantastic adventure for "rocket-minded" youths conscious of the possibilities the conquest of space could offer. They helped create a social and political consensus that mirrored the official culture of mid-twentieth-century America and that found cultural legitimacy in the "man in space" movement of the 1950s.

Hence, astrofuturism is more than a technological enterprise or a parts catalog of means and ends. It represents an attempt to describe futures that are attractive projections of contemporary social and political desires. While futurism is a broad-based phenomenon appearing in everything from military analysis to regional planning and real estate speculation, its clearest cultural expression is in science fiction. It is through science fiction, as a popular literature and as a social phenomenon, that the first-generation astrofuturist consensus made itself felt in American culture. Despite or even perhaps because of its marginal status within the mainstream of official culture, science fiction gave the early space-flight enthusiasts a common ground where they could create narrative models of how spaceflight could be accomplished, its influence on everyday life, and its significance for the course of American civilization.

Representing a mode of technosocial thinking within Western culture, the roots of American astrofuturism extend beyond national boundaries. No matter where they came from, the futurists of the first generation shared a common background in the romantic imagination of nineteenth-century technoscience and exploration. Therefore, when the German rocket team arrived in the United States and began their postwar process of Americanization, they found that they already shared a common language with the native science-fiction community. That commonality was to prove invaluable in years to come because it allowed them to be a part of the infrastructure of periodicals, organizations, and personal relationships that serves as the lifeblood of science fiction.

Through science fiction, the German space enthusiasts were able to find a language with which to communicate their ruling passion to like-minded Americans. In the days before the rise of the 1960s space program, one of the few ways that spaceflight enthusiasts could get their ideas into circulation was through this popular genre and the youth culture it served. In the 1940s and 1950s it was the only space in American culture where their ideas could find an audience that fully embraced their aspirations. It is through science fiction, as a popular literature and as popular science, that astrofuturism came to maturity in the American context. In the next chapter, I turn to Robert A. Heinlein, whose science fiction took the genre to a new level of maturity and defined space travel as an American destiny emerging inevitably out of the national experience.

3. Building a Space Frontier: Robert A. Heinlein and the American Tradition

We are all tired of being stuck on this cosmical speck with its monotonous ocean, leaden sky, and single moon that is half useless. Its possibilities are exhausted, and just as Greece became too small for the civilization of the Greeks, so it seems to me that the future glory of the human race lies in the exploration of at least the solar system!

—John Jacob Astor, *Journey in Other Worlds: A Romance of the Future* (1894)[1]

Astrofuturism is expressed in two contiguous fields, popular science and science fiction. As popular science, its pedagogical mission is explicit: through science journalism, polemical articles, and books, astrofuturists present their program as a pragmatic goal for real-world science and technology. They call upon the authority of science with charts, mathematical equations, and blueprints based on contemporary technology. Willy Ley's *Rockets, Missiles and Space Travel*, for example, was advertised as "the up-to-tomorrow story of rocket development and space-travel prospects."[2] The textbook for rocketry and spaceflight enthusiasm, Ley's text ranges across celestial mechanics, liquid fuels, satellite communication, planetary geology, astronomy, exobiology, and space medicine. But the common reader is not likely to wade through 520 pages of charts, tables, and equations; the book was read primarily by the scientists and engineers who were interested or involved in aerospace projects during the 1950s and 1960s. Despite their desire to authorize their hope for a conquest of space through the dry and respectable discourse of science and technology, astrofuturists have found that science fiction is the most direct way of reaching a popular audience. Astrofuturist science fiction harnesses the pleasure of adventure fiction to mobilize a wide audience. Authors use familiar and entertaining conventions of the popular genre to convince their audiences of the value of the spaceflight project.

The two faces of astrofuturism, popular science and science fiction, are joined forcefully through their constant evocation of a "sense of wonder." A slippery phrase, "sense of wonder" is used by the first generation of science-fiction writers and critics to describe the pleasures unique to science fiction. At its most obvious, the phrase seeks to describe the experience of the sublime, specifically the awe an individual experiences upon confronting a universe infinitely larger than him- or herself. That confrontation is the source of the almost mystic quality that many commentators have detected in such hard science-fiction writers as Arthur C. Clarke and Isaac Asimov. But "sense of wonder" also includes an instrumental component that shifts it away from individual temperament and to a common practical utility. The term is used to define humanity as *homo faber* grappling with an immense universe, comprehending that larger nature through science and subduing it with technology. And ultimately, this characteristic is invoked to distinguish humanity as evolutionarily superior to other animals. Our ability to control and manipulate the natural world through technoscience is the central assumption of space-futurist science fiction. Astrofuturism is at once reverential before the awesome prospect that the universe presents and confidently certain that we can master it.

These conventions of astrofuturist fiction are never divorced from the genre's obsession with method. How humanity advances into the space frontier is at least as, if not more, important than the whys and wherefores. Indeed, authors often will stop a narrative to explain the technoscientific speculation that makes the fictive conquest of space plausible. For instance, the flow of a story might be interrupted as a character or a narrator steps forward to explain Einstein's theory of special relativity, Mendelian genetics, or the mechanics of a rocket. Far from being peripheral to its conventions, this pedagogical mission is an essential characteristic of astrofuturist fiction. Without it, much of the space fiction that has been written since the Second World War would be no different from the space operas of the 1930s. Through accurate presentation of the science and technology of space travel, astrofuturists claim realism for their space future speculations. Thus, it is not surprising to find the authoritative rhetoric of "how to" popular science validating the speculations of the scientific romancer. Indeed, given the context of a society in which technoscience competes with religion to be the dominant explainer of the unknown, science fiction relies on popular science to make the space future convincing as a social, political, and cultural project. In turn, familiar characters and plots domesticate otherwise daunting technical material, mitigating the estrangement that might otherwise create a cognitive dissonance between the futurist vision and the reader. Consequently, futures that claim to differ markedly from the present (and that are, therefore, "wonderful") are often fairly shallow reorganizations of the contemporary status quo.[3]

Often described as the dean of science fiction, Robert A. Heinlein helped define the core conventions of genre science fiction during a career that spanned almost fifty years. In the 1950s, he established his reputation as a writer of hard science fiction (that is, science fiction motivated by techno-science, rather than fantasy) primarily interested in the conquest of the space frontier. In his novels of the 1950s, he created a balance between narrative action and pedagogy that became the hallmark of hard science fiction. Not coincidentally, he almost single-handedly is responsible for the genre's elevation from its low-rent pulp origins to the realms of respectability. Through his Future History stories of the 1940s and his space-cadet novels of the 1950s, Heinlein articulated a vision of the space future grounded in the cultural materials of the nation's present and past. Using the experiences, landscapes, and readings of his own midwestern boyhood, he imagined a human presence in space that would re-create the American myth of western expansion and conquest. His spacemen are representations of the western heroes made familiar in the boys' adventure literature of the early twentieth century: explorers, soldiers, and businessmen who renew middle-class, middle-American values as they pioneer and settle the wilderness of space. These heroes arise within meritocratic, patriarchal regimes that enforce a rough egalitarianism and control the use of science and technology. Theirs is a social order based on an idealized notion of military service. Through the sociomilitary form, Heinlein seeks a human commonality, a "band of brothers" ethic that resolves the racial and ethnic tensions that might impede an expansion into space. By resolving the superficial differences between men, that sociomilitary order allows them to control the technology required to conquer the natural universe.

I intend "sociomilitary" to resonate with Martin Green's term "aristo-military." In his valuable study of the adventure story in American literature and culture *The Great American Adventure*, Green identifies the aristo-military tradition in American adventure literature as a recurrent motif signaling opposition to the nation's early revolutionary egalitarianism.[4] The nation's founding generation adhered to an egalitarian "brotherhood of man" ethic, which was hostile to aristocratic hierarchy as it was represented by the nation's first enemy, the British empire. Green argues that this tradition became central to an

American literature that sought to divorce itself from European traditions and yet found itself, in the period after the Civil War, engaged in an expansion that both mimicked and conflicted with older European imperialisms (for example, the Spanish American War). The aristo-military tradition, in the form of the adventure tale, helped reconcile the facts of American expansion with the nation's democratic self-perception. Green makes a strong case for the adventure tale's significance in American literature as a genre engaged by authors that range from James Fenimore Cooper to Theodore Roosevelt and Norman Mailer. Following his trajectory, I would add that astrofuturism picks up where terrestrial adventure leaves off. With the closing of the American frontier and the difficulty of reconciling terrestrial imperialism with a revolutionary political tradition, the only solution to the limits of American expansion is in the eternal wilderness of outer space. The equality between men that the sociomilitary form imposes from the top down is one sign of the tension between control and freedom that structures Heinlein's narratives. The gender politics of his work are another sign: because of his reliance on the sociomilitary form, Heinlein has difficulty allowing equal places for men and women in his future.

His gestures toward racial tolerance and inclusion signal his acknowledgement that the political appeal of space colonization has to be articulated in the language of democracy and equality. He returns repeatedly to the tension between these two impulses, addressing it most frequently through his female characters. While some female characters are admirable, their significance to narratives and hence to the creation of the future is limited by what he considers essential, because biological, sexual difference. Women can never be fully integrated into the public mission of space conquest. Their biological destiny as wives and mothers, a destiny that Heinlein firmly advocates, forecloses that possibility. Their fate indicates that his future does not break radically with the present. On the contrary, his narratives seek to justify the extension of relationships considered natural in America at mid-century.

At times he simply shifts the line of antidemocratic exclusion from between the races to between the sexes, using his female characters as the foil for the camaraderie of his heroic men. At other times, he turns away from this easy solution and attempts a scenario in which gender is as irrelevant as race. But he is hindered by his inability to imagine gender difference as malleable to resignification, and by his weakness for narrative conventions—heroism, camaraderie, filial devotion—that necessitate a hierarchical, authoritarian social structure in which the extraordinary few distinguish themselves from the ordinary many. The sociomilitary form requires a division between the brave few and the helpless many, the knowledgeable elite and the unruly masses, and, finally, between the rulers and the ruled. Heinlein articulates the core commitments of an astrofuturist science fiction that is faithful to von Braun's synthesis of scientific and military adventurism, and is as sure that the United States always also stands at the pinnacle of intellectual, political, and moral progress. Hence his futures represent an idealized, but fundamentally static view of America at mid-century.

Heinlein was born in 1907 in Butler, Missouri, at a time when its citizens could still remember their state's importance as a gateway to the far western frontier. By birth and temperament, he was situated in a middle-American landscape defined by the great adventure of westward expansion. As a young man, however, Heinlein went east rather than west, graduating from the United States Naval Academy at Annapolis in the class of 1929. He began what seems to have been a promising career in the Navy as Gunnery Officer aboard the USS *Lexington*, the first modern aircraft carrier. Unfortunately, he contracted tuberculosis and had to retire from the service in the early 1930s on a medical disability. That disappointment haunted Heinlein for the remainder of his life, and his nostalgia for his aborted career is apparent in his strong identification with the traditions and mission of the Navy throughout his fiction.[5]

Heinlein spent most of the years of the Great Depression taking odd jobs and getting involved in small-business ventures and local politics. He began to write science fiction as a way of making some quick money. In 1939, *Thrilling Wonder Stories* offered a $50 prize for the best amateur science fiction. Never overly modest, Heinlein believed he could do a better job than most of the writers working in the genre at the time, even though he had never before written for publication. When he finished writing his submission, he thought it too good for *Thrilling Wonder Stories* and sent it instead to *Astounding Science Fiction* (*Astounding*), a better paying magazine.[6] It was a gamble that paid off handsomely, and he quickly became the periodical's most popular writer.

Heinlein's early work helped define what is now called the golden age of science fiction: the roughly twenty-year period of the 1940s and 1950s when genre science fiction was strongly influenced by the editor of *Astounding Science Fiction*, John W. Campbell. Heinlein was part of the stable of writers—along with Isaac Asimov, Lester del Rey, Theodore Sturgeon, L. Ron Hubbard, A. E. van Vogt, L. Sprague de Camp, Clifford Simak, and Jack Williamson—who published primarily in Campbell's magazine, the most prestigious forum for serious science fiction at the time.[7] Through the influence of these authors and their editor the genre matured into a form that emphasized the presentation of technoscientific ideas over pulp adventure. In *Astounding*, science fiction was distanced from its early affiliation with the "gosh-wow" school of gears and gadgets in favor of more rational speculation based on then contemporary science and technology. The future it foresaw had to be constructed either of already available materials or those that could plausibly be developed in the near future. Any writer who wanted to be considered good had to understand the principles of science and the technics of engineering. As a consequence, the short stories and novels influenced by Campbell's revision of the genre became exercises in science popularization as well as popular entertainment.[8] In tandem with the increased emphasis on scientific and engineering verisimilitude came a concern with the effects of technical progress on the social, political, and economic terrain of the future. Isaac Asimov, for instance, defined social science fiction as a literature "which is concerned with the impact of scientific advance upon human beings."[9] Judith Merril argues that Campbell created an atmosphere conducive to a "sociological science fiction" by throwing the genre open to the social sciences, including sociology and cultural anthropology, and thereby encouraged the social thought experiments of Asimov, Heinlein, Sturgeon, and others.[10]

The years of and following the Second World War were a time of extraordinary productivity for Heinlein. During the 1940s, he produced forty-two short stories and six novels. In the 1950s, he reduced his short-story production by two-thirds and focused on both juvenile and adult novels. At the rate of one and sometimes two a year, he ended the decade having published fourteen fulllength books. Heinlein's space-cadet novels of the 1950s allowed him to move away from the pulp ghetto to which science fiction had been confined and to publish in such magazines as *The Saturday Evening Post, Argosy*, and *Town and Country*. He also appeared in more specialized venues such as *Boys' Life*, serving there as the optimistic "apostle of the new frontier of space."[11] He became the first writer of American genre science fiction to place his novels with a major publishing house, Charles Scribner's Sons. Starting with *Rocket Ship Galileo* in 1947, Heinlein and Scribner began a popular and lucrative association that lasted for eleven somewhat turbulent years. Most of the books that he produced during this period belong to his juvenile series. These novels were targeted toward the young adult market even though many of them pushed at the boundaries of what was then considered standard adolescent fare.[12]

In this work, Heinlein presented to his readers the first mature and coherent vision of a potential *American* future in space. He took many of the concepts and speculations of the German rocket team and Americanized them, creating romances placed firmly within the middle-western ethos that formed his own background. The almost inadvertent epic that he created in his Future

History series of novellas and short stories and in the Scribner novels moved a marginal idea from the heavily European influenced traditions of the early rocket societies into the American cultural context. In these texts, he first essayed the integration of images familiar from boys' adventure literature with a technology-based scientific rhetoric. That integration has become a core convention of both the fictional and nonfictional expressions of American astrofuturism.

Despite his insistence on an aggressive, patriarchal capitalism, Heinlein did not create an astrofuturism that was ideologically monolithic. Unlike many science-fiction writers and fans, H. Bruce Franklin regards Heinlein not as a philosopher-king, but as a representative man whose fiction mirrors the contradictions of the society around him.[13] This mirroring and restating of values and tendencies present within American culture accounts in large measure for Heinlein's tremendous popularity and influence. He is by turns an autocrat and a democrat; a hysterical racist and a defender of plurality; the enunciator of an unexamined sexism and a defender of a certain, limited gender equity; an advocate of large-scale, centralized governmental systems and a libertarian exponent of the virtues of small business and decentralized government. In sum, Heinlein is not so much a systematic philosopher or prophet as he is a literary broker of the problems, alternatives, and solutions that continue to preoccupy American culture.

In 1941, Heinlein presented a chart of what John W. Campbell called "the future history of the world" to *Astounding*'s readers.[14] Although it was modeled on a similar effort published by Olaf Stapledon in 1930, Heinlein's chart is modest in comparison.[15] Stapledon's vast scheme symbolized an evolutionary macrohistory; Heinlein limited his historical purview to the time most accessible to his audience, the two to three hundred years around the 1940s. By limiting his scheme to the near future of a culturally recognizable history, Heinlein was able to address themes that were of immediate interest to his audience. This work is aptly described by Robert Scholes's comments on near future fictions, which

draw their power from the cognitive systems of present social science. They are in some sense predictive rather than merely speculative, and they predict on the basis of current knowledge in the fields of political science, economics, psychology, sociology, and the other human sciences. Such fictions often attain great emotional power. . . . They present a noticeable discontinuity with our current situation—but they insist that this altered situation is *not* actually discontinuous, that it is in fact a reasonable projection of existing trends.[16]

Heinlein's future chronology is designed around three major categories: characters, technical data, and social/political events. The heroes of his stories are the pioneers who will lead man to the stars; they are the scientists, engineers, businessmen, adventurers, and poets who work for the space future. Heinlein includes technical sketches of the advances that will make possible man's conquest of space. Transatlantic rocket flight (passenger service), synthetic foods, and the advent of genetic engineering are among the innovations Heinlein foresees. The sociological/political category refers to future history events, including the first rocket to the Moon in 1978, the founding of Luna City soon after, a period of the "Imperial Exploitation" from around 1970 to 2020, "Interplanetary" exploration and exploitation that ends in a period of revolution, an end to space travel for fifty-two years, and finally the rise of the "first human civilization" in the last quarter of the twenty-first century.[17] Accompanying this structure is an additional "remarks" column in which Heinlein emphasizes that the progress of human civilization depends on advances in science and technology, and particularly on the expansion of humanity into space. He represents periods in which the scientific frontier is unexplored and technological innovation stagnates as brief dark ages. These periods, however, are merely temporary recessions from which humanity always recovers.

Whether or not it was intended as serious prophecy, Heinlein's future history chart presents predictions firmly grounded in mid-twentieth-century America's assumptions about progress. Its valorization of social and physical sciences and its devaluation of religious authority echoes the rising prestige of technoscience after the Second World War.[18] But the chart itself is based on the template of the nineteenth century, for that recent past offers numerous examples of the wealth and other benefits awaiting those who contributed their scientific and technical knowledge to the task of conquest. Hence, one of the "dark ages" ends when there is an "opening of new frontiers and a return to a nineteenth-century economy."[19] The space frontier serves Heinlein's America as the New World served Europe: as the tabula rasa on which cultural longings for endless economic expansion and a nostalgic perfectionism can be projected.

Even at the level of plot, Heinlein often presents future events as repetitions of past situations and decisions. As a result the social, political, economic, and cultural past is mirrored in the future, rendering that future recognizable as a smooth and unsurprising extension of the familiar. The conquest of space narrated in Heinlein's future history repeats Euro-American imperial history, complete with the popular narratives that conquest generated. Heinlein and his colleagues did not wish to conquer empty space; they were after the free land to be found on the Moon, Mars, in the asteroid belt, and beyond. Tales of the acquisition and exploitation of this land teach readers how Euro-American civilization can continue to advance through the coming conquest of new worlds.

The episodes of the Heinleinian space epic fall into four phases of outward movement: the Earth-Moon system, the inner solar system, the asteroid belt, the outer solar system, and finally, the most thrilling of destinations, the cosmos. The earliest stories of the late 1940s tell of the first attempts to land on the Moon while those of the late 1950s move on to humanity's presence on a galaxy-wide scale. Whatever else it might be, Heinlein's space future is a big one.

On this broad canvas of discovery and conquest, Heinlein fills in details of social and political problems that closely resemble the paradigmatic events of American history. The American Revolution is used, for example, as a template for *The Moon is a Harsh Mistress* (1966), *Between Planets* (1951), and *Red Planet* (1949). "Logic of Empire" (1941) and *Citizen of the Galaxy* (1957) are both structured around the issues of slavery and freedom dramatized in the Civil War. *The Rolling Stones* (1952) is a refiguration of the western migrations of the nineteenth century with space as the new frontier. "Misfit" (1939) recalls, in part, the social programs of the New Deal. And "Space Jockey" (1947) evokes the world of Mark Twain's classic semiautobiography, *Life on the Mississippi*.[20] But Heinlein is not after historical accuracy; he engages popular myths, not scholarship. The only details of the past worth remembering are those that glorify the men, concepts, and machines that mark the course of democratic science and invention. Providing basic instruction in that history constitutes a major task of the space cadet novels of the 1950s. The boys (and girls) who read these novels are given lessons in space future history: they are taught the basic tenets of its ideology, comprised primarily of faith in the social and political advances they could expect from an American conquest of space and made attractive by promises of adventure and romance.

In the near future novel *Rocket Ship Galileo* (*Galileo*), for example, a signal date is the first atomic explosion on 16 July 1945 at Alamogordo, New Mexico. The young engineer heroes of the story are fully aware of the date and its significance. They also have a "low opinion" of those who are "as a whole incapable of realizing that the world had changed completely" with the arrival of atomic power.[21] Albert Einstein, perhaps the most revered scientist in American science fiction, is mentioned in *Galileo* as a figure with whom young engineers must be familiar. Gregor Mendel is cited in "Methuselah's Children" (1941) and Heinlein's understanding of Mendelian genetics is an important part of the plot.[22] In *Red Planet*, Percival Lowell, an astronomer made notorious at the turn of the previous century by his stubborn insistence on the existence of intelligent life on Mars, is presented as a great scientist rather than one who made an unfortunate interpretive error. Just as Lowell predicted, the Mars of this novel comes complete with canals and natives.[23]

However, in first-generation astrofuturism, the hero who conquers new worlds through science and technology often is not patterned on the likes of Mendel, Lowell, or even von Braun. Heinlein's space-future pioneer is no overt intellectual or aristocrat, but a man or boy of action born in humble but not impoverished circumstances on the midwestern plains. This hero's explorations are funded and driven by an energetic trader's natural values of capitalism and democratic individualism. Heinlein's codification of the type in his future history stories of the 1940s set the tone for a generation of science-fiction writers. Perhaps the most representative of these heroes is Delos D. Harriman, of "Requiem" and "The Man Who Sold the Moon."

Published in the January 1940 issue of *Astounding Science Fiction,* "Requiem" is a poignant story that treats the conquest of the moon as an accomplished fact. In its history, the first man landed on the Moon years ago, regular rocket travel to it is as normal as bus trips between Providence and Boston, and the pioneering days of opening a new frontier are part of a golden past. Heinlein emphasizes the domestication of space by setting the first scene of the story at a country fair in Butler, Missouri. D. D. Harriman arrives there to recruit a couple of down-at-heels rocket jocks for a very strange mission. The rocketeers, reminiscent of the aerial barnstormers who worked similar fairs after World War I, are employed by the Bates County Fair Association to run a carnival ride modeled after the first rocket to land a man on the Moon.[24] A large sign encourages the curious to participate vicariously in the conquest of space:

This WAY to the
MOON ROCKET!!!!
See it in actual flight!
Public Demonstration Flights
Twice Daily
This is the ACTUAL TYPE used by the
First Man to Reach the MOON!!!
YOU can ride in it!!—$50.00[25]

Here we have a mixture of the marvelous with the mundane, the fantastic in the story-filled midwestern landscape made familiar by authors from Mark Twain to Ray Bradbury. Indeed Butler, the eastern Missouri farm town in which Heinlein was born and raised, functions for him as the Mississippi River town of Hannibal, across the state, did for Mark Twain. There he read boys' pulp literature and began dreaming the dreams of adventure and exploration that found expression in his space-future fiction. There he inherited from his grandfather's generation's stories of territorial expansion and colonization, the conquest of the west, and the founding of settlements such as Butler. Heinlein considered these stories integral to his and to his nation's heritage and believed that the experiences they narrated were foundational to American democracy.[26] It is not surprising, therefore, that his future in space extends the western frontier.

In the course of "Requiem," it is revealed that D. D. Harriman is the man responsible for humanity's conquest of the Moon. Even as he opened access to the Moon, however, he found himself trapped on the earth, first by the company he built for lunar conquest and then by his own health. By the time of "Requiem," he is an old and embittered man, despite his wealth and power. Although he pioneered the way to space, he has never been able to go there himself. Harriman's final goal is to set foot on the Moon at least once before he dies, even if it means breaking a law he was instrumental in making. To do so, he has to persuade the rocketeers to take him there. His wealth is not enough to convince these grounded but still heroic spacemen to violate the code of the space frontier. Less sentimentally, the captain of their vessel needs reasons more compelling than cash to buck the system for the sake of one man. Harriman provides that incentive by appealing to a higher law, the passion for new worlds:

> "I don't know whether I can explain it to you or not. You young fellows have grown up to rocket travel the way I grew up to aviation. When I was a kid practically nobody believed that man would ever reach the Moon. You've seen rockets all your lives, and the first to reach the Moon got there before you were a young boy. When I was a boy they laughed at the idea.
>
> "But I believe—I believed. I read Verne and Wells, and Smith, and I believed that we could do it—that we *would* do it. I set my heart on being one of the men to walk the surface of the Moon, to see her other side, and to look back on the surface of the Earth, hanging in the sky.
>
> "I used to go without my lunches to pay my dues in the American Rocket Society, because I wanted to believe that I was helping to bring the day nearer when we would reach the Moon. I was already an old man when that day arrived. I've lived longer than I should, but I would not let myself die . . . I will not!—until I have set foot on the Moon!" (200–201)

Of course, Harriman is not speaking only to these fictional rocketeers; he is also addressing the young men and boys who were habitual readers of *Astounding*. Perhaps this speech inspired some of its readers enough to send their membership dues to the American Rocket Society or to any of the space-cadet fan clubs formed during the 1950s. Harriman's lifelong commitment to a boyhood dream finds a sympathetic resonance in his fictive auditors and invites a similar response from the readers. Having found a kindred spirit, the rocketeers agree to take him on his final trip.

Several science-fiction critics and historians have noted that Harriman is an archetypal point of identification for Heinlein and his readers. Alexei Panshin and Cory Panshin, for instance, point out that Heinlein makes Harriman a contemporary, a character who can speak for the science-obsessed boys who came of age in the early years of the twentieth century.[27] For them, the wide-open frontiers of the nineteenth century were fondly remembered childhood stories that lived on in the popular mythology of boys' culture. Franklin notes that through Harriman Heinlein "eloquently paints a picture of the boys and young men who made pre–World War II science fiction—both those who read it and those who wrote it."[28] This identification is made explicit in another speech the author writes for his character: " 'I wasn't unusual; there were lots of boys like me—radio hams, they were, and telescope builders, and airplane amateurs. We had science clubs, and basement laboratories, and science-fiction leagues,—the kind of boys who thought there was more romance in one issue of *Electrical Experimenter* than in all the books Dumas ever wrote. We didn't want to be one of Horatio Alger's GET-RICH heroes either, we wanted to build space ships. Well, some of us did.' "[29] Through Harriman Heinlein seeks to inspire a new generation with the kind of aspiration that helped create the 1960s Apollo Program.

Heinlein returned to the Harriman character ten years later with "The Man Who Sold the Moon." In this prequel, Harriman represents what Jeffrey Richards has called the "middle-class mercantile exploration-colonization tradition" in the popular imagery of empire.[30] He is a businessman, a latter-day robber baron who takes advantage of the mechanisms of mid-century American consumer capitalism for his conquest of the Moon. The creation of a club for junior spacemen, real-estate speculation, and use of the Moon as a billboard for a popular soft drink are only a few of the schemes Harriman uses in his crusade for lunar conquest. Among the payoffs he and his shareholders expect are the immense profits to be had from lunar diamond mines. Heinlein littered the lunar landscape with diamonds in several of his future-history stories; all you had to do was pick them up to get rich quick. Despite the de-emphasis on the accumulation of wealth implied in "Requiem," Heinlein always implied that wealth would be the reward of any inspired inventor. Space is good business, as well as the proper arena for the exercise of science.

Profit, however, is not the final motivation of the space entrepreneur. It is the windfall from a nobler enterprise—the betterment of mankind. The latter is a project that can be trusted only to the altruism of individuals who have proved themselves worthy custodians by developing extraterrestrial resources. The mercantilistic adventure of "The Man Who Sold the Moon" substantiates this point through an antigovernment rhetoric deployed by Harriman to explain why the U.S. government and its Department of Defense cannot be trusted with the spaceflight dream. Through his character, Heinlein articulates a corporate internationalism that is strikingly similar to that espoused by Arthur C. Clarke and Ben Bova:

"Damnation, nationalism should stop at the stratosphere. Can you see what would happen if the United States lays claim to the Moon? The other nations won't recognize the claim. It will become a permanent bone of contention in the Security council—just when we were beginning to get straightened out to the point where a man could do business planning without having his elbow jogged by a war every few years. The other nations—quite rightly—will be scared to death of the United States. They will be able to look up in the sky and see the main atom-bomb rocket base of the United States staring down the backs of their necks. Are they going to hold still for it? No sirree—they are going to try to clip off a piece of the Moon for their own national use. The Moon is too big to hold all at once. There will be bases established there and presently there will be the God-damnedest war this planet has ever seen—and we'll be to blame."[31]

Harriman's solution is to ensure the proper development of space-based resources by staking a claim to the Moon for himself and his company: " 'I'm not going to let the brass hats muscle in. I'm going to set up a lunar colony and then nurse it along until it is big enough to stand on its own two feet. I'm telling you—all of you!—this is the biggest thing for the human race since the discovery of fire. Handled right, it can mean a new and braver world. Handle it wrong and it's a one-way ticket to Armageddon. It's coming, it's coming soon, whether we touch it or not. But I plan to be the Man on the Moon myself—and give it my personal attention to see that it's handled right.' "[32] Of course, there is no question that only an American corporation headed by a competent and clever white American male can properly develop this frontier. Heinlein did not share the fear of corporate power that Aldous Huxley articulated in *Brave New World*. If Henry Ford could better the lot of humankind with his technology, so can Harriman. Heinlein's only departure from the Fordist paradigm of development is to disregard Ford's anti-Semitism and working relationship with Nazis.

What makes Delos D. Harriman so sure that he is the right person to pioneer the space frontier, open up the space future for humanity, and serve as its shepherd during its formative years? George Slusser argues that Heinlein relies on the seventeenth-century Puritan notion of election to authorize his heroes and elites; hence the evangelical tone inevitably assumed by Heinlein's characters.[33] But that fervor and Heinlein's notions of authority and salvation come by way of the bodies and instrumentalities of nineteenth-century industrial capitalism. If Harriman considers himself to be the master of space exploration, it is because of his obsession, with the very material dream of space conquest. In the service of that obsession, Harriman builds the company that sells the Moon using the tools made available through twentieth-century consumer capitalism. His position as a successful and powerful businessman gives this dreamer the right to determine what should happen to the Moon when his company reaches it. Election may be the rationale, but it is not the source of either the dream or the will to power that motivates it.[34]

Heinlein's message in the Harriman stories is hard-headed: the conquest of space is good business. These stories rely on the methods and characters of mid-century industrial and consumer capitalism to convince readers that this conquest is within reach. Harriman, the bluff, big businessman with brains, is instantly recognizable. By the 1950s, his character type had circulated in American popular culture so long that even Heinlein's telegraphic style is enough to invoke its full dimensions. The methods that Harriman uses to sell the Moon—billboards, radio and breakfast cereal promotionals, real-estate speculation—are neither extraordinary nor fantastic. Even the use of the Moon as a billboard for a popular soft drink achieves a level of banal realism, despite the spectacular nature of the effect. What we may infer from all of this is what Heinlein and his readers understood: that the space future belongs to the Harrimans of the world. In Heinlein's narratives, the right to control new lands and wealth is conferred according one's standing in a meritocratic hierarchy, a position gained by the demonstrable ability to exploit any frontier. In the Harriman stories, both hierarchy and ability is vested in the company; at its pinnacle is a great man who directs the future of humanity. The wonderful dream of new frontiers and American renewal, therefore, is authoritarian even as it professes a rhetoric of egalitarian individualism.

Heinlein's novels, which are equally as pedagogical as his stories, elaborate the political content of his hopes for America's future. *Rocket Ship Galileo* (1947), the first of the juveniles that Heinlein produced for Scribner, marks his introduction to a market beyond the confines of science-fiction magazines. On the cover of the 1947 paperback edition, a short blurb announces that the book is "The classic moon-flight novel that inspired modern astronautics."[35] This is standard publishers' hyperbole, but in the case of *Galileo* it is not far off the mark. Many of the scientists and engineers who became important in America's space effort received their first introduction to the technology of rocketry and to the spaceflight idea as a serious movement through this novel and others of its kind.[36] The novel recounts how a trio of teenage boys and their young mentor, Dr. Cargraves, a scientist who worked on the atom bomb and was "mentioned" for the Nobel Prize, salvage a rocketship and go to the Moon.[37] After overcoming the usual obstacles, including the objections of the boys' parents, they succeed brilliantly. The rest of the book is a melodrama in which the explorers find that a group of Nazis have beaten them to the Moon and are planning a lunar-based takeover of the earth. The novel is significant in Heinlein's oeuvre because in it he establishes the basic themes and conventions that inform not only the remainder of his work, but also that of many other writers: he introduces the audience to the people who lived and breathed rocketry before the war; indicates the elements of the wonderful dream that drives their work; describes the values necessary to become a pioneer in space; shows us what type of *man* will go out there; presents the techniques and methods needed to get into space; and even provides a list of books that combine the elements of the wonderful dream and the practical knowledge necessary to make it work.

From the very beginning of *Rocket Ship Galileo*, the reader is thrust into a world that many members of the old rocket societies would have found familiar. The curtain rises on a primitive testing range where our young heroes experiment with the fundamentals of rocketry: "The three boys huddled against a thick concrete wall, higher than their heads and about ten feet long. It separated them from a steel stand, enclosed to the ground, to which was bolted a black metal shape, a pointed projectile, venomous in appearance and ugly—a rocket. There were fittings on each side to which stubby wings might be attached, but the fittings were empty; the creature was chained down for scientific experimentation" (7). For readers in 1947, this image would have recalled the frightening days of the Second World War when the V-2 rocket enabled a reign of terror against England. But the image also makes it clear that the rocket is a "creature" under the control of man. It is, in fact, a "model rocket" (7). Heinlein knew his audience and knew that many of his readers had been involved in model aviation and rocketry in the postwar years, often conducting similar experiments in their own backyards.[38]

It is easy now to recognize that the idea of backyard engineers building anything that could get to the Moon is far fetched. And Heinlein, who was in a position to know, realized the fantastic nature of his fictional propositions. In a letter to his agent, he indicated awareness of the technical questions raised by his presentation: "*Young Atomic Engineers* [*Galileo*'s working title] contains two conventional deviations from what I believe to be reasonably possible; [*sic*] I have condensed the preparation time for the trip and I have assumed that four people can do work which should require more nearly forty. Otherwise, I regard the techniques used in the story, and even the incident, to be possible albeit romantic and in some respects not too likely in detail. But I *do* expect space travel and I expect it soon."[39] This expectation of space travel in the not too distant future allowed Heinlein to rationalize his use of the "romantic" techniques standard in boys' invention stories since the 1890s.[40] His concern for the "reasonably possible" was overridden by his desire to sell the space future in a package readily accessible to his young audience. Moreover, his echo of the early amateur efforts of the *Verein für Raumschiffahrt* (Society for Space Travel) and the American Interplanetary Society gives his readers a tradition to which they could belong and an informing mythology for the wonderful dream.

That mythology places the young engineers in an astrofuturist lineage, linking youthful dreams to the practical yet glamorous world of the Nobel-class scientist. In the process, Heinlein makes explicit the connection between science fiction and the astrofuturist project. The connecting link could be called the Heinlein Bookshelf, for the author peppers his space-future epic with the titles and the names of writers he considers important in the pursuit of the dream. When Dr. Cargraves examines the clubhouse bookshelves, he finds material that convinces him that the young engineers are serious about the spaceflight dream:

A low, wide padded seat stretched from wall to wall opposite the chemistry layout. . . . [B]ookshelves had been built into the wall. Jules Verne crowded against Mark's *Handbook of Mechanical Engineering*. Cargraves noted other old friends: H. G. Wells' *Seven Famous Novels*, *The Handbook of Chemistry and Physics*, and Smyth's *Atomic Energy for Military Purposes*. Jammed in with them, side by side with Ley's *Rockets* and Eddington's *Nature of the Physical World*, were dozens of pulp magazines of the sort with robot men or space ships on their covers.[41]

On these bookshelves, mass-produced popular texts and canonical works of science fiction exist cheek by jowl with textbooks teaching the latest techniques in science and engineering. The textbooks evoke the school culture of 1950s science and technology; they also authorize the speculative adventure of the romances. The Eddington volume signals the importance of science popularization and the value of an informed and enthusiastic public. The Ley text performs the same function and gains additional significance because the author is an old-time promoter of the dream. In his juvenilia of the 1950s, Heinlein repeatedly emphasizes the importance of books, especially math and science textbooks. Library books especially are regarded as priceless; not returning one is as close as Heinlein ever comes to having a character consider a mortal sin.[42]

The engineering titles are not figments of Heinlein's imagination; they are real books that can be found in libraries, bookstores, or schools. He presents them as the intellectual backdrop to the wonderful dream. Together they are the canon that connects the author, his audience, and the German rocket team that (at the time of *Galileo*'s publication) was working at the White Sands Proving Ground in New Mexico. Cargraves, who may be considered the fictional persona of the author, makes the connection explicit: "He pulled down a dogged-eared copy of Haggard's *When the Earth Trembled* and settled his long body between the boys. He was beginning to feel at home. These boys he knew; he had only to gaze back through the corridors of his mind to recognize himself."[43] Dr. Cargraves's recognition is based on a shared body of knowledge, notion of heroism, and a racial and gendered position that is romantic in motivation yet instrumental in operation. The centrality of a textual canon is evident when he asks the boys to join him in a jaunt to the Moon:

> "All my life I've wanted to see the day when men would conquer space and explore the planets—and I wanted to be part of it. I don't have to tell you how that feels." He waved a hand to the bookshelves. "Those books show me you understand it; you've got the madness yourselves. Besides that, what I see out on your rocket grounds, what I see here . . . shows me that you aren't satisfied to dream about it and read about it—you want to *do* something. Right?"[44]

With his talk of conquering space and exploring the planets, Cargraves evokes the myth of heroic terrestrial exploration and conquest. Going to the Moon is a "madness" sanctioned not simply by the backyard experiments of the young engineers, but by the books they read.

Most space enthusiasts of the first generation were converted to the project through reading Verne, Wells, Haggard, and other men whose social and political landscapes were defined by the empires of the nineteenth century. Heinlein simply recycled that canon for his young readers. The "scientific romances" of these canonical writers were part of a larger movement in popular literature and literacy, which sought to shape the moral character of young men (and women) by instructing them in the goals and projects of their culture. Likewise, papers and magazines for boys adhered to the tenets of a popular imperialism that celebrated the rhetoric of European exploration and colonization. In this literature, coming of age stories in which the young cadet becomes a proper soldier went hand in glove with a benign imperialism emphasizing the white man's burden. Central to the boys' culture that developed through and around this literature was a technocratic militarism that defined progress as mastery over man and nature. From the boys' literature of the late nineteenth and early twentieth centuries, astrofuturism learned the romance and pleasure of empire, the importance of providing detailed descriptions of machines and the laws by which they work (primarily those used in the service of war); stories of uniformed service, the centrality of military values to the construction of masculine identity; and the white man's burden with its rigid hierarchies of race, gender, and class. Citing Haggard and, by extension, others who sang the song of empire in boys' literature, Heinlein appropriates a canon for the space future. The imagined past of empire becomes the history of the future.[45]

Heinlein invokes the popular and technoscientific canon and its heroes in the name of an optimistic social vision that imagines a space future that belongs to a technocratic elite. Using the conventions of military service popular in boys' adventure literature, he imagines an egalitarian future in which all but sexual difference will be tolerated or, at least, overlooked. In *Rocket Ship Galileo*, for example, Heinlein starts at the simplest level of tolerance for his audience: tolerance of the differences among white Americans. One of the young engineers of the Galileo Club is Jewish and another is German American. They are shown working harmoniously together in a world that had only recently survived the terrible implications of anti-Semitism carried to genocidal extremes. Here, Heinlein gives us a picture of noble white Americans overcoming their ethnic and religious differences in service to the greater goal of space exploration.[46] His model for this type of tolerance is taken from the South African romances of one of his canonical authors, H. Rider Haggard. The greatest hurdle in Haggard's "band of brothers" stories is the acceptance of Jews into heroic communities of white men who gather in opposition to black Africans. But as Patrick Howarth points out in his study of Haggard, while the novelist creates a Jewish trader, Jacob Meyer, who behaves heroically in *Benita*, the fear of miscegenation serves as the pretext for the anti-Semitism of other, more favored characters.[47] Heinlein's avoidance of this source of antagonism between his characters is made possible by the absence of women from his novel. In this boys' story, the specter of miscegenation is not allowed to spoil the camaraderie of the young engineers because the bond between them is not complicated by the intrusion of female characters. When sexually mature and unmarried women do appear, as they do in his adult novels of the same era, so does racially and ethnically motivated intolerance.[48]

Ostensibly the Heinlein space stories of the 1950s present a future pioneered by *all* of humanity, not simply the small elite valorized by the popular literature of the Great Exploration. Names such as Chiang, Wong, Costello, Ito, Singh, Shiruko, and Murthi are scattered throughout the space-cadet novels. Set against a galaxy-wide canvas in which human diversity has increased through contact with extraterrestrial environments and intelligences, these names signal

to the reader that tolerance should be the norm rather than the exception. However, Heinlein does not often confront the reader with an African, Asian, or
Indian character as the narrative focus of a story. The sole exception to this rule
is his 1954 novel, *The Star Beast.*

In *The Star Beast*, Heinlein presents an ethic of tolerance that supersedes
difference, whether that difference occurs between humans or nonhuman intelligent species. In this novel, we find that as humanity explored the universe
beyond its own planet, it discovered other sentient races. A Community of
Civilizations, a liberal federation in which the various human and nonhuman
races interact on equal footing, has been formed. In fact, Heinlein imagines that
mankind's contact with extraterrestrial sentients might have a profound effect
on our definition of humanity. He writes, "Once the human race had made contact with other races having interstellar travel the additions to the family of legal 'humans' had come so fast that a man could hardly keep up; the more
mankind widened its horizons the harder those horizons were to see."[49] The
equality of these various humanities is based on an assumption of both intellectual and technical parity. Unlike many of his colleagues, Heinlein does not
assume that humanity must be technically superior to every other species it
encounters.

The principle of tolerance enunciated as the foundation of the Community
of Civilizations is codified in the Customs of Civilizations, a body of law that
defines the rights and duties of all the sentient races of the Federation (56).
Given Heinlein's emphasis on education, it is not surprising that the Customs
replace the Constitution and the Pledge of Allegiance in their elementary education, and that characters can quote sections of it on demand: " 'John Thomas
[Stuart XI] frowned and dug into his memory. 'Beings possessed of speech and
manipulation must be presumed to be sentient and therefore to have innate human rights, unless conclusively provided otherwise' " (167). It is obvious that
the Heinlein of this period believes that tolerance of difference is one of the
social ethics necessary if humanity is to be worthy of the benefits of a space
future. Through his sympathetic portrayal of the Right Honorable Henry Gladstone Kiku, a secondary character in the novel, Heinlein suggests that expansion into space will prompt moral as well as technological progress. Kiku is a
Kenyan who, as Under Secretary of the Department of Spatial Affairs (Dep-
Space), heads the agency that mediates between the Community's member races
and enforces the Customs of Civilization.[50] Heinlein's choice of an African
man for this position allows him to make a point about humanity's inability to
find unity among its own species before the space age. Kiku reflects, "He was
aware intellectually that he himself was relatively safe from persecution that

could arise from differences of skin and hair and facial contour for the one reason that weird creatures such as Dr. Ftaeml had made the differences between
breeds of men seem less important" (83). That Kiku has only an intellectual
awareness of the prejudice leveled at people of color as a result of past exploitation and colonialism implies a space future in which race-based antagonisms have been resolved by humanity's contact with extraterrestrial sentients.
Heinlein revises the problem that future intra-human racial tolerance may result from the exaggeration and displacement of difference. A change for the
better occurs only when space travel opens up the opportunity for contact with
intelligent extraterrestrials, and again because human beings learn to defer, not
progress beyond, their habit of making physical characteristics matter.

As Under Secretary of DepSpace, Kiku has to work with several extraterrestrial races, among them the snake-like Rargyllians. Unfortunately, his
pathological fear of snakes extends to sentient beings who resemble the terrestrial species, and he can barely contain his revulsion at the prospect of working
with the Rargyllian Dr. Ftaeml. Given his milieu, the character feels a certain
amount of guilt: "He knew that he should not harbor race prejudice, not in *this*
job" (83). Eventually he comes to like Ftaeml, but only after a buddy-making
crisis, hypnotherapy, and a lot of pills. Heinlein's point here is that racism is a
peculiar attitude that can be overcome with the right environmental stimuli. By
having an African, a potential victim of racism, struggle with his own racialist
feelings, Heinlein defines intolerance as an historical human problem that can
be left behind without a serious accounting.[51] When Kiku overcomes those
feelings, he proves his worth and standing as a space-future hero.

That the space-future hero is free of race prejudice is axiomatic with Heinlein. Greenberg, whom Kiku is grooming for the Under Secretary position when
he retires, is a human Martian colonist who rises above Kiku's more earthbound sensibilities: "Greenberg had grown up in the presence of the Great
Martians and had dealt with many other peoples since; he did not expect 'men'
to look like men and had no prejudice in favor of human form. Ftaeml was, to
his eye, handsome and certainly graceful. His dry chitinous skin, purple with
green highlights, was as neat as a leopard's pelt and as decorative. The absence
of a nose was no matter and was made up for by the mobile, sensitive mouth"
(101). Heinlein continues with sardonic humor: "He glanced at the medusoid's
tendrils. Pshaw! they weren't snakelike. The boss must have a neurosis as big
as a house. Sure, they were about a foot long and as thick as his thumb, but
they didn't have eyes, they didn't have mouths or teeth—they were just tendrils. Most races had tendrils of some sort. What are fingers but short tendrils?"
(102). What indeed. Heinlein makes racism a neurosis, a disease that gets in

the way of seeing the objective truth. And as disease, in the hopeful techno-scientific milieu of the space-future epics, it can be cured. Through Kiku and Greenberg, we see Heinlein establish the optimistic faith in progress on all fronts—political, cultural, psychological, and technical—that has become a core convention of the genre.

At first glance, the social order that Heinlein presents in his future Community of Civilizations, underscored by the rule of law embodied in their Customs, seems to be quite attractive. It is a liberal, egalitarian social order, based on an ethic of tolerance and universal rights. However, the increase in tolerance that Heinlein represents as a primary social benefit of the space future does not arise organically from man's conquest of space. Although he seems to believe that expansion into space is the necessary precondition for such a development, tolerance must be imposed and maintained from the top down by a scientifically and technically trained elite. In *Space Cadet* and *Citizen of the Galaxy*, that elite is sociomilitary in nature; in the Harriman stories, it is based on the robber baron/big business paradigm; in *The Star Beast*, a bureaucratic model takes precedence. In each case, its members are either scientifically and technically trained or have ready access to those who are.

In Heinlein's early work, it is sociomilitary hierarchy that allows the most effective imposition of an egalitarian social and political regime. In *Space Cadet* (1948), for example, the author creates a Space Patrol Academy that includes youth from all over the solar system and a great variety of cultures. A few of them eventually become members of the Patrol, an elite organization that leaves the comfortable illusions of non-Patrol culture behind. The racial etiquette that Heinlein imputes to the service evokes a foreign legion–type reluctance to discuss a man's past. As far as the patrol is concerned, that past does not matter; all that does matter is allegiance to the patrol. Racism is represented as a breach of form that does not go unpunished, for it violates the band of brothers unity that is a core value for the Space Patrol. In *Citizen of the Galaxy*, Heinlein maps out the punishment for racism by a member of the Guard (a variation on the Space Patrol): "Decibel Peebie was convicted (court trial was waived when Brisby, pointed out how the book could be thrown at him) of 'Inciting to Riot, specification: using derogatory language with reference to another Guardman's Race, Religion, Birthplace or Condition previous to entering the Service, the Ship being, etc.'—sentence three days B & W, sol., suspended, reduction one grade, ninety day probation in ref. B & W, sol., only."[52] Whatever prejudices or affiliations one might have held in civilian life, they are to be left there. The band of brothers share a necessary commonality that sets them apart from and makes them effective guardians of the civilian world, indeed of civilization itself. If that high calling does not suffice, then the uniform code of military justice enforces unity.

Although Heinlein is ostensibly egalitarian, his attraction to the efficiency of hierarchic organizations leads him to justify deferring actual democracy indefinitely. Again, the Honorable Henry Kiku is his spokesman:

"[T]his society has been in crisis ever since the first rocket reached our Moon. For three centuries scientists and engineers and explorers have repeatedly broken through to new areas, new dangers, new situations; each time the political managers have had to scramble to hold things together, like a juggler with too much in the air. It's unavoidable.

But we have managed to keep a jury-rigged republican form of government and maintain democratic customs. We can be proud of that. But it is not now a real democracy and it can't be. I conceive it to be our duty to hold this society together while it adjusts to a strange and terrifying world. It would be pleasant to discuss each problem, take a vote then repeal it later if the collective judgement proved faulty. But it's rarely that easy. We find ourselves like pilots of a ship in a life and death emergency. Is it the pilot's duty to hold powwows with passengers? Or is it his job to use his skill and experience to try and bring them home safely?"[53]

For Heinlein, an actually functioning democracy is not very useful in moments of crisis or for handling the complexities of technological change. The building of a new civilization is too important to be left to the will of the people. He sees no contradiction in using hope for future democracy as a justification for present oligarchy. The future social order is necessarily technocratic, for only scientifically and technically trained pilots have the knowledge and skills required to lead society out of the dangerous shoals that modern technology encounters. They are the pilots of "Spaceship Earth," to use Buckminster Fuller's term; docility is the role assigned to the citizen passenger.

Heinlein justifies this division of narrative labor most frequently by imposing it upon a binary division of gender. As we have seen, intra- and interspecies tolerance in Heinlein's space future is worked out using the conventions available in boys' literature. In that genre and in science fiction, its lineal offshoot, the most significant relationships occur not between men and women, but between men. Since women normally are excluded from the top ranks of the military-style hierarchies that govern society, they are not involved in the important relationships of captain and cadet, father and son.[54] Having no rank within this system means that women are irrelevant except as subjects to be protected, prizes to be won, or malign threats to be defeated. If the patriarchal military paradigm is the most efficient model of social organization, then women have little role in defining their future. Instead, they represent the masses in whose name the elite must fight. Without them, Heinlein's spacemen would have nothing to rise above, no one to serve and protect, and hence no way to define themselves or the nature of their heroism.

Women do not always serve this function for Heinlein. In one important exception, *Starship Troopers,* Heinlein toys with the possibility of making all citizenship contingent on military service. In this text, he avoids trapping women in second-class citizenship by making them members of the Navy. Indeed, only women captain the great ships that take the troopers from one planetary battleground to another. The reason that they do so is quintessentially Heinlein: women are better than men at the advanced math required for faster-than-light travel. Note, however, that this is a separate but equal system, for Heinlein does not imagine a parity that would blur an absolute distinction between the two sexes. Again, in the 1949 story "Delilah and the Space Rigger," Heinlein takes the position that qualified women should be allowed to make their contribution to the conquest of space. The story is set in the first space station situated 22,300 miles above the Earth (just where von Braun and Ley said it should be), the jumping-off point for the great conquest. The challenges of building a space station are met by science and technology; the real problem is people.[55] The story begins when a new radioman arrives at the station and the supervisor discovers that the new man is a woman. She was not filtered out of the job pool because she has an intentionally non-gender-specific name: G. Brooks McNye. The central problem of the story arises from McNye's clear competence in her job despite her sex. As a result, the supervisor cannot dismiss her on any grounds other than her sex. His position is that McNye will be a disruptive influence on the all-male crew of the space station, impairing their efficiency and serving as a perhaps unwitting catalyst for worker unrest. His anxiety, of course, goes deeper. As the title of the story indicates, McNye's presence evokes the fear that the conquest of space will somehow be "feminized," that spacemen will be emasculated by the presence of a woman. The supervisor also complains that he feels sabotaged by the Fair Employment Commission, which does not allow gender to be mentioned on its forms " 'except where it's pertinent to the job' " (175). The fear of a political intervention that might disrupt an efficiently functioning status quo is combined with the social discomfort of redefining gender roles. After a series of misadventures in which "the Boss" disrupts the business of the station by trying to keep McNye away from the men (or is it the men away from her?), he finally relents and allows that there might be a place for women in the pioneering stages of space development (182). In the end, the story acknowledges the advent of women as helpers on the space frontier as a logical inevitability. Eventually, the pioneers will become settlers and, however regrettable, the wilderness of space will have to be civilized.

Heinlein narrates the settlement period in his 1952 novel *The Rolling Stones*. In this domestic adventure, he combines the ritual boy's coming of age tale and adventurous exploration with an account of family life on the space frontier. The multigenerational and extremely talented Stone family includes several capable women. Hazel Stone, the anarchistic grandmother, is honored as a member of the generation that pioneered lunar colonization. She is also a competent, even gifted engineer who left her profession in disgust because of the sexism prevalent within it: " 'I saw three big, hairy male men promoted over my head and not one of them could do a partial integration without a pencil. Presently I figured out that the Atomic Energy Commission had a bias on the subject of women no matter what the civil service rules said. So I took a job dealing blackjack.' "[56] The mother of the family, who is invariably referred to as Dr. Stone, is a medical doctor who is unflinchingly dedicated to her oath. Captain Stone, the father of the family, resigns himself to the knowledge that he has no control over her in this area. In the course of the narrative, Dr. Stone is given several opportunities to prove her bravery and her value. The presence of these female characters in *The Rolling Stones* implies that for Heinlein, character and expertise are the most important criteria for space pioneers

Nevertheless, unlike race, sex can never be made irrelevant. In *Citizen of the Galaxy*, Heinlein creates one of his more interesting female professionals, Dr. Margaret Mader.[57] In this novel, he introduces the Free Traders who reserve important places for women within the sociomilitary command structure of their ship-based culture. The Chief Officers of their ships, for example, are always women; that position makes them the heads of the Free Trader families in matters of commerce and diplomacy. Dr. Mader is a cultural anthropologist who is conducting a study of the Free Trader culture. She describes the division of labor they maintain between men and women: "The Chief Officer is boss. It surprised me . . . But it extends all through the People. Men do the trading, con the ship, and mind its power plant—but a woman is always boss. It makes sense within its framework; it makes your marriage customs tolerable."[58] The marriage system to which Dr. Mader refers is "patrilocal": it is based on the exchange of women between ships, with wives joining their husband's families. The biological imperative behind this custom has to do with the maintenance of genetic diversity among the People. It is a custom made necessary by traditional restrictions on marriage outside of the ship culture. Mader notes that while girls often have to be dragged kicking and screaming from their home ships, they resign themselves to the situation very quickly: "If a girl catches the right man and pushes him, someday she can be sovereign of an independent state. Until she leaves her native ship she isn't anybody. . . . But if men are boss, girl-swapping would be slavery; as it is, it's a girl's big chance."[59] One might ask how this differs from "catching" a promising doctor or lawyer and being trapped in the position of having to realize one's ambition through the manipulation of a husband. Indeed, women become chief officers not on the basis of their abilities, but by virtue of marriage to a captain. Since they are excluded from other senior positions within the Trader command hierarchy, we might well wonder how a woman's competence can be realized if her value on the marriage market is not high enough to enable her to land "the right man." Be that as it may, for Heinlein, the military-style position of chief officer is a sign that ambitious and competent women may attain some kind of public power, if not freedom on the space frontier.

While the space juvenilia was titularly defined as "boys' literature," Heinlein did give some thought to the young women who read his work, even though they constituted a minority of his readers.[60] Several of his young female characters are intellectually brilliant, impertinent in the face of authority, and brave to a fault. Often they outshine their duller male companions by several orders of magnitude. Betty Sorenson of *The Star Beast*, for example, has a mind that operates "with the humming precision of a calculator."[61] Mata, a Free Trader in *Citizen of the Galaxy*, is an expert firecontrolman and "a valuable fighting man."[62] Patricia "Peewee" Wynant Riesfield of *Have Space Suit—Will Travel*, the daughter of a Nobel Prize winner, is a self-confessed and actual genius.[63] Holly Jones of "The Menace from Earth" is in a hurry to get her degree so that she can work as a spaceship designer.[64] As with Heinlein's boy heroes, the girls's competence lies in the area of applied math and engineering. According to the values of his space-future epic, they can be members of the technocratic elite that will pioneer and create the future.

The early Heinlein did believe that women have the capacity to play an important role in the expansion of mankind into the space frontier, as scientists, engineers, medical people, anthropologists, and military officers. Yet he always presented sex as the factor that limits the decisions they can make about careers and their place in the space future. Their male colleagues hold on to gender bias with a tenacious grip, often despite evidence that their attitudes are dysfunctional. For example, Jim, the hero of *Red Planet*, thinks that girls should "stay out from underfoot" when important things are happening.[65] Another character in the same book believes that education is wasted on girls because they tend to get married. Don of *Between Planets* is so puzzled by female behavior, he speculates that they are "much odder than dragons (Venusian extraterrestrials). Probably another race entirely."[66] By presenting bright and competent girls in a space future dominated by powerful men, Heinlein creates a critical distance from the naturalized sexism of boys' literature.

Heinlein's view of sexism as a flaw in otherwise heroic male characters parallels his view of racism as presented through Kiku. Sexism and racism are individual failings, not institutional hindrances. Unlike race, however, sex cannot be easily disregarded. Heinlein's libertarian individualism prompts him to view race as a superficial difference between people. Sex, however, is another matter. It is a fundamental biological difference that marks the limits of Heinlein's social imagination. Despite his professed egalitarianism, it is clear that the social and political contributions of women to his space future are confined largely within the sphere prescribed by reproduction, marriage, and domesticity. We find in his stories that it is unmarried women and girls who most often have independent personalities and make the greatest contributions. This changes when they become sexually mature and take on the roles of wives and mothers. In other words, if they do nothing that sets them apart from men, women can be part of the sociomilitary command structure as, in effect, honorary men.[67] The masculine norm can remain undisturbed if women are allowed to assimilate into it and if cultural assumptions about romance and reproduction are suspended or ignored. But when women are also girlfriends, wives, or mothers, they represent a difference disruptive to the efficient operation of any professional environment or mission.

A good example of how one of Heinlein's smart and sassy female adolescents takes on a woman's estate is found in *The Star Beast*. At the end of the novel, DepSpace has to decide who to send as a part of a diplomatic/cultural exchange with a newly contacted extraterrestrial empire. Betty Sorenson, who has shown intelligence and grit thus far in the novel, impertinently negotiates with Kiku regarding the terms under which she and John Thomas Stuart XI (her beau and the titular hero of the piece) will accompany a diplomatic mission to an extraterrestrial race:

"Just a moment, Mr. Kiku. There are one or two other matter[s]. Just what are you doing for John Thomas?"
  "Eh?"
  "What's the contract?"

"Oh. Financially we mean to be liberal. He will devote most of his time to his education, but I had thought of giving him a nominal title in the embassy—special attaché, or assistant secretary, or some such."

Betty remained silent. "Of course, since you are going along, it might be well to give you a semi-official status, too. Say special aide, with the same salary." It would give you two a nice nest egg if you return . . . when you return."

She shook her head. "Johnnie isn't ambitious. I am."

"Yes?"

"Johnnie is to be ambassador to the Hroshii."[68]

Betty goes on to negotiate a sharp political deal in which John Thomas is given rank and pay similar to that of an ambassador, though without the authority. She is given neither. Despite her claim to a radical individualism and a healthy respect for her own gifts, Betty is shown taking on the traditional job of wife to an important man, a role that she engineers. She is content with fulfilling her ambitions through her future husband. Her role in the new embassy is to be that of wife and mother, and no provision is made for her own education. Nor will she be compensated for the labor she will perform behind the scenes to further her husband's career. At the end of their interview, a bemused Mr. Kiku asks, "Miss Sorenson . . . how does it happen that you do not ask to be ambassador yourself?" Betty makes no response to this question, leaving us to assume that the answer is self-evident. Betty's brilliance and Johnnie's ignorance are a function of their sexual immaturity. As they grow into adulthood, they will assume the roles proper to their sexes. A reversal will occur in which she will become the mother to his father, taking on the placid imperturbability peculiar to Heinleinian mothers (251).

For Heinlein, the biology of sex creates the differences that mandate a gendered division of labor and power within the family. Those differences encourage a familiar separation between the public and the private worlds of his space future. Because of their traditional roles as mothers and nurturers, women cannot become a direct part of the sociomilitary command structure that drives the conquest of space. They are not part of its adventure, nor are they central to the public hierarchies that mark the progress of humankind. They are in space to create the domestic sphere, the haven that is both refuge and prize for the men who don uniforms to protect them. One of Heinlein's juvenile heroes explains the division between father and mother as a simple dichotomy that defines his world: "I have talked more about my father but that doesn't mean that Mother is less important—just different. Dad is active, Mother is passive; Dad talks, Mother doesn't. But if she died, Dad would be like an uprooted tree. She makes our world."[69] In terms of his understanding of sex and the gender roles that our culture allows, therefore,

Heinlein's space future is a direct projection of the public/private culture of the 1950s.

In effect, Heinlein tries to have it both ways: by punishing racial injustice, he establishes the political benefits of the space future; by clinging to reproduction-based sexual inequity he assures us that the future will be comfortably familiar. He is both uneasy with and drawn to the divisions between rulers and ruled that characterize his own world. Seduced by the prospect of being one of the rulers, he ultimately accepts that someone must embody the ruled. Hence Heinlein's conscious ethic of democracy, egalitarianism, and tolerance camouflages an authoritarian, hierarchical, and deeply intolerant future. By defining cultures in which females are dominant as being literally nonhuman (*Between Planets, Have Space Suit—Will Travel*, and *The Star Beast*), Heinlein sets the boundary for legitimate human futures. His example became paradigmatic for astrofuturists of his and following generations.

Heinlein established the foundation of astrofuturist ideology in the 1950s. He took the notion of space travel from the confines of boys' adventure literature and articulated it with the concerns of white, middle-class, college-educated men of his era. He and his publisher were able to exploit the popular hunger for any material that could make the technoscience of the late 1940s and 1950s legible within American culture. By the end of the 1950s, through his space-cadet novels, Heinlein had helped usher in a new age for science fiction. As the first science-fiction writer to appear in hard covers under the auspices of a major publisher, he reached an audience of readers, both juvenile and adult, that had been unavailable to the genre in its incarnation as pulp literature. Novels such as *Rocket Ship Galileo, Space Cadet,* and *Have Space Suit—Will Travel* were recommended reading for young adults in libraries and schools. If a youngster had to read science fiction, then Heinlein was the author of choice. He was integral to the cultural apparatus that tied astrofuturism into the mainstream of American culture. His technical and social speculations described the conquest of space as a project arising out of American history, American character, and the resolution of American problems. Central to his understanding of that history were the values codified and mythologized by America's self-conception as a democratic, egalitarian power finding constant renewal on new frontiers.

His concept of a desirable or rational social future, however, relies on techno-military hierarchies to do the job of conquering the space frontier and maintaining human control over its resources and potentials. The sociomilitary form made it possible for Heinlein to connect the strange notion of a future in space with the familiar one of militaristic exploration and adventure in exotic lands. It evokes a familiar cultural landscape in which the hierarchies of age (the untried cadet and the "old man"), gender (men and women), ethnicity (the convention of the Scots engineer and the Anglo commander), class (the buffoonish lower-class sidekick and the aristocratic hero), and race (human and nonhuman) can be reinscribed onto unfamiliar territory. Relying on the hierarchies implicit in the sociomilitary form to lend a kind of cultural reality to his space futures, Heinlein unwittingly undermines his own egalitarianism.

4. Will There Always
Be an England?
Arthur C. Clarke's New Eden

"But it's not paradise we're going to be making down here on this planet. It couldn't be, there'll be humans in it, you see."

—Peter F. Hamilton, *The Reality Dysfunction*[1]

Prelude to Space

Of all the authors in this study, perhaps the best known and most influential is Arthur C. Clarke. His renown is due partly to his longevity: Clarke's career spans the entire length of the space-flight movement from its beginnings in the early rocket societies to its current incarnation as integral to the popular culture of science. It leads us from the conjoined adolescences of science fiction and rocketry in the 1930s, through their maturation in the space race of the 1950s and 1960s, their appropriation into the military and entertainment cultures of the 1970s and 1980s, to their resurgence within the globally networked electronic knowledge systems of the post–cold war era. As a writer and as a spaceflight advocate, he has been a strong, continuous bridge between the two genres that carry science to the general reading public. The bulk of his fiction advocates the idea of a conquest of space, while his nonfiction and popular science extend the scientific and ideological basis for the space future illustrated in his stories and novels.

Unlike Heinlein, Clarke's conquest of space is not obsessed with an endless reiteration of the sociomilitary form. The pattern of his social future is taken from the international community of science as it existed in the late nineteenth and early twentieth centuries. Clarke follows H. G. Wells in idealizing Western science and scientists as an open and altruistic discursive community capable of creating a world order that serves all of humanity. Articulating a sensibility quite different from Heinlein's, Clarke imagines a future run by civilians. Hierarchies are not as clearly defined, culture is not as static, and the desire for an end to atavistic behaviors, such as war, is more pronounced. The conquest of space that Clarke seeks is one predicated on the expansion of human knowledge and social welfare. It is less totalitarian in design and more effective as a statement of democratic intent than that of Heinlein. If it is fair to see Heinlein as a conservative, then we must view Clarke as a liberal working within the conventions of astrofuturism to reform their imperial subtext.

Clarke also takes us from the United Kingdom and its terrestrial empire to the United States and its continual search for democratic renewal on an ever-receding frontier. As with the German futurism we inherit through von Braun, Clarke allows us to trace the subcutaneous links between English political history and the American attempt to transcend it. Throughout his popular science and science fiction, Clarke depends upon a progressive view of imperial history. As a self-consciously liberal writer and thinker, he has attempted to envision a space future that salvages the recent past of Western civilization and extends its benefits to the entire human race. The trajectory of Clarke's writing allows us to trace a loss of faith in the transformative power of the astrofuturist vision following the breakdown of the classic spaceflight agenda at the end of Project Apollo. The imbrication of his early work in the grand narratives of Western exploration and boys' adventure literature constrains his astrofuturism, for he imagines the conquest of space as an imperial project in a world grown too small for terrestrial empires. He entertains identities and histories that arise from outside the orbit of an Anglo-American hegemony, but cannot authorize a future using that material. In other words, the futurism of the early decades of his career is traceable to the imperialist narratives popularized early in the twentieth century. But in a series of collaborative novels written in the 1990s, he revises the optimistic teleology of the space age in response to the social movements of the 1960s and 1970s. An obdurate humanity fractured along the lines of race, class, and culture seems harder to move, less likely to use well the utopian opportunities presented by a space frontier. The recovery of faith requires a resolution of our discontents within space-future landscapes designed and nurtured by a black woman. Through that figure, Clarke asks if human expansion into space can be led by, and can answer the justifiable discontent of, those who have been disenfranchised by previous territorial expansions.

In many respects, Clarke's early life parallels that of H. G. Wells, the literary progenitor to whom he is most often compared. Clarke was born in 1917 on

England's Bristol Channel in the parish of Minehead. His father Charles was a demobilized Army officer who had married soon after the First World War and turned his hand to farming. His failure and early death left Clarke's mother Norah alone to raise Arthur and his siblings.[2] Before the 1870s, such a background would have meant that the young Clarke could have expected nothing more than to follow in his father's footsteps as a farmer or as an apprentice in some trade. However, the late nineteenth-century educational reforms that had saved Wells from life as a tradesman did the same for Clarke. His studiousness and his talent for mathematics marked him out in the Minehead school system, and he was encouraged to take the Civil Service exam as soon as he was of age. Passing the test with flying colors, Clarke left the rural community of his birth for a job in London as an accountant in "His Majesty's Exchequer and Audit Department."[3]

Clarke's work as a government accountant was not particularly edifying. His primary responsibility lay in shuffling the payroll numbers for government-run schools. However, since he usually finished his work early in the day, the job left him plenty of time to pursue his true passions: science fiction and membership in the British Interplanetary Society (BIS). Clarke had become a BIS member shortly after he moved to London; many of the BIS's prewar meetings were held in his cramped Charing Cross Road flat and in a nearby pub. Despite its success in publicizing its cause and the engineering and literary luminaries it attracted before the war, the BIS was a poverty-stricken group existing on the margins of respectable scientific and technological discourse.[4] Yet in later years, Clarke would look back on those days with the kind of nostalgia that only age, vindication, and comfortable circumstances allow.

These early days ended, however, with the arrival of the Second World War. Clarke stayed with auditing long enough to be moved out of London during the Blitz along with the rest of his department. Seeking a more active role in the war effort, he joined the Royal Air Force. Although desperate for young men to staff England's defense against the German attack, the RAF did not send Airman Clarke to the front line as a pilot. His background made him more valuable in quieter, less ostentatiously heroic pursuits, such as the effort that turned early radar into an effective instrument of war. As a Flight Lieutenant, he was put in charge of the ground-controlled approach (GCA) radar apparatus that had been developed by Luis Alvarez and his Radiation Laboratory team at MIT. Clarke credits this experience with triggering the line of thought that lead to "Extraterrestrial Relays," the technical paper on which rests his reputation as a scientist.[5] Published in the British radio journal *Wireless World* in 1945, it was the first serious technical article on the possibilities inherent in telecommunications satellites placed in geosynchronous orbit. Although, as Clarke himself points out, it marks the initial conception of the idea and not its final realization, the paper is an important document in the history of technology because it appeared at the moment when the communications satellite became a technical possibility. Even though few realized it at the time, Clarke's paper was one of the first indications that some advanced military technologies of the war might be turned to peaceful purposes.

For Clarke, the war was a monumental but momentary diversion. After its end, the generous postwar subsides for ex-servicemen allowed him to continue his education at King's College London. In 1948, he graduated with First Class Honors in physics and mathematics. By that time, he had several technical papers to his credit and in all likelihood could have built on his wartime and academic training to pursue a career in electronic engineering.[6] His commitment to the spaceflight movement and his facility as a writer, however, quashed any incipient career as an obscure functionary of big science. Instead, he set to work rebuilding the network of contacts and relationships that made up the BIS. Before the war, the BIS had been part of an international network of amateur rocket societies dominated by young men who dreamed of the technology that would make possible the conquest of space. Because British law restricted experimentation with explosive fireworks, the society retained its initial focus on promoting spaceflight rather than moving to the practical development of early modern rocket technology. As a result, despite its groundbreaking conceptual studies in the technology and methods of spaceflight—many of which were "rediscovered" during the American space program of the 1960s—the BIS retained the aura of impractical speculation. However, the technological advances that the war fostered forced a public reassessment of the technology, if not of the aims of space enthusiasts, and conferred a certain respectability on the BIS. As chairman of the society during the crucial years of its reemergence and growth, Clarke assumed responsibility for explaining its aims to the general public. Thus, during his undergraduate training at Kings College, Clarke became interested in the fictional and nonfictional explanation of the spaceflight movement that was to define his future career.

In 1951, Clarke published his first book, *Interplanetary Flight,* a basic primer on the technology and methods of spaceflight. The response to it convinced Clarke and his publishers that another less technical, more popular work was needed, "for the benefit of all those who are interested in the 'why' and 'how' of astronautics yet do not wish to go into too many scientific details."[7] In *The Exploration of Space*, published that same year, he presented many of the themes that were to recur repeatedly in his work: the importance of history and technology as predictive guides, the inevitability of the conquest of space, the deflation of techno-myths such as explosive decompression of the human body in airless space, and the difference between good science fiction and pulp. The book follows the general format pioneered by David Lasser and Willy Ley in the United States and reiterated by many astrofuturists during the 1950s: the literary grounding of "the Dream" in Western utopian fiction, a tour of the solar system, a discussion of the rocket, and speculations on designs for spaceships, lunar bases, and space stations.[8]

In the early 1950s, Clarke very quickly established himself as a popular writer of science fiction and expository science. His success made it possible for him to leave his job as an indexer for *Physics Abstracts* and devote his full attention to writing. Over the next few years, he laid the foundation of his reputation as one of the most literate and intelligent science-fiction writers of the 1950s, matching Heinlein in his rate of production. In novels such as *Islands in the Sky* (1952), *The Sands of Mars* (1953), *Against the Fall of Night* (1953), and *Childhood's End* (1953), Clarke presented a rigorously imagined space future based on what astronomy could surmise about worlds beyond Earth's atmosphere and on technological speculations from the rapidly aging members of the old rocket societies. His fiction was complemented by his close contacts with those working on technical developments and organizing the companies that would form the backbone of 1960s aerospace industry. His nonfictional work in this postwar period was a combination of popular science and speculative technoscience. In the successors to *Interplanetary Flight* (1950)—*The Exploration of Space* (1951), *Going into Space* (1954), *The Exploration of the Moon* (1955), and *The Making of a Moon* (1957)—Clarke introduced the technological theory of spaceflight, educating a growing audience in topics such as rocketry, nuclear power, astronomy, and the possibility of extraterrestrial intelligence. These books are important because they document how the public was educated in the new science and technology of the 1950s, specifically by being encouraged to place new developments in technoscience within the grand narratives of history, civilization, and future progress.

More ardently than many of his contemporaries, Clarke believes that the continued evolution of civilization depends on the conquest of space. The use of the term "evolution" in this context is deliberate, for Clarke believes human history to be the expression of a biological imperative toward perfection. He inherits a Western historical teleology that understands humanity to be climbing a ladder rising from the "primitive" to the "modern." The West's political dominance during the nineteenth and the early twentieth centuries convinced many of its intellectuals, including Clarke's literary progenitor, Wells, that European civilization was positioned at the top of the ladder of human achievement. For Clarke, the West's advances in science and technology ensure its position as the vanguard of the human race. That tendency to evaluate a culture through its technical accomplishments, its comprehension and control of the material world, has remained constant throughout his career.

Clarke's techno-evolutionary theory of history and civilization emerged in the mid-1940s when he came under the influence of historian Arnold Toynbee, while considering "the cultural and philosophical implications of astronautics."[9] Early in 1946, Clarke attended a lecture by Toynbee at the University of London on "The Unification of the World." He wrote of that experience:

He . . . opened my eyes to the highly parochial view we westerners take of human history, which is best summed up by our attitude that *we* discovered the world. Above all, however, I was struck by Toynbee's emphasis on "challenge and response" as shaping the rise and fall of civilizations, and it seemed to me that we would be presented with a classic example of this when the Space Age opened. Here without question was the greatest physical challenge that life on this planet had faced since the distant days when it emerged from the sea and invaded that other hostile environment, the arid, sun-scorched land.[10]

Toynbee argued that the survival and evolution of civilizations are directly related to their ability to respond successfully to challenges, both human and environmental. Without challenge, he warned, any civilization would quickly stagnate and decline. Of course, this idea was not a startling innovation; it was a refinement of notions circulating in British intellectual circles for quite some time. Its attraction for Clarke lay in Toynbee's attempt to create a history that made Darwinian evolution a tenet of historical law. Given that foundation, historiography would then be a scientific enterprise with predictive power.

In the immediate postwar era, Toynbee's lecture on "The Unification of the World" must have seemed to Clarke like a ray of hope in a world that had only narrowly missed destruction. Like many of his generation, Clarke was concerned about the destructive power that technology had unleashed during World War II. It became clear to some that war had to be displaced as the primary generator of human ingenuity and technological advance. Using Toynbee's "challenge and response" thesis as a lens through which to view the immediate postwar world, Clarke turned to the spaceflight movement as the solution to the concerns of the day. The confluence of Toynbee's ideas and Clarke's spaceflight enthusiasm resulted in a lecture the latter gave before the BIS, entitled "The Challenge of the Spaceship." This paper marks a defining moment in Clarke's career and in his space-future advocacy: it was his inaugural lecture as chairman of the society, and it established the themes to which he would return repeatedly in his fiction and nonfiction. In the essay's several parts, Clarke attempts to place the new rocket and nuclear technology in the context of human history and progress; discusses the basic motivations behind the conquest of space; presents his hope that nationalism and imperialism (that is, politics) will cease to be a factor in human relations as a result of the philosophical and moral improvements brought about by spaceflight; and indicates that the space frontier may be the safety valve necessary for the preservation of civilization.

Clarke begins with the thought that "an historian of the twenty-first century, looking back past our own age to the beginnings of human civilization, will be conscious of four great turning points which marked the end of one era and the dawn of a new and totally different mode of life."[11] He goes on to describe spaceflight as the most recent of four revolutions that have marked the progress of humankind. Spaceflight and the development of nuclear energy share equal significance with the "invention of agriculture" and the "taming of fire" (66). Acknowledging the difficult task of convincing an often harshly skeptical public of the validity and the importance of spaceflight, Clarke nevertheless rues the tendency to mix a high flown rhetoric of imperial glory with the crassest of utilitarian motives and greedy speculations about the unlimited resources of the space frontier. Speaking to his audience of the faithful, he reveals what he considered to be the only acceptable and lasting motive behind the spaceflight venture: a simple, emotive, creative impulse that he considers "beyond analysis," but that he likens to composing music, painting a picture, writing a book, solving an equation, or exploring the world (67–68). In other words, Clarke views the exploration of space as something that is undertaken only secondarily as a purely rational project:

Any "reasons" we may give for wanting to cross space are afterthoughts, excuses tacked on because we feel we ought, rationally, to have them. They are true, but superfluous— except for the practical value they may have when we try to enlist the support of those who may not share our particular enthusiasm for astronautics yet can appreciate the benefits which it may bring, and the repercussions these will have upon the causes for which they, too feel deeply. (68)[12]

For Clarke, therefore, the core of the spaceflight movement is composed of those who seek the conquest of space not for any material gain, but for the thing itself. This represents the idealism that underscores his otherwise instrumental reliance on evolutionary history.

Perhaps the most interesting theme "The Challenge of the Spaceship" reveals is Clarke's ambiguous evaluation of imperialism and nationalism. Like most children of his generation, Clarke had grown up with the popular imperialism of the early twentieth century. The boys' adventure literature of his youth unabashedly extolled the glories of empire.[13] In 1938, when a young science-fiction fan, Clarke wrote his first piece of popular science for the British fan magazine *Scientifiction*.[14] "Man's Empire of Tomorrow" combined a survey of the known solar system with a pamphlet for imperial opportunities. After the war, Clarke became less sanguine about empire and its future prospects. Eight years later in "The Challenge of the Spaceship," he condemned empire as an "extreme form of nationalism" that cannot survive the move onto the space frontier. The conquest of space will force an "evolution" from the selfish tribalism of empire to a "world outlook."[15] Nevertheless, in response to C. S. Lewis's criticism that the spaceflight movement represents ambitions of infinite imperial expansion to which "the destruction or enslavement of other species in the Universe, if such there are, [would be] a welcome corollary," Clarke replies: "I would point out that Empires—like atomic bombs—are self-liquidating assets. Dominance by force leads to revolution, which in the long run, even if indirectly, must be successful. Humane government leads eventually to self-determination and equality, as the classic case of the British Empire has shown and is still showing. Commonwealths alone can be stable and enduring, but Empires must always contain the seeds of their own dissolution" (76). At this juncture, despite his discomfort with imperialism, Clarke is unable to dismiss completely its "benevolent" British manifestations. His primary concern is for the stability and perhaps even the ascendancy of his own nation. He warns that the BIS membership should be vigilant against "the menace of interplanetary imperialism," implying that such a thing might be established by the United States—which at that time controlled nuclear technology—without "world-wide technical and political agreements well in advance of the actual event" (73).

Clarke's anti-imperial rhetoric is at odds with his assumption that "conquest and empire" are necessary for human evolution and civilization. Indeed, his progressive history defends the possibility of imperial benevolence on the grounds that it readies subject peoples for self-government and equality with "advanced" cultures, an advance that presumably they could not have achieved if left to their own devices. His belief that without the imperial impulse civilization would stagnate and decline was borrowed from the cultural theories of such late Victorian scholars as the anthropologist J. D. Unwin and the classicist Sir James Frazer. These men held that human societies only advanced when they were actively expanding their material production and political influence. The theory found ardent partisans on both sides of the Atlantic in the late nineteenth century. Clarke reminded his audience of an aphorism coined by Frazer and repeated by Unwin: "Intellectual progress, which reveals itself in the growth of art and science . . . receives an immense impetus from conquest and empire" (4). But Clarke also believed that the latest war was an ample testament to what could happen if imperial contests over limited resources and cultural practices were allowed to continue. With the exponential rise in the destructive power of Western science and technology, the civilized impulse toward empire could lead to the destruction of humanity. The only solution to this dilemma, Clarke told his audience, is "Interplanetary travel . . . the only form of 'conquest and empire' compatible with civilization" (72).[16] Here he can imagine no template for the space future's expansion of the human imperium and salutary effect on civilization but that of European exploration and domination.

"The Challenge of the Spaceship" also helps explain Clarke's influence in the American astrofuturism of the 1950s and 1960s. Despite his upbringing in Britain, Clarke was heavily influenced by his childhood reading of American science fiction. As a result, he integrated quintessentially American notions of frontier into his thought at an early age. While he often used "frontier" in its European sense of boundary or borderline in much of his early work, he also followed the American usage with its connotation of free wilderness and unoccupied space. Just as the west served nineteenth-century Americans as an outer space into which the discontent and adventurous of the Old World or the east could escape, Clarke's imagined space frontier offers the challenge that will save us from future decadence and destruction: "The crossing of space—even the sense of its imminent achievement in the years before it comes—may do much to turn men's minds outward and away from their present tribal squabbles. In this sense the rocket, far from being one of the destroyers of civilization, may provide the safety-valve, that is needed to preserve it."[17] Here is the hope that the new rocket and nuclear technologies would be used to gain access to "an outlet for dangerously stifled energies."[18] The conquest of the space frontier, therefore, becomes "the moral equivalent of war," giving scope to the imperial impulse without spilling human blood; it is imperialism without empire.

The relationship between history and empire that Clarke articulates in "The Challenge of the Space Ship" provides the thematic foundation of his first science-fiction novel, *Prelude to Space* (1951). In the novel, he emphasizes the historical importance of the conquest of space by introducing a historian as the principle point of view character: Dr. Dirk Alexson, an American historian, is the trained observer who will record the events around the first flight of the spaceship *Prometheus*. Alexson is not a historian of science and technology or of the western frontier. Rather, he specializes in renaissance Italy: his thesis focused on the life of the Medici family of Florence. When he begins his association with Interplanetary, the scientific body that develops space exploration, he finds himself untrained in and somewhat fearful of science, out of touch with the political and technological currents of the modern world. His personal journey in the novel is a progression from that position to one of enlightenment and commitment to the space future. His relative ignorance in science allows Clarke to use him as an interlocutor through whom the reader can be educated. Alexson's advanced degree, however, makes him an intelligent observer rather than a buffoon. As a result, he also becomes the moral expert through whom the reader can judge the activities of the men at Interplanetary. And, of course, the fact that he is a renaissance historian positions him nicely as the witness to and recorder of the beginnings of a new renaissance through the conquest of space.

The central historical issue with which Alexson wrestles is whether the conquest of space represents an advance in human relationships and the comity of nations, or is the beginning of the end. He finds plenty of arguments for and against the endeavor as he conducts background research on Interplanetary's maiden lunar voyage and interviews its members. The most troubling is an anti-imperialist argument that reads human history as one of unreasoning violence and greedy immorality, and "conquest and empire" as anything but benign. Those skeptical of Interplanetary's goals extend the anti-imperialist and -racialist arguments familiar since the late nineteenth century: *"Since Man, they argued, had caused so much misery upon his own world, could he be trusted to behave on others? Above all, would the miserable story of conquest and enslavement of one race by another be repeated again, endlessly and forever, as human culture spreads from one world to the next?"*[19] Clarke attempts to answer this question by countering with the anti-imperialism of his fictional astronauts. Interplanetary's Director-General announces the society's intention to put men on the moon with the assurance that their purpose is not to annex "the Moon in the name of this or that nation." Rather, it is an adventure embarked upon by a group of scientists from all over the globe who will render nations and nationalism obsolete through their work. These scientists are to represent all humanity in its quest for a destiny beyond the earth: " 'There are no nationalities beyond the stratosphere: any worlds we may reach will be the common heritage of all men—unless other forms of life have already claimed them for their own.

'We, who have striven to place humanity upon the road to the stars, make this solemn declaration, now and for the future:

'We will take no frontiers into space.' "[20]

Interplanetary embodies this anti-imperialist sentiment. In the years before the cold war space race, Clarke imagined that the conquest of space was so tremendous a project that no single corporation or country could muster the resources necessary to pursue it. If so, any space venture with a hope of success would have to be international in scale.[21] Interplanetary's space program is an international venture supported by the political goodwill of several nations, the resources of international aerospace corporations, and the coordinated skills of scientists and engineers from around the globe. "About a fifth of the staff are American, and I've heard every conceivable accent in the canteen. It's as international as the United Nations secretariat, though the British certainly provide most of the driving force and the administrative staff." According to Alexson, Interplanetary is a hybrid, a "typically British compromise."[22] The internationalism that Clarke has in mind is securely contained by the dominance of the United Kingdom and the United States in the association. Its compromise extends to diversity of accent, but not to any challenge to the easy ascendancy of predominantly white, English-speaking peoples.[23]

For Clarke, as for his ideological mentor Arnold Toynbee, internationalism is the next step after empire. The people formerly subordinated to the imperial ideal can be raised through technology into a commonwealth that will make the joint conquest of space possible. Within that commonwealth, national and cultural divisions will be eliminated as people organize around the same technoscientific goal. Clarke makes the Heinleinesque point that no matter their differences in social background or national and cultural origins, the people working at Interplanetary are essentially the same. Alexson wonders, "apart from their accents, it's very difficult to see any real distinction between the different nationalities here. Is this due to the—to put it mildly—supranational nature of their work? And if I stay here long enough, I suppose I shall get deracinated too" (18). Nation and race become simply a matter of accents, linguistic accidents that do not distract the scientists and engineers of Interplanetary from their primary goal. Spaceflight gives them a new country to achieve.

But again, even as he calls for an international space effort Clarke assumes the influence, if not the domination, of Britain. On the eve of superpower control of space technology, it was still possible for Clarke and other members of the BIS to imagine that the British might play a decisive role in the conquest of space. Indeed, Interplanetary is little more than an international version of the BIS. Clarke often points out in the book that the Americans—even though some of them are members of Interplanetary—are not convinced that the conquest of space is a worthwhile project (4). It is the heirs of the British Empire, therefore, who must accept the noble burden of space exploration. This is especially evident in the final countdown that accompanies the launch of the "Prometheus" to the Moon. Instead of a human voice counting backwards from ten to one, we get the bell of the world's most famous clock tower: "In Westminster, halfway round the world, Big Ben was preparing to strike the hour. . . . Dirk remembered that for a half a century Englishmen all over the world had waited beside their radios for that sound from the land which they might never see again. He had a sudden vision of her exiles, in the near or far future, listening upon strange planets to those same bells ringing out across the deeps of space" (138). Thus begins a powerful scene in which Clarke describes the launch of the first manned mission toward a world beyond our own. The depth of feeling the author musters here derives from his faith that the first flight to the Moon will represent a pivotal historical moment. For him, that moment encapsulates all that has come before in human history and all that will, perhaps, follow. Significantly, the most immediate and salient history of that moment is the British Empire, an empire that in Clarke's prose survives through the BBC World Service. In this scene, members of the future commonwealth are all exiles from the motherland. The formerly colonized members of the terrestrial commonwealth are absent, perhaps because they cannot be represented as part of an enlightened realm that stretches across space and time. The walls of race and nationality are too steep to climb. The radiophonic voice of Big Ben becomes the cultural icon not only of past British empires, but also of the future British empire that humanity may build in space. Thus space itself becomes a frontier with Greenwich and Westminster at its heart.

The significance of the empire in Clarke's space future is clarified by the presence of a tertiary character who appears toward the end of the novel. The nightwatchman who watches over the lunar ship, *Prometheus,* in the final days before its launch is Ahmed Singh, a Sikh law student. In Singh's portion of the plot, Clarke is careful to counter the racist supposition that "blacks" (interchangeable with Indians in mid-century British usage) are lazy and cannot be counted on to do a proper job.[24] It is true that when a saboteur creeps up to the *Prometheus,* Singh is asleep. But that is expected, and the alarm system around the ship alerts him to the danger.[25] Singh represents the subaltern who has been assimilated into the world the Europeans have made, and his presence represents Clarke's space-future pluralism. However, his low position within Interplanetary (nightwatchman) and his status as a student emphasizes the division of labor represented by British leadership in the project. The subaltern subject is always in the position of tutelage to his Western superiors and must prove his worth within the institutions designed and controlled by the West, even in the future. The internationalism of the novel arises from Britain's experience with empire and the effect that it has had on the world's peoples. As such, the pluralism it advocates is one in which the power relationships between peoples in a postimperial world remains unchanged.[26]

Clarke's use of imperial subalterns indicates that his rhetoric of pluralism covers an implicit hierarchy, a status quo that the writer perhaps could not help but endorse. Political and social power will flow in patterns similar to those that underwrote the popular literature of imperial Britain: the dominance of English-speaking people and culture, racial hierarchy (though liberalized), the absence of women within the adventure, and a renaissance that will allow Western culture to improve without end. The hopes of the future ride on the peaceful use of new technology to conquer new territory, and the control of that technology guarantees the contemporary and future status quo:

[It's] only a logical extension of what mankind's been doing since history began. For thousands of years the human race has been spreading over the world until the whole globe has been explored and colonized. The time's now come to make the next step and to cross space to the other planets. Humanity must always have new frontiers, new horizons. Otherwise it will sooner or later sink back into decadence. Interplanetary travel's the next stage in our development, and it will be wise to take it before it's forced upon us by shortage of raw materials or space.[27]

This passage makes it clear that there are, indeed, no new ideas in astrofuturism in the late 1950s. By the time *Prelude to Space* was written, earlier space futurists had rehearsed most of the arguments for and against going out into space long before the rest of the English-speaking world could believe in the premise. The idea of space futurism hung around at the margins of the general cultural discourse, awaiting its chance. Its advocates simmered until they found a moment when they could connect to the mainstream and achieve the kind of influence that would make possible a general political mobilization toward their goals.

The novel ends years later, long after the successful conclusion of the first voyage to the Moon, as Dirk Alexson reviews a lifetime's work. He has completed his six-volume history of the dawning years of the space age and now lives on the Moon, retired from his distinguished career as Professor of Social History at the University of Chicago. It is the end of the twentieth century and medical advances hold out the hope of an extension of life long past that possible on the Earth (141–42). Humankind has moved far into the inner solar system, and "Man" is "gathering his strength . . . for the leap to the outer planets" (142). For the Clarke of *Prelude to Space*, the next fin de siecle will not be the end of progress, the end of empire, or the end of history, but the beginning of a brave new millennium: "As he saluted the dying century, Professor Alexson felt no regrets: the future was too full of wonder and promise. Once more the proud ships were sailing for unknown lands, bearing the seeds of new civilizations which in the ages to come would surpass the old. The rush to the new worlds would destroy the suffocating restraint which had poisoned almost half the century. The barriers had been broken, and men could turn their energies outwards to the stars instead of striving among themselves" (142–43). We turn our energies out to a conquest of space rather than the conquest of terrestrial nature and nations. Humanity embarks on a shared project that draws together its disparate peoples: "Out of the fears and miseries of the Second Dark Age, drawing free—oh, might it be forever!—from the shadows of Belsen and Hiroshima, the world was moving towards its most splendid sunrise. After five hundred years, the Renaissance had come again. The dawn that would burst above the Apennines at the end of the long lunar night would be no more brilliant than the age that had now been born" (143). This final paragraph of the novel clarifies what is at stake for its author: Clarke's first novel ends by offering us a Wellsian choice between obliteration and a glorious beginning.

By the late 1950s, Clarke was comfortably situated in his professional life as a popular science/fiction writer and as a member of the British Interplanetary Society. He was in great demand as a lecturer and expert on the coming space technologies. However, his personal life seems to have taken a turn for the worse. An acrimonious divorce ousted him from what could have been a comfortable life as a "boffin" and sent him out into the world.[28] In 1956, he moved to Sri Lanka (formerly Ceylon), an island-nation just off the southeastern coast of India that had gained its independence from the British empire in 1948.[29] This removal from the center of imperial Britain to its periphery makes Clarke unique among the major Euro-American writers of science fiction.

Clarke's sympathetic relationship to his adopted home has been unwavering, although perhaps influenced by the remnants of the benevolent face of imperialism. In the late 1970s, Lester James Peries, the eminent Sri Lankan film director, became interested in directing a film based on an early novel by Leonard Woolf. Woolf, whose principle fame lies in his work as a cofounder (with his wife Virginia Woolf) of the Hogarth Press and as a member of the Bloomsbury group of writers and thinkers, began his adult life as a colonial administrator in Ceylon from 1904 to 1911. After he left the colonial service, partly

because of disgust with the ineffectual nature of British imperial rule and partly
to marry Virginia Stephen, he wrote *The Village in the Jungle* (1913). Peries, a
friend of Clarke's, cast the writer as Leonard Woolf in his film of the novel
Beddagama (1980). Thus Clarke found himself in the robes of a colonial judge
administering British justice in the outposts of empire. It was a role with which
he discovered a natural affinity: "As I sat on the bench in my borrowed judicial
robes, I was not in the least conscious of acting a role; even the camera and
lights did not break the spell. The courtroom was a time machine that had carried me back to the beginning of the century. . . . If Leonard Woolf could have
looked through my eyes, as I sat on the dais he had occupied so many times, he
could not have told that seventy years had passed."[30] Clarke was sixty-three at
the time of the film's production; Woolf had been in his late twenties during his
career as a member of the Ceylon Civil Service. Clarke's intense nostalgia
for lost empire and youth complicates our understanding of the technological
progressivism that dominates his reputation. The futurist calls into being the ju-
ridical dominion of the past, sweeping away the political and technological
changes that allows Peries to ironize the Raj through his command of a modern
medium. Instead, Clarke implies that the old forms are ever present, overriding
any notion of a future made by the culture and people of Sri Lanka independent
of Western contrivance.

In his essay on Woolf and the filming of his novel, Clarke accurately
points out that when Woolf left the Ceylon Civil Service he had become disenchanted with the Raj and with the role of colonizer. Woolf had graduated from
Cambridge a committed believer in the civilizing mission of the British Empire. From his point of view, the motivation for British dominance was not the
greedy exploitation of conquered peoples, but their uplift and assimilation into
the modern world. But his experiences as an Assistant Government Agent
(AGA) in Ceylon convinced him that "even the most benevolent imperialism,
for all the good that it undoubtedly brought in terms of peace, justice and im-
proved standards of health and education, could not be morally justified."[31] His
semiautobiographical novel *The Village in the Jungle* was only his first expression of the anti-imperialism that resulted from his Ceylonese experience.

Clarke's romantic identification with the Leonard Woolf of pre-Bloomsbury
days revises our understanding of the kinds of anti-imperialism available in
the late empire and deepens our understanding of Clarke's own position in the
postcolonial world. On the one hand, the futurist sympathizes with the young
AGA's initial attraction to benevolent imperialism and he accepts Woolf's
eventual discovery that empire is not a morally tenable project. On the other, he
stops far short of the older man's conviction that the benefits of industrial

modernity do not justify antidemocratic domination. For Clarke, the transformative power of technology can dissolve the barriers between "modern" and "pre-modern" cultures, but it must proceed from and belong to the "modern." Clarke's Wellsian scientism creates an anti-imperialism that justifies an English presence in Sri Lanka after the end of colonial domination.

Woolf's retreat to England was, in part, due to his belief that the imperial system overestimated the ability of "natives" to absorb the intellectual and physical gifts of Western science and technology.[32] Clarke uses his post-colonial experience to counter this modernist pessimism, describing, for example, how the "natives" ran the satellite station that allowed him to communicate with a science-fiction convention in Washington, D.C.[33] His nostalgia for Woolf's imperial past coupled with his belief in the transformative power of technology rescues the benevolent imperialism that failed to convince the AGA. It promises the equitable distribution of scientific and technological advance to all the world's peoples, but retains initiative as a Western prerogative. This stance is predicated on the denial or repression of political choices that might set conditions on technoscientific transfer. Clarke believes it more likely that the social and political order will be changed by technology rather than the other way around. Moreover, he is certain such exchanges will liberate its beneficiaries. He has often argued, for example, that communications satellites will bring about an increasingly free flow of information and thus will make tyrannies harder to impose.[34] In short, Clarke's Sri Lankan experience did not alter immediately the progressive, redemptive history invoked in "The Challenge of the Spaceship." The change, when it does come, is all the more difficult and complex.

The Fall of the Garden

In the late 1980s, Clarke began rethinking many of the themes he had addressed earlier in his career. After astrofuturist hopes were dashed by the scaling down of the American space program, he had to reexamine his faith that the space future would follow inevitably from contemporary social mores or some transcendent technocultural drive. Nor could the space future be predicted as the logical consequence of scientific progress and technological innovation. The Soviet and American space programs of the 1960s had proved that humanity had the capability to conquer space (or, at least, a small portion of it), but it became evident that those gains did not guarantee that the species would explore, exploit, and colonize the space frontier. For Clarke, this meant that many of the themes on which he had built his career within popular science and fiction had to be reexamined. That reassessment took place not so much in Clarke's popular science, of which he wrote less as the years went by, but in his fiction. In his science and opinion articles, Clarke remained optimistic, continuing to profess that science would bring about an almost utopian future. A good example of this is the coffee-table futurism of *July 20, 2019*, a tourist guide to the new consumer goods that technoculture might make available.[35] But in his space future fiction, Clarke exchanges his early, optimistic evolutionism for a troubled recognition of race-based inequities as the principle impediment to a human apotheosis.

The novels that most clearly represent the changes that occurred in Clarke's representation of the space future are *Rendezvous with Rama, (Rama)*, *Rama II, The Garden of Rama,* and *Rama Revealed.* Together these books constitute a post-Apollo space-future epic, a record of the change from social and political optimism to a pessimism about the old space-future utopianism. *Rendezvous with Rama* (1973), authored as the Apollo program tottered to a close, focuses on humanity's first encounter with evidence of extraterrestrial sentience. The book's only concession to the social upheavals of the 1960s is that its ship culture is represented as pluralistic and blind to the differences signaled by race, class, creed, and sex. *Rama II* (1989), cowritten with space-systems engineer Gentry Lee, describes a second encounter and a world that is grimmer and less successful in its conquests than that depicted in the first Rama novel. *The Garden of Rama* (1991) moves on to a third encounter in which a representative sample of the human race inhabits a technological utopia provided by the Ramans, an experiment in astrofuturist social engineering that goes wrong. And the final novel, *Rama Revealed* (1993), presents the narrative of the previous novels as a test of humanity's evolutionary fitness by the mysterious Ramans. Written over the course of almost twenty years, these novels chart the disintegration of the pioneering consensus in astrofuturism and illuminate Clarke's attempt to find an accommodation with the heterogeneity of the post-1960s world.

Rendezvous with Rama (1973) was published shortly after the last Apollo mission visited the Moon in 1972. As a result, it still reflects many of the conventions that marked the first generation's consensus: the notion that the conquest of space will be an extension of a human imperium; use of the recent past as a template for the social and political institutions of the future; the projection into the future of a sociomilitary enterprise with a clearly defined hierarchy of responsibilities and skills; an ethic of the genius of science as represented by specific individuals; and confidence that even the most frightening and insoluble problems can be overcome by scientific advancement. As Clarke is working from within a liberal internationalism, we find that technical skill is no respecter of rank, or national origin. Even sergeants exhibit skills that can, in certain situations, require them to take over command responsibility from higher officers. In *Rama*, white women and people of color are an integral part of the central team of "spacemen," and national or cultural "others" are integrated into sameness by anglophonic names.

Rendezvous with Rama is essentially a first contact novel, premised on the conceit of the first undeniable visit by an extra-solar artifact to human space. The artifact, a gigantic and seemingly untenanted spaceship, enters the solar system for a short time and raises more questions than it answers about its creators and purpose. For our purposes, *Rama*'s importance lies not in the mystery of the spaceship's origins, but in what the novel reflects of the time in which it was conceived and written. *Rama* itself is a cultural artifact of the astrofuturism of the early 1970s. It also represents one of the first fictional treatments of physicist Gerard K. O'Neill's space-colony concept.[36]

The social backdrop of the story is a familiar extrapolation of contemporary life. Clarke supposes that by the latter part of the twenty-first century, humanity will have resolved its merely local differences and created a global government. While the novel wastes no time investigating the political arrangements that exist on the earth, we can assume from acquaintance with Clarke's other novels that it has become a relatively peaceful world. Interspecies conflict occurs not between the people of the earth, but among the various worlds of the solar system that humanity has colonized. Following the model of the United Nations, the worlds of Earth, Luna, Mercury, Mars, Triton, and others form the United Planets, a place where the sovereign worlds can work out differences and formulate joint policy. Clarke's use of the United Nations model indicates that he wants to sidestep the possibility that an imperial Earth will be the final governing authority in a space future. He is committed to a federal system that allows room for diverse political systems and social subjects. Yet it is also clear that that federalism nevertheless is hierarchical, with Earth as its dominant partner. Our world remains the center of a human-dominated solar system and, Clarke's federalism not withstanding, in his late twenty-first century, humankind is in the process of mastering the solar system. Much of the descriptions of the human colonization of Mercury and proposals for terraforming Venus or warming up Jupiter and Neptune have to do with wielding tremendous technological forces to tame natural worlds for human colonization and exploitation. Clarke's scenario is reminiscent of the school of painting that featured advanc-

ing trains and telegraph lines, cut tree trunks, and scattering Indians to celebrate the technological conquest of the American West.[37]

Liberal narratives of first contact in science fiction and the popular culture
at large are of interest because they can imagine a perhaps humiliating limit to
the human imperium heralded by triumphalist space futures. The presence of
some other out on the space frontier evokes both threat and opportunity, for it
implies that there may be a limit to our control and domination of the natural
universe. The possibility of the existence of sentient beings who are not us, or
even evolutionarily related to us, raises the fear and hope of active opposition
to the conceit that all of creation is a human birthright. In conservative hands,
the tale of galactic empire preserves a human-dominated future in which mankind never meets an alien who can contest his mastery. However, Clarke works
from the presupposition that a truly advanced technology, such as that used for
space travel, necessarily represents a corresponding advance in moral and political sensibility. He assumes that any space-faring species with the patience
and tools to traverse extrasolar space will have evolved to the point where it
controls its own as well as physical nature. In this optimistic evolutionary
schema, the tragic history of European exploration will not be repeated by any
correspondingly advanced race that might reach us. The danger, rather, will
come from the fearful, and by contrast, primitive human response to contact
with an intelligent other. This constitutes Clarke's answer to liberals and pro-
gressives who suspect that astrofuturism is nothing more than an excuse to extend humanity's past crimes onto an endless playing field. He counters with his
faith that the conquest of space will civilize the human race, making it fit to
meet any extraterrestrial intelligence in a spirit of good will. First contact will,
therefore, be an opportunity for human and nonhuman intelligences to share
knowledge and to grow together.

Furthermore, Clarke's commitment to a liberal space future in *Rendezvous
with Rama* includes a sense that the social landscape of the future might differ
from our own present. This is drawn most clearly in his representation of gender relationships and family structure. Most of the narrative focuses on the
crew of the *Endeavor*, the spacecraft that happened to be in the right place to
rendezvous with the alien artifact. Its crew is composed of the standard group
of technocratic military explorers made familiar by over a century of Anglo-
American popular literature. Its members function both as the representatives
of humankind and as the very best that the species has to offer. They are mixed
along the lines of gender and race. This mixing is most effective in terms of
gender, for white women are integral to the crew. By making the chief surgeon

of the ship a woman and by giving a female noncommissioned officer command responsibilities during a crisis, Clarke attempts a response to criticism that spaceflight is a masculinist fantasy. He makes sure that the reader understands that the competence of the *Endeavor*'s women is never questioned by the ship's men; it is simply an unremarkable fact of life.[38]

Race is an equally unremarkable characteristic of the *Endeavor*'s crew. The East Asian, South Asian, and Hispanic men who play significant roles in the narrative do so with the barest mention of their backgrounds. Only the cues of naming and skin color break the implicit assumption that all the novel's characters are Caucasian. The commander of the *Endeavor*, William Tsien Norton, for example, can only be suspected of mixed Anglo-Asian parentage because of his middle name and the meticulous technical competence ascribed to him.[39] Nowhere in the book is there evidence of the jealousies, resentments, or doubts that might arise should the same characters be placed in the actual history of their world. Representing as it does a plural cross section of humanity and organized into the institutional structure of space-born military explorers, the crew of the *Endeavor* is the social model that liberal futurists hoped might resolve the domestic tensions of mid-century America. Here men and women of color are assimilated into a common tradition, a common culture, and a commonly recognized system of merit. We are familiar with this convention through Heinlein's space-cadet novels of the 1950s and in the television crews of the various *Star Trek* series. But noteworthy in Clarke's articulation of the convention is his clear vision of the historical tradition that mandates the techno-military foundation of a pluralistic space future.

Clarke patterns the adventure of *Rendezvous with Rama*, the fictive exploration of a new world, after the voyages of Captain James Cook (1728–79), the English explorer who contributed much to the mapping of the New World and made terra incognita accessible to late eighteenth-century Britain. The spaceship *Endeavor* is named in honor of the ship that Cook commanded when he circumnavigated the globe in the late 1760s. Commander Norton, our point-of-view character, is well aware of the *Endeavor*'s lineage and is fascinated by the historic ship and its captain.[40] He keeps a portrait of Cook above his office desk and when he has a difficult decision to make, he routinely asks himself what his famous predecessor would have done.

By the time *Rendezvous with Rama* was written, canonizing the old heroes of imperial exploration was not without its problems. The morality of European adventure in the New World had become an issue that the political mainstream was forced to address as traditional Western historiography came under fire in the early 1970s. In the astrofuturism of that era, a writer's political position corresponded to his or her position in relation to the central narrative convention of imperial exploration. For Jerry Pournelle, Larry Niven, and many other space-opera specialists, the militaristic overtones of geographic exploration (past and future) are a necessary component of any future social order we can imagine.[41] The "exploration by warfare" that so troubled opponents of late nineteenth-century imperial adventure is presented by this faction as the most exciting and important aspect of exploration, for it validates the power of Western science and technology to overwhelm natural and cultural opposition. For writers such as Clarke who oppose crude jingoism, such narratives undermine the moral authority of any civilizing mission that the West might conduct on the space frontier. They also deny the possibility that explorers might be instructed positively by the new worlds and cultures they encounter.

In *Rendezvous with Rama*, therefore, Clarke attempts to liberalize and update Captain Cook's image and defend his utility as a model for his pluralistic crew by pointing out that he was an unusually humane man in an age of patriarchal sadists: "Cook had been not only a supreme navigator, but also a scientist and—in an age of brutal discipline—a humanitarian. He treated his own men with kindness, which was unusual; what was quite unheard of was that he behaved in exactly the same way to the often hostile savages in the new lands he discovered."[42] Regardless of the validity of this claim, its implication here is clear: the good will of one explorer justifies the belief that the Western tradition of scientific exploration is an appropriate model for a future in space. The most desirable future is one in which all the world's peoples assimilate the traditions, values, and skills privileged by this model, dismissing perspectives that may dissent or differ from that mainstream. At this juncture, Clarke's liberal pluralism has little room for a space future defined by cultural traditions or experiences other than those of the Royal Navy and European colonial empires.

Sixteen years passed between the publication of *Rendezvous with Rama* and its sequel, *Rama II*. In that interval, science fiction underwent a metamorphosis, which changed its method of production and the expectations of its audiences. It became a regular feature of bestseller lists, six-figure advances were negotiated for individual works by prominent authors (including Clarke, Heinlein, Asimov, and Sagan), and film options involving millions of dollars became commonplace. All in all, the economic stakes in the genre rose exponentially. *Rama II* and its immediate successor, *The Garden of Rama*, in part reflect the voracious appetite of the burgeoning market for science fiction. They also articulate a brand of astrofuturism that attempts some response to the changed expectations of their readers. Clarke, science fiction, and liberal astrofuturism had been affected by the demographic changes that took place in spaceflight advocacy, science fiction, and among those interested in space futures. Individual writers, as well as groups, began to define the space future from perspectives that, though still informed by the central tenets and technologies of the field, extended beyond those unique to white, middle-class males in the mid-twentieth century. Younger and more progressive liberals such as Carl Sagan articulated a new and very popular vision of the space future that consciously opposed the legacy and mythology of colonialism; instead, it was open to the influence of other cultural traditions and to the possibility of heterotopia on the space frontier. Vonda N. McIntyre, for example, took the cold war liberalism of *Star Trek* and Gerard O'Neill's space-colony concept and brought to it her own style of antiracist feminism.[43] This raised the hackles of some reviewers who disliked her presentation of complex marriage and homosexuality on the erstwhile virginal and heterosexist space frontier. With Allen Steele came a writer willing to lampoon the pretensions of the first-generation astrofuturists. Through his working-class heroes, Steele introduced the question of how the space future might look from the point of view of labor rather than management.[44] Octavia E. Butler combined a mutant sociobiology with a subversive reading of race and gender, and in one of her futures presents a humanity that has little power to define the conditions of its survival as a species.[45]

In response to changes in science fiction, which broadened the kind of futurist inquiries and alternatives that could be entertained, Clarke dispensed with a long held distaste for authorial collaboration to work with a neophyte science-fiction writer, Gentry Lee.[46] Lee's interest in writing science fiction seems to derive from the same impulse that drove many other second-generation space scientists into the field: an intense affection for the literature and frustration with the pace and direction of the American space program. Following other career scientists in astrofuturism, he turned toward fiction as a way of escaping the constraints of his working life. His work with Clarke was, in fact, part of a motion-picture project that was underway before the famous writer was approached to join the effort. Early in their collaboration, Lee found more free time on his hands when Galileo, an unmanned interplanetary probe designed to investigate Jupiter and its moons, was put on hold by the 1986 *Challenger* explosion. Clarke's suggestion that they collaborate on a sequel to *Rendezvous with Rama* came at the right time.

Their joint production of the Rama series presents one long narrative that begins with hope and cycles through tragedy. Despite the several decades of earthly time that separate the first two sequels, the relativistic speeds at which the main protagonists travel allow the authors to create a coherent point of view through a single set of characters. In *Rama II*, the central protagonists are again

drawn from a group of cosmonauts dispatched to investigate a new Rama artifact. The crew of the *Sir Isaac Newton* are, of course, the best that the world
has to offer: scientists, engineers, pilots, journalists, and military officers, many
with IQs that place them at genius level. Hence the range of skills necessary
to explore *Rama II* comes from a pool of applicants much larger than that of
the military. Indeed, only two of the principle characters are career officers.
Since, however, these military officers are the titular heads of this technical
elite, the crew follows the sociomilitary model of the *Endeavor* almost as a re-
flex. *Rama II* is primarily a transitional novel, a bridge between the first and
third volumes in the sequence. It allows the authors to reintroduce the reader to
the central concepts established in *Rendezvous with Rama* and to restage the
future history that supports the narrative.

My treatment of the Rama sequels is organized around the utopia introduced in the third volume of the series, *The Garden of Rama* (1991). The plot
of that novel concerns the building and implementation of a utopian community called New Eden. Situated in the third Raman space colony, New Eden is
designed by humans but serves primarily as an experiment through which we
and the mysterious Ramans can observe the likely effect of paradise on a representative sample of humanity. Hence the novel is a speculation about the
likely outcome should the people and problems of the contemporary world
come into contact with the paradise made possible by extraterrestrial technology. As in the books that precede it, *The Garden of Rama* is concerned with
what happens when people find evidence of extraterrestrial intelligences. But
since the creatures who designed the Raman space colonies never appear, the
central issue of the narrative becomes how the human race conducts itself when
confronted with the mysteries of the space frontier. The primary business of
these novels, therefore, is to explore the adequacy of human relationships and
knowledge to the project of creating a better future. Solving the enigma of the
Ramans becomes secondary as the mystery of human behavior in space-future
utopia deepens.

The character who codesigns the social experiment at the core of the
Rama sequels is Dr. Nicole des Jardins, "a statuesque copper brown woman
with a fascinating French and African lineage."[47] She enters Clarke's space-
future epic as the chief life sciences officer of the *Sir Isaac Newton*. Her centrality suggests the importance of the issues raised by race and gender in Clarke
and Lee's space future. My reading will explore the limits of the liberal pluralism represented in her portrayal. I will then expand my analysis to consider the
utopia she designs and the flaws, both intentional and unintended, which lead
to its failure. I will argue that the failure of the New Eden experiment is due

both to the problems that the authors build into their narrative utopia and to the unexamined presuppositions that inform their address of culture and community. These presuppositions include: that simplistic dichotomies explain the relation between Western ways of knowing and those which are considered primitive or other; the assimilation of outsiders into a static and unchanging Western culture represents the solution to contemporary social ills; and the belief that heterosexual marriage will provide the solution to the problem of racial/cultural difference.

In a genre in which the narrative point of view is invariably that of a white man, giving center stage to a black woman is cause for some reflection.[48] What the authors intend, it seems, is to extend the pluralism evident in Clarke's previous work. In so doing, they express optimism about the possibility of an egalitarian future. In the *Rama* novels, Nicole des Jardins is, in fact, the defender of order, the mother and judge of a new race, and the madonna who represents the best human values and virtues. She is, we are told, not only an accomplished medical researcher and technologist, but also an Olympic gold medalist. To cap her desirability as an icon of minority achievement, she is also described as a statuesque beauty who, more than any other cosmonaut, has made the world curious about the mystery that surrounds her life and accomplishments. Over the course of *Rama II* and *Garden*, des Jardins functions as the bridge between the two sides of a racial and cultural abyss. As the daughter of a white French historical novelist and a black woman of the West African Senoufo people, des Jardins is a symbolic meeting of white and black, Western civilization and a primitive, native culture, a miscegenation of the rational and the pre-rational.

At no point are we led to believe that des Jardins' centrality to the self-conscious pluralism of the *Rama* sequels means that she represents, as a woman of color, a denial of what is traditionally understood as Western civilization. From the history given about the character, we find that she is primarily motivated by her desire to assimilate into mainstream French culture, a culture represented by her loving father and her girlhood heroines, Joan of Arc and Eleanor of Aquitaine. So great is her devotion to these icons that she enters a national competition for a girl to represent Joan of Arc at a celebratory pageant and throws herself into it "with a fervor that both thrilled and worried her father."[49] Unfortunately, she finds that, in the words of her father, France wasn't "ready for a copper-skinned Joan of Arc" (427). Racism is still a significant social fact in the metropole of the twenty-second century, and assimilation is still the dominant means of combating it. The racial slight she receives during the Joan of Arc affair may be disillusioning, but it also creates Nicole's driving passion to prove herself. Again, she is intent on proving her worth within Western culture, against its defining notions of racial hierarchy. Her triple-medal win in Olympic track-and-field events (a sport that is dominated by African American men and women in our own day) is the result of her effort to show the world that she can play by its rules and still win.

She proves her point, rides high for a few glorious moments, and then encounters the stigma of race again. This time it arrives in the form of the man she chooses to love. Shortly after the Olympic games, she meets and conducts a torrid affair with Prince Henry, the future monarch of England. The authors imply that birth-control technology will not have advanced significantly in two hundred years; in fact, they do not mention that such a thing exists. Her brief romance with the prince produces a daughter whom Nicole names Genevieve. While on earth, des Jardins never reveals to the royal sire that he is the father of her first-born child. And even though he suspects, he does not try as hard as he might to find out: Clarke and Lee imagine that the racial politics of twenty-second-century England would still move to prevent the elevation of a black woman to royal rank (281). Nicole raises her daughter with the help of her own father, fending off the media's attempts to determine patrimony. It is evident that Clarke and Lee intend des Jardins to be a paradigm for how a responsible racial and gendered "other" responds to discrimination. And through her character they privilege the strategy of nonconfrontational accommodation favored by middle-class liberals in the 1950s and 1960s. Her position as codesigner of the New Eden colony and her role as its first judge signals the hope that a particular form of pluralism will define future social order. Her name is a further cue that she is to be the dark Eve of political hope.

Des Jardins allows Clarke and Lee to test their space future vision against the racial divisions that separate humankind. Although her mother Anawi Tiasso, "a jet-black African woman of uncommon stature," died shortly before Nicole's adolescence, she remains a defining, if underground, presence in her daughter's life (277). Through Tiasso's "blood" and culture, des Jardins is given some access to the authors' image of African folklife and mysticism. Before her death, Tiasso attempted to introduce her daughter to her African roots through cultural events and a harrowing coming-of-age quest. She told the often resistant Nicole that even though she was growing up in France, part of her was and would always remain African. This suggests that the authors believe there is a place in the future for cultural traditions and perspectives other than those defined by the West. Clarke's familiarity with Sri Lankan history and culture and his use of it in novels such as *The Fountains of Paradise* lends substance to this claim.[50] However, it is also clear that Nicole's relationship to her African heritage is one of estrangement rather than embrace. Her principal, defining contact with her mother's people occurs during her childhood and is severed by her mother's early death. In maturity, her experience of the Senoufo and their traditions happens not through human encounters, but through waking and sleeping dreams and brief, shamanistic encounters with her maternal grandfather. In other words, she has no contact with her African heritage that might be defined as occurring on the level of workaday human relationships. Her conscious life and experiences are defined exclusively by Western/Francophone culture; her relationship with her mother and her mother's people happens only through the unconscious.

Overtly, Nicole des Jardins's dreams are represented as aberrations that have no place within the rational traditions of the West.[51] While des Jardins cannot ignore her dreams and often finds comfort in them, she is generally unable to interpret them, especially since she lacks the knowledge of and advisors within the culture that engenders them. Moreover, she often fears that she is in danger of losing her mind and her anchoring in reality because of them. The incompatibility of her dreams with the rational, knowable world is dramatized through her abortive attempts to discuss them with the white men who share her journey out of the solar system in *Rama II*. Richard Wakefield, the brilliant English electrical engineer who becomes her husband, and Michael O'Toole, the American general who will eventually father two of her children, are dismissive. They jointly decide that her dreams are nothing more than "the psychotropic reactions of a drug liable individual."[52] Given obvious authorial sympathy for the protagonist, this attitude is clearly the wrong one. The reader is cautioned against making the same mistaken evaluation.

Des Jardins's dreams dramatize a cultural split, a Cartesian dichotomy that opposes the European to the African, the modern real to primitive illusion. The modern, rational consciousness finds its counterpoint in that of the premodern, nature-bound unconscious. Clarke and Lee are aware of this dichotomy and use it deliberately to authorize the liberalism of their futurist narrative. That liberalism is found not in any effort to erase the boundaries set by the dichotomy but in authorial attempts to attribute a positive function, however condescendingly, to its negative term. Des Jardins's dreams provide metaphors for mysteries thought to fall outside of Western ways of knowing. They allow her access to understandings not readily accessible through her socialization as a French woman and as a highly trained medical doctor. It is clear that des Jardins's access to these dreams are a function of her race and gender: it is no accident that her African heritage comes from her mother, while her father represents the high tradition of European literature and history. Therefore, the cultural dichotomy that Clarke and Lee present to us is a conventional one in which dreams and emotional sensitivity characterize women and the world outside Euro-America, while waking reality and scientific rationality are the province of men and what Nicole calls "our Western culture."[53] Race, gender, the unconscious, and Africa combine to form the boundaries of the enclosed Western culture that extends into space.

This gendered, cultural dichotomy creates an unresolved tension in des Jardins's character that reveals what the authors can and cannot allow in their future. Clarke and Lee can imagine that the material presence of racial, gendered, and cultural others is possible in the space future. However, they represent any subjectivity or political position based on that presence as subterranean, and insist that any successful nonwhite character must be assimilated within the intellectual and social traditions they consider normative. Hence while the West extends itself onto the space frontier in overt material and intellectual ways, the Rest survive only as a repressed, inarticulate instinct. They manifest themselves as a disturbing racial memory whose inclusion seems like a positive survival, but whose impact is largely ineffectual. While Clarke and Lee may intend des Jardins to function as a racial and gendered insider through the medium of her dreams, her estrangement from a nuanced black/African social context and her flat political response to her position as a black woman in the metropole—she is never allowed to display even a moment of anger or doubt—compromises her role as a representative of the Rest. She is, in essence, a token.

It is also important to note that Nicole's function as a woman and as a representative of Africa rests on what the West is not. For if, as a token, she stands as a kind of caricature of biracial "otherness," her position must be measured against the authors' presentation of an equally caricatured West. Clarke and Lee assume that Euro-American culture is monolithic, rational, technocratic, and impervious to the unconscious or the extra-rational. In this West, everything is known or knowable, measured or measurable. There is no room, therefore, for evangelical religion, porous cultural boundaries, or the stuff that dreams are made of. Even the Christian subtext of the narrative leaves little room for the unknown, for knowledges and practices that come from outside a unitary Western tradition. When questions of faith arise, they are presented as part of a rational search that confirms Western science, history, and theology, even in the ostensibly alien. Clarke and Lee's overall desire to justify Western ways of knowing, even as they critique its racism, forces them to create what they hope to avoid: another version of salvation history through astrofuturism.

Through Nicole des Jardins and New Eden, Clarke and Lee use the history of racism and slavery to critique an earlier astrofuturism's endless reproduction of the nineteenth century in space. They wish to create the image of a future that breaks with the imperial logic of the past, a potential utopian future in which "all men are brothers." In so doing, they point out the flaws inherent in the old astrofuturist reliance on salvation through the creation of a technological utopia. However, their reliance on the normative strategy of racial and cultural assimilation limits the alternatives they can imagine. By the end of *The Garden of Rama*, they replace the failed technological utopianism of the past with a biological utopianism that calls for the erasure of difference through miscegenation. Humanity's "brotherhood" is made clear on the morphological level as racial difference is erased through intermarriage.

In *The Garden of Rama* (1991), a third version of the Rama space colony arrives in the human solar system. This time, however, the gigantic spacecraft carries a human family headed by des Jardins and her engineer husband, Richard Wakefield. Within the space colony is New Eden, the utopia sponsored by the mysterious Ramans and designed by the couple for human settlement. Their mission is to secure a representative sample of the human race that will cover as wide a range of human occupational, cultural, and racial groups as possible.[54] In a transmission to the human world, the Ramans demand that these representatives be collected and sent to rendezvous with Rama III in Mars' orbit. In response, earthly authorities send two thousand people on their way to the Rama space colony. As it is not generally known that Rama has returned and made its demands, the fiction is created that the two thousand colonists will help to reestablish the Martian base, which was abandoned during The Great Chaos. When the three colony ships arrive at Mars, the truth is revealed and the humans on board find themselves forced to take part in the Raman's utopian experiment.

As its name implies, des Jardins and Wakefield intend New Eden to be a paradisiacal setting in which a human community can pursue its destiny without the distractions of poverty, ignorance, and war. In design, the utopian plan owes much to the middle-class space colonies that O'Neill imagined in the 1970s and, by extension, to the garden city concepts so popular in the transAtlantic planning community early in the twentieth century.[55] Its Central City and residential villages set in a pastoral landscape are familiar in the satellite cities conceived in the 1920s by regional planning advocates such as Lewis Mumford and Benton MacKaye. This intellectual genealogy indicates the assumptions about the nature of the New Eden community that are crucial to its viability: the community will be centered around middle-class professionals who themselves will be members of nuclear families organized around the heterosexual couple; members will focus on educational attainment and "rational" government as primary social goods; they will reside in a park-like setting that will foster organic community and encourage shared parenting. A certain amount of functional diversity is built into this model in order to ensure the variety of skill required by an isolated community. There is no doubt, however, that New Eden's tillers of the soil will be gentlemen-farmers in the Jeffersonian mode. Des Jardins and Wakefield do not take into account the effect of people or relationships coming from outside of that mainstream in the design of their utopia. They make no allowances for the effect of history or the will to power.

When the Mars colonists arrive at New Eden, the lack of foresight inherent in its design aids in the unraveling of paradise. Indeed, during the first year of the New Eden colony, the new communitarians segregate themselves along the racial, national, and class lines of the current social order. The garden city plan that splits the community into four villages around a central city facilitates the re-creation of familiar hierarchies and civil conflicts. The group of highly motivated, pluralistic, middle-class professionals who arrive on the first colony ship cluster around the Des Jardins-Wakefield clan in the southeast village of Beauvois (named after Nicole's home in France). The Europeans, East Asians, and white Americans who could not fit into Beauvois settle down in Positano, the southwestern village. Blacks and browns, Mexicans, Hispanics, African Americans, and Africans move into San Miguel. And the "Orientals" (following the authors' terminology) cluster in the village of Hakone. To make life in New Eden even more topical, the authors throw in the devastating effects of an AIDS-like retrovirus, RV-41, with all its attendant social and political implications. The metaphoric links between disease, homosexuality, and race that accompany AIDS help underscore authorial engagement with the problem of difference. By the end of the novel, New Eden gives up the bright promise of utopian renewal and becomes a militarized state shaped by racism, homophobia, misogyny, and disease intolerance. The forms and textures of contemporary politics are abstracted and reproduced in the novel's examination of the space future. By recasting the contemporary world in the New Eden colony, Clarke and Lee go against the expectation that the colonization of space will provide an escape from terrestrial problems. These futurists fully expect humanity to carry its discontents into the space frontier.

Ideally New Eden is a thought experiment that allows the writers to work through the possible effect of the space future on the contemporary world. Clarke and Lee ask an important question: given advanced technology, knowledge that there is a civilization more advanced than our own, and an environment that eliminates the need for competition, could humanity put aside its pettinesses and create an optimal life for all? This question directly addresses the presupposition central to astrofuturism's technological utopianism—the belief that the conquest of space or a civilian expansion into it will solve the national, cultural, and racial conflicts that divide humanity. As I have argued, Clarke spent much of his early career establishing and defending this belief. In company with Lee, he now goes beyond his early work and confronts the limits of the astrofuturist creed. By introducing into the New Eden experiment the very problems that it is designed to solve, Clarke and Lee create what seem to be insurmountable obstacles for the colonists, problems that cannot be solved by the wave of a high-tech wand or by the fresh start provided by a new land. Race and class are the categories Clarke and Lee use to comment on the possibility of a utopia modeled on aspirations common in twentieth-century America, but where people maintain the habits of mind that lead to unjust societies.

The Mars colonists arrive at New Eden supposedly on equal footing with one another and the native utopians. Our expectation is that this space future community will allow humanity to leave antagonisms behind in the old world, for they have the opportunity to start fresh in a paradise where all physical needs are provided for. In a move that is positively platonic, New Eden is even provided with human "biots," biological robots who can perform all of the repetitive and tedious tasks necessary in a viable settlement. The colonists should become a uniform elite who, unburdened by the necessity of creating a laboring class among themselves, will use their abundant leisure to pursue self-improving culture. In essence, the biots are the slaves on whose labor Clarke and Lee's new republic will prosper. But the use of the human biots raises psychosocial problems that undermine New Eden from its inception and sets up unfortunate historical resonances that would compromise any social experiment based on this techno-model.

When human biots are first proposed, the authors have des Jardins raise objections that "people would be terrified if they couldn't tell the difference between humans and machines."[56] Even though her objection is dismissed by her husband (on the grounds that she has read too much science fiction), the utopian designers settle upon a compromise that will make it easy for human colonists to distinguish between person and robot: the creation of robotic classes patterned after readily identifiable historical personages. As a result, the human biots that Raman technology produces are made to resemble Abraham Lincoln, Albert Einstein, Kasunari Kawabata, and their own fictional heroine, astronaut/poet Benita Garcia. The only exception to the distinguished historical personage rule is that of the Anawi Tiasso class, patterned after Nicole des

Jardins's mother. This bizarre exception allows us to begin unraveling the reasons why humanity cannot make a fresh start, not even in a New Eden.

The residents of New Eden cannot tell the difference between a human biot and the person on whom it is modeled except through a conscious effort of will. This is dramatized in the text when Nicole wakes up from a several-year-long hibernation and stares into the face of her long-dead mother. It is only after some confused cognition that she recognizes that it is one of the Tiasso robots that she helped design.[57] The problem here is that with even an intimate knowledge of the technology involved—by no means a sure thing even among the Mars colonists—the temptation to anthropomorphize humaniform robots would be overwhelming. Speculation on the possibility of misidentification, both comic and tragic, is common in contemporary literature. And some of the more thoughtful writers, such as Philip K. Dick and Marge Piercy, have explored the question of what moral and civil rights self-aware machines in human form would have.[58] There is no guarantee that humans would be at all rational or consistent in their separation of the humanoid form into distinct "real" and "artificial" classes. In the case of Nicole and the robot who replicates her mother, would a familial similarity encourage people to misidentify Nicole as nonhuman and, therefore, a part of the laboring biot classes? Moreover, this creation of a new class of servants defers resolving the propensity to organize social relations by castes and classes. The connection between the New Eden experiment and the orthodoxies that supported nineteenth-century American slavery are too close for comfort.

Within the traditions of Western liberalism, it is clear that human biots are designed to solve the problems created by the division of humanity into classes in which a few benefit from the labor of many, and some lead lives of ease while the Rest are required to serve that leisure. The robot, it has often been imagined, would make it unnecessary for one group of people to subjugate another in pursuit of a civilized life. We quickly realize, however, that the robot represents an evasion, not a solution. It is not surprising that the racial and gender divisions apparent in contemporary culture are mirrored in the hierarchy of labor represented by the human biots. The Abraham Lincoln biots function as the colony's general secretaries and domestic helpers; the Albert Einstein biots run the colony's infrastructure as engineers; the Kawabatas are the creative artists who handle most of the cultural functions of the community; Benita Garcia's class work as security and sanitation workers; and health care is handled by the Tiasso class. In this revealing passage, Clarke and Lee reestablish the racial and gendered hierarchies that inform New Eden's social order: "The hamburger stand in Central City was completely run by biots. Two Lincolns managed the busy restaurant and four Garcias filled the customer orders. The food preparation was done by a pair of Einsteins and the entire eating area was kept spotless by a single Tiasso. The stand generated an enormous profit for its owner, because there were no costs except the initial building conversion and the raw materials."[59] There is a certain comedy in the image of iconic scientific and political greats balancing the books and slinging hash, but the images of Latinas trapped in service jobs and des Jardins's African mother swinging a mop brings one up sharply. Also troubling is the ironic idolatry that domesticates Lincoln's cultural significance as the figure representing democracy and freedom from slavery. The social hierarchy embedded in the controllable technology of the human biots indicates the future desired by late capitalism, one in which human frailty and unpredictability does not interfere with profit. Through Raman technology human slavery is decontextualized and perfected. The moral and historical significance of holding people in bondage for their labor to support a free society is suppressed and replaced by the dream of a slavery that hurts no one. New Eden suggest that no matter how far we proceed into the future, the function of progress will be to *re*produce the same, rather than to produce anything different or better. The utopian moment that the biots are supposed to represent is disrupted by the technological reconstruction of a Western racial evolutionism that would freeze social relations in predetermined forms. The biots can only mimic the society that they serve, one in which an evolutionary ladder of race and gender remains intact to determine life chances and aspirations. Anglo-American men are at the top, Jews are next in line, Hispanics and Blacks after them, and women are at the bottom.

Through the human biots, Clarke and Lee set up a confrontation between the technological utopianism at astrofuturism's core and the necessity of a change in the way our culture desires the future. In *The Garden of Rama*, they suggest that the reinscription of a slave-based racial hierarchy on the space frontier is the likely result of any human conquest of space that reiterates the political understandings common in America at mid-century. That this is not desirable is shown by the New Eden utopia's rapid descent into a warfare state divided by race and class. The biots, designed as a benign extension of liberal paradise, become objects of terror when they are used in an assassination plot to destroy political opposition. They become mad, insurrectionary monsters who disturb the peace of the natural order.

It is not long before des Jardins finds herself the target of racial epithets, confronting a lynch mob while protecting the tattered shreds of New Edenic law. Nicole begins to realize that her paradise is unraveling and laments " 'that everything I have done or am doing is absolutely useless' " (342). Her husband, Richard Wakefield, tries to comfort her, but cannot reassure her: "you must remember you're dealing with human beings. You can transport them to another world and give them a paradise, but they still come equipped with their fears and insecurities and cultural predilections. A new world could only *really* be new if all the humans involved began with totally empty minds, like new computers with no software and no operating systems, just loads of untapped potential" (342). It seems that there is no way out of endless repetitions of the status quo, unless humans become biots. From Wakefield's point of view, the fault lies not in technology, but in history and biology. Human beings, he believes, are genetically incapable of putting aside their differences: "Nothing I have seen here in New Eden or on Earth suggests to me that humanity is capable of achieving harmony in its relationship with itself, much less with any other living creatures. Occasionally there is an individual, or even a group, that is able to transcend the basic genetic and environmental drawbacks of the species. . . . But these people are miracles, certainly not the norm" (342–43). *The Garden of Rama*, therefore, questions the dominant tradition of American technoscience, for here human nature replaces technology in determining the politics of the future. Humanity is not allowed to escape itself by moving out onto the space frontier. In Clarke and Lee's formulation, humankind is prevented from achieving paradise by its history and its biology, its genetically and environmentally determined identification with terrestrial models of hierarchy and identity.

However, the possibility of escape is essential to the literary and cultural tradition from which astrofuturism springs. The genre's practitioners and fans turn to it to imagine an escape from terrestrial gravity, an escape from culture, an escape from history, perhaps even an escape from the normal, consumerist identities imposed by a middle-class-oriented capitalism. Even as Clarke and Lee critique the failure of astrofuturism to take seriously the politics most likely in the creation of a human imperium in space, they are constrained by the necessity to honor its commitment to salvation. Working within the tradition, the authors still hope that space can provide some opportunity for transcending the human condition. Interestingly, this opportunity arises from race, the very thing that is destroying the space colony.

As racial polarization deepens New Eden's political crisis, we are asked to consider the necessity of a change of attitude, a fundamental reevaluation of the way whites think about race. This is dramatized again through Nicole des Jardins. Looking over the ruin of New Eden's utopian dream, she muses,

I was too black to be Queen Nicole of England, or even Joan of Arc in one of those French anniversary pageants. I wonder how many years it will be before skin color is no longer an issue among human beings on Earth. Five hundred years? A thousand? What is it that the American William Faulkner said—something about Sambo will be free only when all of his neighbors wake up in the morning and say, both to themselves and to their friends, that Sambo is free. I think he is right. We have seen that racial prejudice cannot be eradicated by legislation. Or even by education. Each person's journey through life must have an epiphany, a moment of true awareness, when he or she realizes, once and for all, that Sambo and every other individual in the world who is in any way different from him or her *must* be free if we are to survive. (91–92)

The authors' antiracism is in bold relief at this moment. In the context of an astrofuturist text, it implies a critique of the racialism that was a silent partner to first-generation astrofuturism and in the creation of the original astronaut corps for the 1960s space program. Despite its egalitarian rhetoric, Clarke and Lee imply that the space future, as it was understood before and during the 1960s, could not have offered hope "for all mankind," given its complicity with prevailing Anglo-American attitudes on race. The technological fix of the space future fails, along with educational and legislative reform, to change the cultural commitment to racial hierarchy. Having discredited the link between technological and social progress but needing to retain the space future's utility as an avenue of salvation, the authors are left hoping for a spiritual transcendence. It is faith, rather than the technological mastery of space or the transformative power of its innocence, that will and must change the human heart. Leaving nothing to chance, the authors are quite explicit in putting forward this proposal. Having raised tremendous barriers to the realization of space-future utopia with the poor material provided by humanity, they lead the reader to the hope that salvation is possible through faith and the human capacity to forgive. They dramatize that salvation as a reconciliation brought about by the possibility of interracial marriage, as exemplified in a subplot leading to marriage between one of des Jardins's daughters and a doctor who came to the New Eden colony on the prison ship.

Dr. Robert Turner arrives at the New Eden colony as part of the convict population, looking for a new life and possible redemption for his past. He quickly becomes indispensable to the colony as the head of its hospital and the researcher who is leading the effort to find a cure for the AIDS-like RV-41. In due time he and one of des Jardins's daughters, Ellie, are drawn to each other and he asks her to marry him. Before that marriage can be consummated, however, Dr. Turner feels that he has to reveal the sins of his past and, more importantly, to ask her forgiveness. The story he tells is one in which race, sex, and murder collide in an American dream gone sour. He begins, "I was thirty-three years old and blindly, outrageously happy. I was already one of the leading cardiac surgeons in American and I had a beautiful, loving wife with two daughters, aged three and two. We lived in a mansion with a swimming pool inside a country club community about forty kilometers north of Dallas, Texas" (331). Here the authors establish the basic parameters of an Anglo-American success story. Dr. Turner is young and at the beginning of a stellar career. He and his family live in the upper-class version of a beautiful home with a white-picket fence, in a wealthy community, safe and secure, well distanced from the problems that inhere in a society riven by the effects of a race- and class-based distribution of resources. However, Turner finds that his distance from social degeneration and failure is a tragic illusion. He comes home one night to find frightened security guards at the entrance to his community and police and reporters clustered in his driveway: "My wife was lying under a sheet on a cot in the main hall beside the stairway to the second floor. Her throat had been slit. I heard some people talking upstairs and raced up to see my daughters. The girls were still lying where they had been killed—Christie on the floor in the bathroom and Amanda in her bed. The bastard had cut their throats as well" (331). Turner's American life moves from dream to nightmare. The destruction of his family is, for him, the destruction of innocence. An emotional numbness and a lust for revenge takes its place. It is when Clarke and Lee provides an object for Turner's hatred that we get some glimmer of the connection between race and salvation: "The police had a suspect in less than a week. His name was Carl Tyson. He was a young black man, twenty-three years old, who delivered groceries for a nearby supermarket. My wife always used the television for her shopping. Carl Tyson had been to our home several times before—I even remembered having seen him once or twice myself—and certainly knew his way around the house" (332).

The racial core of an American nightmare sharpens. The wall around Turner's country-club community is raised not simply as a sign of wealth, but to ward off the discontents of a system in which race is principle hurdle to opportunity. In his role as a delivery boy, Tyson is granted access to a paradise he can achieve in no other way. As a burglar who commits murder, he violates his parole, breaching not only the physical wall separating inside and outside, but the social and political barriers between wealth and poverty, the famous cardiologist and the delivery boy, the white and the black, life and death. As the authors describe the physical evidence against Tyson, it is both ambiguous and conclusive. Its persuasiveness rests on whether one accepts the story presented by the prosecution or the defense. Turner is, however, convinced that Tyson did indeed commit the murders and he expects summary conviction and execution

(332). This racial nightmare gains topical resonance as the case becomes famous, and Tyson is able to retain the services of a famous lawyer to argue his side. It is then that the politics of race enters explicitly into the narrative:

"During the defense portion of the trial, I really began to have my doubts about the American judicial system. His attorney made the case a racial issue, depicting Carl Tyson as a poor, unfortunate black man who was being railroaded on circumstantial evidence. His lawyer argued emphatically that all Tyson had done on that October day was deliver groceries to my house. Someone else, his attorney said, some unknown maniac, had climbed the Greenbriar fence, stolen the jewelry, and then murdered Linda and the children." (333)

Turner, American society, and its judicial system are not able to judge the robbery and murder on the basis of the evidence alone. Carl Tyson is black and, therefore, guilty of the desire to steal privileged lives and property. Carl Tyson is innocent because he is a black man who is being made to suffer by a system that considers him guilty by reason of his color. As the trial comes to an end it becomes clear that, in this case at least, the latter argument is stronger than the former, and Tyson will be acquitted.

For Turner, this is an unforgivable abuse of the law: "I went insane with righteous indignation. There was no doubt in my mind that the young man had committed the crime. The thought that he might be set free was intolerable" (333). The doctor then decides that justice will be served, no matter the verdict or the consequences: "When the acquittal was announced, there was an uproar in the courtroom. All the black people in the gallery shouted hooray. Carl Tyson and his attorney, a Jewish guy named Irving Bernstein, threw their arms around each other. I was ready to act. I opened my briefcase, quickly assembled the shotgun, jumped over the barrier, and killed them both, one with each barrel" (333). With this act, Turner himself crosses the wall, the divide between prosperous citizen and heroic/criminal vigilante. In doing so, the character invokes the violence that is partner to American racial conflict. He acts to seek the restoration of a violated status, but the authors take the trouble to present his move as a crime that brings not freedom or restoration of paradise, but a more certain damnation. Turner continues his confession:

"I have never admitted before, not even to myself, that what I did was wrong. However, sometime during this operation on your friend Mr. Diaba [a Nigerian RV-41 patient that he and Ellie work to heal] I understood clearly how much my emotional outrage has poisoned my soul for all these years. . . . My violent act of revenge did not return my wife and children to me. Nor did it make me happy, except for that sick animal pleasure I felt at the instant I knew that both Tyson and his attorney were going to die." (333–34)[60]

After confessing this bathetic story of racial tragedy, Turner turns to des Jardins's daughter and asks for her forgiveness and her hand: "Although I may not be worthy, I do love you, Ellie Wakefield, and very much want to marry you. I hope that you can forgive me for what I did years ago." Ellie does not respond to either the tenor or the content of the story that her suitor relates. Instead, she responds to her feelings for Turner, and on them bases her judgement of him and his proposal: "I do know what I feel when I think about you is wonderful. I admire you, I respect you, I may even love you. I would like to talk to my parents about this, of course . . . but yes, Dr. Robert Turner, if they do not object I would be very happy to marry you" (334). In this exchange between Turner and Ellie, Clarke and Lee offer a solution to the tremendous problems inherited by their space future paradise. Only through a marriage between white man and black woman can the discontents that are destroying the New Eden colony be resolved. Only through forgiveness of past sins can humanity achieve the paradise that is the core dream of the space future.

Within the confines of the Rama novels, the impulse to marry away racial, class, and ideological discontent is activated by the lack of agency ascribed to minority characters. By this, I do not mean that des Jardins and other minority characters are background figures who do not get enough to do. To their credit, Clarke and Lee make these characters something more than cardboard cutouts, passing scenery. However, as Ellie's lack of response to Turner's story shows, there is a curious lack of depth to Clarke and Lee's minority characters. Neither Ellie nor her mother are allowed a moment to consider the implications of Turner's account, even to make so mild a statement as "how sad" or "how tragic." In order for the authors' space future to work, in order for the transcendence of earthly bickering to occur, people of color have to suspend any identification with a past in any way different from that sanctioned by the mainstream of American (Western) culture. Any notion of separate or local identities based on specific and partial histories within Western or world culture, therefore, have to disappear in order for New Eden to become a paradise. And with that disappearance comes the necessary innocence, the freedom from sin that marks the characters of all but one of des Jardins's children. The result is a static, hermetically sealed future that cannot admit differences that matter even as its liberal elements search for such a possibility.

In any case, we should note that Clarke and Lee's use of interracial marriage elevates biological determinism to the level of a spiritual faith. It is in no way inconsistent with earlier work in the Clarke canon, such as *Imperial Earth* (1976), in which the author implies that the cure for American racial troubles is the creation of an ivory-colored humanity for which difference and otherness is a thing of a primitive genetic past. In that novel, racial prejudice ceases to exist on earth because humanity is moving to the point at which "we're all the same shade of off white."[61] People on Earth who regret this development are represented as obsessed with the past. Space colonials, however, never think about it. When confronted with evidence of a mild race consciousness, Duncan Makenzie, the point-of-view character, does not know what to think: "Duncan looked at him for a moment with puzzled incomprehension. He had never given any more thought to his skin color than to that of his hair; indeed, if suddenly challenged, he would have been hard pressed to describe either. Certainly he had never thought of himself as black; but now he realized, with understandable satisfaction, that he was several shades darker than George Washington [not the original], descendant of African kings."[62] This, I suppose, is progress.

In the Rama novels, we have a morally directed natural selection that will solve the problems of race and class. In other words, the space future is not assured through legislation, education, or political struggle, but through biology. According to the biologically based, culturally assimilative pluralism that these astrofuturists develop, our historical and political problems are so intransigent as to be hardwired into our genes or our brains. They can only be escaped through biology. By the end of *The Garden of Rama*, we find ourselves considering a solution to human problems that is strikingly similar to that proposed by Harriet Beecher Stowe in the final chapter of *Uncle Tom's Cabin*. Stowe ends her 1852 novel by imagining that the salvation of Christian civilization might be accomplished through a marriage between the black and white races. The biologically inherent qualities of one (the intelligence and aggressiveness of the white) will complement the other (the natural Christianity of the black) to create an Anglo-African utopia in Africa that will lead the rest of the world into a new age.[63] Through their insistence on a biological/evolutionary solution to human problems, Clarke and Lee unwittingly reiterate the romantic racialism inherent in the future that Stowe desired. The similarity between the solutions presented in these novels shows us the incredible durability of biological determinism, even in liberal thought. It is a theory that finds its initial justification in Christian religion and its continuing influence through certain readings of Darwinian evolution.

Through Clarke and Lee's work, we trace one direction taken by astrofuturism by the end of the 1980s. While, for the astrofuturists, the space frontier continues to represent the last, best hope for humankind, it also becomes contested terrain. It is no longer possible to imagine that the conquest of space will happen easily or that its benefits will reform completely the human condition. Instead, the social renaissance represented by the occupation of space is threatened by conflicts between the pioneers. Reading the Rama series, it becomes clear that the optimism of *Rendezvous with Rama* derives from the assumption that a narrowly defined Anglo-American culture will dominate the space frontier. Its vision of the future as a liberal plurality, therefore, rests on the assumption that differences of identity, culture, and character are superficial, leaving only those of reproductive biology. The pessimism of the first and second sequels arises from a discomfort with the specter of a polyglot future composed of social identities and political agencies coming from outside of the mainstream. It is the potentially criminal threat which those agencies represent that jeopardizes the social experiment of the New Eden community.

In the social future of the Rama novels, therefore, there is "good" culture and there is "bad" culture, culture that is modern and Western and culture that is retrograde and primitive. This simple dichotomy describes Western, African, and Asian cultures as sketchy outlines with little concession to depth or complexity. As a result, the future that Clarke and Lee describe presents a reductive view not only of "other" identities and cultures but of those traditions considered "mainstream" in the West. However, through narrative and character, Clarke and his cowriter hope to convince the reader that the future vision they offer is inclusive and progressive. This ideal represents the core of their liberal vision. Once the problem of diversity is solved, they assume, all breeds and conditions of "men" will find harmony on the space frontier. Whether or not we are convinced by its execution we must accept the sincerity of the effort.

5. The Domestication of Space: Gerard K. O'Neill's Suburban Diaspora

It is in the long run essential to the growth of any new and high civilization that small groups of men can escape from their neighbors and from their governments, to go and live as they please in the wilderness. A truly isolated, small, and creative society will never again be possible on this planet.

—Freeman J. Dyson, "A Space-Traveler's Manifesto" (1958)[1]

The Second Generation

All second-generation astrofuturists, whatever their political persuasions, have found it necessary to respond to changes in American society by persuading the public of the democratic uses of the space future. Until the political upheavals of the 1960s, American science fictionists rarely imagined that the future might be one of social or economic movement.[2] According to the astrofuturism articulated by von Braun, Ley, Heinlein, Martin Caiden, and others, the space future was not meant to change contemporary social, political, or economic systems, but to make them more efficient, faster, wealthier, and less vulnerable to attack from external forces. In other words, the conquest of space would reinforce a familiar status quo with new wealth and provide it with an eternal frontier for expansion.[3] The writers who follow are preoccupied with the question of social movement; they have had to address the role of various racial and national groups, find an expanded place for women, and either defend or revise the astrofuturist assumption of improving human social and political structures through the conquest of space.

With the breakdown of its older consensus, astrofuturism has had to remake itself to salvage the hope of a future in space.

Up to this point, the histories of rocketry and the spaceflight idea had proceeded hand in hand. In large part, the search for legitimacy that characterizes the period from the late 1920s to the early 1950s had been resolved by the international demand for better weapons-delivery systems. With the Soviet Union's *Sputnik*, the "peaceful" pursuit of producing carrier rockets in the race for space gave the technology a certain ideological respectability outside military circles. In a modern version of the Cinderella story, the early rocket amateurs moved from the fringes directly into the mainstream of international politics within the span of a single generation. The tremendous velocity of rocketry's development is evident in the often printed juxtaposition of two photographs: the first shows the young von Braun carrying an experimental rocket to a primitive test site in Germany; the second shows a much older von Braun dwarfed by the monstrous bulk of the *Saturn V* on an American launch pad.

But as the visionaries of the rocket team faded from the institutional structure of NASA, the popular culture of the space race fizzled. There was something of a crisis of leadership within the spaceflight and astrofuturist communities. When von Braun died in 1977, for example, the National Space Institute was left without its most famous and authoritative fundraiser. The spaceflight agenda was edged out of the limelight by pressing domestic and international issues, and eventually the old vision of the first generation was buried in the congressional budget hearings of 1971.[4] The reduction of funding for a manned space program and the eventual cancellation of the Apollo project broke the link between first-generation astrofuturism and the political coalition that made the space race possible. Thousands of engineers, technicians, and scientists lost their jobs as NASA scrambled for political and fiscal survival in congressional hearing rooms. As a result most of the next generation of space futurists found themselves working outside the national space program. As the power of the old rocket engineers declined, the core of astrofuturism moved out of the halls of policy and back into the popular culture and literature of science fiction and, for the first time, into the classroom. The futurists of the second generation tend to be academic scientists and popular writers of science fiction and popular science rather than engineers in government service.

They also represent a greater diversity of personal and professional affiliations than did their predecessors. With rare exceptions, first-generation astrofuturists had been middle-class, university-educated professionals trained in applied science and engineering. Many were active in the aviation and aerospace industries of the 1950s and 1960s. Without exception, they were white and male, empowered by their positions in a society divided along the lines of race, gender, and class. The breakdown of consensus in early 1970s astrofuturism was, therefore, one of demographics as well as content. The criticisms of the left and the social and political initiatives of the 1960s pushed astrofuturism to represent a widening segment of the American population. By the mid-1960s and increasingly during the 1970s, the producer and consumer populations of science fiction began to include increasing numbers of white women and people of color.[5] By 1977, NASA's space shuttle program included a "New Breed" of astronauts which produced the same effect for the national space program.[6] These developments had important ramifications for the popular understanding of the space program and for the creation of usable social futures on the space frontier.

Because of these demographic shifts, individual astrofuturists began including previously excluded groups in narratives of an American-dominated space future. Astrofuturism became explicitly politicized in a way that revealed divisions in a community whose public quarrels had traditionally concerned only the technical issues of getting into space. As a result, a political spectrum has emerged within American astrofuturism that roughly mirrors that existing in the general culture. The astrofuturist left is heavily weighted toward academic science and is populated by men who have spent most of their careers within university classrooms and laboratories. Carl Sagan, a planetary astronomer, was a full professor of astronomy and department head at Cornell University until his death in 1996. Prior to his death in 1992, Gerard K. O'Neill had a solid reputation in high-energy particle physics and spent much of his career shuttling between Princeton University, MIT, and NASA laboratories. William K. Hartmann, a planetary geologist who moonlights as a space artist and science-fiction writer, has worked as a university professor, research scientist in private industry, and NASA consultant. Brian T. O'Leary, an astronaut-trainee and physics graduate student at the University of California, Berkeley, during the days of Haight-Ashbury and "the Revolution," has spent his career on some of the most prestigious campuses in the scientific community, including Cornell, Berkeley, the California Institute of Technology, and Princeton. Freeman Dyson, a prominent physicist, was a participant in the Orion Project, a late 1950s government program to build nuclear spacecraft for the first crewed mission to Mars, and has spent the greater part of his career at the Institute for Advanced Studies in Princeton. As graduate students and professors, these men have been immersed in the academic culture and were directly influenced by the decade of campus unrest that began in the mid-1960s. By contrast, those ensconced in corporate, government, and military institutions were insulated from the political struggles that transformed intellectual life on university campuses.

Others—such as Jerry Pournelle, James P. Hogan, Ben Bova, and Gene Roddenberry—came to astrofuturism with professional affiliations other than those of scientist and engineer. They worked primarily as science fictionists, carrying forward the tradition of hard-science extrapolation that they believe represents the core of the genre while also grappling with the challenges of the times. Roddenberry, for instance, liberalizes the medium considerably by fostering a vision of an American future in which the contemporary status quo can be expanded to incorporate all cultures and subject positions, irrespective of race, class, or nationality. As conscious literary and ideological descendents of Robert Heinlein, this group of futurists also grapples with what critics identify as the "right-wing and tough minded" politics encouraged in the genre by John W. Campbell during his reign as editor of *Astounding Science Fiction* in the 1940s and 1950s.[7] Whatever their differences, members of this loosely defined group see themselves as the freedom-loving inheritors of first-generation futurism and, beyond that, of the founders of the American republic. In the context of their time and in light of attempts to move American politics to the left, their defense of astrofuturist conventions often has a defiant, confrontational tone.

But even conservative space futurists did not remain unaffected by the debates that were occurring in the streets and on campuses. Like their more liberal colleagues, they could not assume their audiences would have a political language consistent with or favorable to their own. In this atmosphere, the future became a battlefield, and both liberals and conservatives claimed the high ground by virtue of their alienation from the governmental and institutional forces that were hindering the great leap into space. Conservative astrofuturism differs from the liberal in its reluctance to attack the cultural and economic foundations of those forces. While the left imagines space as the site of utopian experimentation, the right is content with creating narratives in which a middle-American social reality holds sway. Forced to address issues of race, gender, and class, conservative writers cling to what they considered to be core American values, and thereby challenge the right of the radicals to set the nature and content of the debate.

One of the most powerful and enduring legacies of the Apollo program is the image of a blue, cloud-shrouded planet suspended in the void of space.[8] With this image, for the first time in history humanity saw the true compass of its world, and some understood its small scale and fragility. When R. Buckminster Fuller, a long-time designer and advocate of futurist solutions, saw the photograph, he coined the term that became the catchphrase of a generation:

"Spaceship Earth."[9] The image of the Earth as a beautiful and finite cradle served as a focus for Americans whose political and social sympathies tended to the left, revitalizing their concern with the effects of science and technology on the home of life-as-we-know-it. Many ecologists point to the Apollo image as the catalyst and founding emblem of the new environmentalism that gained momentum in the late 1960s; "Spaceship Earth" became an enduring cultural icon in 1970 when the first Earth Day was organized. The picture of the "Big Blue Marble" fostered a serious debate about the sustainability and effect of exponential growth as the primary goal of industrial civilization.[10] The debate helped form the modern study of futurology in the late 1960s, which, in turn, drew together scientists, industrialists, and activists interested in addressing the problems generated by industrial capitalism. One of the earliest and most prominent group of futurologists called itself The Club of Rome.[11]

Founded in 1968, the club was primarily concerned with the impact of scarcity on political freedoms. Its first meeting in Rome focused a decade-long debate on the human and natural resources required to sustain the West. Participants decided that in order to evaluate the prospects of industrial civilization, a systematic resource study was needed that would factor in variables such as population growth, resource availability, land use, pollution, and so forth. The club supported the work of a group of MIT-based researchers whose work in "world dynamics" provided the global model required to evaluate the grand scale and long range implications of industrial growth. Using a sophisticated (for that time) computer model, the MIT team, headed by Donella Meadows and Dennis Meadows, considered several scenarios that projected the effects of unrestrained industrial and population growth and of several policies designed to avoid a disastrous collapse. Their findings were published in 1972 as *The Limits to Growth*, a text that continues to define the debate even today.[12]

The continuing relevance of *The Limits to Growth* has to do with the controversy surrounding the MIT team's negative conclusions on the sustainability of an ever-growing industrial civilization given the Earth's limited resources:

Every day of continued exponential growth brings the world system closer to the ultimate limits to that growth. A decision to do nothing is a decision to increase the risk of collapse. We cannot say with any certainty how much longer mankind can postpone initiating deliberate control of his growth before he will have lost the chance for control. We suspect on the basis of present knowledge of the physical constraints of the planet that the growth phase cannot continue for another one hundred years.[13]

The limits thesis created a firestorm in academic, industrial, and government circles. It also attracted the interest of the astrofuturist community. Three years after the publication of the MIT team's work, one of the second generation's most prominent members, Ben Bova, recalled, "The MIT study evoked immediate howls of protest and delight. Some said the book was a mathematically accurate forecast of a doom that we must work hard to avert. Others said it was a grab bag of poor assumptions and unwarranted straight-line extrapolations. As of this moment, the debate rages on. And the clock is ticking."[14] The limits thesis directly challenged the central assumptions of industrial capitalism, assumptions that amount to a faith in unlimited opportunities for progress and in technology's near magical ability to extract earthly treasures for human consumption. Any dissent from this position was (and is) rejected as pessimistic by those who feared its threat to the ideological foundation of industrialism. However, much of the heat that the debate generated came not from any doubt that the results of the MIT study were valid, though many did question its methods, but from fear of its implications. Despite the MIT team's bid for scientific dispassion, it is clear that its members were disturbed by what they found. The *Limits to Growth* model forecasts the end of a way of life; it implies that the prosperity that the industrialized nations enjoyed in the 1950s and 1960s cannot be sustained into the distant future. By implication, any hopes that the developing world might have for pulling even with the West through unbridled growth are unjustified. Moreover, the consequences of reaching the planet's limits by creating a global industrialism will be dire: the re-creation of preindustrial economies of scarcity, the failure of democracy, and the rise of a variety of totalitarianisms. The socioeconomic imagination of industrial capital had finally caught up with a century's worth of dystopian warnings and science-fiction potboilers.

In order to avoid the inevitable collapse of industrial civilization, the MIT team advocated an "equilibrium state" in which "population and capital are essentially stable [and where] the forces tending to increase or decrease them [are] in carefully controlled balance."[15] This means, of course, that the global economy and its informing values would have to switch from a policy of never-ending growth to a steady state. The limits-to-growth theorists hoped that this latter policy would still enable a future in which the "soft" areas of human art and science could grow without constraint (175). They also hoped that the elusive goal of universal equality might be realized as economic values moved to emphasize exchange rather than accumulation. Certainly, they profoundly wished to avoid a world in which diminishing resources would destroy any chance that these changes could occur. In defense of their hope that a no-growth policy might foster a better world, the researchers wrote: "One of the most commonly accepted myths in our present society is the promise that a continuation of our present patterns of growth will lead to human equality. We have demonstrated in various parts of this book that present patterns of population and capital growth are actually increasing the gap between rich and poor on a world-wide basis, and that the ultimate result of a continued attempt to grow according to the present pattern will be a disastrous collapse" (178). In the end, *The Limits to Growth* is a critique of the ideology of progress in so far as that ideology rests on a thesis of endless growth and limitless accumulation. It also calls into question the primacy of the industrial revolution as the last, determinant stage in the economic and political evolution of humankind.

Many study groups formed to poke holes in the limits thesis.[16] The astrofuturist response ranged from the reactionary dismissiveness of the ideological camp around science-fiction publisher Baen Books to the left-liberal intervention represented by "radical Saganism."[17] Despite such variation, all astrofuturists offered the same solution to limits: the exploration or exploitation of space. Ben Bova put the case succinctly when he noted that "several science fictionists—including Arthur C. Clarke—immediately pointed out that the MIT scientists automatically assumed that the earth is a closed system. The MIT team didn't consider that humankind now has the ability to draw natural resources from elsewhere in the solar system. This is perhaps the major flaw of the MIT study."[18] The main thrust of the astrofuturist response to the limits thesis came from the same environment that engendered it, the university subculture of science-oriented experts. Of central importance to second-generation futurists is the place of science and technology in modern life, most specifically in relation to the social and political problems then on the national consciousness.

A key figure in the astrofuturist response is Gerard K. O'Neill, a Princeton physicist whose early specialization in high-energy physics became the springboard for his contributions to space science and astrofuturism. During the mid-1970s, O'Neill's technical experiments and social futurism shifted the conquest of space to what he calls a "humanization of space." His revision helped revitalize both spaceflight activism and astrofuturist hopes following the disappointing aftermath of Apollo. In his revision of astrofuturism, we see a sustained attempt to articulate an adequate response to the criticisms of the left. Here too we see the astrofuturism, of the last thirty years beginning its odd dance between the militaristic, technocratic conventions endemic to the genre and the need to present a future responsive to contemporary calls for a democratic and plural social order. O'Neill's solution to contemporary political discontent relies on a rhetoric of diversity and social experimentation. But that rhetoric is undermined by his reliance on the suburban ideal: a tradition of middle-class environmental planning, which emphasizes the value of family and domestic life. As a result, the futures he designs are an extension of, in Robert Fishman's words, "bourgeois utopias."[19] I understand O'Neill's astrofuturism to be a literary extension of the suburban boom of the immediate postwar era and of values cherished by the middle class. In the mid-1950s, O'Neill was a young college professor living in Princeton, New Jersey, a town well served by that boom and exemplifying the bourgeois retreat from urban life. In response to the restlessness and discontent he saw on campus and in the cities of the 1960s, O'Neill proposed the extraterrestrial development of space colonies that would be a safety valve for the terrestrial pressure cooker. Colonies in space, he argued, would provide the new lands necessary for the indefinite extension of suburban development and would allow sufficient room for the diversity and growth he believed necessary for the survival of the human species.

In the 1969–70 academic year, it was O'Neill's turn to teach Physics 103, one of the general physics courses for Princeton undergraduates. As he prepared his topics and assignments, he found himself thinking about the way the world outside was affecting the university's routine: "In that . . . period the horrors of the war in Southeast Asia had provoked a revulsion against authority and against technology on American university campuses. . . . Students who sensed that they had talents in science or engineering were on the defensive, accused by their colleagues of being 'irrelevant,' or in another catch phrase of the time, 'counter-productive.' "[20] While O'Neill was sympathetic to some of the political and social concerns voiced in the "student revolt," the challenge that it presented to academic authority and particularly to that of academic science disturbed him. He was well aware of how science and technology could be and had been abused by the pursuit of power. However, he could not agree with the Luddites of the counterculture that they were inherently evil. From his point of view, they had been the instruments of good more often than of evil. He hoped he could prove through the Princeton physics curriculum that science and technology were, in fact, relevant to the great issues of the day. For O'Neill, therefore, the physics survey took on more than normal significance. His students would have to be taught not only its fundamentals but its social function:

Given the peculiar problems of 1969 on a university campus, it seemed that we should attack the question of the place of the scientist and the engineer in the society of the next decades. Clearly, the days of blind trust in science and in progress were past. Not only because of the self-doubts and questionings of the would be scientists themselves, it was important to examine problems relevant to the issues of the environment, of the amelioration of the human condition, and of the interaction between science and society.[21]

Figure 2. Gerard K. O'Neill memorably portrayed as an icon of popular culture in the 1970s. Cartoon by Jonathan Vankin and Steve Vance. Reprinted, by permission, from *The Big Book of the '70s,* ed. Jonathan Vankin (New York: Paradox Press/DCCOMICS, 2000), 123.

The task of the scientist and engineer, O'Neill believes, exceeds that of developing better transistors or more ingenious ways of dominating the natural world. The dignity of the professions demands that they contribute to the ideals of a society and that science be seen as a significant catalyst of valuable reform.[22] O'Neill's plan for colonizing the high frontier answered what he considered a pressing need to relegitimize the social role of science.

Therefore, when O'Neill asked an advanced section of Physics 103 to address the problem of whether "a growing industrial civilization" can remain anchored to the surface of a planet, he was not joking, as Erik Bergaust has supposed, or pursing an abstraction.[23] He was responding to students who were questioning the relevance of the basic physics curriculum and the scientific professions to contemporary social problems. He was also interested in countering the commonsense appeal of terrestrial limits as a necessary condition of any improvement in civilized life. He writes, "I have always felt strongly a personal desire to be free of boundaries and regimentation. The steady state society, ridden with rules and laws, proposed by the early workers on the limits to growth was, to me abhorrent."[24]

Like many Americans of his generation, O'Neill believed that the American way of life could only be guaranteed by plenty of elbow room. His response to the pessimistic limits-to-growth debate advocated the colonization of a territory that would allow national growth to continue ad infinitum, guaranteeing an eternal regeneration of the social, political, and economic constants of American values. Quoting Robert L. Heilbroner, O'Neill argued that in a technological civilization "held by law to a steady-state condition, freedom of thought and of inquiry would be dangerous, and would probably be suppressed" (246). His theory of the colonization of space is predicated on the belief that colonizing the high frontier by building orbital space colonies will allow the human race to avoid the dangers of overpopulation, pollution, famine, war, and tyranny that were the bugaboos of the limits debate. By opening up the resources of the solar system, space colonies would provide "room for growth at a moderate rate for many thousands of years" (247).

O'Neill's account of the development of his ideas for the humanization of space reveals two changes in astrofuturism at the beginning of the 1970s: the influence of opposition from the left and the consequent reorientation of the political goals of the second generation. O'Neill bridged the divide between astrofuturism and its critics as technophilic elements of the left came to embrace his speculative technology. Historians of the 1960s have been fascinated by those who dropped out of the industrial system integral to American life.[25] They have focused on the agrarian ideals that informed the various communitarian ventures of the time, experiments designed to show that Americans could live without the large-scale systems of late capitalism. Because those systems are supported and maintained by big science and technology, communitarian dissent has often been condemned as a wrong-headed Luddite revolt. Certainly this is the stereotype cherished by mainstream defenders of science and technology such as Gerald Holton. Less well known is the fact that many dissenters were not machine breakers; rather, they embraced alternative technologies that they hoped could be democratic and not militaristic or wasteful. It is this segment of the left that embraced O'Neill's space-colonization proposal as an alternative technology that could provide a sane, sensible, and humane solution to pressing problems. Despite O'Neill's reservations regarding the conflict between many social revolutionaries and the dominant culture, initial support for his ideas came from technophiles on the left.

The Portola Foundation (later known as the Point Foundation) of San Francisco, founded to fund projects for radical social change, gave O'Neill the moral and financial support that led to the First Conference on Space Colonization in 1974. The foundation was famous in communitarian circles for its publication of *The Whole Earth Catalog*. Opposing industrial capitalism but eschewing a reactionary stance toward invention, the catalog enumerated pragmatic tools with which to build alternatives to the mechanisms and institutions of the consumer society. Its articles, reviews, product entries, and mail-order service made it easier for those involved in communitarian and utopian ventures to find the goods, services, ideas, and methods necessary for their work.[26] Interested in what would become known as "appropriate technology," some of the catalog's editors and writers were much taken with the speculative technology O'Neill championed.

For O'Neill, however, these energetic young communitarians were a last resort. Several frustrating years followed the inspirational physics seminar of 1969–70, during which he approached all the standard public and private foundations for funds to conduct research and hold conferences on space colonization. Early versions of what would become his seminal article went the rounds of the standard scientific journals, where they provoked reactions ranging from shocked disbelief to polite disinterest. As an academic scientist, it was only natural that O'Neill sought professional legitimacy for his ideas. This, in itself, marks a change between first- and second-generation space futurists. Before *Sputnik*, the space future had not been the driving force behind the professional lives of von Braun, Ehricke, Rudolph, and their colleagues. It was, at most, a hobby that put a benign face on work primarily devoted to the creation of powerful weapons systems. This changed with the futurists of O'Neill's generation.

By the mid-1970s, they were no longer directly connected to the massive structure of national defense, which had lent legitimacy to the first generation. Dis-
connected from a short-term strategic rationale, the exploration of space
became a topic of minor importance on the national agenda. O'Neill realized
that this state of affairs made his work politically marginal and compromised
hope of serious consideration. He could not take the easy road of presenting
space colonization as science fiction; he had to make the case for it as a practical project well within the profit-driven ordinary work of technoscience.[27] As a
result, he was desperate to find fora where space colonization could make the
transition from airy speculation to definite proposal.

In 1974, the Portola Foundation gave O'Neill the boost he needed by
granting six hundred dollars toward the First Princeton Conference on Space
Colonization. "The Establishment will be forced to recognize the existence of
your work by filling out forms and generating a lot of red tape," the foundation's officers reasoned. "Within many institutions that is the only reality that
is understood."[28] Through the institutional structure established for grants at
Princeton came public notice in the form of newspaper articles, wider recognition in scientific circles—especially in light of the concurrent publication of
O'Neill's seminal article in *Physics Today*—and NASA interest in sponsor-
ing further small research grants. The success of that first small conference laid
the groundwork for a much larger and more professional meeting the following year.

For the second conference, NASA and the National Science Foundation
came forward with grants, giving the event the cache of official recognition.[29]
The American Institute of Aeronautics and Astronautics (AIAA, the most recent incarnation of the aforementioned American Interplanetary Society) sent
its blessing and eventually published the conference proceedings. Many eminent names within aerospace and academic science were on hand to read papers and lead learned discussion. As a result, the space colonization idea began
to move rapidly away from its humble grassroots: "In the organization of the
second conference, it was important to maintain a high level of professional expertise and seriousness. A year earlier, we had been a small, happy band of
revolutionaries; now, with increasing recognition by professional and governmental bodies, it was both desirable and necessary to adopt a conservative and
pragmatic approach. As a title I chose 'Princeton University Conference on
Space Manufacturing.' "[30] O'Neill's quick movement toward the "conservative
and pragmatic" included offering the space-colonization idea as the answer
to the social and political debates of the 1970s. Popular notice made him a
celebrity, specifically because his grand technological vision of orbiting space

Figure 3. Artist's conception of an O'Neill space colony commissioned for the 1975 NASA Ames/Stanford University Summer Study. *Interior of the Stanford Torus,* painting by Don Davis. Courtesy of NASA.

colonies seemed to widen the previously narrow social range of people that would have access to a space future. O'Neill seemed to be throwing the doors of the aerospace industry and the space future open to all the people.

As new spaceflight organizations such as the L-5 Society—named after one of the gravitationally stable Lagrange points that O'Neill identified as a suitable site for a space colony—were formed to promote his vision, the political style and demographics of spaceflight advocacy changed. Michael A. G. Michaud records that the L-5 Society's "leading personalities had backgrounds in protest movements, notably those connected with the Vietnam War, the environment, and women's rights."[31] The inclusion of these controversial issues on the sociopolitical agenda of its members caused tension within the space advocacy community and on the political left. These tensions rose to the surface in a debate on the space-colony concept that appeared in the *CoEvolution Quarterly* in the mid-1970s.

The *CoEvolution Quarterly* was founded in 1974 with some of the profits from the Portola Foundation's successful *Whole Earth Catalog* operation.[32] When the catalog was first published in 1968, much of its audience consisted of communitarians who formed the core of the new environmentalism.[33] Continuity between the production staffs of *CoEvolution* and the catalog insured that the same general goals would be pursued by both publications. In accordance with the traditions of the *Whole Earth Catalog*, the magazine's editorial policy focused on the question of lifestyles alternate to those sanctioned by twentieth-century American industrial capitalism. In other words, it was a bastion of earthbound environmentalism and a certain amount of free-thinking, and the last place on Earth one might expect to find an active debate on the technical feasibility and the sociopolitical merits of space colonization.

As the founder of the catalog and *CoEvolution*'s first editor, Stewart Brand undoubtedly was aware of the excitement that O'Neill's ideas caused among other members of the foundation. But it was "a chance remark by a grade school teacher" that convinced him that those ideas should receive an airing in his magazine:

She said that most of her kids expected to live in Space [*sic*]. All their lives they'd been seeing "Star Trek" and American and Russian Space activities and drew the obvious conclusions.

Suddenly I felt out-of-it. A generation that grew up *with* Space, I realized, was going to lead another generation growing up in Space. Where did that leave me?

For these kids there's been a change in scope. They can hold the oceans of the world comfortably in their minds, like large lakes. Space is the ocean now.[34]

He concludes that the only possible response to this situation was to find out as much about the subject as he could, embrace it, and put it before his readers for debate.

Readers of the *CoEvolution Quarterly* were not so much interested in the technical aspects of O'Neill's vision as in its social and political implications. For many of them, space colonization was symptomatic of an industrial culture run wild. In response to a query from Brand, for example, Lewis Mumford, a respected observer of utopias, wrote: "If you were familiar with my analysis in the 'Pentagon of Power' you would know that I regard Space Colonies as another pathological manifestation of the culture that has spent all its resources on expanding the nuclear means for exterminating the human race. Such proposals are only technological disguises for infantile fantasies."[35] In a less dismissive response, environmentalist and nature writer Wendell Berry agreed with Mumford and pointed out that O'Neill's concept falls prey to "every shibboleth of the cult of progress." Berry also stated that the space-colony idea was "superbly attuned to the wishes of the corporate executives, bureaucrats, militarists, political operators and scientific experts who are the chief beneficiaries of the forces that have produced our crisis."[36] Others worried that it would divert us from solving problems here on Earth. Dennis Meadows, a member of the MIT team that first enunciated the limits-to-growth thesis, doubted the efficacy of a "new frontier" as a solution to the environmental and social problems of the human world. Instead, he believed, what is "needed to solve these problems on Earth is different values and institutions—a better attitude toward equity, a loss of the growth ethic, and so forth. I would rather work at the root of the problem here."[37]

No doubt O'Neill was chagrined by the tenor and quality of the criticism that his idea attracted. While he saw himself as apolitical, his vision of a humanization of space was liberal in conception and intent. In seeking to address the limits to growth through an integrated system of space manufacturing and the concept of satellite solar power (SSP), O'Neill hoped to use space to harvest a host of material and social benefits for the earthbound. He proposed large artificial structures at the gravitationally stable Lagrange points between Earth and the Moon. These "pressure vessels," which would contain all of the requisites to sustain earthly life in comfort, would serve as safety valves against the increasingly apparent environmental limits encountered by growing populations, the exhaustion of nonrenewable resources, pollution, energy, and food production. O'Neill and his colleagues imagined that once the first colonies were established, using lunar-based resources, the number could be exponentially increased. Not only would they insure an endlessly expanding frontier but, unfettered by earthly constraints, humanity's intellectual range would increase correspondingly, and in turn make possible exploration and exploitation of the solar system. The end result of all of this activity (if the species survived) would be the creation of a Dyson sphere, a mammoth construct composed of thousands, perhaps millions of space colonies surrounding our sun at the general distance of Earth's orbit.[38] At that point, humanity would be efficiently exploiting all of the energy that the sun produces and creating, so the logic goes, a civilization of immense material power.

In a speech given before the World Future Society in 1975, O'Neill declared, "The human race stands now on the threshold of a new frontier, whose richness surpasses a thousand fold that of the new Western world of five hundred years ago."[39] The new abundance promised by that space frontier did not depend on new knowledge or far-off technological breakthroughs, but on the simple willingness of the race to invest in the national space program. O'Neill imagined that by using the NASA shuttle fleet (then in the early stages of construction), the initial components of a space colony could be in orbit by the late 1970s and the first one, Island One, could be ready by 1990 (10). With access to the unlimited energy and materials of free space, the colonies would allow "a continuation rather than the arrest of the industrial revolution" (10).

At the time of the space-colony debate, the energy crisis topped the list of problems awaiting the resolution promised by expanding the industrial revolution beyond the limits of our terrestrial environment. When OPEC nations began to set oil prices with the future in mind (that is, in response to the reality that oil is a limited resource), they created political and economic consternation in the West and inconvenienced millions of consumers. America's political leadership of that era directed attention to a search for alternatives to energy dependency, not to war. Responding to the opportunity, O'Neill hoped that the idea of SSP would generate support for space colonization even from space-colonization skeptics (16).[40] He reasoned that solar power satellites would be cheaper to build in free space, where they would have access to a free and utterly reliable generator—the sun. The energy captured would then be transmitted to receiving stations on Earth, slaking the thirst of the planet's energy-hungry industries. Moreover, the satellites would in turn provide the economic base for space colonies. Because of space-based manufacturing and the building and maintenance of communication satellites, O'Neill supposed that an SSP program would allow future space colonies to return Earth's initial investment in space colonization many times over.

The benefits of SSP would not be limited to space colonies or to the consortium of Western nations with the resources to build them. O'Neill hoped that along with providing the promise of economic and political independence for the space colonies, SSP would help supply the conditions for a more generous relationship between what he considered developed and developing countries:

Because of widespread concern over decreasing energy and materials supplies, we are now viewed by many as exploiters of scarce resources. This has been a significant factor in hostility toward the US and toward other industrial nations. With a program of power plant construction at L5 we could return, at little cost in energy and materials from the earth, to our traditional role as a generous donor of wealth to those in need. In this case the wealth we could provide would be in the form of energy to third-world nations, and ultimately of "beachhead" colonies for their own progress. The L5 project would give us the opportunity to act with generosity, yet with little cost to our own national resources. (18)

Here O'Neill optimistically imagines that with the development of space colonies and SSP, America would become an energy exporter rather than importer. He is confident that if the United States develops space-based resources, a trickle-down effect will ensure globally shared wealth. The dystopian scenarios of a World War III battle over diminishing resources, a war conducted along racial lines, would thus be avoided.

Furthermore, space-based solar power stations would answer the concerns of environmentalists as well, for solar power entrepreneurs would avoid the cost of lifting heavy components out of the planet's gravity and the environmental damage caused by tons of rocket exhaust. They would also provide the planet with a clean source of energy: "If this development comes to pass, we will find ourselves here on Earth with a clean energy source, and we will further improve our environment by saving, each year, over a billion tons of fossil fuels, now lost to heat and smoke in driving our electric generators. Given a worldwide market which may be several hundred billion dollars by the year 2000, probably the industries at L5 will grow rapidly in numbers and size, to satisfy so urgent a demand."[41]

Finally, according to the numbers generated by several O'Neill-led study groups, the creation of new space colonies "at the fastest possible rate" would create a safety valve for our terrestrial population. Overpopulation was an abiding concern of "whole earth" sentiment in the early 1970s. Paul Ehrlich's *The Population Bomb* was the most popular of a series of demographic studies that expressed anxiety regarding the Malthusian consequences of unfettered growth.[42] To their warnings, O'Neill added:

[T]he productivity that we have achieved already on Earth, when employed in the energy-rich, materials-rich environment of space, could lead within less than two generations to a production-rate of new land area great enough even to accommodate the population increase rate of Earth. If the number of people on our planet rises to ten billion, and if its rate of increase goes unchecked, that rate of increase will be 200 million people per year. . . . it would require [another] thirty years from the completion-date of the first community before new lands would be increasing more than fast enough to cope with such demands.[43]

Providing additional space and the locus of material abundance for new populations, O'Neill's space colonies would also be a place where the discontented could escape from the power of terrestrial authorities. Liberal astrofuturism meets the American left in their shared critique of an increasingly repressive industrial civilization. Despite his wish to extend industrial civilization ad infinitum, O'Neill sees that it has certain unfortunate limitations, including a hostility toward cultural diversity: "[O]ne of the unpleasant characteristics of modern industrial life is that regional differences tend to be ironed flat by the economic pressures toward uniformity. The differences between small villages in separate countries are now far less than they were a generation ago, and something has been lost in that transition."[44] What has been lost might also be termed humanity's capacity to adapt to unfamiliar circumstances or even to imagine that life might be lived differently and that common experiences might have various meanings in disparate classes and cultures. This tendency toward diversity—which some believe to be an essential aspect of human character—is also essential to humanity's ability to adapt to different environments. Lose that ability, the logic goes, and humankind loses its ability to survive. Lose the tendency toward diversity and we also lose the ability to solve the social and political problems that confront us. And that loss would be dangerous in a world where man-made power can scrub the earth clean of civilization and most complex life-forms.

But space colonies, O'Neill argues, while extending industrial civilization, would simultaneously, albeit paradoxically, relieve "the pressures toward uniformity." Access to the limitless abundance of the space frontier would eventually create opportunities for diversity that would enlarge social, political, and economic freedoms:

I would think that in the long run, the tendency toward community diversity, the diversity of governments, diversity of the ways people choose to live, the kinds of architecture that they choose to have, and so on, would be enormous. Which is, I think, in exact contrast to the way that things are going on the surface of the Earth at the present time. And I believe that if someone were to look back on this whole business from the vantage point of say a hundred years further in time, probably the economic factors, which loom so large to us, will seem then to be relatively unimportant, because they won't be able to appreciate from their presumably much wealthier vantage point, what our problems were like. But the question of diversity and of the opening up of new possibilities and new frontiers, both of the body and of the mind, I suspect will come to be regarded as the most important contribution that these ideas have made.[45]

The argument that cultural diversity would be a highly desirable result of space colonies persuaded many astrofuturists on the left. Carl Sagan, for example, began revising a long-held skepticism about the human exploration of space because O'Neill's grand idea offered the possibility of utopian experiments on the space frontier. With an eye toward the relevance of space colonization to contemporary concerns, Sagan substituted the term "space city" for "space colony," arguing, "I think 'Space Colonies' conveys an unpleasant sense of colonialism which is not, I think the spirit behind the idea."[46] With this gesture toward eschewing the imperialist traditions of astrofuturism, Sagan registers his belief that "The idea of independent cities in space—each perhaps built on differing social, economic or political assumptions, or having different ethnic antecedents—is appealing, an opportunity for those deeply disenchanted with terrestrial civilizations to strike out on their own somewhere else. In its earlier history, America provided such an opportunity for the restless, ambitious and adventurous. Space cities could be a kind of America in the skies. They also would greatly enhance the survival potential of the human species."[47]

Both Sagan and O'Neill embraced the space frontier as the arena in which the American experience as utopian experiment could be replayed and vindicated. The pioneering space community would seek a new way of life in much the same way as early Euro-American migrants to the American West sought their various paradises. Explaining space colonization through the mythologized history of American expansion allows O'Neill to develop its politically liberatory potential. However, that potential derives not from specific political commitments, but solely from the expectation of an eternally renewable freedom, or escape:

Escape from outside interference will be an option open to a community in space, unless military intervention occurs to prevent it: there will always be the possibility of "pulling up stakes" and moving the habitat to a new orbit far from the source of the interference. In history we have many examples of groups, not least among them our Pilgrim ancestors, who have been permitted to escape from coercive situations. Usually those who remain behind justify that permission by something equivalent to "We're better off without those trouble makers." The space communities would be in contrast to the classical Utopias in part because they could escape so much more successfully.[48]

O'Neill assures us that diversity will be maintained in space because communities there will be able to isolate themselves from the home world and from one another. If all else fails, they can protect their isolation from conflict by moving ever outward from the Sun. Space proffers an endless supply of elbow room for individuals and communities that may wish to escape the strictures of civilization. And the disharmonious elements of any space habitat would find it easier to accept exile than to resist or challenge community standards. Unfortunately, this vision of the space future implies that heterogeneity is rejected, not embraced. Human diversity across the space frontier is purchased with the support of locally intolerant monocultures. Local intolerance is the principle feature of space colonies that can more firmly police their physical and symbolic borders. The hope that the space future will represent an increased capacity for tolerance, a greater facility at addressing sources of conflict among humankind, is set aside. Permission to depart, which O'Neill intends as an expression of tolerance, mystifies the expulsion of difference and the suppression of dissent. It becomes evidence not of a greater liberality but of more complete totalitarianisms. O'Neill does not see the contradiction in allowing the suppression of diversity in the name of diversity. In his space future, the heterogeneity of the whole is assured by the homogeneity of the parts. Thus a "separate but equal" doctrine defines the limits of O'Neill's hopes for peace. Within this strand of astrofuturism, we find that political differences are not resolved, but escaped. The dream of a good and just society, a democratic commonwealth, which depends on diversity of opinion and persons for its health, is deferred.

O'Neill's emphasis on escape rather than struggle for reform indicates some tension between a desire for genuine political alternatives and resistance to prescribing the nature of those alternatives. The latter stems from his fear of becoming a "new age" guru and from his wish to reaffirm the values and privileges common to the white middle class at mid-century. As bold as he is in scientific and technical speculation, O'Neill is reluctant to consider explicitly the full social and political implications of his work. While he hopes that the space habitat would provide a forum for diversity and an escape from governmental interference for the dissident, he also presents it as a form empty of stable political meaning.

In contrast, and very much by intent, I have said nothing about the government of space communities. There is a good reason for that: I have no desire to influence or direct in any way, even if I could, the social organization of the details of life in the communities. I have no prescription for social organization or governance, and would find it abhorrent to presume to define one. In my opinion there can be no "revealed truth" about social organization; there can only be, in any healthy situation, the options of diversity of experimentation. Among the space communities almost surely there will be some in which restrictive governments will attempt to enforce isolation, just as such governments do on Earth. (235)

Resisting the temptation to become a cult leader (in the manner of Brian O'Leary, for instance), O'Neill casts space colonies as open technological platforms whose content could be determined by their residents. His desire for government and corporate sponsorship led him to de-emphasize political goals in favor of promises of immense shareholder profits. Indeed, concerned that his humanization of space might be dismissed as utopian, O'Neill was careful to distance his ideas from the utopian tradition.

O'Neill's reading of classic utopian and communitarian adventures reveals that they have at their heart an often unresolved tension between external freedom and internal discipline. The communitarian ventures of the nineteenth century often foundered on this tension, either because the conflict between the commune and the world around it was too disruptive (as with the Mormons before they settled in Utah) or because the internal rules were so rigid that the group never achieved enough internal diversity to become a viable community (as with Bronson Alcott's Fruitlands). O'Neill hoped to avoid these dilemmas by denying that he had any specific agenda for space communities and by emphasizing differences between American utopianism and the humanization of space. The fundamental flaw that he finds in traditional utopias and in the communes of his own experience is their inability to couple their new social ideas to progressive or even appropriate technology. Traditional utopias tended to use the technology of the surrounding culture or looked backward to a more "primitive" or "restrictive" technology (236). According to O'Neill, space colonization would avoid the antitechnological taboos of communitarianism and couple social experimentation with forward-looking technologies: "The humanization of space is no Utopian scheme: the contrast is between rigid social ideas and restricted technology, on the part of the Utopias and communes, and the opening of new social possibilities to be determined by the inhabitants, with the help of a basically new technical methodology, on the part of the space communities" (236).

O'Neill's humanization of space is not a utopian venture justified by some new sociopolitical arrangement but a technological initiative that will produce or extend the range of earthly experiments. In other words, space colonization will be an extension of an ideal American pluralism. Social experimentation and diversity will be tolerated in space because of the wealth available there and because of the vast distances between human communities in the void:

In space, where free solar energy and optimum farming conditions will be available to every community, no matter how small, it will be possible for special-interest groups to "do their own thing" and build small worlds of their own, independent of the rest of the human population. We can imagine a community of as few as some hundreds of people, sharing a passion for a novel system of government, or for music or for one of the visual areas, or for a less esoteric interest: nudism, water sports, or skiing. Of the serious experiments in society-building, some will surely be failures. Others, though, may succeed, and those independent social laboratories may teach us more about how people can best live together than we can ever learn on Earth, where high technology must go hand-in-hand with the rigidity of large-scale human groupings. (237)

If these social experiments are to be the expression of similarity and consensus, then the smallest evidence of difference—hobbies, tastes, faiths—is enough to prompt emergencies that split space-future communities. This is a demand for a homogeneity that has never been achieved on Earth. Disturbed by the radical political diversity of his time, O'Neill takes a stand against politics altogether. He does not hope that we might address our differences rationally or that a wide range of temperaments, behaviors, cultures, and colors may be accommodated in the worlds we devise. He imagines an infinite regression of space habitats organized around affiliations and preferences that range from the trivial to the profound. The possibility that the space future might afford greater opportunities for the communication of social and physical knowledge, that it might herald the advent of a truly democratic commonweal, is scattered among an archipelago of private resorts or petty tyrannies. Again, it is space technology and the possibility of escape through endless growth that it provides that guarantees continual experiments in "free" society. No specific political commitment structures O'Neill's vision. His liberalism requires no ideological adherence to a cause, but only optimism in the benign effect of high technology and infinite space. In other words, for O'Neill, freedom is guaranteed by machines and space, not by human desire or practice.

It is not surprising that critics looked through O'Neill's emphasis on diversity and his denial of any specific social or political agenda and saw both his anxiety and a default politics. Wendell Berry, no friend of O'Neill's technocratic leanings, sums up critical dissatisfaction when he calls the space-colony idea "conventional."[49] Despite his effort to resist prescribing the governance of space colonies, O'Neill's narratives describe a social order easily recognizable as an idealized version of mid-century America. A comment from Allen Steele's *Clarke County, Space* (1990) illustrates the problem: "Ever seen the early artists' conceptions of O'Neill colonies, back when they were first thought up in the last century? The biospheres were pictured as wall to wall tract housing, complete with backyard barbecue grills. Looked like New Jersey in orbit. Space as a giant suburb."[50] To make space colonization attractive to a wide audience, O'Neill promised to satisfy middle-class desire for retreat from public engagement into a private utopia. In the late 1960s and 1970s, America's great cities were no longer lands of opportunity; instead, they embodied the failure of the American dream with their poverty, civic corruption, racial unrest, civil disobedience, and violence. They signify the world that must be escaped by flight into space. In an era of white flight and rapid suburban sprawl, the city became an icon of the nation's disenchantment with itself. As middle- and working-class whites abandoned the caldrons of American hybridity and sought refuge in homogeneous suburbs, the city also became synonymous with racial heterogeneity and, in turn, people of color became emblems of crime, poverty, and urban blight. Given that escape is the only option that O'Neill can imagine, and given that in both instances escape is motivated by fear of alterity and a passion for homogeneity, it is difficult to detect the difference between white flight in the America of the 1970s and the humanization of space by the common people he imagines. In neither case is the political imagination usefully extended. The regenerative promise of a new frontier falls before business as usual.

O'Neill's radical technological platform echoes the conventional, even banal escapes that have been available to the American middle class since Frederick Law Olmsted's plan of Riverside, Illinois, in 1868.[51] Thus, his futures make sense to us from within familiar landscapes, which allow the pursuit of happiness without sacrifice or change. J. B. Jackson describes the suburban ideal as "middle landscapes" that reconcile city-bred conveniences with the regenerative qualities ascribed to nature. Thus O'Neill opposes the machine-city perfectionism envisioned by early twentieth-century futurists and allies his futurism with a suburban ideal that can represent wealth and peace. However, his space suburbs rely on highly refined technologies of automation, communication, transportation, and energy production. The escape into the middle landscape of space is no flight from industrial production or invention; rather, it is an exploration of technology's humane possibilities. The suburban form that anchors his space future is a technological fix that can replace the grim military-industrial finishes of space conquest with the soft-green textures of a tranquil domesticity.[52]

The early space habitats designed by von Braun looked like the interiors of submarines; O'Neill wanted his colonies to resemble his idea of the most comfortable and attractive parts of Earth. He follows the planning tradition initiated by Patrick Geddes that locates the origin of civilization in the valleys of

Europe and takes them as the ideal setting for the good society.[53] O'Neill, in turn, creates valleys in orbit to continue the evolution of bourgeois civilization:

it is interesting to consider some of the possibilities for modeling directly attractive portions of the Earth. We think of a valley area two miles by twenty as rather small, but it is surprisingly large when compared to some of humankind's favorite places. Most of the island of Bermuda, including the lovely south coast areas named after the English shires, could be modeled rather well within about half the length of a space-community valley. . . . We may expect that, in common with our ancestors who chose wistfully to call their frontier "New England," at least some of the settlers in space will model their cities and villages on the prettier areas of Old Earth.[54]

In this passage from *The High Frontier*, O'Neill assumes that the first human designs of worlds in space will seek to replicate the familiar, not embrace the new. Their task will be to create environments that foster a familiar and comfortable life of leisure:

Island One [the first space colony] will be small, though far less crowded than many Earth cities, and it can be attractive to live in. The inhabitants can have apartments which will be palatial by the standards of most of the world. Each apartment will have a private garden, bathed every day in sunshine at an angle which will correspond to late morning. Even within the limits of Island One and its water supply the colonist can have beaches and a river, quite large enough for swimming and canoeing. . . .

Even within Island One the new options of human-powered flight and of low-gravity swimming and diving will be possible, and the general impression one will receive from a village will be of greenery, trees, and luxuriant flowers, enhanced if the village chooses to run with the climate and plantlife of Hawaii. Heavy industry can be located outside but nearby, so that no vehicle faster than a bicycle will be needed within the community. (124)[55]

For any student of American planning history, the above description of Island One invokes the ideology and designs that marked the plans of the garden city movement during the 1920s. Although denying any prescriptive intent, through his description of the physical environment to be created in a space colony, O'Neill presents his vision of an ideal space future. The result is a recasting of the middle-class suburban ideal in the seemingly empty reaches of outer space. The flight to the suburb becomes a metaphor for O'Neill's imagined retreat from public engagement into private utopias of endless leisure and domestic bliss.

That this is O'Neill's intention is clear from the "common man epistles" that he inserts into his space-future narrative. These are letters written to the folks back home by future space colonists. O'Neill patterns these letters after those sent by early European colonists in America describing their experiences and the riches of their new frontier (201). O'Neill's space colonials are not the action-adventure heroes of imperial exploration, the stern techno-military elite of the 1950s, or the youthful dissenters of the 1960s and early 1970s, but middle-aged Americans who are the space future's "salt of the earth." His description of the typical pioneer couple is revealing: "Unlike those youthful immigrants who might be in the majority, this is imagined to be a couple whose children have grown up, married, and established families on Earth. Work experience and a record of stability and responsibility could be important factors influencing the 'selection committees' which will play an important role inevitably in determining who goes to the early communities, though with the passage of time it can be expected that eventually most of the people who may wish to go to L5 will have the opportunity of doing so" (202). The emphasis on family, stability, and responsibility reads like the catalog of traits required of mid-century good citizens who believe simultaneously in the democratic process and in the inadvisability of fighting city hall. They are not promising material for the incipient social or political experiments supposedly endemic to the high frontier. The common man epistle serves an important function for O'Neill's futurism, for it implies that the future is not limited to a small elite— an accusation commonly leveled at the spaceflight community of the 1960s— but welcomes ordinary folk as well. It is based on the second generation's understanding that viable human communities require stable social and physical environments. In short, we need a domestication of space.

For O'Neill, this domestication means that the humanization of space must not be undertaken only by a professional middle class made up predominantly of white Americans. For it to work, it must be an endeavor undertaken by a broad cross section of the global populace. The scientific and technological elite essential to the smooth running of any space venture are kept in the background; in the foreground are farmers, factory workers, and low-level technicians. This plan for a future social order in space is perhaps designed to persuade congressional funding committees and their constituents. It does not raise the specter of revolutionary change that might threaten the status quo. Instead, it offers comfortable assurance of an expansion that will enlarge and enrich the established order. Change is limited to a pluralism that maintains familiar social hierarchy by extending its privileges to the erstwhile disadvantaged. Yet in his rosy vision of future social order in the high frontier, O'Neill avoids acknowledging that his common people necessarily must represent an elite group selected and tested by an elite group. At least initially, the process of migration to the space frontier would be controlled by the needs of nation-states and their corporate clients. Social engineering, not wild and wooly experimentation, would be the dominant characteristic of life in space.

By denying the possible utopian aspects of a humanization of space and taking the seemingly moderate approach of an apolitical techno-prophet, O'Neill valorized a space future that was both open-ended enough to allow for (undescribed) social experimentation and prescriptive enough to allow for an endless extension of contemporary life and customs. In the long run, this meant that the technocratic and astrofuturist left's embrace of O'Neill's vision did not preclude a similarly fervent endorsement from the right. O'Neill's influence on the astrofuturist community has, therefore, been tremendous. His space-colonization proposal provided a technological vision that, for the first time in thirty years, came from outside the institutional matrix of government, industry, and the military. In contrast to the ballistic missiles and surveillance satellites that represents the best efforts of previous futurists, O'Neill's' open-ended scheme for space colonies, solar power satellites, mass drivers, and lunar mining colonies seemed humane because it is a technological infrastructure designed to promote the expansion of civilization rather than its destruction. As a result, writers, scientists, and spaceflight activists from across the political spectrum arose to embrace the new vision. Early O'Neill followers T. A. Heppenheimer and K. Eric Drexler came to the vision as pro-technology students and produced widely read books and articles explaining its utopian dimensions.[56] Carl Sagan and Freeman Dyson, academic scientists who regularly indulged in popular speculation, used the space-colony idea as the focal point for discussing a wide range of liberal social concerns.[57] Science-fiction writers such as Mack Reynolds, Arthur Clarke, and Ben Bova have generated near future adventures that speculate on the relevance of O'Neill's work to social, political, and even biological evolution. And others, such as popular science/science-fiction writer Jerry Pournelle, became involved in the vigorous spaceflight activism of the late 1970s and early 1980s while seeking support for an O'Neill-based agenda in Washington.

The Suburban Frontier

O'Neill's commitment to a suburban future is obvious in his 1981 sequel to *The High Frontier*, *2081: A Hopeful View of the Human Future*. Distinguishing his work from the speculative literary tradition of Bellamy and Orwell, O'Neill argues that his predictions are "consistent with the histories both of technology and social interaction."[58] Preferring the certainties of forecasting technological advance to making "social predictions," O'Neill valorizes technology as the principle "driver of change." Efforts to direct the course of social affairs are restricted to the consumption of industrially distributed invention. In seeking to sever links with the socialism prevalent in literary utopias, the futurist installs capitalism as the economic system that best serves the human desire for physical comfort and cultural fulfillment. O'Neill excises from consideration any future offering significant social change on two grounds: 1) while technology does change, human nature does not, and 2) it is impossible to predict or even choose the direction of social change.

Because he underestimates the impact of political struggle, O'Neill forecasts a future in which technological invention secures the spatial separations around race and class characteristic of American life. In this future, class is tightly aligned with the alterity signaled by race. Although O'Neill insists that any future technological advance must serve all humankind, he represents a prosperous, white middle class as its most immediate beneficiaries. Political and economic hope hinges on the willingness of these North Americans to share technology and expertise with less fortunate peoples and nations. The entitlements that O'Neill imaginatively bestows on them require that they serve as Earth's benefactors. The salvation of the white middle class creates something of a representational crisis in *2081*. As we have seen, diversity is an important value in O'Neill's future vision. Yet he is unable to represent it within the model community he imagines as a desirable material goal. The difficult alterities symbolized by race or culture (language, religion, and so forth) are placed in analogic exile in his future. The Other is in another town, city, nation, or space colony, but not next door.

Thus, it is in *2081* that O'Neill reinvents the segregationist ethic that was a principle feature of American culture in the first half of the twentieth century. His belief in the immutability of the human character and his unwillingness to represent new social relations certainly open him to this charge. Waterford, Pennsylvania, the model town that embodies his optimistic view of the future, replicates the covenanted, gated communities of thirty years ago. The boundaries and hierarchies marking its race, gender, and class positions are presented as stable and enduring a century hence, while difference has been domesticated as a commodity available for easy consumption. Waterford's white, middle-class citizens inhabit a culture of consumption that makes nothing of its own but must import the signs of culture from elsewhere. O'Neill's argument for future diversity therefore contains a catastrophic tension between an unmarked whiteness representing technological modernity and a marked blackness (racial/

cultural others) representing the atavistic survival of preindustrial culture as tourist trophy or exotic spectacle. His belief that a vigorously enforced local homogeneity will produce safety, freedom, and prosperity reproduces what we might justifiably call a liberal segregationist ethic. There is a rupture between O'Neill's egalitarian claims for the suburban form and his presentation of it as a working social order.

Homogeneity is a desirable attribute of O'Neill's imagined communities and integral to his wish to maintain the pleasures of regional differences.[59] While social and political experimentation would be the rule in his space future, O'Neill has clear notions about the kinds of communities that will prosper. They are likely, he argues, "to be . . . strongly motivated toward peaceful cooperation and constructive hard work."[60] Reasoning from the colonial and frontier experiences of the Americas, the futurist opines that "it is clear that the early settlers in space will be exciting people: restless, inquiring, independent; quite possibly more hard-driving and possessed by more 'creative discontent' than their kind in the Old World."[61] He hopes, however, for a limit to the adventures his space pioneers might pursue:

A very small number are likely to be criminals, revolutionaries, or members of extremist sects, eking out a precarious existence on the fringes of civilization, as such groups have done historically. But in their nature such groups will need to prey on, attack, or obtain converts from society, and therefore won't go far beyond its physical boundaries. Dependent as they will be on society, they are also unlikely to be large-scale independent builders of new colonies; indeed, if any are as self-destructive as the notorious "Jonestown" sect, they won't leave anything for the future beyond lurid headlines and a bad taste.[62]

In other words, large-scale successful dissent is made impossible by the very nature of the space frontier. Although O'Neill can hardly be faulted in his desire to avoid recurrence of the Jonestown debacle, all too often restrictions against "criminal," "revolutionary," or "extremist" movements are levied also against the type of "creative discontent" that O'Neill prizes. In fact, the destructive potential inherent in the creative makes any innovation dangerous to the standing order. Fear of the creative leads logically to an authoritarianism that would suppress the confluence, essential to any real democratic experiment, of competitive and often antagonistic ideas and persons.

O'Neill represents his model future community, Waterford, as an attractive paradigm of middle-class probity and consumption. This gesture, more than anything else, limits the type of diversity that he can represent. Ideal space communities require a material abundance in which luxury and adventure are the mutually supporting strands of everyday life. The denizens of O'Neill's future worlds manifest the same qualities that David M. Potter discovered in the Americans of his 1954 sociological treatise, *People of Plenty*.[63] Potter argues that Americans are defined primarily by the material abundance our continent makes available. Wealth beyond mere subsistence accounts for the freedoms and prospects that are, according to him, unique to this nation. As we have seen, the transformative potential of resource windfalls assumed by this argument is a common presupposition in astrofuturism. O'Neill relies upon it to shore up his promise of an inexhaustible prospect in space. Access to that cornucopia will allow American civilization to break the cycle of rise, decline, and fall discovered by both academic and popular histories since the days of Edward Gibbon and Brooks Adams. In this manner, American exceptionalism is married to the astrofuturist prospect of an endless space frontier.

O'Neill's goal is nothing less than the creation of a solar system–wide society of abundance. And that abundance inevitably is linked to consumption of the energy and goods produced from extraterrestrial sources. The defining presupposition of *2081* is that the ordinary culture of white American middle-class professionals is a reasonable template for the texture of an abundant future. The book dramatizes the advantages of that life and defends it against the charge of exclusivity by reason of race or nation. Because the bounty of space will create a surfeit of luxury and knowledge, the instinct for hoarding wealth will diminish. At a stroke, the principle source for human conflict—the struggle over the control, exploitation, and distribution of resources—will be extirpated. In this account, the grounds for racism and cultural hatred would evaporate, opening the door to the survival of all races and to the evolution of the species.

"Life in 2081," the narrative heart of *2081*, elaborates O'Neill's technological utopianism and allows us to test the boundaries of the diversity for which he strives. Following utopian conventions, the story dramatizes the material and cultural advantages of a future that is at once familiar and strange. Eric C. Rawson, the story's narrator, is a space colonist who undertakes a grand tour of the planet Earth in 2081. He is a guest in the old world, a naive eyewitness who can direct us in admiring and puzzling over the machines and manners of its inhabitants. Following each of his reports, O'Neill provides a "factual commentary" sketching the developments that license his social and technical speculations (108). The typical utopian journey takes the protagonist from the familiar to the strange. The men of Charlotte Perkins Gilman's *Herland* (1915), for example, travel from Europe to the remote South American locale of her feminist utopia. O'Neill, however, reverses direction and takes his eyewitness from the strange to the familiar. If distance is a device offering an escape from the quotidian in the traditional adventure or literary utopia, then Eric's grand tour allows his creator to stage a confrontation between the innocence fostered by the space-colonial future and the troubles of a big and complex planet.

The difficulties of daily life are evident even as Eric marvels at the luxury and technical sophistication enjoyed by his informants. Terrestrial life, he realizes, is hostage on the one hand to the irritation of high taxes and political despotism and on the other to the dangers of terrorism and nuclear war. By implication, the space colonies of the future may lack the technocultural privileges of the home world but are free from the tensions caused by racial, national, and economic conflict and the uneven distribution of resources that persists on Earth (218). Indeed, Eric's home, Fox Aggregate, is "a permanent human society [founded] on the principles of nonviolence, free of weapons and so remote that it will never be troubled by the continuing wars of Earth" (106). The Fox Aggregate is a locus of freedom and plenty while the Earth is still divided between haves and have nots. Earth is the site of antagonistic alterity, signaled by racial and national differences, while space colonies eliminate heterogeneity as the price of domestic peace. Since Rawson is guided by the affluent of Earth's denizens, we see the future planet at its best. But around our narrator we also catch glimpses of the way heterogeneity is managed through strategies that aim for containment, commodification, and segregation.

Our correspondent travels to Earth on the *Dandridge M. Cole,* "a small ship designed for cargo and passenger service over long-distance routes" (108).[64] The ship is appointed with conveniences for both body and mind. Small domestic robots called "pups" do all of the service work such as table waiting and laundry (110). And the stateroom walls come equipped with displays that one "could call up for showing more than a hundred thousand works of art from the museums of the Inner System" (109). The ship's dining room is "a revolving restaurant, looking outward on all sides from a great height, through panoramic windows, to the lights of a city surrounded by water with mountains beyond" (111).[65] Narrator and reader are positioned as privileged inhabitants of a culture comfortable enough to turn its achievements into readily consumable commodities. The artfully rendered urbanism that Eric enjoys is a tame version of the real thing. That is the point: the restaurant provides an environment that aestheticises earthly places with no fear that either natural accident or human infelicity will disturb a pleasant evening.

Encapsulated here is the social ecology that Eric discovers on his grand tour. The future is best imagined as a restaurant in a luxuriously appointed hotel, even if the food (as is to be expected) is a bit bland. O'Neill's admiring asides to Disney's theme parks and the mall-like hotels of architect John Port-man indicate that his physical planning references are culled from the commercial vernacular of world's fairs and recreational tourism. The architectural experiments of Paolo Soleri, R. Buckminster Fuller, and the Archigram group—O'Neill's contemporaries who sought to integrate human needs with environmental concerns—have little or no effect on his own practice. Rather, he creates a collage of already available futurist images—yesterday's tomorrows, as Joseph Corn calls them.[66]

This is particularly evident in O'Neill's focus on mobility and the means of transportation throughout his space-future narrative. Following his three-month trip on the *Cole*, Eric's itinerary includes arrival at a space station, a shuttle to an equatorial spaceport, and a supersonic jet to Cincinnati where he meets one of his old-world relatives (116). His guide then shepherds him onto the "floater," a nationwide, high-velocity subway that takes them to Erie, Pennsylvania, and then onto an automated automobile and highway system (125–29, 135–37). Eric's trip proceeds as planned, on time with no rough spots or inefficiencies of service. Speed, efficiency, and silence are the hallmarks of the services he enjoys. The appeal of this fantasy lies in its banality. It is the dream of effortless mobility promised by technological progress, modernity, and futurity for the past two centuries.[67] In O'Neill's fable, baggage and passengers always arrive on time and in the right place. There are no misunderstandings or delays and the food, when it is offered, is not bad (112).

The material promise made here is that the future will offer the individual unprecedented freedom of movement. This freedom, however, is purchased from unseen authorities who monitor every movement made by private citizens. Eric discovers that a "credit anklet" is essential to security and consumption in the world of tomorrow. With the anklet, one may purchase goods and services without making any visible sales exchange. The wearer is freed from such petty inconveniences as waiting in line to board a plane. The device also records the location and identity of its wearer. Eric is told that "unless I couldn't stand the notion, I would a lot better off letting the immigration guards at Freeport Seven (a space station) put an anklet on me. If I didn't, I would be annoyed by time-wasting delays at every national border, and I'd be hassled at every residential town, museum and shopping enclave" (116). Thus the individual surrenders a great deal of autonomy for the sake of ease in commercial transactions and increased security. O'Neill allows Eric to feel some small discomfort at this "loss of privacy" and speculates that residential enclaves would enforce Privacy Acts to restrain the use of information gathered via the anklet (153).

Nevertheless, the residents of earth seem to accept loss of their privacy and believe that if one is innocent one has nothing to hide. O'Neill argues in the expository section following Eric's introduction to Waterford's surveillance system that a "loss of privacy" would perhaps prevent crime and certainly would ensure its swift punishment: "What would it be worth in loss of privacy to know that one's child could walk any street, day or night, and be safe from molestation, even in a world where a potential deliberate murderer could move thousands of miles in a single hour? What would it be worth to know that one's home was safe from burglary or arson, because no stranger could approach it without being monitored and identified by the town's police computer? A good deal I suspect" (158). In this world, a line is drawn between those who are se-cured by the system and those who are not. Alterity is not eliminated, but mechanized and hardwired into the system, with class as its primary sign. This future is described aptly by Robert Fishman's term "bourgeois utopia." It offers security and ennoblement to a middle class hoping to maintain its privileges in an environment characterized by alienation and dissent. In principle, this means a future in which only one's bank balance matters. O'Neill justifies his prophetic creation of enclave towns such as Waterford by pointing out the growing popularity of gated communities and shopping malls, which privatize the public world and ideally create secure spaces for leisure, work, and con-sumption (158–59).

Waterford, Pennsylvania, is an enclave town, an enclosed garden city whose citizens enjoy a uniformly high level of prosperity, security, and leisure. Productive activity is not a matter of necessity, but is chosen for self-cultivation and pleasure. The key characteristics of this community are stability, security, efficiency, and silence. Everyday life is shaped by the mechanisms that support a smooth transfer of goods and persons from place to place. Service is relegated to nonhuman agents (robots) who replace domestic servants and the industrial working class. O'Neill assumes that those who formerly undertook routinized work or even skilled craft have found a place in middle-class vocations. Ser-vice positions such as bartending, cooking, and gardening are obsolete except as diverting recreations (139, 163, 177). High culture must be imported and is collected in living spaces devoid of local, personal, or political histories. O'Neill's Waterford is what Paul Goodman and Percival Goodman call a "city of efficient consumption."[68]

Eric's tour of Waterford is hosted by the Tehaney family, distant relatives who introduce him to the private side of life in the future. His report on the new town is dominated by appreciations of its physical amenities. Its completely artificial ecology (Paolo Soleri would call it an arcology) ignores the heavy snowstorm sweeping the unroofed world outside.[69] The community's residents live in a controlled climate, which separates them from the inconvenience of seasonal change. The lushness of its foliage lends the place the atmosphere of a rich and very exclusive Hawaiian resort. Indeed, the title of the chapter in which this description appears is "Honolulu, Pennsylvania." The suburbanites of Waterford are on permanent vacation. This connection is underscored through a description of the luxurious finishes of the Tehaney home:

The house seemed much like those in one of our Polynesian-climate colonies, with plenty of open space, high ceilings and thick roof beams in natural wood. The floors at the entry level were terra cotta tile, and large windows opened onto courtyards and gardens rich with tropical flowers. We climbed stairs with a carved wooden railing to a carpeted level where Jeannette showed me to my suite, with bedroom, balcony, bath and exercise room. She showed me the controls for the stereo, the video, and the lights, and added that if I just spoke in a normal tone in any room the house computer would hear me and carry out my instructions. (138)

The Tehaney house is more a five-star hotel than a private home (155). Eric is later informed by Arthur, the couple's robot butler, that his shoes will be shined if they are left outside his suite door (154).

O'Neill is careful to provide a life for the Tehaney's that is both outrageously luxurious and dead common. Take away the youth maintained by "anti-aging drugs" (138); the robot servant of all work who serves drinks, washes dishes, and gardens; the open-air town-car, which is both mobile bar and living room; and the RV big enough to carry a "small sauna and gym" (224) and you have a family that would have been called typical in the 1950s. Dad is a consulting engineer while Mom takes care of the house and works part-time at a travel agency. Daughter is a college student working toward a degree in ecology and is rebellious enough to want a more venturesome life than that enjoyed by her parents. She, quite naturally, will immigrate into space (172). This vision of middle-class paradise seems isolated from the rest of the world by its privilege. It is a deliberate portrayal of suburbia as paradise. The family seeks out difference through travel and collection—in other words, as sites of tourism and appropriable commodity. It does not encounter heterogeneity in the course of daily life; indeed, the world of 2081 is designed to prevent such encounters.

The principle that drives O'Neill's narrative of Eric's grand tour is the future elimination of the differences that cause conflict. However, the author is troubled by the tendency of industrial capitalism to create monocultures, which strip away regional variations.[70] He prizes diversity as a source of pleasure and as important to the survival of the species. Creating a future that satisfies both his desire to eliminate alterity as grounds for conflict and his wish to retain it as a virtue of the human character forces a neat set of separations into his narrative. As Eric approaches and tours Earth, he is struck by the great variety of race, language, and culture that he finds there. On his arrival at the orbital station, he observes: "I passed through an automatic door to a small room where two male guards, tall, and strongly built, and smiling, were waiting. They were coffee-colored and looked splendid in their Freeport Seven 'Constabulary' Bermuda shorts and tall helmets."[71] This description establishes racial variance as an exotic feature of the home planet. It is a signal difference from the homogeneity we assume for Eric's colonial home. Eric is the beneficiary of a diaspora, which has scattered communities into separate enclaves by race, language, religion, ideology, what have you. Each space colony is something like a seventeenth-century New England village, only large enough to support a single kin. And this scale-imposed uniformity provides the foundation for a peace and prosperity that requires the voluntary exile of any person or group who will not conform to the organizing principle of community. Diversity is thereby served in a way that minimizes the chance of conflict or competition.

Meanwhile, Rawson encounters the planet's multiplicity as a scenic luxury of his tour, a confection to be consumed like any other delicacy he encounters. However, it is also apparent that Earth's gorgeous heterogeneity is the danger that stimulates its peoples' obsession with security. The future Earth that Eric explores is at once a Disneyland and a purgatory. When Eric arrives in New York City, O'Neill's interest in Disney urbanism as the template for the organization of public space in the future is revealed: "The venerable Walt Disney commercial empire had established around the turn of the century one of the largest 'theme parks' in the country, on a bulldozed, reclaimed piece of New York city that had once been a slum. We spent two days there without seeing the wintry weather outside. Nations, companies, and multinational corporations all maintained permanent exhibits in the park, and I spent much of the first day touring their displays and learning a great deal from them" (196). This fantasy approvingly mirrors the Model City and other urban renewal schemes of the 1970s. It also presages Disney's "cleaning up" of Times Square in the 1990s and what architectural critics have called the "malling of America."[72]

Other nations similarly benefit from the prosperity created by space-based resources. Africa is the site of many "success stories" boosted by a satellite-fostered trend toward universal education and economic prosperity.[73] The continent's status as the site of wild nature insures a healthy ecotourism catering to travelers such as Eric. The United Kingdom has completed its transition from an industrial/imperial power to an international theme park "because the country was making so much money out of tourism that it didn't need to produce much" (208). Eric falls "in love with England" because of "the small scale of their shops and restaurants," the unchanged appearance of "the legendary London cabs" and "the Peter Pan statue in Kensington Park" (209). When an alternate culture is actually lived and not simply commodified, the signs of its difference from the normative, unmarked culture of Anglo-America are confined to domestic life. Thus, the future Japan maintains peace between ancient tradition and modernity by holding apart their expression: while the daughter of a typical Japanese family wears "a stylish skirt and blouse that might have come, and perhaps did, from a Paris boutique" in public, at home she appears "clad in a kimono, with her hair and face made up in a style I recognized from prints by Hokusai" (217).

When not thus contained as commodity or cloistered eccentricity—that is, when difference actually makes a difference—non-Anglo-American cultures are blamed for the continuing ills of future earth. Culture is the catalyst of the political turmoil that nurtures dictatorship, economic privation, and societal insecurity. In his expository notes for Eric's trip abroad, O'Neill explains: "We North Americans are fortunate that our ancestors, frontier colonists and emigrants, were forced to develop for survival a pragmatic, positive attitude toward inventions and mechanisms. It helped us a great deal to make the most out of the first centuries of industrialization. Unfortunately, the cultural heritage in some of the nations that need industrialization most is very different and constitutes a barrier to urgently needed technical development" (219). Americans are an exception to the rule because their culture was determined by access to a frontier. The frontier was the crucible in which the peculiar dynamic of American abundance and progress was born. Other cultures are not so fortunate. The dangers that Eric encounters during his world tour are an index of earth's diversity. The planet not only is too small for a growing industrial civilization, it is also not big enough to maintain peace within its heterogeneity. According to this logic, it is the Earth's heterogeneous population that prevents humanity's growth beyond poverty, stupidity, and annihilation. Apropos the African situation, O'Neill has an amateur historian, another of Eric's guides, opine "that the most successful nations [are] those with homogeneous populations, because homogeneity eliminated one source of violent conflict" (205). The homogeneity apparently enjoyed by the Japanese (and by the Tehaney family) is used to reinforce this lesson (213).

The removal of Eric's space-colony home from the terrestrial purgatory of nuclear weapons and terrorism is presented as a privilege that the people of

Earth may envy but, because of their heterogeneity, would find hard to emulate. Hence the solution of Earth's discontents is two-fold: the inward turn to suburban enclaves such as Waterford and the outward dispersal into space as new colonies. O'Neill's astrofuturism thereby resolves alterity by breaking the human race up to preserve it. The world may be saved if an efficient version of the lifestyle the American middle class enjoyed in the 1950s can be exported globally and if the planet has access to space-based land. This version of astrofuturism gains a freedom that may avoid conflict, but it sacrifices the possibility that we might use our circumstances to develop a polity that can live with difference democratically.

O'Neill's astrofuturism, therefore, solves the problem of alterity on Earth, and specifically in America, by imagining that space-colonial settlements would function best as homogeneous satrapies. This is a defensive prospect that uses the great distances of outer space to create rigid boundaries between putatively irreconcilable human groups. Diversity is a factor of the diaspora as a whole, not of its constituent parts. Thus, O'Neill casts the century-old separate but equal compromise onto the grand scale of his future.

6. Ben Bova: Race, Nation, and Renewal on the High Frontier

Perhaps, as we place the extraterrestrial domain into the service of all people, we may be permitted to hope for the greatest benefit of all: that the ugly, the bigoted, the hateful, the cheapness of opportunism and all else that is small, narrow, contemptible and repulsive becomes more apparent and far less tolerable from the vantage point of the stars than it ever was from the perspective of the mudhole. After all, should we not take a cue from the fact that since the beginning, we have always placed our dreams and aspirations among the stars?

—Krafft Ehricke[1]

Beyond the Limits?

Ben Bova's significance to astrofuturism derives from his canny responsiveness to the fora and stratagems used by spaceflight advocates in pursuit of their dream. In the 1960s, he was deeply involved in the immense public and private institutional structure of the space program. In the 1970s, he found himself on the outside looking in, writing popular science and science fiction in the hope of keeping the dream alive in Apollo's aftermath. As editor for *Analog Science Fiction/Science Fact* and *Omni*, he became a prominent force in adjudicating the field's shift toward the political left. In the 1980s, he became president of the National Space Institute (NSI) and helped organize a grassroots lobby for the spaceflight agenda in Washington. His spaceflight advocacy, therefore, has covered almost the entire range of expression available to a second-generation futurist. Bova's work serves as a test case for the impact of the liberal persuasions of second-generation astrofuturists on the narrative conventions established by a largely conservative first-generation consensus. Specifically, Bova's interventions allow us to query the extent of revision possible in the context of a shifting political terrain.

Bova was president of the NSI during the time of its merger with the O'Neill-inspired L-5 Society. Through that merger and Bova's response, we see how sharply the spaceflight community was divided over the political implications of their dream. The merger between the two groups is significant because it encapsulates the conflicts that occurred between technophiles from the middle to the left of the American political spectrum in the late 1970s and early 1980s. The bulk of this chapter is devoted to gauging the effect of that conflict on Bova's astrofuturism, in both its fictional and nonfictional iterations. Bova's astrofuturism is a direct response to the political moment of its production. While relying on the sociomilitary and boys' adventure conventions of earlier futurists, Bova attempts a revision that eschews the narrative of imperial conquest for one of pluralistic inclusion. The narrative of a human advance into space becomes one of secular salvation rather than one of greedy acquisition. Indeed, he argues that the only way to resolve contemporary social and political ills, especially those involving poverty and race, is to develop space-based technology and industry. In scenario after scenario, narrative after narrative he hammers home this point: the security of democracy and the expansion of the American experiment can only occur through opening a new, perhaps endless, frontier.

The trajectory of his career makes Bova a test case for examining astrofuturism's ability to respond to the challenges posed by its critics. While deeply committed to the core values and ordinary practices of the genre, Bova has nevertheless sought to reconfigure the social relations it assumes. As a result, race, as an emblem of all the injustices that must be addressed by the space future, has become an increasingly prominent feature of his work. His futures seek compelling strategies for including formerly excluded individuals from the space-future adventure. Initially in the novels of the Kinsman saga, those strategies are found in precedents from Euro-American history and, more narrowly, in the sociomilitary form as represented by the U.S. Air Force. Bova, like others of the futurists we have examined, takes the military as the model of a meritocratic organization that can satisfy calls for a society based on equality of opportunity rather than arbitrary hierarchy. In this way, Bova imagines a space future that is more colorful than the present but which is ruled by values and systems familiar in contemporary American life. The future of the Kinsman novels is not designed by and "for all mankind," but is an American future ruled by a disciplined elite who direct an international and putatively democratic order. As a result, these futures become an improving mirror of things as they are rather than a prophetic glimpse of things that might be.

However, Bova grew dissatisfied with this solution to America's racial problems and made resolution of a history of racial injustice the central problematic of his 1990s novels *Mars* and *Return to Mars*. In these texts, he takes on the challenge of recuperating the tradition of scientific exploration foundational to the astrofuturist project while disentangling that ideal from the histories of conquest and dispossession that accompanied and perhaps even enabled its pursuit. He does so through his mixed-race protagonist whose combination of European and Navaho lineages holds out the possibility of redeeming the history of America's conquest, transcending national divisions, and integrating the races in joint progress toward a common future. By granting authority to control space settlement to the Navaho nation, Bova points to space as the new frontier that offers a fresh start, a chance not to repeat our past mistakes. Although we should not underestimate the challenge Bova poses to astrofuturist conventions by closing the Mars novels with a new Eden possessed by a dark-skinned Adam and Eve, questions about the efficacy of replacing white men with red men in a relatively stable narrative of benevolent ownership take us up to the limits of liberal astrofuturism. Bova proves that the wonderful dream is sufficiently flexible to welcome the formerly dispossessed into its ranks. But whereas the openness improves the lot of the newcomers, their assimilation does not pose a substantive challenge to the core of the genre. Their impact is limited to saving astrofuturist ideals and its connection to past imperialisms, and does not extend to revising its foundations.

Bova came to science, technology, and spaceflight through the science fiction he read as a boy. His first novel, written at the age of eighteen, was rejected without explanation by the genre's major publishers until an editor clarified the political stakes involved: "Finally one editor was kind enough to invite me to his office and explain that his company would not publish the novel, even though it was 'no worse than most of the science fiction we print.' The main reason for their rejecting the novel was that Senator Joseph McCarthy, then at the height of his power as a witch-hunter, would persecute any writer, editor, or publisher who dared suggest that the Russians were in any way superior to Americans."[2] According to Bova, this early experience gave him a valuable lesson in the limits of permissible expression in popular culture.

After graduating from Temple University, Bova found "a good job in journalism" at a small paper in the Philadelphia suburbs. However, his eyes were "full of stars" and the attractions of a secure job as a small-time newspaperman paled before the opportunities opening up in the burgeoning aerospace industry of the late 1950s. With no scientific background or technical training to speak of, the young reporter talked his way into a job as a technical editor at the Glen L. Martin Company of Baltimore, Maryland. At the time, the Martin Company, a pioneer in aviation, was under contract to the U.S. Navy to develop the new liquid-fueled rocket technology of the Second World War. Working for two years on Project Vanguard, Bova gained a ground-floor view of America's nascent space and defense industry.[3] Despite the difficulties with being in what was considered at the time a marginal technology and living through Vanguard's failure to challenge Russia's success with *Sputnik*, working on the rocket was a romantic and exciting adventure for Bova. His job at Martin meant that he was playing an active part in making the spaceflight dream a reality.[4] When his work with the aerospace pioneer ended, Bova relocated to the Boston suburb of Everett and took a job at the Avco-Everett Research Laboratory. Working in its public relations department during the 1960s, he discovered the connections between the space program and the Department of Defense that would provide the realistic texture of his near-future fiction. Reentry vehicles for ICBMs and the gasdynamic laser were among the projects he observed in development and that he helped present to government and industrial customers.[5]

During the 1960s, Bova led something of a double life. By day he worked as a sober corporate executive, guiding the marketing division at Avco. By night (and on weekends and holidays, no doubt), he maintained his position as a prominent writer of "hard science fiction." While writers such as Joanna Russ, Samuel R. Delany, and Ursula K. Le Guin were creating a New Wave in the genre, expanding its literary potential, Bova remained science fiction's version of a "moldy fig." He clung to the straightforward storytelling and technocratic values that many of its old hands treasure as the core of the genre. In his fiction and nonfiction, Bova spoke to and from the community of aerospace engineers, describing fairly accurately its political positions and representing its technical knowledge.

As the national program fell apart in the afterglow of Apollo, its NASA-focused industries laid off many ardent spaceflight advocates and futurists. It became apparent that the aerospace industry was no longer the cutting edge for the kind of activism and commitment that would fulfill the spaceflight agenda. In the early 1970s, Bova followed the lead of many fellow space futurists and left the aerospace industry to devote his full attention to science fiction. In 1972, shortly after the death of John W. Campbell, Jr., he accepted the editorial post at *Analog Science Fiction/Science Fact*. From that prominent position, Bova generated controversy by asserting his opinions regarding the connection between politics, society, and science and technology. He came to the magazine

as an unreconstructed New Frontier, Kennedy liberal identified with a pluralistic domestic agenda and a tough, cold war–inspired foreign policy. In his
editorial policy, he broke with the political conservatism that had informed
Campbell's leadership. Bova's editorial decisions included publishing stories
that raised questions of gender, race, and public policy, in ways that distressed
some *Analog* readers.

Consider, for instance, his serialization of Joe Haldeman's antiwar novel,
The Forever War. Haldeman was a veteran whose experience in Vietnam took
him to the antiwar movement and allowed him to bring the war home to the
science-fiction community. *The Forever War* explores the brutal lives of soldiers in a galactic war, alienated from the society for which they fight by the
relativistic distortions caused by interplanetary travel. The narrative is both a
metaphor for Vietnam and a critical reappraisal of the glorious militarism of
Robert Heinlein's *Starship Troopers.*[6] But despite the controversy this and
similar works generated among conservative readers, Bova's mixture of technoscience and politics was successful. In the mid-1970s, he was awarded four
Hugos, the Science Fiction Achievement Award, for best magazine editor.[7]
Over the next two decades as a writer, as the editor of *Analog* and editorial
director of *Omni* (the first mass market science-fiction magazine), and as president of the pro-space National Space Institute, Bova became a leading sup-
porter of the embattled national space program and a notable space-future
visionary.

Previous "space cadets" had worked with the Congress and various administrations to win the space race and had received a collegial welcome in the
halls of government. Those of Bova's generation found themselves standing
outside and often in an adversarial relation to the institutional matrix of government and industry. The new space advocacy groups of the late 1970s and early
1980s, such as the NSS and the Planetary Society, went to Washington with the
aim of representing "the people" rather than industry or NASA. They were reduced to the status of a special interest competing with other special interests,
such as civil and women's rights, education, conservation, gun control, and
so forth. The formerly enfranchised found themselves competing as one of the
disenfranchised for the attentions of their elected representatives.

In 1983, Bova became president of the National Space Institute (later the
National Space Society [NSS]), a Washington-based spaceflight group founded
with the help of Wernher von Braun. NSI was created by the National Space
Club in 1974 to be a "Navy League for space."[8] In its early days, the organization was supported by NASA and was meant to serve as the agency's interme-

diary between the taxpayer and the rest of the government. The institute also found allies within the aerospace industry: during Bova's tenure as president, a membership drive designed to solve the organization's financial woes was supported by industry contributions. But because of this alliance and in the highly politicized atmosphere of space activism during the 1980s, space activists on the left criticized the NSI as an "industry flack" and a "NASA fan club."[9] Fearing an escalation of cold war ambitions, critics objected to a conquest of space that would empower government and business at the expense of the common citizen.

Bova countered this fear of centralized power with his conviction that the space future would not be possible without the full participation of government and industry. Searching for the political high ground, however, he emphasized that the NSI should be a "citizen's advocacy group rather than a functionary of government or business."[10] Because he wanted it to be an activist group promoting the spaceflight agenda and the benefits of a space future to the ordinary citizen, he spent much of his time as president fostering the NSI's merger with the L-5 Society. As Bova explains it, by combining the forces of the two groups, the merger would create a powerful new advocacy organization. It would give the L-5 Society stability and an entry into the Washington scene, while the NSI would have access to the L-5's energy and cadre of young activists. The merger between the L-5 Society and the NSI took a little more than two years to consummate, and the factional strife that made it a bitter and contentious marriage had not been resolved when Bova resigned the presidency in 1988. During that time, Bova kept NSI members informed of merger negotiations and the issues involved through his column in the society's monthly magazine, *Space World*. Here we get the flavor of the political and social differences that had to be negotiated between the astrofuturist left and the right, as well as some insight into Bova's own position as what Todd Gitlin would call a "managerial liberal": a moderate who had to find common ground between the old (NSI) and the new (L-5).[11]

Bova noted in a column halfway through the merger, "NSS is a tightly-organized, centrally controlled society. The L-5 Society is a looser federation of various chapters, with a more open and democratic operating system."[12] The president goes on to contend that because of the L-5 Society's democratic character, the organization's history was rife with factional struggle that often seemed a prelude to chaos. The management styles of the two groups reflected deep divisions along the lines of age, political orientation, and "commitment":[13] "L-5 people tended to be more liberal politically, more inclined to activism in the pro-space cause, and intensely interested in the management of their organization. NSI people tended toward more conservative politics, confined their activism to programs initiated and carried out by the Washington headquarters, and seemed content to let Washington insiders run the organization."[14]

The differences between the two groups are exemplified in the conflict over the name of the new organization. Central to the controversy was the retention of "National" in defining the organization. Bova argued repeatedly that retaining the first two words of the NSI's handle was necessary because of the recruitment drive, sponsored by the aerospace industry, to which the institute committed itself before the merger. He maintained that it would have been disastrous to change names in midstream.[15] With the help of a market-research firm, both groups agreed that "Space," an important and significant indicator of their purpose, had to be kept. However, some members of the L-5 Society took exception to "National," objecting that because the spaceflight project was international, the expanded group should not identify itself with or privilege any one country. The dissenting L-5ers also thought their organization was treated as a junior partner in the new organization; indeed, under the merger arrangements, the NSI, as the National Space Society, seemed to retain more of its public character and continuity that did L-5. It looked like the NSI was making a satisfying meal out of the L-5 without paying for it: "Some L-5ers saw our unilateral name change as a slap against them. They still resent it. The merger agreement, as it now stands, says the membership of the combined organization will vote on the name after the recruitment drive is ended. There is opposition to this among the L-5 people; some of them want to vote on the name immediately. NSS is opposed to that."[16]

The seemingly trivial name debate continued throughout Bova's tenure as president of the space advocacy group as the most public indicator of the factionalism that plagued the organization until his resignation. Bova's enthusiasm for the merger came from his belief that the NSS should be an "activist organization" in the spaceflight movement. From his point of view, the differences between L-5 and the NSI were not as important as their shared conviction that the nation should pursue the space option with all deliberate speed. Bova hoped that he could find some middle ground between the right and the left that would translate into an effective space activism. However, as the 1986 *Challenger* disaster played itself out in the national media and among pro-spacers, as the recruitment drive showed no sign of reaching its goals, and as the organization's financial problems and its factional strife continued unabated, it became apparent that the merger had done more to weaken the NSS than to strengthen it.[17] While the 1988 presidential campaign ground on with no indication that any of the major candidates had any interest in making national space policy a campaign issue, Bova grew increasingly bitter about the internal battle being waged within the NSS.[18] By November 1988, he informed the membership of his resignation and turned his attention back to his creative work.

Bova has never wavered in his belief that access to the tremendous prospect of the space frontier will motivate the maintenance and extension of rights guaranteed by the U.S. Constitution. Along with more conservative astrofuturists, Bova believes that wealth is necessary for the sustenance of American values and institutions. When he talks about a space future as the only way to ensure the survival of the human race, he is concerned specifically with the survival of the "American experiment." His brand of liberalism was influenced by the election of John F. Kennedy to the presidency of the United States in 1960. Bova, who was 28 at the time, identified with the new president's youth and his New Frontier rhetoric. Kennedy's most important claim on Bova's political conscience, however, came from his pioneering support of an aggressive national space program. The fact that such support was motivated by an anti-Soviet military strategy and not the spaceflight dream did not, at the time, cause Bova or his contemporaries to doubt the sincerity of the government's initiative. What matter that Kennedy and his men did not come from the ranks of spaceflight enthusiasts and astrofuturists? The important thing was that the most powerful executive in the land had thrown his weight behind a project that could give Americans new worlds to conquer. The art of political compromise, after all, has always made strange bedfellows. From the vantage of later years, Kennedy would become, for Bova, the last resident of the White House who "knew how to lead": "He pointed us to the Moon, and we got there so swiftly and well that to many Americans it still seems like an easy stunt."[19] For Bova, the end of the Kennedy presidency marked the end of good leadership in the White House as administration officials and Congress turned their attention to the Vietnam War and pressing domestic issues.

Bova's position on post-Camelot politics is evident in his reaction to the 1986 *Challenger* accident. He laid the blame for the tragedy not on the doorstep of NASA or its contractors, but in the front parlors of the Nixon administration and Congressional liberals: "built into [Space Shuttle] design were several engineering short cuts that were forced on NASA by the politicians. In a sense, the Space Shuttle design supervisors were Richard Nixon, Ted Kennedy, William Proxmire, Walter Mondale, George McGovern, and the faceless bureaucrats at OMB [the Office of Management and Budget]."[20] Even when he lobbied the government as NSS president, Bova often found himself in opposition to both the right and the left on Capitol Hill. As a result, it is difficult to label him as belonging clearly to either the right or the left. He thought of himself as belonging to neither extreme; instead he followed a third course, which he called "promethean."

Bova's Prometheanism in effect is a liberalism that presumes the efficacy of technological solutions for political as well as material problems. The free frontier of space here stands for renewal because it calls for the acquisition and deployment of powerful technical skills and knowledges. Improvement in social relations is the by-product of meeting exotic environmental challenges with the best available instruments. As a political agenda, Bova's Prometheanism is shaped by its foundational commitment to space colonization. He explains his position in *The High Road*, the closest thing to a direct public statement of policy that the NSI was able to muster in the early 1980s. His affiliation with the group is prominently displayed on the cover of the paperback edition, and the jacket copy identifies the author as "our most visionary futurist."[21] *The High Road* can be read as a companion to Gerard O'Neill's *The High Frontier*, for both books were written in partial response to the limits to growth debate, which raged during the 1970s. Bova agreed with O'Neill's conclusion that the "no growth" solutions advocated by the limits-to-growth futurists were undesirable given a pessimistic view of political realities and human nature, and unnecessary given the vast prospect of space. *The High Road* differs from O'Neill's book in its direct explication of a political position and in its array of desirable and undesirable future scenarios from which the reader could chose.

In *The High Road*, the political world is divided between three groups: the Luddites, the Establishment, and theIsm. The nature of the Luddites is clear from Bova's use of the name for the early nineteenth-century machine breakers who resisted the disruptive influence of textile machinery on their lives. In the political world of the 1960s, the Luddite was often identified with the left in a contemporary iteration of the early resistance to industrial capitalism, which led to Marxism, socialism, and various efforts at instituting labor and consumer protections.[22] Bova is not unsympathetic to the inheritors of these causes; indeed, he points out that "Much of what these groups are trying to achieve is necessary and good. They are among those who have been fighting carcinogenic additives in our foods, unsafe factories, unsafe cars, and unhealthful environments."[23] On the other hand, he does not believe that direct political struggle has any effective role in improving the life of the common citizen. For Bova, the potential for social good lies not with any human agency, but derives from the power of the machine to transform nature into wealth that can be distributed to improve the lives of men and women. Describing the fate of the Luddite movement, Bova contends:

Today the descendents of those displaced craftsmen live in greater comfort and wealth than their embattled forebears could have imagined in their wildest fantasies. Not because the labor movements have eliminated human greed and selfishness. But because the machines—the machines the Luddites feared and tried to destroy—have generated enough wealth to give common laborers houses of their own, plentiful food, excellent medical care, education for their children, personally owned automobiles, television sets, refrigerators, stoves and all the other accouterments of modern life.[24]

Hence Bova reasserts the optimistic futurism that was a signal feature of middle-class life in the 1950s and that embraced aviation and spaceflight as symbols of inevitable prosperity.[25] According to this sentiment, progress can result only from benign change in material circumstances, not from improvements in human morality or government. Any human intervention, then, especially that of an irrational left, can only hinder, not help, the distribution of the goods that science and technology create.

Bova supports this vision of progress through the Horatio Alger–like narrative that he identifies in his own life as he measures the distance between himself and his immigrant forebears:

I am the son of a laboring man and a descendent of Italian peasants. I grew up in a row house that could most kindly be described as "modest." Yet I took it for granted that I could listen to the finest musical artist with the click of a switch. I could read the works of the greatest minds of civilization simply by walking down the street to the public library. I could admire masterpieces of painting and sculpture by riding a trolley to the Philadelphia Museum of Art. And by stepping into the Fels Planetarium of the Franklin Institute, I could begin to see the wonder of the wide, starry universe.[26]

The fruits of the Industrial Revolution gave Bova access to a world unavailable to his ancestors, immured as they were in primitive material circumstances. Technological progress allowed him to move from his working-class background into the middle class. This personal narrative is a familiar one in American political mythology, but its articulation here replaces the characteristic "luck and pluck" of Alger's heroes with technology as the necessary agent for change. It also allows Bova to de-emphasize the importance of political movements and social agency in the Americanization that European immigrants of his parents' generation underwent, and with them the possibility that the "world of opportunity" he encountered as a young man was not created without very real conflicts involving human actors.

In opposition to the Luddite, Bova offers the Promethean, a being who embraces technology and the changes that it brings. He or she believes in progress and the improvement, even perfection of humanity through ever more refined knowledges and inventions. While the Luddite looks backward and clings to the past, the Promethean rushes toward the future. The Promethean, in short, is convinced that technoscience is a force for human good more often than for evil: "It was technology, the Private Discussionans point out, that freed the slaves. . . . The steam technology that ushered in the Industrial Revolution killed off slavery. Not the religious moralists. Not the revolutionary firebrands. Not the kindly plantation owner or the hardheaded businessmen or the working free man. It was the machines. Once the looms spun by themselves, once steam power became cheaper than muscle power, slavery withered and died" (45). Any historian of technology, labor, or abolition can produce ample evidence to challenge Bova's reductive history. The transition from preindustrial to industrial culture was by no means smooth, nor did it automatically ensure that everyone within the social and political order shared in the fruits of that transition. However, the simple, optimistic determinism that Bova displays gives him the epistemological foundation necessary for creating attractive American futures. If the technological revolutions of the past can be said to have "ended slavery," then those of the future may be called upon to ease or abolish the incipient totalitarianisms and rebellions of the present. For Bova and other technological futurists of his time, any limit to growth represented the possibility that technology might be used for totalitarian ends, for scarcity would force the many to accept the dominance of the few. He realizes that this is just what the so-called Luddites fear, that technology has been and will be used to enslave rather than liberate, to enfranchise technocratic elites at the expense of a new class of "techno-peasant."[27] However, this realization does not translate into an acceptance of Luddite reasoning, which holds that the only way to avoid a dystopian future is to dismantle the centralized technological infrastructure that may make it a reality.

Bova's most powerful argument against the Luddite position derives from his theory of the relationship of technology to human survival. He asks what would happen if the beneficiaries of modern technology and scientific advance were to trade it all in for early modern and/or preindustrial technology, as suggested by some radical utopians. His answer is that we would have to accept the death of millions: "If we turned our backs on technology, if we closed the factories and shut down the power plants and went back to organic farming and returned to 'nature,' billions of people would die in a very few months. Assuming they would be content to die peacefully, of starvation and disease, without riots and revolutions and wars."[28] According to Bova, the human cost of the Luddite position is that it will call into being the very catastrophes that it wishes to avoid, empower the technocratic elites it dreads, and ensure the failure of liberty and the success of totalitarianism. He goes on to attack what he identifies as a crucial blindness in the Luddite view of desirable social orders in a world that de-emphasizes technological development and growth. He asks:

Who would die? The ghetto dwellers of every major city in the world? The villagers and herdsmen of India, Ethiopia, Guyana, Mali, Indonesia? The teeming millions of China and Japan?

The Luddites who campaign for a simpler world tacitly assume that they—white, affluent, educated—will be the survivors and beneficiaries of the "simpler" world they desire. A leaky assumption at best (44).

Bova's charge that the Luddite vision of the future, as articulated by certain communitarian and environmentalist elements of the New Left, might be racist and politically particularist is a stinging indictment. By contrast, he implies that the Promethean position, with its recognition that the steam engine "destroyed" slavery rather than extending its lease in the American economy, is more likely to generate futures that will resolve the inequities of past and present. He expands his thesis to imply that the money spent on Great Society programs of the 1960s did little, if anything, to alleviate the problems of the poor, especially those of urban blacks and Latinos. The money devoted to the welfare state thus would be better spent if it were invested in high technology industries, such as computers and electronics, related to the exploration of space. He believes that this investment would do more to alleviate inner-city poverty than anything the War on Poverty had tried, because investing in space would create jobs on earth:

The money is not spent *in* space, it is spent *on* space. Actually it is spent here on Earth, on jobs for American workers and profits for American companies. It is not merely the aerospace industry that makes profits. It is not scientists and engineers alone who receive paychecks. Every dollar spent on space has a multiplier effect in the national economy. Scientists buy groceries, believe it or not. And houses, clothes, cars, baby bottles, newspapers, heating fuel, tobacco, liquor, furniture, household appliances, electricity, even toothpaste and toilet paper. They employ plumbers, housepainters, letter carriers, baby sitters, electricians, television servicemen, physicians, grocery clerks, secretaries, beauticians, barbers, dentists, and even psychiatrists. (208–9)

The indirect "multiplier effect" of space investment, rather than direct engagement with the causes and consequences of poverty, will make Americans rich. And, more importantly, it will offset the danger of political revolution here on earth.

In the political ferment of the 1970s, Bova's arguments for the economics of space did not go unchallenged. Dissent came from Congressional liberals who defended the Great Society programs desired by a goodly portion of their constituencies, and from a newly invigorated left that questioned the cost of a space frontier in light of pressing domestic problems. The political voice that served as the iconic focus of liberal/left dissent from the space vision and its economics came from the nation's black community:

> Whenever I recite the economics litany in public, I am always asked, "What's in it for me?" Usually the questioner is a black man who sees that the space program may be great for white engineers who live in nice suburban developments, but has a suspicion that it won't do anything for the black ghettoes of our cities.
>
> Yet an expanding space program that has a positive impact on the national economy can improve life in the cities, even in the urban ghettoes. When the economy improves, everybody benefits. Job opportunities increase at all levels. (211–12)

Bova's authority for the space future as solution to the nation's ills is again his own experience, this time in the aerospace engineering community. In an interesting passage in *The High Road*, he recounts the experiences of a group of RCA engineers who initiated a space science program in a New Jersey high school. Here they leave the cloister of their professional lives and discover the urban poor: "What they found, once they actually visited the school, shocked them to their souls. Illiteracy. No books. Hostility to any stranger. Total indifference to learning. And yet a spark was there, a yearning for something better than the ghetto had to offer. With lumps in their throats, the sleek white middle-aged RCA scientists and engineers 'got down' with the black and Hispanic teen-agers of Camden High. Both sides learned a lot" (213). What the professionals learned was that, given a chance, the students they encountered could become excited and intellectually stimulated by projects in science and technology. Under their guidance, the students designed experiments that could be taken into orbit by the space shuttle. In this instance, the students could see that their efforts had meaning and effects in the real world. Bova concludes, "It was never skin color nor economic level nor inherent IQ that held those kids in the ghetto. It was isolation from the real world, the world of opportunity. RCA presented the teen-agers with an opportunity to reach beyond the ghetto. The students responded" (213).

These passages indicate the mix of ideological elements from which Bova draws to bolster his arguments for investment in space. He exhibits faith in elites, particularly scientists and engineers, to use their knowledge and position to benefit the less fortunate. When, in his fiction, he recognizes the danger that exploitative political and economic elites pose to any ameliorative order, he turns again to the transformative power of the space frontier and is reassured that the scale of its abundance will defuse the selfish impulses of its pioneers. Because there will be more than enough to go around, benefits eventually will trickle down to those who wait their turn. But if this faith in experts and trickle-down economics positions him on the right of the political spectrum, Bova's faith in the machine also resonates, however unself-consciously, with a similar faith expressed in the scientific socialism of Marx and Engels. And his self-conscious Prometheanism does borrow something from leftist critiques of "the Establishment," which he identifies as "a mix of major corporations and federal agencies. Between them, they make most of the business and governmental decisions for the US" (47). Bova's definition and critique of the Establishment seems limited to the moment when Americans became interested in national energy policy during the oil crisis of the mid-1970s. The greatest sin that he identifies in the Establishment is that its policies lack long-term vision. The Establishment all too often focuses on short-term profits for corporations, readily available resources, and the maintenance of political power (48–55).

In Bova's political grammar, the Establishment and the Luddites form an oppositional dichotomy that marks the battleground on which space policy has to fight. "Here is the basic power struggle of our century," he writes, "the centralizers vs. the decentralizers; the big vs. the little; the corporations vs. the people" (56). His Promethean would split the difference between the two, creating a third way toward the high road to space and thence to an abundant life for planet Earth's inhabitants. Bova believes that space would provide room enough for the preferred technologies and political styles of both sides: "Will the riches brought back from space benefit the cause of centralization or decentralization? My suspicion is that it will help us all, and that the wealth awaiting us in space is so vast that it will overwhelm today's arguments between Big and Little, just as the discovery of America silenced the wars between Christianity and Islam" (57). The exploitation of space renders irrelevant the disagreement between right and left in American political practice. Only in this way, Bova believes, can a space future be assured.

Bova's preferred method of underlining the possibilities inherent in the space frontier is to write narratives that present what Darko Suvin would call "optimal" and "pessimal" alternatives. These scenarios amount to miniature science-fiction tales whose purpose is to sketch out the near future in relation to the social, political, and technological parameters that Bova deems relevant. The four futures outlined in *The High Road* focus primarily on the domestic consequences of taking the road to space. The first three narrate what Bova thought would happen if the spaceflight initiative remained a low priority for the American government and the people. These futures take place before the presidential election of 2000, and they amount to a referendum on whether or not the United States will survive to be a dominant power in the twenty-first century. Future One is that of a nation in economic decline: "There are forty million unemployed in the United States of America. Ever since the economic Collapse of the late 1980s, the national standard of living has plummeted until now, at the turn of the century, most Americans live no better than their forebears did two centuries ago" (65–66). In this future, the American century has ended, and the nation's citizens have become economic refugees suffering political oppression at home and fearful contempt abroad. Bova establishes the energy crisis of the 1970s as the first shot across the bow of the nation's prosperity. In that context, the only way to avoid this dystopia is to develop space-based energy resources, starting with the solar-power satellites championed by O'Neill.

Future Two sets out what would happen should the nation decide not to pursue the mixture of ground-based nuclear and space-based solar resources that Bova advocates. Relying instead on coal, American industry is productive enough to provide full employment. However, the economy offers little leeway in the pursuit of life, liberty, and happiness. It also exacts a horrendous toll from the environment:

Coal saved America from going under. Sure, some of the medical people give out scare stories about the rising rates of cancer and lung disease, and the few eco-freaks that haven't been rounded up still write their underground tracts about acid rain destroying the Great Lakes and the croplands of the Midwest. But who pays attention to those nuts? Nobody who wants to work regularly.

There's oil to be had, if your company can afford it. And if your corporate executives know how to speak Arabic. (65–66)

The xenophobic edge to this future points to the connection between nationalist sentiment and moderate to conservative astrofuturism. If the argument can be made that space-based resources will undermine the ability of Arab countries to hold the energy-hungry West at ransom (or to demand a "fair" price based on the ancient laws of supply and demand—it depends on your point of view), then Bova is willing to make it. This is the kind of flexibility from which political coalitions are built.

Future Three measures the social impact of what might happen if America does not bring itself to "do the right thing." Here Bova imagines that the government's inability to distribute equitably an energy tax exacerbates the already cruel disparities in American society: the rich, who can afford solar-power systems for private homes, are allowed to escape the increasingly high taxes designed to "punish" the use of oil and gas. The taxes, of course, are instituted with the stated intention of saving the environment. The poor, who cannot afford to "go solar," have to pay them. The result is an armed conflict that throws race into bold relief: "Civil War has begun in the United States. On one side, the ghetto dwellers of the big American cities: mostly black, brown, yellow. Against them: the affluent middle class of white and blue-collar workers who live in the suburbs and the farmers. In the middle: the federal government (mostly white) and the US Army (mostly black)" (83). The ensuing civil war divides the armed services along racial lines and prompts the president to suspend the upcoming election while attempting to hold the Soviets at bay (84).

These pessimal futures constitute what Bova understood to be the main parameters of futures effected by lack of access to the space frontier. Poverty, racial conflict, the breakdown of Constitutional protections, environmental damage, and the loss of superpower status—a catalog of ills that could end the American experiment. Future Four moves from the pessimal to the optimal. It does not, however, delineate a perfect world. Starvation and unemployment continue to plague the Third World, but solar-power satellites and space stations orbit the earth, providing the energy needed by developing nations. Space creates "new jobs and income" for their citizens and allows the industrialized nations to wean themselves from dependence on Mideast oil. In Bova's scheme, this is a world with a future that is open to all. The problems of overpopulation, poverty, political terror, and war—all inevitable consequences of the limits to growth—have been defused by access to the limitless potentials of space.

It is important to note that in this optimal future, Bova moves the focus of his scenario from the domestic scene to the stage of international politics, as though it is not necessary to detail the benefits of space-born economic abundance at home. Instead, a rosy picture may be painted of the kind of benefits that the Third World can expect. What is left unsaid is the very real political changes and dislocations that might result from a U.S.-led exploitation of space. At the moment when Bova could explain just how this new abundance would fulfill the promises of the American system, he averts his (and our) gaze. Certainly this is an inspired stratagem if one hopes to build coalitions with powerful elements of the culture that might not like the nature of changes inspired by space-born wealth.[29]

Brothers in Arms

Bova's fiction mirrors the political indeterminacy evident in his nonfiction, mixing engagement with questions from the left with a conservative, if pragmatic, acceptance of the importance of governmental and military resources to the spaceflight dream. Again, Bova hopes to resolve the two warring tendencies in American politics with the material and spiritual benefits gathered from the exploration of space. For him, the high road to space is not to be taken as an extension of terrestrial imperialism; indeed, he has often remarked that the conquest of space is a ridiculous concept. Instead, the space frontier is to be the site of political, social, and economic renewal. The expansion into space is the only way that the values he believes central to Western civilization and the American experiment can survive in the new millennium.

Bova's social, political, and technological program of human salvation in the space future is most explicitly drawn in the space future epic he has written around the life of Chester Arthur "Chet" Kinsman. Drawing from by now familiar materials, he began work on Kinsman's story in the late 1950s writing a novel that, according to the author, "predicted the space race of the 1960s."[30] This was the inaugural work that publishers, fearful of the power of the House Un-American Activities Committee, refused to publish. Evidently a story in which the Soviet Union appears as a not unsympathetically drawn technological rival was too hot to handle. Undaunted and encouraged by Arthur C. Clarke, Bova continued to develop the ideas and characters that were to form the background to the Kinsman story. During the 1960s, pieces of his space future appeared in several science-fiction magazines and anthologies. In the late 1970s, the writer revised and collected these pieces into a pair of novels, *Millennium* (1976) and *Kinsman* (1979), updating his near future in light of contemporary events. In 1987, Bova released the novels as a single narrative, *The Kinsman Saga*, which describes the full trajectory of Chet Kinsman's life from his early days as a military jet jockey with the "right stuff," to his successful establishment of the first lunar colony as an independent nation, and finally to his death in a space station.

Part of what makes *The Kinsman Saga* and its early versions interesting in the context of astrofuturism is its fictive representation of aerospace history, its retelling of contemporary events in a form accessible to a popular audience. Bova calls upon the heroes and narrative strategies common in popular fiction to make sense of the largest technoscientific project of the postwar era. Through Kinsman, we are given an insider's view of military aviation during the early days of jet propulsion at Edwards Air Force Base, the test pilot subculture from which the first astronaut corps were recruited, the glory days of the national space program (with Chet Kinsman replacing Neil Armstrong as the first man on the Moon), and the establishment of a joint American/Soviet city on the Moon by the end of the twentieth century. As events outpaced his imagination, at least with regard to putting men on the Moon, Bova came to perceive the Kinsman stories as mythic biography and political extrapolation rather than prediction. As the protagonist whose character invests Bova's space future with its claim to moral authority, Kinsman is designed to embody a political sensibility that is both liberal and pragmatic. He wanders through Bova's epic as a tragic hero, starting as a fairly innocent space cadet whose personal life and the business-as-usual-politics of a world quickly running out of options delivers the hard knocks necessary for his maturity. Through him, we know that the future will have a uniquely American character. And in a gesture now conventional to astrofuturism, we measure the validity of the future through its incorporation of racial others: "Kinsman himself is a symbol. A young American male, full of the adventure of flying, who brings both love and death to the pristine realm of outer space. In *Millennium*, he becomes a Christ figure, and his closest friend, Frank Colt, takes on the role of Judas. Colt himself symbolizes the dilemma of the black man in modern America" (ix). While Chet Kinsman is symbolic of American hope, Frank Colt symbolizes American fears of the destruction of hope. Bova's creation of a credible American future rests in large measure on resolving the symbolic and political dilemmas represented by Colt. Bova's experiment implies that if Colt can become an active agent in an astrofuturist narrative, then the constellation of problems represented by race in America can be solved. Chet Kinsman is a type familiar from Heinlein's space-cadet novels of the 1950s: the technophilic, middle-class white male who is the key to future salvation. He is also a grown-up spaceman whose family background, career in the U.S. Air Force, and coming of age in the 1960s place him in a recognizable historical moment. Locating Kinsman's story in the near past and future of contemporary history allows Bova to address directly the political and social issues of his era. Using the didacticism that remains an important feature of hard science fiction, Bova allows Kinsman to take part in political discussions, which reveal the parameters of the character's sympathies. As the scion of a family of Main Line Philadelphia Quakers, Kinsman is heir to a political tradition that might be called establishment liberal. As he explains to a group of student activists in a Berkeley coffee bar, " 'an uncle of mine is a U.S. Senator. My grandfather was Governor of the Commonwealth of Pennsylvania. Several other family members are in public service. I've been involved in political campaigning since I was old enough to hold a poster' " (13). Like all families who have a tradition of public service and believe in the responsibility of power, the Kinsmans are expected to follow a well-defined trajectory from cradle to grave. Since they take their Quakerism very seriously, Chet inherits a pacifism that is at odds with the demands of his chosen profession. Despite his protestations that he is in the Air Force only because of his desire to become an astronaut, his commission makes him the family's "black sheep" (43).

The political traditions the Quaker Kinsmans evoke and Chet's partial alienation from them serve a double function. First, it allows Bova to establish early on that Chet Kinsman is motivated by the highest ideals available within the mainstream of American political culture: freedom, equality, and a desire for social justice. Despite his role as a career Air Force officer, the reader is asked not to view him simply as a militaristic patriot. Second, in the tradition of boys' adventure literature, the reader is expected to sympathize with Chet through his alienation from his family and to admire his independence. By the end of the epic, it is clear that our hero is simply following his own path to the fulfillment of the family's best traditions. It is only his desire to become an astronaut that has led him away from playing the role of dutiful son. In the end, he will prove true to his heritage by making the lunar nation of Selene possible, and thereby allowing for the fulfillment of the American Quaker tradition of founding a new society in a new world.

In Bova's near future narrative, Chet Kinsman's Quakerism as well as his membership in the armed forces lend him a moral and pragmatic authority. His pragmatism derives from Bova's position that the spaceflight dream can only be fulfilled with government and, therefore, military support. Kinsman's position in the Air Force allows him to move from the role of jet pilot to that of astronaut. Whenever he is distracted from that goal and commanded to do the job of a highly trained military officer, Chet agonizes over the likelihood that he might be forced to take another human life. Playing out this conflict in Kinsman's basic philosophy and his space future aspirations, Bova describes the "high ground" essential to his future vision.

The space politics of *The Kinsman Saga*'s raison d'être develop against the backdrop of a near future in which economic and political repression is the order of the day. Bova shows the reader a nation that still sets the pace for the free world but whose core values are falling victim to its pursuit of the cold war, its overpopulation, and the limits of natural resources. The result is widespread poverty, McCarthy style witch-hunts, and global militarism:

America was on a wartime footing, almost. The oil shock of ten years ago had inexorably pushed the United States toward military measures. The Star Wars strategic defense satellites that could protect the nation against Soviet missiles were being deployed in orbit, despite treaties, despite opposition at home, despite—or because of—the Soviet deployment of a nearly identical system. Unemployment at home was countered by a new public-service draft that placed millions of eighteen-year-olds in police forces, hospitals, public works projects, and the armed services. Dissidence was smothered by fear:

fear of dangers real and imagined, fear of government retaliation, fear of ruinous unemployment and economic collapse, and the ultimate fear of the nuclear war that hovered remorselessly on the horizon waiting for the moment of Armageddon. (170–71)

This essentially is an updated version of the dystopian scenarios that Bova describes in his popular science. Chet's world is one in which superpower rivalry, domestic unrest, and the curtailment of civil liberties are symptomatic of the material and spiritual limits, which the earthly environment imposes on industrial civilization. Kinsman believes that the only way disaster can be avoided is by founding a new society beyond the Earth's envelope that will set an example for the world, even if it has no immediate benefit for the millions who will never travel into space:

"We've got to start someplace. And we've got to start now, right *now*, before we sink so far back into the mud that we won't have the energy or the materials or the people to do the job. Civilization's cracking apart, Diane."

"And you want to run away from the catastrophe."

"No! I want to prevent it." Realizing the truth of it as he spoke the words, Kinsman listened to himself, as surprised as Diane at his revelation. "We can build a new society on the Moon. We can set an example, just the way the new colonies of America set an example for the old world of Europe. We can send energy back to the Earth, raw materials—but most of all, we can send hope." (193–94)

If humanity can get "out there," all its problems will be solved. Each man and woman will have the resources of a millionaire, and the human race will reach the moral and physical perfection often dreamed of in Western religion and philosophy.[31] In this dream, human salvation or utopia does not result from political movements or ideologies, but from the pragmatic calculations of heroic individuals (and the groups they lead) to gain control of those resources. In *The Kinsman Saga*, Chet Kinsman is the individual who offers humanity that measure of control.

The appropriate question to ask here is whether Bova's pragmatism leaves the existing political and economic order intact as humanity goes out onto the space frontier. On Earth, Kinsman is part of a governing structure that borrows valor from the mobilization of its citizens through military hierarchies. To some, the military is a desirable solution to various demands from the left because it incorporates minorities (the men first) and women (of whatever color) into a formerly racialized status quo without upsetting "traditional" privileges. In a society that by mid-century was aware that American prestige abroad might be damaged by the color line at home, the appeal to the sociomilitary form constitutes a negotiated settlement between social tradition and innovation. The American social experiment, which Bova hopes the space future will foster, depends in large part on how the question of race is resolved. In *The Kinsman Saga*, this resolution is embodied in the figure of Frank Colt, the Negro, Black, Afro-American, African American (to quote what he has been called in the various versions of the Kinsman story) Air Force officer, who is Kinsman's best friend, rival, and, eventual successor.

Franklin Colt is the very model of an angry black man circa 1968 trying to make it in a white man's world. Kinsman meets him at Vandenberg Air Force Base during his first assignment outside the academy. From the beginning, it is clear that Colt is not a easy man to get along with. He is aware of his position as the only black in the Air Force's astronaut corps. He makes certain that he has what it takes to succeed in the system and is equally certain that he will not be allowed to do so because of his race.[32] Paranoid and hot-tempered, Colt's attitude and prowess earn him the nickname "Black Napoleon," and isolation. In the conversation that introduces Colt to the reader, Kinsman is asked to consider the importance of race to the black lieutenant's isolation:

"He's a black loner in an otherwise white outfit."
    "That's got nothing to do with it."
    "The hell it hasn't."
    Kinsman started to reply, hesitated. There were a dozen arguments he could make, three dozen examples he could show of how Colt had deliberately rebuffed attempts at camaraderie. But one vision in Kinsman's mind kept his tongue silent: he recalled the squad's only black officer eating alone, day after day, night after night. He never tried to join the others at their tables in the mess hall, and no one ever sat down at his.[33]

Colt's social isolation is underscored by his position as the best pilot in the squad and the highest scorer on the corps training test. In the symbolism of *The Kinsman Saga*, Colt represents both Kinsman's shadow self and, in a strange way, his apprentice. Although they represent radically different social backgrounds, both men come from Philadelphia, the "City of Brotherly Love" (35). They are the top men in their squad, blessed with an intuitive knack for operating and maintaining the technology fundamental to their jobs, and are touched in similar ways by the awe that visits the true astronaut when confronted by the majesty of space (54). In the end, it is the kinship that they find on the high frontier that allows them to remain friends, despite the insider/outsider social dichotomy that they represent in the narrative. Without Kinsman, Colt could not survive in the Air Force; without Colt, Kinsman's space future dream cannot survive.

Chet Kinsman serves as Colt's mentor despite the latter's strong personality, in part because of Kinsman's status as an insider. Whenever the two get into a sticky situation, together or apart, Kinsman is able to protect them both through his use of family connections and the rule book. After an escapade in which Colt and one of the women from their squad seek relief from the claustrophobic condition of their space shuttle by taking an unauthorized EVA (extravehicular activity), Kinsman places himself between them and older officers with a very thin lie. Shortly afterward, a suspicious but grateful Colt asks him, "Why'd you do that?" He responds, "Frank, you've memorized the book of regulations but you haven't figured out the people yet. He won't kick us out for something *I've* done. Not unless it's a lot more serious than this" (47). Bova's portrayal of Kinsman's willingness to protect Colt from the prejudice of their superiors allows him to depict the character as an insider without prejudice. By risking a little, Kinsman makes room for "others" within the Air Force's white, male hierarchy.

Bova's use of Frank Colt within the saga is important because of the author's attempt to imagine a minority character who speaks both to the political conflicts that rage around race and to his hopes for resolving them through the colonization of new worlds. As an angry young black man, Colt rides the knife edge of outright opposition to a racist society and chip-on-the-shoulder assimilation. His motives for joining the Air Force and becoming a pioneer in its aerospace program are both personal and political, a consequence of family history and the very real cost of dissent in an unjust society: " 'I don't just wanna be good,' Colt was saying. 'I got to be the best. I got to show these honkies that a black man is better than they are.' " " 'You're not going to win many friends that way.' " " 'Don't give a shit. I'm gonna be a general someday. Then we'll see how many friends I got' " (64). Colt goes on to explain how the example of his brother taught him the price of a more militant opposition to the status quo:

"My brother, he's all hot and fired up to be a revolutionary. Goin' around the world looking for a war to fight against oppression and injustice. Regular Lone Ranger. Wanted me to join the underground here in the States and fight for justice against The Man.

"Underground? In the States?"

"Yeah. FBI damn near grabbed him a year or so back."

"What for?"

"Hit a bank to raise money for the People's Liberation Army."

"He's one of those."

"Not anymore. There ain't no PLA anymore. Most of them are dead. The rest scattered. I watched my brother playin' cops and robbers . . . didn't look like much fun to me." (64)

Hence both of Bova's main protagonists have been tempted to join radical dissent against the establishment and both have found reasons to resist temptation (14–19). But, according to the political logic that Bova wants to establish, this does not mean that they have been co-opted. Colt, in particular, opts for a conscious strategy of working inside the system to beat it:

"So I decided I ain't gonna fight The Man. I'm gonna *be* The Man."

"If you can't beat 'em . . ."

"Looks like I'm joinin' 'em, yeah," Colt said, with real passion in his voice. "But I'm just workin' my way up the ladder to get to the top. Then *I'll* start giving the orders. And there are others like me, too. We're gonna have a black President one of these days, you know."

"And you'll be his Chief of Staff."

"Could be." (65)

Frank Colt is not supposed to be an Uncle Tom, but a closet revolutionary. Yet despite what seems to be a radical edge to his polemic, it soon becomes clear that Colt, unlike Kinsman, has no vision of a social order that is an alternative to the one within which he operates. While Kinsman can imagine a future in which humanity is freed from the burden of the armed status quo that he otherwise defends, all of Colt's energy, skill, and intelligence is harnessed to the goal of proving himself. His amorous adventures with white women, his "black but better than thou" pose, and his patriotic anticommunism indicate a man who desperately wants to belong.

Not surprisingly, as Colt advances in rank, he becomes less of an adversary of the system and more its staunch defender. Bova implies that this movement is not so much a process of Colt selling out as of a nation that improves as the world around it worsens:

Colt's superpatriotism always surprised and embarrassed [Kinsman]. Childhood prejudice, he knew. Blacks were anti-Establishment when you were a kid and you expected them all to be anti-Establishment forever.

But America was truly multiracial now. There were black generals, Hispanic bank presidents, Oriental board chairmen. The talk was that there would be a black President before much longer. (160)[34]

As Bova's future America changes to fully assimilate its former slaves and aliens, Colt becomes more comfortable with his role inside its borders. However, the improvement of race relations on earth is more apparent than real. Chet may think that America's multiracial face indicates improvement, but Colt knows better. He fears the fate of his militant brother who "fought for what he believed in: black power. Wound up in a shittin' hut in Dahomey, in

Africa, hidin' out from the FBI and CIA and Lord knows who else" (392). That fate throws doubt on the efficacy of overt militancy as a successful political strategy. Colt learns his lesson and chooses the only other path open to him, participation. Because Colt is not interested in serving the system but in owning it, Bova presents him as much more dangerous than his brother whom the system crushed with contemptuous ease. Like Kinsman, Colt works for the system in pursuit of private goals that are more important, in the final analysis, than the establishment he ostensibly serves. Within the logic of his position, therefore, Colt's defense of the system is more self-interested than patriotic or oppositional.

Be that as it may, while Frank Colt evolves into a valuable ally in Kinsman's campaign to create a permanent human settlement on the Moon, it is still Chet Kinsman who has the unique vision and motivating force that opens the door for the new social alternatives that the colony represents. He does so by putting together a political and economic package that combines military, government, and corporate interests. Kinsman's package contains an argument for the efficacy of implementing the Strategic Defense Initiative (SDI), which Bova advocates in his popular science.[35] It also establishes the space frontier as the only alternative to a Great Society, which Bova believes will fail. In convincing a liberal senator not to block legislation for the lunar base, Kinsman enumerates the failings of liberal social policy and his belief in space colonization's ability to salvage the human race without overt liberal activism:

"A solid industrial base in orbit. Shipping lunar ores to orbital factories can start the ball rolling on the solar power satellites and all the other peacetime industries in space that will help people on Earth. Opening the door to all the raw materials and energy in space. New jobs. New Technologies. New industries. Space is our escape hatch, Neal. If we use it wisely we can put an end to the causes for wars on Earth. . . .

"Everything else is taking from Peter to pay Paul. That's what causes wars, Neal: trying to steal a bigger slice of the pie. All those welfare programs you're pushing, all they do is prolong the misery. Space operations can open up new sources of wealth, make the pie bigger."

"For the rich. For the corporations."

"For everybody! If you do it right."[36]

Here we have the core of Bova's futurist pragmatism. He accepts the neoconservative rhetoric embedded in advocacy for SDI and antiwelfarism for the sake of a space frontier that will serve as a safety valve for all the discontents of American civilization. Through his unique negotiation of the interests represented by this rhetoric, Kinsman becomes a blue-suited savior offering a chance of escape and renewal on the high frontier.

At the end of book one of *The Kinsman Saga*, "Kinsman," that frontier is described as American-dominated. The end result is a *pax americana* enforced by American control of space resources and the high ground of earth orbit, despite Bova's espousal of global partnership. Book two of the saga, "Millennium," presents a space future that is shared across the division of the iron curtain and in which nationalism, not racism, is the primary obstacle. As Kinsman works to transform the American/Soviet moon mining colony/hospital complex into the nation of Selene, he finds that lunar independence has wider implications than the creation of a new player in the game of nations. Selene, through its control of Star Wars technology, satellite-based control of the weather, and its position on the threshold of the solar system's vast resources, can usher in a new era of peace and prosperity for all humanity. By the end of the book, Colt, who opposes independence for reasons involving patriotism and fear of a racial holocaust, authorizes this new era by joining the cause in the last moments of Kinsman's life. In Bova's symbolic schema, Colt transcends the role of Judas and takes on the mantle of Peter, the rock on which the church of the future is to be built (565–66).

To reach the point where nations on the space frontier will transcend the petty nationalisms of the old world, Bova has to find some way of legitimizing the revolution Kinsman leads. If Chet is to be the George Washington of a new, postnational world, then his alienation from allegiance to the United States of America, the ancient repository of the rights of man, has to be explicated.[37] Thus, the initial reason for Selene's revolution has to do with Kinsman's desire to prevent the final conflict between the United States and the Soviet Union, in order to prevent the end of the human world.[38] The second reason has to do with the foundations of patriotism and duty to one's country. Bova has Kinsman raise the question of whether the cause of freedom is being served by the United States and, hence, whether Americans opposed to the revolution act according to the fundamental values of their country:

"Think about it," Kinsman said. "Look at what's happening down there. Fuel shortages. Food shortages. Riots. More people in jail than on the streets. Army patrols in every city. Curfews. Surveillance. What the hell kind of nation is that?" . . .

Kinsman shook his head. "The two of you—open your eyes. That wonderful land of the free and home of the brave—it's gone." With a chill in his heart, Kinsman realized it was something he had known for years, but ignored, buried, hid away from his conscious thoughts. "That beautiful nation died in 1963, while we were still kids. May someday it'll be beautiful and free again, but not the way it's going now. Not if it's subjected to nuclear attack." (428)

Naming the moment of the loss of America's most cherished values is a powerful but ambiguous move. It locates Bova as a member of the generation that
adopted John F. Kennedy as *their* president, the man who would lead the nation
to new heights of greatness and fulfillment, whose loss meant that the utopian
moment of American renewal never came. Chet might be excused for believing
that American innocence died with Kennedy. However, believing this makes
the struggles to fulfill the American dream that occurred after Kennedy's death
seem irrelevant to our future condition. Identifying 1963 as the final moment of
the American dream before its resuscitation in the lunar nation of Selene allows
us to avoid serious consideration of the militant politics of race and gender that
followed. Perhaps Bova understands subsequent decades as a time when extremes of the political spectrum captured the political landscape and created the
militarized America of which Chet complains. This passage suggests that what
followed after that moment, the conflicts and changes by which the 1960s are
remembered, represents the decline of a nation, the shredding of the American
experiment. Here an expansion into space is presented as a technical fix for the
Earth-bound efforts—including the civil rights movement, the war on poverty,
and the women's liberation movement—that sought to reform the American
political system. If we go to space, we can avoid the difficult political conversations forced by these struggles and avoid as well the need to create equity in
our common public life.

Thus, in *The Kinsman Saga*, the locus of freedom moves from the American west to the space frontier. The United States is no longer the protector of
the free world but a source of oppression. Limited by the Earth's environment,
it can no longer afford its democratic ideals. Selene, synthesized from the Soviet and American colonies on the Moon, creates a new nation that forces the
world to transcend national identities and rivalries. The leaders of an otherwise
powerless United Nations recognize that Selene's membership and access to
its overwhelming technological power represent the possibility of peaceful
world government (498). Bova's space future, therefore, proceeds beyond an
argument for the human colonization of space and toward the ethical ideal of a
world government that would benefit the peoples of all nations. The United
Nation's Latin American Secretary General, Emanuel De Paolo, explains that
global problems cannot be solved by nations. In fact, the selfish insistence on
national sovereignty is the greatest impediment to the resolution of the world's
ills: "Each nations [*sic*] considers itself sovereign, a law unto itself, with no authority to hinder its actions. All nations, even the youngest of Africa and Asia,
demand complete authority to do as they wish within their own borders. What

they accomplish is stupidity! Population crises, famines, racial massacres. And eventually, inevitably—there is war" (535).

Bova's background as an employee in the American aerospace industry and his pro-space lobbying on Capitol Hill makes the internationalist political solution that he presents in *The Kinsman Saga* startling. As a propagandist, we would expect him to argue for a continued expansion of an American empire on the space frontier, in the manner of his predecessors. Instead, he dispenses with a patriotic commitment to an unlimited American future for one which transcends and fulfills that commitment in more generous form. De Paolo points out to Kinsman that Alexander Hamilton foresaw the problem of nationalism: "He wrote, 'Do not expect nations to take the initiative in developing restraints upon themselves' " (536). Through Hamilton, Bova invokes the authority of America's revolutionary past to underwrite the "treasons" the UN and Selene commit against earthly sovereignty. Moreover, De Paolo appeals to historical precedent again by invoking the same evolutionary teleology common to European and American imperialisms:

"You believed you were acting to save your world—your Selene—from being destroyed by decisions made here on Earth. Then you found that perhaps you could save the people of Earth from destroying themselves. Now we offer you something much grander, and much more difficult to achieve: a chance to rid the Earth of the curse of nationalism. A chance to move human society to its next evolutionary phase. A world government is the only chance we have to avoid global catastrophe." (539)

By gaining its own sovereignty, therefore, Selene continues a pattern of evolutionary historical development. The only way to ensure the survival of democratic values—the promise of life, liberty, and prosperity for all—is to impose them on a recalcitrant populace, and thus to follow the course of empire and utopia from the West to outer space. In essence, Bova would agree with fellow futurist Buckminster Fuller that for the inmates of spaceship Earth, it is either "Utopia or Oblivion."[39]

Red Man on a Red Planet, a Scientific Romance

Transcending or forgetting the past is a recurrent gesture in astrofuturism. It encodes a hope for something better and it serves as a balm for the wounds caused by our histories. But can the space frontier really be "for all mankind" if it is directed by a white elite committed to an extractive capitalism? Is it to be the triumphalist reinvention of an American nation that mythologizes the costs of its past? Are people of color equals in the space future vision or only clients who may visit the frontier as long as they behave? Can a nonwhite character carry the visionary burden of the space future in a medium that is often considered the exclusive preserve of white males? What would happen if a minority character were to direct the wonderful dream?

In the 1990s, Ben Bova's astrofuturism offered some answers to a nation divided by its racializing practices. For Bova, race-based inequities became emblematic of the range of terrestrial ills that had to be addressed, in fact could only be addressed by the space future. Whereas social renewal in the Kinsman series is the gift of a white patriarch, in his planetary novels of the 1990s, it is directed by black, Hispanic, and Native American men. In *Mars* (1993) and *Return to Mars* (1999), the writer reverses the field of race and nation to heal historic hurts. If astrofuturism provides an escape from the social and political problems we have inherited from older generations, then the history addressed by Bova's Mars novels is that of the European-led conquest of the Americas. Bova conducts a frontal assault on this problem with James Fox "Jamie" Waterman, a half–Native American (Navaho) geologist who is the central protagonist of the novels and a symbolic liaison between the planets and the races of his author's space future.

The First Mars Expedition of *Mars* plays out the venture in fairly straightforward von Braunian terms, with a dash of O'Neill thrown in for flavor. The expedition that arrives at the fourth planet is a multiracial armada sponsored by an international consortium of governments. Following von Braun's lead in *The Mars Project*, Bova imagines a technical infrastructure reminiscent of the grand engineering projects and progress narratives of the early twentieth century. The operational hierarchy of the Mars explorers is also familiar, represented by the astronauts and cosmonauts who shepherd the scientific staff. The only concessions made by the imagined engineering of the expedition to the discoveries of post-Apollo spaceflight are its solutions for avoiding the long-term physiological problems associated with microgravity and its use of advanced computing to ease expeditionary labor. Unfortunately, the novel also supposes the reinvention of an industrial infrastructure that was dismantled in the 1970s. It is, therefore, almost retrogressive in its appeal to astrofuturist conventions.[40] The second expedition of *Return to Mars* is another matter. It exchanges the still powerful legacy of German-American big science for a downsized "cheaper, faster, better" model suited to the fiscal constraints of the 1990s.[41] In this environment, the new instrument of planetary exploration is the Mars Direct system pioneered and championed by aerospace engineer Robert Zubrin.[42] Zubrin's model for small-scale, crewed planetary exploration moves

Bova away from the government-sponsored, brute force projections avowed by both von Braun's paradigm and O'Neill's revision.

Zubrin values the small, privately funded ventures that succeeded in conquering the Arctic and the Antarctic in the early twentieth century. He argues that the manned space program of the 1960s was no different from the great Victorian expeditions—gigantic, unwieldy affairs that often ended in spectacular failure.[43] Only when explorers avoided government or military sponsorship did they succeed in their goals. Zubrin notes the willingness of Roald Amundsen to live off the land and follow the examples of circumpolar peoples in his effort to understand and survive in the new lands he encountered. In *Return to Mars* (*Return*), Bova follows Zubrin's logic, imagining an expedition cut off from government support and political compromise. The writer's goal is to produce a fiction whose heroic planetary explorers can "go native" without interference. The result is a utopian vision of planetary exploration that seeks credibility through a protagonist who can live on Mars and speak for the planet. Addressing a culture that sorts talents and sensibilities into racial categories, Bova makes that native speaker a Native American.

As half-Navaho, geologist Jamie Waterman is marked by the political reality of being "other" in a white man's world; as the sympathetic center of the Mars novels, he articulates the potential of the wonderful dream. He is the soul of the first Martian expedition and he becomes the formal and spiritual leader of the Second Expedition. He supplies the emotional and political motivation for the successful discovery of extraterrestrial life and intelligence. He also establishes the first legal claim to a piece of Mars and hence defines its use. By the close of *Return*, Bova's aim is clear: it is possible that a Martian future might be neither white nor black but Navaho.[44] This implies that an extraterrestrial future will not be an escape from race but its transformation. That transformation begins by finding something positive in racial difference.

The positive characteristic supposed for Native Americans is a unity with nature, an essentially noble savagery. In the early 1970s, this customary compliment found new expression in a famous public service campaign that helped domesticate the new environmentalism. The Keep American Beautiful campaign, "People Start Pollution, People Can Stop It," was first broadcast on Earth Day, 22 April 1971. Iron Eyes Cody, an actor who specialized in Indian roles during the mid-twentieth century, created a memorable icon as the first American who shed a tear for a violated land. The power of this stereotype in the ordinary culture is indicated by its evocation in *The Quiet Crisis*, the manifesto for a managerial environmentalism, written by the Secretary of the Interior in the Kennedy and Johnson administrations.[45] The widely available image of aboriginal Americans as the overwhelmed representatives of a violated land help establish the stakes of Bova's project. In the course of the Mars novels, Jamie develops an intellectual and emotional relationship to the red planet. His author has him claim the new world as a scientist and as a Navaho who speaks for its long-dead aboriginal inhabitants. It is his role to save Mars for science and to defend it against the exploitative usages of organized greed. Thus, Bova designs a character who can represent a new world order, an alternative to a corrupt status quo.

In an interview he gave in 2000, Bova is explicit about the link between landscape, character, and race. For Jamie's author, the Navaho are people of the land and represent a way of being in the land unavailable to whites. Bova notes that as a white character, Jamie could not have intervened in the discourse between race and nation: "Actually, when I first started plotting out the original novel *Mars*, the central character was a white-bread American geologist, and it just didn't work out. So finally I came to a realization that this guy is part Navajo. So we went out to New Mexico for a month or so and absorbed the area and that's when I started writing the novel."[46] The half-Navaho Waterman does for Bova what a monoracial character cannot: he serves as the nexus of a web of political and cultural connections that brings the Earth and Mars together. Waterman functions as the link between the geology of Earth and the areology of Mars, and as a liaison between races. And at the level of character development, he reconciles the races in his own person by coming to terms with being both white and Navaho. Bova comments, "Although Jamie is very white and very Western, he still has that [Navaho] streak in him. Indeed, Mars and Earth, the two different planets, can be seen as symbols for the two parts of Jamie's soul. I think that in *Return to Mars* he has finally resolved those differences."[47] The resolution that Bova presents is simultaneously biological and political. In the context of a space future defined as "American," Waterman represents the desire to articulate an expansive project that will create a partnership between the descendents of previous generations of colonizers and colonized. In astrofuturism, Waterman is distinguished as a character who can represent race, science, and an environmentalist's sensibility toward the Martian landscape.

What does it mean to be a liaison? Jamie is familiar yet strange by reason of race, class, and profession. He is familiar as a biracial child who is raised in Berkeley by parents who are college professors. He is thereby removed from many of the experiences and from the class position of those who live on reservations of the sort visited by Bova in New Mexico. Waterman's Navaho father, once an angry young man, has assimilated into the "white" patterns reserved for successful academics.[48] In the social world of his family, Indianness and middle-class success are mutually exclusive categories. Waterman explains, "My father has spent most of his life trying not to be an Indian, although he'd never admit it. Probably doesn't even realize it. He earned a scholarship to Harvard University. He married a woman who's descended from the original *Mayflower* colonists. Neither one of them wanted me to be an Indian. They always told me to be a success, instead" (193). He goes on to admit that "They were never active in Indian affairs and neither was I" (194). As a consequence, Waterman "was brought up to be a white man" (235). In his starkly divided racial world, the only way he can become a scientist is by ignoring the political implications of his father's history. Jamie's only contact with his Navaho heritage occurs during the summers he spends on the reservation with his grandfather, Al Waterman, a successful businessman who never forgets his roots (64).[49] " 'If it weren't for my grandfather,' " Jamie says, " 'I'd be more white than you are. He taught me to understand my heritage, to accept it without hating anybody' " (194).

From this history of racial antagonism, Bova argues for a politics of integration. Waterman is sympathetic in the narrative because he does not choose political radicalism. Instead, like Kinsman, he embraces a liberalism that rejects both the radical cultural nationalism of political organizations such as American Indian Movement (AIM) and the white nativism of his mother: " 'I'm the descendant of Indians. My skin is darker than yours. But if you take our brains out of our skulls, Mikhail, you wouldn't be able to tell the difference between them. That's where we really live. In our minds. We were born on opposite sides of the world and yet here we are together on a totally other planet. That's what's important. Not what our ancestors did to one another. What we're doing now. That's the important thing' " (194). What matters is not skin color but gray matter, the intelligences in our skulls. On Mars, we will relearn the significance of that human essence and will strip away the superficialities we have inherited.

But integration does not mean leaving behind a personally meaningful history. Unlike his father, Waterman has not completely given up his connection to Navaho culture. When the first expedition lands on Mars, he impulsively speaks a Navaho word of greeting instead of the footprints and flags speech set by the American government: "He had already forgotten the lines that had been written for him a hundred million kilometers ago. He said simply, 'Ya'aa'tey' " (12). Waterman publicly denies that he intended to make an oppositional statement honoring the experience of a conquered people. The narrator's description of the moment, however, demonstrates an alienation from business

as usual: "Finally it was Jamie's turn. He felt suddenly weary, tired of the pos-
turings and pomposities, exhausted by the years of stress and sacrifice. The excitement he had felt only minutes ago had drained away, evaporated. A hundred
million kilometers from Earth and they were still playing their games of nations and allegiances. He felt as if someone had draped an enormous weight
around his shoulders" (12). By speaking the language of a colonized nation/
people, Waterman throws off the weight of the old world and nations jockeying
for power. Here Bova suggests that the physical distance between the Earth and
Mars will not matter unless it can be measured culturally. *Ya'aa'tey* provides
that cultural distance, a distancing gesture that clears away old boundaries by
magnifying a buried New World speech. With the word, Bova attempts to articulate something new, to provide a different direction for American culture
based on its suppressed, untaken alternatives. Waterman brings Native American culture with him to Mars, and thus speaks for a relationship to the planet
that seeks to avoid old conquest narratives.

It would not mean that the character speaks from the political choices
available to contemporary Native Americans. The neat social segregations of
Bova's portrayal leave little room for political choices contrary to mainstream
common sense. Explaining what we should make of his speech, Waterman
notes that, "I've never been active in politics of any kind, on campus or afterward. I vote every election day, but that's about it. I consider myself to be an
American citizen, just like you do" (148). Although the character demonstrates
awareness of key incidents in Native American history such as Wounded Knee
and the Trail of Tears, he does not follow that history into AIM or any other
position that would imply a radical exercise of Native American identity. His
relapse "into the language of my ancestors" is instinctual rather than lived or
thought, a simple and atavistic response to the sight of a new world from a
character who apparently carries reverence for land in his noble, savage genes
(90).[50]

It is his lack of political commitment that authorizes Waterman's ability to
speak as a minority figure within the circle of Bova's future vision. If he were
to find common cause with or claim sympathy for the "Indian activists" who
embrace him as a hero in *Mars*, he would not be able to serve his author as a
sympathetic bridge between the white and nonwhite worlds. Hence Waterman
has no ongoing political or social connection to the Navaho. This does not
mean that he lacks affiliations altogether. As an American citizen, he claims a
place within a nation that includes, we presume, Native Americans. More importantly, he identifies himself as a scientist; his political defense of himself and
of the Mars project rests on that identification. His status as a representative of

professional science allows him to de-emphasize the more widely available claims of race and political identity:

"I'm speaking to you from the planet Mars. This afternoon my fellow scientists and I discovered water here. That is far more important than the color of my skin or the nature of my political activities. For the first time in our exploration of the solar system we have found water in a liquid state on another world. You should be interviewing us about that, not over a few words I spoke at a very emotional moment in my life. All the others of our team spoke in their native languages when they gave their first words from Mars. I spoke in mine—spoke the only words of Navaho that I really know. And that's all there is to it. Now let's stop this bullshit and get on with the exploration of Mars." (148–49)

From within astrofuturist discourse, Waterman gives priority to the ideals of science over any possessive investment in culture, politics, or history.[51] His idealism reads like a manifesto demanding an individual's right to choose the conditions of his work without regard to any commitments beyond his own wants. It fits neatly with the futurist sentiment that the scientific exploration of space heralds the setting aside of terrestrial histories and modes of being. It wrestles with past habits for the sake of a promise that would dispose of them. Waterman's scientism lays out a prospect in which old political categories, ethnic particularities, and national hatreds become irrelevant. If Jamie belongs anywhere politically, it is with the party of space. The British Interplanetary Society sweatshirt he wears as casual dress indicates his commitment to a tradition and lineage with claims beyond race and nation.[52]

Bova's engagement of race and nation addresses a question central to astrofuturism in the years since the shattering of Project Apollo's institutional consensus: if it is an American-led adventure patterned after the expansionist projects of the nineteenth century, can the conquest of space avoid recapitulating the intolerances, scandals, and murders of its historical precedents? In *Return to Mars*, Bova takes up the question by foregrounding race in the personal struggle between Waterman and a young geologist, Dexter Trumball, the son of the wealthy white businessman who bankrolls the voyage. In order to head off an exploitative landgrab by Daryl Trumball's group of venture capitalists and to prevent Mars from being ruined by the same forces that ruined the American west, Waterman contacts the president of the Navaho nation. For most of the book, his position can be described as a stand for science against the exploitative capitalism represented by Dex's father, who wants to profit by promoting tourism to Mars.[53] While Dex argues that his father's proposed profiteering is "inevitable," Waterman turns to the Navaho to postpone that fate. The Navaho president accepts his proposal with these words:

"The Navaho people accept the responsibility of claiming utilization rights to the areas of Mars explored by the Second Mars Expedition," the president said slowly, as if reading from a prepared script. "We intend to hold it in trust for all the peoples of Earth, and to encourage the careful scientific study of the planet Mars and all its life-forms, past and present.

"We recognize that Dr. James Waterman, whose father was a pure-blood Navaho, will be our people's representative on Mars while this claim is officially filed with the International Astronautical Authority." (376)

This move creates an interesting twist in our understanding of the future that Bova imagines. In *Mars* and for the first 370-odd pages of *Return*, we have been safe in the assumption that the future will leave behind the American regime of race and nation. The exploration of Mars will be a multicultural, international affair that will call into question all our ethnic particularities. Those who persist in translating national rivalries (Ilona Malater, the Russian-hating Israeli biologist of *Mars* [43, 545]) and ethnic hatreds (Daryl Trumball's explicit racism in *Return*) represent a bad old order that must be defeated (378). What we find instead is not that race and nation have been made irrelevant, but that they have undergone a speculative refashioning that heralds the renewal of a race and the birth of a nation. Dex puts it all in perspective, noting, "My old man's gonna pop an artery over this! The Indians pull a land steal on the white men! Wow!" (371).

Waterman, a politically centrist character who in *Mars* denied any interest in an identity politics, in *Return* uses the political instrument of Navaho sovereignty to claim Mars. It is quickly apparent that that claim will not be a simple extension of middle-class notions of a "diverse" community, but a land that will produce a Navaho future in space. On learning that the International Astronautical Authority will recognize the Navaho claim as "legal and binding" (378), Jamie clarifies his intentions to fellow future Martian, Vijay Shektar:

He heard her laughing. "The Navaho reservation is now bigger than the States, isn't it."

"If you take in all of Mars, yes. But this isn't part of the reservation it's—"

"Don't take it so seriously!"

"But it is serious," he said. "I'm hoping that this will motivate Navaho kids to get involved in Mars, to study science and mathematics, to—"

"To become Martian?"

He took a breath. "Yeah, maybe. Eventually. Someday." (402)

The Martian prospect is revealed as an extension of the schoolwork conducted by the RCA engineers of *The High Road*, a liberal reconciliation between "the world of opportunity" and the restricted lives lived in reservations and ghettos.[54]

Unlike the white engineers who came from outside with the uplifting knowledge of space science, Waterman's role is that of the minority "insider," the role model who can inspire the disadvantaged to new ambitions. In the biblical terms Bova used to explain Kinsman's biracial salvation narrative, Waterman becomes the Moses who leads his people out of Egypt to a new planetary frontier. As a prophet of a space-born millennium, he synthesizes the racial and directive roles of Frank Colt and Chet Kinsman.

The political maneuvering that establishes a Navaho (Indian) Mars literally bubbles up from Jamie's unconscious in the dreams that link him to his late grandfather, the genocidal history of contact between white and red men, and the shamanistic interchapters establishing the scientific/mythic links between the Earth and Mars. When Waterman produces a political solution to the Mars problem and acts as a Navaho in a political world, it reads as a *deus ex machina*, an techno-spiritual fix much like the ultimate weapon that has saved the day in so many space operas. Nevertheless, we should note Bova's attempt to shift the astrofuturist paradigm by suggesting that a human space future could, in principle, be pioneered by people of color. This is astonishing in a genre that assumes that the space future and science itself are the exclusive properties of the white West. To imagine that the various indigenous peoples, or Indians, of the Earth might stand as the defenders of science is to reverse the hierarchy of knower and known, ruler and ruled. And it is also significant that this future supported by capitalism seeks to slip its economic bounds into a utopian space that does not call for the uncritical extension of a corporate or consumer civilization.

Finally, on first reading, it appears that Bova has broken with the technological determinism that is the constant of his long career. Mars is not an automatic fix for the Earth's problems; on the contrary, the forces of greed and power which have wreaked havoc on earth, if allowed to proceed unchecked, could do the same in the new land. Human intervention in the form of a political solution is required to avoid that possibility. But a closer consideration reveals that the technological fix is not abandoned. Bova always promises that expansion into space will solve otherwise intractable terrestrial problems. The Mars sequence ends before he substantiates that claim. Let us borrow the narrative strategy of his popular science and consider two hypothetical scenarios: 1) control of Mars's resources empowers the Navaho and allows them to improve their lot on earth, or 2) the move to Mars gives the Navaho, through their representative, a chance to leave behind the history of their dispossession and start over.[55] In either case, the technological fix reemerges. In effect, Bova implies that the only option available to those dispossessed by the previous course of exploration and settlement is to repeat that project on another world. By joining the race for space, they will gain the opportunity to control not only their own destiny, but also that of two worlds. Within astrofuturism's discursive field, they have no alternative but to follow the course of empire and to prove that they can repeat its history without its flaws.

Through this gesture, Bova suggests that the astrofuturist ideal can be separated from its imperial baggage. In his novels, he seeks to separate disinterested scientific exploration from its use in projects of conquest and exploitation. Bova tries to shift the von Braunian paradigm by arguing that its political commitments are not necessary to the wonderful dream; indeed, the realization of the dream is hampered by the ideological residue of the space age. He proposes that the core astrofuturist ideals of liberty, brotherhood, and knowledge can be validated by nonwhite adherents once freed from the wastelands of the Earth.[56] If we have forgotten how to be scientists, the Navaho will remind us of the common good that results from pursuing knowledge for its own sake. Conveniently, Bova's indigenous Martians are long extinct, thus the Navaho need not fear visiting the brutal past on a new race. By taking up the mantle of science, they will slough off the bad conscience of the Western scientific tradition and validate the propriety of its fundamental principles. In the process, they perform the role that people of color often undertake in liberal systems: atoning for the sins of their conquerors by succeeding within the systems established by conquest.

Here we come up against the limits of a liberal astrofuturism. Bova offers the various Indians or indigenous peoples of the Earth a chance to be history's winners, and that is no small accomplishment. His paradigm shift proves that astrofuturism can make room for people (or at least men) of color, but can their inclusion change astrofuturism further? As there is no future that is not an extension of exploration and colonization, as the motion of history is inextricable from that progress narrative, new agents have to repeat old stories. At its worst, this is assimilation, not integration. New agents, however, do not have to repeat old stories faithfully; if they may be counted on to improve upon the past, then they can redeem its best aspirations. If the disenfranchised look to an elite to create the technology that creates this opportunity, the elite must look to the disenfranchised to use the technology in a manner that will take the human race to its next evolutionary leap. At its best, theirs would be a joint enterprise that would benefit all its participants.

7. On Mars and Other Heterotopias: A Conclusion

The ship is the heterotopia par excellence. In civilizations where it is lacking, dreams dry up, adventure is replaced by espionage, and privateers by the police.

—Michel Foucault[1]

If the interventions of interlopers such as George Takei, Homer Hickam, and Nichelle Nichols recover the emancipatory and utopian motivations of the space future, their presence in the actual and fictional places of space exploration holds astrofuturism accountable to its promise of a frontier that will free all of humankind. Indeed, the development of twentieth-century astrofuturism is the story of America's response to the claims of marginalized peoples. I have focused on the scientific utopianism at the heart of astrofuturism in order to interrogate the alternative societies that it can imagine. American culture persistently projects itself onto other times and different landscapes; this habit strikes me as a move that combines utopian longing with the fantasy of almost unlimited power.

For much of the twentieth century, American dreams of space conquest reflected what Raymond Williams calls "the mood of a rising class, which knows down to detail, that it can replace the existing order."[2] That mood is an index of the technical and political power that the United States enjoyed following the Second World War. But the posture of confidence assumed by the United States in the international arena was accompanied, and perhaps in part occasioned, by the nation's internal crisis of confidence. Even as it rose to global prominence as the bulwark of freedom, America harbored a political culture that mandated the unequal distribution of civil rights. The contradiction between rhetoric and practice was (and continues to be) an open secret that undermined the nation's credibility as it sought moral and political high ground in its ideological war with Soviet Russia. In the gap between promises made and then betrayed, we find the discontents that make a rising class or nation suspect its good fortune. Its members may believe they have no rival and yet fear catastrophic failure or experience the pain of soured expectations. In this nervous condition, they "create a new heaven because [their] Earth is a hell."[3]

Insofar as it has been the expression of a particular class, the spaceflight movement has always demonstrated vulnerability to social anxiety, alienation, and betrayal. In this project, I have used the motif of race to track a majority project's attempts to resolve contradictions between the rhetoric and practice of the American dream, predominantly by expelling all sources of conflict and homogenizing all evidence of alterity. Given its ideological debts, I have asked whether astrofuturism has the resources and the flexibility to serve as an instrument of aspiration and accomplishment for those it has traditionally excluded. Certainly the cold war astrofuturism that promised to extend American ascendancy in perpetuity exemplifies what George Lipsitz has called America's "possessive investment in whiteness." Lipsitz argues that nothing that has been gained or lost by the political and economic struggles of the past century can be understood without reference to the rewards and privileges our society reserves for whiteness. Read through this lens, astrofuturism becomes part of a cover deflecting attention from America's treatment of its racialized minorities and safeguarding the white nation's status as inheritor of Europe's colonial mantle and its standing as the vanguard of technological modernity. The exclusion of women and racial minorities from the pioneering astronauts corps of the 1950s and 1960s was a deliberate gesture whose significance was readily apparent: the segregations of contemporary American life were to be extended into the space future as part of what Lipsitz identifies as "the rewards and privileges of whiteness."[4] The antiseptic interiors and routinized characters of Stanley Kubrick's *2001: A Space Odyssey* (1968) are an ironic portrayal of the heroic white males valorized by the 1960s space program. The mystical transcendence and evolutionary leap offered in the film's final scene takes "the absolute value of whiteness in U.S. politics, economics, and culture" to its logical conclusion on the space frontier. [5]

And yet people of color continue to turn to science in general and to astrofuturism in particular to express their political aspirations and personal longings. Despite its troubling history and unwelcoming practices, this discourse somehow invites the affiliation of those seeking alternatives to a racialized status quo. Consider the example of Neil de Grasse Tyson, astrophysicist and

Frederick P. Rose Director of the Hayden Planetarium of New York's Natural History Museum. When Tyson received his Ph.D. in astrophysics from Columbia University in 1991, he increased the number of black astrophysicists in the United States from six to seven.[6] To do so, he climbed a racial mountain comprised of blacks and whites who insist that African Americans have no business pursuing advanced academic degrees in the sciences. The latter expect blacks to excel in music, sports, or other forms of entertainment, but never in fields that require significant intellectual effort. The former maintains that the political and economic condition of black people is such that those who have the resources and intelligence must enter practical professions that will uplift the race.[7] Jeffrey Allen Tucker, an African American scholar specializing in science fiction, has noted "that for many people—black as well as white—science fiction and African American culture are mutually exclusive."[8] Any African American interested in the pursuit of knowledge is vulnerable to these commonplace sentiments. To be interested in the dream of spaceflight is to reach beyond the boundaries of acceptability in our racialized culture. In post-King America, we may dream only the dreams fit for our race and class.

Fortunately, there are always those who oppose the segregations required by a remarkably obdurate core of vested interests. Family and teachers, black and white, fostered Tyson's interests in math and astronomy. The curators and lecturers of the American Museum of Natural History's Hayden Planetarium provided the courses that fed his curiosity and the role models that made it possible for him to imagine himself in their profession.[9] And the Education Director of the Explorers Club advised him on scholarship programs and travel opportunities that helped him develop his concentration. When he went shopping for an undergraduate education, Carl Sagan invited him to visit Cornell and welcomed him with a compassionate interest that made academic astronomy an attractive career option.[10]

Tyson's education as an astrophysicist reveals the tension between the promise of science and the political reality that has curtailed African American participation in the sciences. Tyson dramatizes the pragmatic value of science in the everyday politics of race as he recounts taping an interview for Fox News on the physics of solar flares. He recalls his reaction upon seeing himself on television: "I had an intellectual out-of-body experience: on the screen before me was a scientific expert on the Sun whose knowledge was sought by the evening news. The expert on television happened to be Black. At that moment, the entire fifty-year history of television programming flew past my view. At no place along that time line could I recall a Black person (who is neither an entertainer nor an athlete) being interviewed as an expert on something that had nothing whatever to do with being Black" (117). Here, then, is the final frontier. "For the first time in nine years," Tyson continues, "I stood without guilt for following my cosmic dreams" (117). As Tyson indicates, his presence on television as a titled representative of science is a powerful statement. It stands for political hopes that place no part of human endeavor beyond the reach of aggrieved communities. It fulfills the social promise often made in the name of rational inquiry.

For Tyson, science is another country, an alternative to a nation in which the gap between rhetoric and practice is incoherent and cruel. His experience of science contrasts sharply with the frequently irrational suppressions of thought and person he sees as part of everyday life.[11] By contrast, he writes, "the laws of physics apply everywhere on Earth and in the heavens and are independent of social mores. These same laws were beginning to serve as one of my intellectual anchors amid the irrationalities of society" (20). The disinterestedness and rationality of science evoke hope for an equally rational world in which rules apply without favor to everyone.

Tyson's critique of the 1960s space program complements that of prominent civil rights leaders, such as Ralph D. Abernathy, who protested its extravagance:

Space exploration is generally a good thing, but while my formative years were coincident with NASA's Mercury, Gemini, and Apollo programs, I am far from being a space zealot. I saw who was going into space. The astronauts were predominantly military officers representing the branches of the armed forces. There were no women anywhere in the pipeline, and the chosen ones all wore crew cuts at the same time the musical *Hair!* was enjoying 1,750 performances on Broadway. Furthermore, they all seem to have been selected for their steel nerves and their absence of emotional expression. As far as I could tell, the American agenda was not the exploration of space but the American *conquest* of space to gain military advantage. (45)[12]

A space program undertaken as a projection of a militarized white masculinity into heretofore untenanted territory held no appeal for a young man who was both African American and a budding scientist. Indeed, it held little interest for the liberal scientists, such as Carl Sagan, who were his intellectual and professional models.[13] However, for Tyson, the conquest of space, no matter how vast its mobilization, does not exhaust the value of human inquiry into realms beyond our atmosphere. The cold war–era space program, socially illiberal in its implementation, also opened imaginative doors. Speaking for the liberal agendas of science education, Tyson argues that "nothing in this world has the power to inspire forward thinking and visions of the future the way the space program can" (46). He assumes that nestled in the gargantuan machinery of the rocket state is the knowledge that could free us all to participate in making and "imagining a reachable future" (46).

Tyson's criticisms and hopes are echoed by many fellow travellers in his generation, including the writers, scientists, and space advocates who comprise the third generation of American astrofuturism. The generation that came to prominence in the late 1980s and 1990s inherits a rich tradition of literary and scientific exploration. Many of its members, such as Terry Bisson in *Voyage to the Red Planet* (1990), lampoon the restricted political imaginations of their predecessors and condemn the cold war hypocrisy that used the rhetoric of freedom to mask the West's structural inequalities. However, they also honor the potential of the high frontier to provoke speculation about changes in the terrestrial status quo. To this end, astrofuturist writers of the last two decades have pursued postmodern futures that grapple with the claims of peoples whose role as active participants in the advance of human knowledge has been routinely devalued or ignored.

In this incarnation, the spaceflight project is harnessed to the creation of outer spaces that experiment with diversity and hybridity, and break with terrestrial powers that would fix human potential into bounded, governable forms. In these heterogeneous spaces, suppressed histories and talents can flower and the deferred dreams of aggrieved communities can be realized. Their designers seek to reclaim the radical roots of astrofuturism and to fulfill the prospects opened up by the social movements of the 1960s and 1970s. Instead of a perfectly realized "end of history," they imagine futures in various states of democratic constestation and fulfillment. They also reject the assumed superiority of the state-sponsored technological platforms that underwrote the modern astrofuturist vision. In lieu of massive technocratic institutions dedicated to securing a narrow range of race, class, and national interests, we now see technological proposals suited to the small scale of private university research institutes and citizen's space-advocacy groups. Popular narratives that rely on the reflected glory of military adventure make way for stories that explore the utopian potential of science that is not entrained to corporate capital or the projection of national political power. Political hope is expressed neither as monolithic galactic empires and federations nor as racially pure, space-based bantustans whose distance from one another is supposed to guarantee the survival, peace, and prosperity of the species. Hope exists in the invention of heterotopias, spaces that escape the simple oppositions maintained by our possessive investments.

Following Foucault, I define heterotopia as a space that is always material and bounded, partial and transitional, hybrid and momentarily, if ever, homogeneous.[14] Although utopia may never shake the charge of being nowhere at any time, heterotopia is distinguished by always being somewhere and at sometime. It is achievable through available means, and is inhabited by identities and agendas that mirror the complexity of our ordinary world. In heterotopic spaces, thought experiments are run that suspend ordinary rules long enough to allow us to consider alternative ways of being. In heterotopian astrofuturisms, we find fresh potential for space futures that do not depend on the imperatives that govern everyday life. Geographer Derek Gregory writes of Foucault's heterotopias as "marginal sites of modernity, constantly threatening to disrupt its closures and certainties."[15] Third-generation astrofuturists create extraterrestrial heterotopias by changing the bodies and identities that inhabit space futures. In so doing, they extend the astrofuturist engagement with modern technological utopia from a stance of postmodern skepticism. Thus, like the disaporic intellectuals valorized by Cornel West, they mount "an intense and incessant interrogation of power-laden discourses in the service of neither restoration, reformation, nor revolution but rather of revolt."[16]

Allen M. Steele, Vonda N. McIntyre, and Kim Stanley Robinson have sought to reconfigure astrofuturism from the perspective of working class culture, antiracist feminism, and Marxist intellectual history respectively. Their thought experiments force an audit of the investments in whiteness, masculinity, and bourgeois primacy that elsewhere constitute the ordinary business of our culture. The incipient revolts of third-generation astrofuturists target race, gender, class, and nation as regulatory devices that stabilize the potential of bodies and identities in rigid hierarchies. The most promising development from these inheritors of the astrofuturist tradition is the move from utopia to heterotopia; from singularity to multiplicity; from unidirectional growth to multiple space-based projects that answer to the many histories on earth. Writers such as Steele, McIntyre, and Robinson turn away from uncritical celebrations of enlightenment science wielded by an elite, albeit benevolent, few. Instead, these authors imagine a more participatory culture of science and hence a greater spectrum of possible futures. In their novels, we find room for the inclusion of disenfranchised peoples, not as grateful recipients of the largesse of powerful scientists and capitalists, but as active developers of new worlds.

All three writers directly engage astrofuturism's conservative tendencies, either by satirizing its conventions or by troping them away from their intended meanings. Allen Steele, for instance, satirizes the class prejudices of early astrofuturists and the naiveté of their deterministic faith in the beneficent effects of technological advance. His first two novels, *Orbital Decay* (1989) and *Lunar Descent* (1991), respond to one of the oldest dreams of liberal astrofuturism, articulated by Arthur C. Clarke in the 1950s: the creation of a satellite-based global communications network that will force the break- down of old nationalisms, ease social divisions, end tyranny, and result in a grassroots, decentralized global democracy. Steele criticizes cold war astro- futurism's uncritical advocacy of space technology and its blindness to the dan- gers of supporting governmental, military, and corporate space projects. He recognizes, as Clarke and others of his generation did not, that space tech- nology is more likely to be used as an instrument of political repression than as the basis for a global utopia.

In *Orbital Decay,* Steele's working-class protagonists see that in the wrong hands, space-based communications technology can be used to consoli- date and extend the tyrannical power of wealthy governments and their corpo- rate allies:

Y'know, the thing which always got me about the exploration of space was how naively the human race—but Americans particularly—has approached the whole thing. I mean, because we'd proven to ourselves that it was possible to send men and machines into orbit, we always assumed that everything would always work *right*, that people would always do the *right* thing out there, that just being in space would make everything so *right*. Jesus, you would have thought that after 1986, after the *Challenger* blew up and killed seven people because some people at NASA disregarded good advice not to launch that day, that after SDI was proven to be a monstrous sham which knowledge- able people who knew that it couldn't work as advertised tried to foist upon the world anyway, after the L-5 Colony bullshit which even more so-called reliable sources tried to present as being economically feasible and practical . . .[17]

The narrator trails off, leaving us to wonder at the folly of entrusting any rea- sonable space program to governments, corporate bureaucrats, and academic visionaries. According to Steele, the space futures institutionalized in NASA by the von Braun rocket team in the 1960s, O'Neill's space colonization proposal of the 1970s, and the enthusiastic acceptance of the Strategic Defense Initiative by spaceflight advocates such as Pournelle and Bova in the 1980s have all been discredited by subsequent experience.

Conducted through his portrayal of the managerial, middle-class character of Henry George Wallace, Steele's critique raises the question that was often asked of astrofuturists during the 1960s and 1970s: who will pioneer the final frontier? While first-generation authors—including von Braun, Ley, Clarke, and Heinlein—promoted the space future as the next step in human evolution, they represented only a small slice of the human race as fit explorers of the space frontier. A scientific and engineering elite, often in uniform and nearly always organized in military-style hierarchies, was their ideal of the space cadet. Norman Mailer and Tom Wolfe both valorized the type in their journalistic accounts of the 1960s space program.[18] In Steele's version of the space future, however, there must be a place for ordinary, working-class people. While delineating that place, he imagines the class conflicts that might complicate the old technocratic mission. The conflict between labor and management starts, as these things often do, with the relatively minor insistence of workers that they be allowed some degree of autonomy, in this instance expressed as the right to keep pet cats. But Captain Wallace interprets their show of independence, perhaps rightly, as defiance that strikes against the very heart of his ideal of the well-disciplined, smoothly functioning, hierarchical society:

"It wasn't the cats that started this, it was Skycorp, and before them, NASA. It was all the space experts like Clarke and O'Neill, the groups like L-5 and the National Space Society, claiming that outer space was meant to be colonized by the so-called common man." He laughed again. "All the common man is good for is to pave the way for *homo superior*, those who have disciplined themselves—trained their minds, hardened their bodies, become ready to live in this environment. This frontier was never meant for the common man Ed, it was meant for . . ."

He searched for the right word, waving his right hand in the air. "The master race," Felapolous supplied slowly.

Wallace smiled and jabbed an index finger in his direction as he walked away, his eyes searching the floor of the darkened compartment. "Yes, although not by the classic Hitler definition. I would hate to have my theories compared to his."

"No, of course not," Felapolous murmured.[19]

Steele makes explicit the trajectory that leads from first-generation astro-futurism's roots in the oven state of Nazi Germany to its final resting place in the comic-book evolutionism that became popular in the late 1970s.[20] By the end of the novel, it is clear that the cherished vision of the conquest of space by a technocratic elite is bankrupt. Hence we note that the character of H. G. Wallace is a dig at H. G. Wells—a founding father of space futurism—at his most imperially enthusiastic.

But despite his indictment of astrofuturism's most hallowed convictions, Steele is not ready to dispense with the wonderful dream altogether. *Orbital Decay*'s working-class heroes, the novel's principle protagonists, prevent the conquest of space from inaugurating an increasingly complete apparatus of oppression. By the end of the novel, they salvage the democratic hopes that sustain Steele's interest in the space frontier. Interwoven with his satiric review of the blindness and hypocrisy of cold war astrofuturism is a sympathetic portrayal of the blue-collar conspiracy that saves the novel's spaceflight mission. Steele's argument is not with astrofuturism's motivation—the desire to explore and further inhabit our universe—but with its social texture. He is opposed to the almost bloodless vision of the space future that was canonized in Stanley Kubrick and Arthur C. Clarke's 1968 film, *2001: A Space Odyssey*. By narrative convention and design, *2001* presents the space future as a fulfillment of the technological utopianism embodied in the white cities of the modern world's fair movement: clean, bright, patriarchal, Eurocentric, affluent, and supported by a push-button technocracy.[21] This sanitized, pneumatic utopia has been iconographically rendered from the 1930s through the 1960s in such films as H. G. Wells's *Things to Come* and George Pal's *The Conquest of Space*, and in television series from *Star Trek* to *The Jetsons*.

By contrast Steele's future is dirty, dangerous, hard working, and suffused with the popular culture of rock and roll, outlaw bikers, and marijuana. Its characters are culturally and geographically specific, with backgrounds in middle-western and southern American cities. Although he writes of the space future as a man's world, he adheres to a liberal feminism that allows women to be equal partners with the men.[22] Racial diversity among the workers is an unremarkable fact of life, occasioning comment only when white bigotry rears its ugly head.[23] Working-class people are the moral center and the heroes of his future; their preoccupations and tastes shape its norms. And labor's ability to win struggles with management regarding the development of space signals Steel's faith that it is still possible to invest political hope in the wonderful dream.

In short, Steele takes the utopias of boys' adventure fiction, turns their class hierarchies upside down, and speculates about a heterotopian space frontier where terrestrial norms can be suspended and revised. He imagines an else-when in which the common labor essential to survival gains the moral and political stature it is denied on the Earth. His space future is built from the bottom-up rather than from the top-down. Steele is emphatic that space can only fulfill its promise through the agency of ordinary men and women. At the end of *Orbital Decay* and *Lunar Descent*, successful insurrections and strikes enable workers to wrest control of space stations and lunar mining colonies from corrupt, earthbound authorities. We are left with the hope of a better future organized for the good of the common people, rather than for the continuing dominance of comfortable elites.

This preference for multiplicity arising from below rather than uniformity imposed from above is evident as well in the work of Vonda N. McIntyre. In her *Starfarer* series, published in the late 1980s and early 1990s, McIntyre uses Gerard O'Neill's engineering proposals and Robert Heinlein's familial arrangements as a starting point for a nonimperial space future. But she goes far beyond anything her predecessors imagined in her speculations about the malleability of human biology and identity, and consequently proposes multiple transformations of kinship structures, individual identities, and social organization. O'Neill's space future tends to look, as Allen Steele has suggested, something like the affluent suburbs of New Jersey writ large;[24] McIntyre's parodic engagement transforms it into a site of experimentation.[25] Thus, she follows the lead established by Marge Piercy in *Woman on the Edge of Time* (1976) and appropriates a technology strongly figured by masculinist and racist ideologies (even if liberal) for feminist and antiracist ends.

Most obviously, in McIntyre's space future the centrality of a black woman is represented as commonplace. With this gesture, the narrative engages the use of black and female figures in astrofuturist fiction, particularly in texts produced since the 1960s.[26] In the hands of other futurists, such characters exist primarily to authorize Man—the Anglo-American male, the only being capable of representing universal humanity—in his role as author and actor, artist and astronaut. In both liberal and conservative narratives, we are never allowed to lose sight of the fact that the black character is other to the writer and to any imagined reader.[27] And the job of the other remains that of marking the frontier as the place where the regimes of whiteness and masculinity find their apotheosis.[28] McIntyre breaks with these habits by re-creating herself within the text as a black woman: Victoria Fraser MacKenzie shares her first initial, a middle surname and a Celtic patronymic with Vonda Neel McIntyre. The character is neither a flattering foil nor a saintly rebuke; McIntyre exchanges the flatness of otherness for depth of social detail, historical specificity, and imaginative scope. In MacKenzie, she creates a character that is both marginal to the social relations of mainstream science fiction and central to its astrofuturist discourses.

Despite the dissenting work of a handful of black writers, science fiction often assumes that the problem of racism will be solved in the future by the disappearance of race. While intended to improve on the contemporary politics of race, this assumption disregards the historical and cultural specificity of people of color.[29] That specificity, coded as "difference," represents the trouble and danger from which racism is thought to emerge. Eliminate difference and the problem of racism evaporates. Within this logic, the problem of racism can be erased if its victims forgive its perpetrators and if we all forget the history of racialization and the richness of cultural variation.[30] The problem with this solution is that it enshrines white masculinity, unmarked or troubled by culture, race, and gender, as the norm to which all "difference" must assimilate. In this vision, anyone who goes up to space in ships is, to echo Donna Haraway in another context, "necessarily a white boy in moral state, no matter what accidents of biology or social gender and race might have pertained prior" to the great adventure.[31]

McIntyre's characterization of MacKenzie is notable because she allows the character to indulge in the full range of human activity without giving up her historical and emotional affiliations. The history of slavery and racism is presented as informing the future, rather than as a shameful past that we must forget. The *Starfarer* does not require a "band of brothers" who forget all social attachments in their trek to the stars.[32] In choosing to make MacKenzie's family history an issue, McIntyre graces the character with a social specificity rare for black characters outside the bounds of African American writing. The history and experiences of MacKenzie's African and African Canadian ancestors are invoked in the text through the figure of her great-grandmother. When this black woman defends a charter that forbids colonization and exploitation, the history she represents lends urgency and poignancy to her words. McIntyre replaces Vivian Sobchack's "virgin astronaut," the white space hero, but does not attempt to fill his shoes.[33] Instead, her character speaks from and for the victims of colonial heroism and articulates their desire for a different future. Thus, McIntyre's intervention is intended to force scientific humanism to live up to its ideals, and suggests that it can do so only by changing its subject.

The character and spirit of *Starfarer*'s social experiment is signalled further through Victoria Fraser MacKenzie's membership in what she calls a "family partnership," a form of marriage that allows several sexually active adults to cohabit in a socially recognized relationship.[34] Although the partnership resembles polygamy, the family structure in which a spouse can have more than one mate, MacKenzie is quick to clarify the difference between the two: "The technical term is 'family partnership.' It is not as rigidly defined as polygamy. A family partnership is gender-transparent. It does not require a particular mix, like several members of one gender or one member of the other."[35] McIntyre underscores the transparency of the MacKenzie partnership through the nonidentification of an offstage member named Merit. Merit, the family's initiator and "house manager," is the victim of a tragic accident that predates the events narrated in *Starfarers*. Merit's absence gives McIntyre the luxury of not having to describe the character beyond a name and fond memories. In her silence about this character's sex, race, class, sexual preference, and other identifying features, the reader is forced to face his own assumptions regarding the figure that would fit this unmarked space. Identity as a function of racial or gendered specificity disappears, to be replaced by Merit's memory. For this

character, race and gender becomes the most superficial of markers. By implication, the human beings of McIntyre's future can become open to an as yet
unimaginable range of social affinities.[36]

But the MacKenzie family partnership does not imply the advent of a
utopia in which difference does not make a difference. Instead, it is the harbin-
ger of a social formation in which the proliferation of differences provokes a
disruption of norms. In other sections of *Starfarers*, McIntyre entertains the
possibility of an astrofuturist posthumanism, of the sort fictionalized in Bruce
Sterling's *Schismatrix* (1985).[37] Again, it must be emphasized that the family
partnership does not reflect a military structure in which individual differences
are sanded away to create a mechanical sameness. Rather, McIntyre allows for
individual specificity as a part of what has to be negotiated in domestic and
public life. The members of the family partnership do not live in some impossible harmony, but are forced to address the tensions created by Merit's death,
financial stress, and personal differences. An open-ended structure made even
more so by Merit's death, the family is vulnerable also to the influence of
newcomers.

Through the family partnership, we begin to realize that McIntyre's interest in the space future lies in the possible malleability of the markers of individual and social identity. The biographical and historical specificity of her
characters sympathetically emphasizes their differences in a way that evacuates
the content from the notion of "universal man." In fact, the wide range of differences that McIntyre imagines, both artificial and natural, encourages the
speculation that in her space future, there will be as many genders, races, and
sexualities as there are people. The author usurps the universal humanity into
which all must fit, not in order to prescribe a particular alternative to conventional social relations, but to imagine a society built around the freedom to re-
fashion one's self and one's associations. Social and political consensus, if it
occurs, arises out of the affinities that people of very different backgrounds
may find through reasoned argument, common interest, and emotional commitment. It cannot be imposed from above by a mandated similitude of interest,
purpose, or character. Working with the materials she inherits from previous ar-
ticulations of the space-future project, McIntyre finds room to speculate about
social alterity. She avoids the simple humanism that would have social good
automatically flowing from any movement out onto the space frontier. Instead,
she articulates a feminist astrofuturism that reflects a changed and changing political engagement. The negotiations, promises, and compromises of politics do
not disappear, and freedom requires not only eternal vigilance, but also eternal
experimentation.

As do Allen Steele and Vonda N. McIntyre, Kim Stanley Robinson mounts an opposition that is loyal to the transcendence imagined through space exploration but critical of the political and economic assumptions that guided astrofuturism's founding voices. He is third-generation astrofuturism's most deliberately utopian writer for, as he argues, the habitation of new worlds is always and "almost automatically a utopian effort":[38] "The people who put down Utopia as 'pie in the sky,' impractical, and totalitarian—all that is a political stance aiding the status quo, which itself is clearly unjust and insupportable. Utopia has to be rescued as a word, to mean "working towards a more egalitarian society, a global society."[39] But if for astrofuturists such as Jerry Pournelle and Ben Bova, the conquest of new worlds is a flight from terrestrial political conflicts, Robinson responds that the red planet should never be thought of as a convenient escape from the consequences of our actions here on Earth. Rather, the Mars of his imagination is a test site for the innovations required to solve the social and physical problems of our native planet. Robinson's Mars trilogy— *Red Mars* (1993), *Green Mars* (1994), and *Blue Mars* (1996)—is a deliberate strike against the bourgeois fantasy of escape into an unspoiled frontier. In a 1996 interview, he remarks, "I was particularly worried that it would seem that I was proposing Mars as some kind of bolt-hole—that we could let Earth go to hell because we could make an even better second Earth on Mars. That is so contrary to my feelings that I had to make the entire plot say the opposite—that Mars can't function as a bolt-hole, that it can't even exist as a human place, unless Earth is doing well."[40] Hence Robinson offers Mars as a thought experiment that can help us address urgent terrestrial problems. Chief among these is the question of the environmental impact of an exploding human population's aggressive use of the Earth's limited resources.

Although Robinson agrees with Mars Society president Robert Zubrin that Mars is a wilderness that must be domesticated by powerful new technologies, he is skeptical of the frontier metaphors prevalent in contemporary astrofuturism.[41] In the Mars trilogy, his characters grapple with the "intrinsic worth" of the Martian environment on the one hand and, on the other, the need to alter that environment in order to sustain human activity.[42] The conflict illuminates Robinson's position that humankind must rethink its relationship to whatever land it inhabits. The species must learn to think of itself as people of the land and not conquerors, exploiters, or escape artists.

Robinson's rejection of astrofuturism's empire-building conventions is the space-clearing gesture that allows him to offer alternatives. Whereas for Robert A. Heinlein or Arthur C. Clarke the space future is a reflection of nineteenth-century glory, Robinson insists that historical analogies to past revolutions and conquests have little bearing on the future that will emerge from present circumstances. Any representation of terrestrial and space futures must reckon with two centuries of struggles for liberation by subjugated lands and peoples. Hence the history of the future cannot be fully controlled by any single individual or group, ideology, or nation. Robinson's theory of history is self-consciously opposed to the monolithic, capitalist future histories that so engaged science fictionists from the late 1930s to the 1960s.[43] Instead, it engages the strand of space futurism pioneered by David Lasser in the early 1930s. His futures are not the gift of a single privileged people or messiah but emerge from a cacophony of voices that never quite resolve into a single, harmonious choir. Moreover, against the great majority of space-future fiction that entertains us by reconstituting nineteenth-century industrial capitalism on grander scales, Robinson seeks to construct a narrative unregulated by "the mechanistic world view [that uses] the old futures like tired stage sets."[44] Using astrofuturism's resources, he breaks with the technological determinism and political naiveté of his predecessors.

Over the course of Robinson's Mars trilogy, it becomes clear that the human habitation of extraterrestrial spaces does not redeem American history. Rejecting both a redemptive repetition of our past and a triumphant escape from endless cycles of rise and fall, Robinson imagines future history as a slow, nonlinear, often frustrating shuffle of the cards that must constantly reckon with the state of things. Neither a frontier to conquer nor the site of a revolution that leaves Earth behind, Mars is a heterotopia that could change the very nature of revolution. The making of a new world is an enterprise so vast and complex that it changes the course of human history. The historical bloc under which we live undergoes a "phase shift" marked by changes in structures of feeling and social relations that add up to a new culture.

Although Robinson is careful to problematize the analogies that have fixed the meaning of revolution to paradigmatic moments in America, France, and Russia, he acknowledges that these precedents provide the vocabulary we need to interpret phenomena that would otherwise be incomprehensible. The revolution of *Blue Mars* appropriately begins with "a gunshot," echoing Ralph Waldo Emerson's commemoration of the start of the American Revolution as "the shot heard round the world."[45] However, Robinson's future revolution is also heralded by "a bell rung, [and] a choir singing counterpoint."[46] This third and final Martian revolution, he writes, *was so complex and nonviolent that it was hard to see it as a revolution at all, at the time; more like a shift in [an] ongoing argument, a change in the tide, a punctuation of equilibrium* (734, author's emphasis). The crisis that sparks this final revolution is the clash between

Earth's desire to solve the political problems created by overpopulation and un-restrained resource exploitation and Mars' need to protect the fragile new social ecology its inhabitants have established. Given our history and fictional cliches, we expect a final conflict in which one side conquers the other (in the process planting the seeds of the next inevitable clash) or in which both combatants are reduced to preindustrial quiescence or extinction. In seeking a way off the treadmill of these plots, Robinson proposes an acceleration of history that out-runs humanity's violent impulses:

At any point in the process, in a thousand different places, things could have turned vio-lent; many people were furious; but cooler heads prevailed. It remained, in most places, at the level of argument. Many feared this could not continue, many did not believe it possible; but it was happening, and the people in the streets saw it happening. They kept it happening. At some point, after all, the mutation of values has to express itself; and why not here, why not now? . . . This was the moment of mutation, history in the mak-ing, and they could see it right before them, in the streets and on the human hillsides and on the screens, history labile right there in their hands—and so they seized the moment, and wrenched it in a new direction. They talked themselves into it. A new government. A new treaty with Earth. A polycephalous peace. The negotiations would go on for years. Like a choir in counterpoint, singing a great fugue. (745–46)

Here the value of inhabiting another world, with its implications of a tremendous increase in the human ability to manipulate natural forces, lies in our progress toward what Gerard Piel has called the "humane phase" of his-tory.[47] Thus, in the Mars trilogy, Robinson not only rescues utopia from the in-tellectual backwaters of twentieth-century literature, but also makes credible the possibility of change from one historical era to another. That latter option is directed toward the here and now, for his task is to destabilize the structures of feeling that nurture our inequalities. The utopia he imagines does not banish change and struggle because it exists inside a history that is never finished.[48]

In his account of the rise of *homo ares*, Robinson imagines humanity transformed by its interaction with the advanced technoscience that allows it to make Mars inhabitable. His hopes for our terrestrial and space-based future is articulated powerfully in his description of the revolution as a resolution be-tween two human species:

On the coast of Tempe, the new Kampuchean settlers got out of their landers and went to the little shelters that had been dropped with them, just as the First Hundred had, two centuries before. And out of the hills came people wearing furs, and carrying bows and arrows. They had red stone eyeteeth, and their hair was tied in topknots. Here, they said to the settlers, who had bunched before one of their shelters. Let us help you. Put those guns down. We'll show you where you are. You don't need that kind of shelter, it's an old design. That hill you see to the west is Perepelkin Crater. There's already apple and cherry orchards on the apron, you can take what you need. Look, here are the plans for a disk house, that's the best design for this coast. Then you'll need a marina, and some fishing boats. If you let us use your harbor we'll show you where the truffles grow. Yes, a disk house, see, a Sattelmeier disk house. It's lovely to live out in the open air. You'll see.[49]

The new Martians are humans who have gone native and become the people of their new land. They appear with all the signs of racial difference we have been conditioned to recognize as threatening or amusing: the topknot as a sign of cultural difference; bows, arrows, and furs that signal their technological commitments; and "red stone eyeteeth" to signal physical difference from terrestrial humanity. The Martians have become the "natives, "primitives," and "Indians" of imperial adventure, but they are also the inhabitants of a scientific utopia, the possessors of a technological inheritance that trumps the military hardware deployed by terrestrial authority. Hence a powerful new social ecology has resignified the meaning of race. Their knowledge, indeed their creation of the land and their choice to hunt it with bows and arrows, indicate an order opposed to the extractive industrial capitalism represented by the settlers' guns. They are the "future primitives" who Robinson hopes will supplant the commonplace industrial futures imagined by astrofuturists such as Gerard O'Neill and Robert Heinlein.[50] And he imagines them to be the hybrid descendents of all the African, Asian, and European varieties of humankind. Moreover, the settlers are not the white Europeans of our own colonial heritage, but people who were the colonized of the recent past. Race and difference have not disappeared; they have been complexly troped and reassigned in light of past miseries, present desires, and future hopes.

This space future contains all the scientific and narrative conventions we have come to expect, but they are opened to possibilities not imagined by Robinson's predecessors. Robinson regards astrofuturism as a collection of "utopian statements of desire, full of joy and hope and danger, re-opening our notion of the future to a whole range of wild possibilities."[51] It is in this way that science and its fiction may be used as resources for addressing the political hopes of peoples who struggle for futures unfettered by authoritarian injunctions to accept what is. Robinson embraces the potential that astrofuturism and science fiction represents for his generation: "I love this part of the literature: the thought-experiment that attacks social problems and suggests solutions, utopian goals, or envisions societies that we might then work towards. It seems to me that that's one of the most important things that it does, and it doesn't necessarily have to be like taking castor oil. It can be playful, and it can be fun to read, and yet still be a way of increasing the meaning of our lives and sharpening our political will."[52] Finally, astrofuturism expresses the desire to bring together science and art in a concerted engagement with the questions we address in our private and political lives. By these means, we shape our responses to contemporary politics and maintain our skill at discovering other places and inventing other futures.

What is at stake in narrative constructions of a future in space has never been as simple as refurbishing power. Astrofuturism has also been motivated by a desire to push the boundaries of convention, to exceed the physical and social imperatives that structure the contemporary order. Trends in third-generation astrofuturism indicate that even the most conservative and obdurate instruments of power have in them potential that can be tuned to other agendas. Astrofuturism represents the kind of dreams that can arise from within our ordinary culture; although contained within the boundaries of the dominant cultural hegemony, such dreams also nourish dissent. McIntyre, Steele, and Robinson all engage elements of our ordinary culture that have been nourished poorly by our dominant institutions. Herein lies the dynamism of recent history and the force that will shape whatever future we encounter.

Heretofore, the spaceflight movement has been considered almost exclusively within the frame of its complicity in the dominant projects of a regnant America, a nation solely concerned with burnishing its image abroad and achieving an unambiguous victory over its ideological, economic, and political rivals. Although this research agenda is undeniably important, by itself it is inadequate. The astrofuturism of the spaceflight movement is by turns an extension of exploratory dramas that celebrate conquest and exploitation and those that seek wildernesses that are free from the powerful hierarchies of our world. We might consider what help there is in this tradition for communities suffering the political and economic consequences of mendacity, bigotry, and greed. Their engagements exemplify our ability to imagine just social orders using the materials at hand, seizing help from unexpected quarters. It is through this kind of imaginative work that we develop the tools we need to change the future.

Abbreviations

ABMA	Alabama Ballistic Missile Agency
ADU	American Democratic Union
AEC	Atomic Energy Commission
AIAA	American Institute of Aeronautics and Astronautics
AIS	American Interplanetary Society
AMNH	American Museum of Natural History
ARS	American Rocket Society
BIS	British Interplanetary Society
DLP	David Lasser Papers, University of California, San Diego
EWP	East West Players
HUAC	House Un-American Activities Committee
JPL	Jet Propulsion Laboratory
MIT	Massachusetts Institute of Technology
MSFC	George C. Marshall Space Flight Center
NASA	National Aeronautic and Space Administration
NSF	National Science Foundation
NSI–NSS	National Space Institute–National Space Society
RHG	Robert H. Goddard, *The Papers of Robert H. Goddard*, Vol. 2, 1925–1937, ed. Ester C. Goddard and G. Edward Pendray (New York: McGraw-Hill Book Company, 1970)
RHG II	The Papers of Robert H. and Ester C. Goddard, Box 13, Special Collections, Robert H. Goddard Library, Clark University, Worcester, Mass.
SFE	*Science Fiction Encyclopedia* (1st ed.)
SSI	Space Studies Institute
VfR	*Verein für Raumschiffahrt* (Society for Space Travel)
WAA	Workers Alliance of America
WPA	Works Projects Administration

Notes

Introduction

1. See Frank H. Winter, *Prelude to the Space Age—The Rocket Societies: 1924–1940* (Washington, D.C.: Smithsonian Institution Press, 1983).

2. The term "hard science fiction" denotes a form of science fiction that conforms to the physical laws observed by contemporary scientific knowledge. It is defined in opposition to fantasy, horror, and other subgenres, which imagine emotional or spiritual forces intervening in the operation of physical reality. Writers such as Charles Sheffield, Gregory Benford, and Robert L. Forward (all trained physicists) argue that hard science fiction is the core that justifies and stabilizes a genre that the public mind all too often confuses with fantasy. Kim Stanley Robinson, restive about the extra-literary policing implied by the term, has argued that it represents more a "hardness of attitude" than any strict adherence to the disciplines of science (Kathryn Cramer and David G. Hartwell, "Kim Stanley Robinson Interview," *Readercon 9 Report*, ed. Evelyn C. Leeper and Mark R. Leeper, *ReaderCon 9* [*July 13, 1997 Convention Report*] 21 August 2000 <http://www.fanac.org/Other_Cons/ReaderCon/r97–rpt2.html>). For more on the history of the term and the controversy that surrounds it, see *Hard Science Fiction*, ed. George E. Slusser and Eric S. Rabkin (Carbondale: Southern Illinois University Press, 1986) and Allen Steele, "Hard Again," *New York Review of Science Fiction* 46 (June 1992): 1, 3–5.

3. Cramer and Hartwell, "KSR Interview."

4. The classic study of the construction of the west in dime novels is Henry Nash Smith's *Virgin Land: The American West as Myth and Symbol* (Cambridge, Mass.: Harvard University Press, 1982 [1950]), 90–120. See also Jane Tompkins, *West of Everything: The Inner Life of Westerns* (New York: Oxford University Press, 1992).

5. Peggy Deamer, "The Everyday and the Utopian," *Architecture of the Everyday*, ed. Steven Harris and Deborah Berke (Princeton, N.J.: Princeton University Press, 1997), 215.

6. Howard Segal, *Technological Utopianism in American Culture* (Chicago: University of Chicago Press, 1985).

7. My argument is influenced by Emily Martin's definition of science as an active matrix that allows for a traffic between its inside and outside. See "Citadels, Rhizomes, and String Figures," *Technoscience and Cyberculture*, ed. Stanley Aronowitz, Barbara Martinsons, and Michael Menser (New York: Routledge, 1996), 97–109.

8. William Sims Bainbridge, *The Spaceflight Revolution: A Sociological Study* (Seattle: University of Washington Press, 1976).

9. Winter, 13–17.

10. Walter A. McDougall, *"... the Heavens and the Earth": A Political History of*

the Space Age (New York: Basic Books, 1985); Howard E. McCurdy, *Space and the American Imagination* (Washington, D.C.: Smithsonian Institution Press, 1997); Dale Carter, *The Final Frontier: The Rise and Fall of the American Rocket State* (New York: Verso, 1988).

11. Constance Penley, *NASA/Trek: Popular Science and Sex in America* (New York: Verso, 1997) and Henry Jenkins, *Textual Poachers: Television Fans and Participatory Culture* (New York: Routledge, 1992).

12. I borrow the term "poaching," as does Jenkins, from Michel de Certeau's *The Practice of Everyday Life* (Berkeley: University of California Press, 1988). His analysis of consumption as a productive activity informs the whole of my argument, as does his insistence that even the most oppressively dominant discourse (he gives the example of the Spanish colonization of the Americas) is vulnerable to appropriation and rearticulation (31–32).

13. Sharon Traweek, "When Eliza Doolittle Studies 'enry 'iggins," *Technoscience and Cyberculture*, ed. Stanley Aronowitz, Barbara Martinsons, and Michael Menser (New York: Routledge, 1996), 37–55 and *Beamtimes and Lifetimes: The World of High Energy Physicists* (Cambridge, Mass.: Harvard University Press, 1988); Emily Martin, "Citadels, Rhizomes, and String Figures," *Technoscience and Cyberculture*, 97–109; and Donna J. Haraway, "Teddy Bear Patriarchy: Taxidermy in the Garden of Eden, New York City, 1908–36," *Primate Visions: Gender, Race, and Nature in the World of Modern Science* (New York: Routledge, 1989), 26–58.

14. Daniel Leonard Bernardi, *Star Trek and History: Race-ing Toward a White Future* (New Brunswick, N.J.: Rutgers University Press, 1998) and Michael C. Pounds, *Race in Space: The Representation of Ethnicity in* Star Trek *and* Star Trek: The Next Generation (Lanham, Md.: Scarecrow Press, 1999).

15. Robert Scholes and Eric S. Rabkin, *Science Fiction: History, Science, Vision* (London: Oxford University Press, 1977), 188.

16. In *The Lathe of Heaven*, Ursula K. Le Guin satirizes this desire to create an undivided human race in which "all men are brothers" by briefly turning the entire human race gray (New York: Charles Scribner's Sons, 1971).

17. Brian W. Aldiss with David Wingrove, *Trillion Year Spree: The History of Science Fiction* (New York: Atheneum, 1986), 428.

18. Recent scholarship on Delany as a writer of science fiction and fantasy is exploring this territory. See Jeffrey Allen Tucker, "Sense of Wonder: the Postmodern Projects of Samuel R. Delany" (Ph.D. diss., Princeton University, 1997) and his online essay "Studying the Works of Samuel R. Delany," *Wired for Books* (online database) cited 25 April 2002 <wiredforbooks.org/scifi/delany.htm>.

19. Peter Nicholls, ed., *The Science Fiction Encyclopedia* (Garden City, N.Y.: Dolphin Books, 1979), 467.

20. See, for example, Joseph Corn's treatment of technological prediction as "a predominantly male exercise," which produced a literature that seems unmarked by race or class (Joseph J. Corn, "Epilogue," *Imagining Tomorrow: History, Technology, and the American Future*, ed. Joseph J. Corn [Cambridge, Mass.: MIT Press, 1986], 225).

21. Toni Morrison, *Playing in the Dark: Whiteness and the Literary Imagination* (Cambridge, Mass.: Harvard University Press, 1992).

22. Donna J. Haraway, *Modest_Witness@Second_Millenium.FemaleMan_Meets _OncoMouse* (New York: Routledge, 1997), 151.

23. Haraway expounds this argument in "Situated Knowledges: The Science Question in Feminism and the Privilege of Partial Perspective," in *Simians, Cyborgs, and Women: The Reinvention of Nature* (New York: Routledge, 1991), 183–201.

24. Thulani Davis, "The Future May Be Bleak, But It's Not Black," *Village Voice*, 1 February 1983, 17.

25. For an incisive examination of the politics behind the criticism of mass culture, see Dick Hebdige, "Towards a Cartography of Taste," in *Hiding in the Light: On Images and Things* (London: Routledge/Comedia, 1988).

26. Dwight Macdonald, "A Theory of Mass Culture," reprinted in *Literary Taste, Culture and Mass Communication Vol I: Culture and Mass Society*, ed. Peter Davidson, Rolf Meyersohn, and Edward Shils (Teaneck, N.J.: Somerset House, 1978), 173.

27. Macdonald, 175–76 and Hebdige, 57.

28. For the political implications of the 1960s youth culture, see Todd Gitlin, *The Sixties: Years of Hope, Days of Rage* (New York: Bantam Books, 1987).

29. Jazz, as an outgrowth of African American culture, was often treated contemptuously by mass-culture critics, such as Evelyn Waugh, who tended to see black culture as emblematic of the corruption of American (popular) culture (see Hebdige, 50–71). Between the 1920s and 1940s especially, this prejudice was shared by intellectuals on both sides of the Atlantic. Not all white intellectuals, however, condemned jazz as the sign of a great cultural malaise. After the Second World War, many liberal and leftist intellectuals, black and white (e.g., Norman Mailer, Kingsley Amis, and Leroi Jones [Amiri Baraka]), hailed it as the manifestation of a heroic, oppositional force representing the best of Western/American culture. See Andrew Ross, "Hip, and the Long Front of Color," in *No Respect: Intellectuals and Popular Culture* (New York: Routledge, 1989), 69–101 and Kingsley Amis, *Memoirs* (New York: Summit Books, 1991), 52–53, 65–70. Along with films, cricket, and the wireless, Amis lists science fiction as "one more indisputably good thing" (52). His enthusiasm for the genre led him to write in the genre *The Alteration* (New York: Viking Press, 1977) and, more famously, the critical appreciation *New Maps of Hell* (New York: Ballantine Books, 1960), an influential evaluation that helped dignify literary attention to the genre.

30. Marge Piercy is best known within science fiction as the author of *Woman on the Edge of Time*, an antiracist feminist utopia (New York: Knopf, 1976). Ishmael Reed is important for Davis's argument because, like Delany, he disrupts our expectations of black and white characters, for instance, in *The Terrible Twos* (New York: St. Martin's Press/Marek, 1982), creating the kind of cultural slippage against which Davis warns.

31. African American science fiction has reached a watershed with the release of an anthology delineating its history and its prospects, *Dark Matter: A Century of Speculative Fiction from the African Diaspora*, ed. Sheree R. Thomas (New York: Warner Books, 2000).

A recent addition to the list of science popularizers includes Neil de Grasse Tyson,

Frederick P. Rose Director of the Hayden Planetarium in New York. Since his appointment in 1996, the astrophysicist has become the most prominent African American science writer since Benjamin Banneker published his almanac in the 1790s. Tyson is the author of two collections of his popular astronomy pieces: *Merlin's Tour of the Universe* (New York: Columbia University Press, 1989) and *Just Visiting This Planet* (New York: Doubleday, 1998). He has also authored an autobiography, *The Sky Is Not the Limit: Adventures of an Urban Astrophysicist* (New York: Doubleday, 2000). Apropos the themes of my investigation, it is worth remembering that Banneker, a largely self-taught astronomer, is most famously remembered for his correspondence with Thomas Jefferson. His letter, published as an introduction to his 1793 almanac with Jefferson's reply, claims the "rights of human nature" announced in the Declaration of Independence for African Americans. The claim is grounded in Banneker's ability to do the mathematical work required for his almanac. Long before the scientific and technological utopias of the coming centuries, science was drafted into the project of human emancipation. See Silvio A. Bedini, *The Life of Benjamin Banneker* (New York: Charles Scribner's Sons), 152–56, 280.

32. See the list of newspaper and online reviews, "October Sky (1999)," Rotten Tomatoes (database online), cited 14 August 2000 <www.rottentomatoes.com/movies/browse/1085865/reviews.php>.

33. Homer H. Hickam, Jr., *October Sky: A Memoir* (New York: Dell Books, 1999 [1998]), 1.

34. Some allowance was made for male students who could escape this fate by excelling at football and winning athletic scholarships to college. They are, however, the exception that proves the rule.

35. An illustration of the segregationist ethic dominant in the American south at mid-century can be found in Oak Ridge, the nuclear industrial and scientific community established by the U.S. government in 1942. Fermi and Samra note that the "negro hutments" allocated to the town's black inhabitants "were separated by a fence within a fence so that members of the white community were hardly aware a 'Negro Village' existed at all." Physical invisibility was underscored by denial of civic amenities. The hutments sat on dirt floors, and lacked window glass, and black children had no access to local schools (Rachel Fermi and Esther Samra, *Picturing the Bomb: Photographs from the Secret World of the Manhattan Project* [New York: Harry N. Abrams, 1995], 58).

36. In the film, their roles are merged with that of white machine-shop workers to create a heroic black character, Leon Bolden, a World War II veteran who flew with the Red Tails, an all-black bomber escort squadron. The film character is emblematic of a resistance to racism that is patriotic instead of radical. Consequently, it allows the filmmakers to de-emphasize the significance of racial segregation in the social order Hickam remembers. In the film, Bolden is on a first-name basis with Homer's father and mother, even though the senior Hickam is the mine supervisor and, therefore, his boss.

37. Note that one of the sources for Captain James T. Kirk and his Starfleet was C. S. Forester's portrait of Horatio Hornblower and the Napoleonic-era British Royal Navy. Forester died in 1966, the year that *Star Trek* began its first season on television (Stephen E. Whitfield and Gene Roddenberry, *The Making of Star Trek* [New York: Ballantine Books, 1968], 28).

38. *Star Trek* is often said to have been ahead of its time as a television show addressing contemporary issues from a liberal perspective. In a recent interview, Peter Fonda argues that the 1960s counterculture frightened the general American public with its more outrageous behavior (Gregg Kilday, "Icon: Survival of the Fittest," *Madison*, September 1999, 118–25). If that is so, then we might consider *Star Trek* an alternative that allows audiences to imagine nonthreatening change, and to defer that change for three centuries. Roddenberry's Starfleet allows the extension of democratic guarantees while providing a military order that mobilizes heterogeneity for the exploration of space. Racial and ethnic diversity is institutionalized in a future that does not threaten predictable, contemporary command structures. Contemporary shows such as *Room 222* and *Mod Squad*, however, indicate that Roddenberry and Desilu Studios were sailing the prevailing winds of network television. *Mod Squad* premiered in the 1968 season as the networks searched for a formula that would capture the interest of young audiences by appearing "relevant." Castleman and Podrazik note, "With Pete, Julie, and Linc involved in cases as timely as the evening's headlines, ABC could exploit current issues such as youth rebellion, drug abuse, and racial tension while making sure the legitimate authority always triumphed in the end" (Harry Castleman and Walter J. Podrazik, *Watching TV: Four Decades of American Television* [New York: McGraw-Hill, 1982], 208). The original *Star Trek* series followed the trend toward topicality during its three-year run. Notable episodes include "Let That Be Your Last Battlefield," on race (which first aired 10 January 1969); "The Way to Eden," on a misguided youth culture or cult group (which first aired 21 February 1969); "A Taste of Armageddon," on the Vietnam War (which first aired 23 February 1967). Network interest in speaking to contemporary audiences affected the career of more than one black television actor. Lloyd Haynes, the star of *Room 222*, was initially contracted to be a regular player on *Star Trek* as the communications officer of the *Enterprise*. After working on the second pilot of the series, "Where No Man Has Gone Before" (which first aired 22 September 1966), the *Room 222* opportunity came up and he asked to be released from his contract. Nichelle Nichols was hired to replace him (George Takei, *To the Stars: The Autobiography of George Takei, Star Trek's Mr. Sulu* [New York: Pocket Books, 1995], 235–36). However, we should not discount the political hope symbolized by *Star Trek*'s social vision. Roddenberry's future allows us to imagine a time when we do not recognize race as a source of danger. This is explicitly illustrated during an exchange between Lt. Uhura and a being calling himself Abraham Lincoln in the *Star Trek* episode "The Savage Curtain" (which first aired 7 March 1969). *Star Trek*'s innovation at the time lay in its projection of a future in which race does not matter, certainly not as it did in real life.

39. Takei continues that work today. See his "Diversity in Television," *Asian American Artistry* (database online), cited 23 July 2000 <www.asianamericanartistry.com/articles-takei.html>.

40. Roddenberry's original pitch for the series emphasized its similarities to the popular early 1960s horse opera *Wagon Train* (1957–65). Roddenberry also argued that any hopeful future would lower the barriers between women and high office. He therefore imagined that women in command of starships would be ordinary and unremarkable. This supposition proved too much for test audiences and network executives in that pre–women's movement decade (Whitfield and Roddenberry, 128).

41. Daniel Bernardi, "*Star Trek* in the 1960s: Liberal Humanism and the Production of Race," *Science-Fiction Studies* 24 (1997): 217–18.

42. Takei, *To the Stars,* 238–39.

43. In fairness, Bernardi's general interest in the institutions and individuals that made the program does include actors (210). I suggest only that his analysis can be pushed further to take seriously those moments when minority actors actively intervene in the production process, even when the results of their interventions seem small or ambiguous.

44. Takei records that when he began work as a professional actor in the television industry of the early 1960s, an Asian actor could expect to be cast as "the classic stereotype" of the "bumbling comic servant with a funny accent and a high-pitched laugh" (197). Among the more prominent such characters on network television during that time was "Hop Sing," the cook and comic relief for NBC's *Bonanza*, played by veteran actor Victor Sen Yung. His insistence on breaking with stereotypes sometimes meant that Takei had to refuse parts that he considered too buffoonish or offensive (198).

45. Tula Lake, California, was a maximum-security facility for Japanese and Japanese American "disloyals." Takei's family was relocated there after his parents answered "no-no" to questions 27 and 28 of a Loyalty Questionnaire. Takei lists the two questions:

No. 27. Are you willing to serve in the Armed Forces of the United States on combat duty wherever ordered?

No. 28. Will you swear unqualified allegiance to the United States of America and faithfully defend the United States from any or all attack by foreign or domestic forces, and forswear any form of allegiance or obedience to the Japanese emperor, to any other foreign government, power, or organization? (42, italics in original)

These questions were designed as a pledge of allegiance. Takei records that the internees did not overlook their political significance: "The substance of American citizenship—most vitally, freedom and justice—was torn away from us, but now we were not to be denied the 'responsibility' of citizenship. Japanese Americans had the right to be killed for a country that had humiliated them, stripped them of property and dignity, and placed them behind barbed wire" (43).

46. Mrs. Takei's decision indicates one of the ways in which the trans-Pacific history of the Takei family came into conflict with the patriotic nationalism of the 1940s. Although he was raised and educated in the United States, Norman Takei was a Japanese citizen by reason of birth. According to immigration law at that time, he could not become a naturalized citizen. Emily Takei was American born, as were her children. She feared that the wartime paranoia that interned her family would break it apart if her husband were deported as an "enemy alien"—a real enough possibility with the passage of Public Law 405 and the abrupt closing of the internment camps. She sacrificed her birthright in a desperate gamble to prevent the dissolution of her family (44–45, 55–57).

47. Takei's family also experienced the trauma of wartime casualties. His mother's sister, "Aunt Ayako," and her baby died as part of the atomic bombing of Hiroshima (59–60).

48. The move to the new theater was completed in March 1998 when EWP

opened the David Henry Hwang Theatre in the Union Center for the Arts. Takei's prestige in the Asian American community may, perhaps, be indicated by the following anecdote: Vinod Sekhar, a Malaysian businessman who had promised $500,000 for the new theater, doubled that amount to a cool million in exchange for dinner with Takei. Mr. Sekhar is reported to be a "huge *Star Trek*" fan ("$1 Million for Union Center," *Little Tokyo News* 2, no. 1 [January/February 1997] [database online] cited 19 July 2000 <http://www.janet.org/ltnews/ltnews21_uctr.html>).

49. Bernard C. Nalty, *Strength for the Fight: A History of Black Americans in the Military* (New York: Free Press, 1986).

50. Takei closes his account of the 442nd by quoting President Truman's words at the White House ceremony honoring their unit: " 'You fought not only the enemy, but you fought prejudice—and you have won' " (58). At this point, Takei is triumphant, but we do not have to be. It would not be too far from the truth to call Truman's blessing the valedictory of a Pyrrhic victory. Many Japanese American soldiers received the same "thanks" from their fellow citizens that black servicemen and women found on returning home. As the civil rights era dawned in the 1950s, it became clear that the Second World War was only the opening salvo in a much longer struggle.

51. "HERO, A Tribute to George Takei" was presented by the EWP on 14 November 1998 as a benefit performance for their new space. Among the guest performers were Takei's *Star Trek* colleagues, Nichelle Nichols, Walter Koenig (who played Ensign Pavel Chekov in the original series), and Garrett Wang (who played Ensign Harry Kim in the fourth Star Trek series, *Star Trek: Voyager* [1995–2001]) ("EastWest Players Honors George Takei with a Benefit Performance of Comedy and Music on November 14, 1998," *Asian American Theatre Review* [database online], cited 21 August 2000 <www.abcflash.com/a&e/r_tang/ Takeitribute.html>).

52. Nichelle Nichols, *Beyond Uhura: Star Trek® and Other Memories* (New York: G. P. Putnam's Sons, 1994), 160–63. See also Allan Asherman, *The* Star Trek *Interview Book* (New York: Pocket Books, 1988), 69; Herbert F. Solow and Robert H. Justman, *Inside Star Trek: The Real Story* (New York: Pocket Books, 1996), 244–45; J. Alfred Phelps, *They Had a Dream: The Story of African-American Astronauts* (Novato, Calif.: Presidio, 1994), 62.

53. Nichols, 164–65; Phelps, 62. Nichols's prominence in the black community was ensured by a cover story run by *Ebony* magazine ("A New Star in the TV Heavens," *Ebony* [January 1967], 70–72, 74, 76).

54. Nichols, 219–25.

55. Phelps, 62–65. LeVar Burton, who played Lt. Cmdr. Geordi LaForge in *Star Trek: The Next Generation* (1987–95), explains the importance of public representation via popular culture to members of disenfranchised groups: "Mae Jemison, the first African-American woman in space—she flew on the shuttle—became a scientist first, and then an astronaut, because she saw Nichelle Nichols on the original Star Trek series and said, 'You know what? That's for me' " (*Trekkies*, dir. Roger Nygard, Paramount Pictures, 1997). The genealogy of influence continues to Burton himself, for he too has seized the language of aspiration provided by science fiction to author his own hopeful future narrative, *Aftermath* (New York: Warner Books, 1997).

56. Nichols, 224; Penley, 19; Jesse Katz, "Shooting Star," *Stanford Today* (July/

August 1996), 38–41. *Stanford Today Online* (database online) cited 11 August 2000 <www.stanford.edu/dept/news/stanfordtoday/ed/ 9607/9607mj02.shtml>.

57. Dissatisfaction with NASA is fairly widespread in the spaceflight movement, although the grounds for criticism vary. See, for example, Gordon R. Woodcock's critique of NASA's post-Apollo performance in "Wanted: Pioneers for the Space Frontier," *New Destinies: The Paperback Magazine* 7 (spring 1989), 177–200. In Penley's terms, Jemison may have become disillusioned by the practice, but not by the theory (19). Penley takes care to account for the reasons that women might *not* be interested in the space program run by NASA. She notes that writer Ellen Willis, writing after the deaths of Christa McAuliffe and her crewmates, recounts that she had grown up "curious about the stars and space exploration," but lost interest until she saw someone like herself being recruited into the astronaut corps. "Willis says that she was so alienated from the WASP space cowboy version of spaceflight that she missed watching the moon landing on TV. . . . Like many women she passed it up out of anger that NASA's iconography left her no room for fantasies of women in space" (58).

58. Jemison's experience is consonant both with constant traffic between science fiction and contemporary spaceflight and the link that some African Americans have made between the spaceflight dream and political empowerment.

In the documentary *Trekkies*, Nichelle Nichols recounts, "There were two little girls, around nine years old, eight years old, when Star Trek first came on. And one of them told me years later, 'I looked on that television and I saw you, I saw this black lady, and I ran through the house screaming: Come quick, come quick. There's a black lady on television and she ain't no maid.' And she said, 'I knew right then and there I could be anybody I wanted to be. I could be anything I wanted to be.' And so she decided to be a superstar. And her name is Whoopi Goldberg" (*Trekkies*, 1997).

59. The Planetary Society has been actively arguing the case for Mars since the early 1970s. The group's founders, Carl Sagan and Bruce Murray, were involved in the robotic exploration of the planets during the 1960s and 1970s, far from the limelight generated by the manned space program. They also exemplify the dual role of professional scientist/engineer and popular science proselytizer common in the field. See Bruce Murray, *Journey into Space: The First Thirty Years of Space Exploration* (New York: W. W. Norton, 1990), 350–51, and Carl Sagan, *Pale Blue Dot: A Vision of the Human Future in Space* (New York: Random House, 1994), 355.

60. Kathy Sawyer, "Bush Urges Mars Landing by Year 2019," *The Washington Post*, 12 May 1990, A6 and James Gerstenzang, "Bush Pegs 2019 for Next Giant Step for Man-On Mars," *Los Angeles Times*, 12 May 1990, A14.

61. Norman Spinrad, *Russian Spring* (New York: Bantam Books, 1991); Allen Steele, *The Labyrinth of Night* (New York: Ace Books, 1992); Ben Bova, *Mars* (New York: Bantam Books, 1992); Kim Stanley Robinson, *Red Mars* (New York: Bantam Books, 1993).

Chapter 1

1. David Lasser, excerpt from "Remark by David Lasser to Los Angeles Chapter," AIAA, June 16, 1982, Airport Marine Hotel, Los Angeles, California, "Questions to David Lasser," Box 1, Folder 4, t.s., David Lasser Papers, University of California, San Diego, question no. 32.

2. G. Edward Pendray, *The Coming Age of Rocket Power* (New York: Harper & Brothers, 1945), 118.

3. The magazine was published by Hugo Gernsback, the Luxembourgian "father" of American science fiction, from 1930 to 1936 (Brian Stableford, "Wonder Stories," *The Science Fiction Encyclopedia*, ed. Peter Nicholls [Garden City, N.Y.: Dolphin Books/Doubleday & Company, 1979], 662–63).

4. Beryl Williams and Samuel Epstein, *Rocket Pioneers: On the Road to Space* (New York: Julian Messner, 1958), 171–72.

5. Pat Jefferson, "David Lasser: Rocketry Pioneer," *AIAA Student Journal* 26, no. 3 (fall 1988): 2.

6. David Lasser, "Questions to David Lasser," Box 1, Folder 4, t.s., DLP, 1. The former organization is probably the Hebrew Ladies' Maternity Aid Society, an international women's league with Canadian and U.S. branches (Norma Baumel Joseph, *From Immigration to Integration: The Canadian Jewish Experience, A Millennium Edition* [database online] cited 18 September 2001 <www.bnaibrith.ca/institute/millennium/millennium12.html>). The Volunteer League is a liberal organization founded by Newark's Jewish community in 1901 to provide "non-discriminatory care to people of all spiritual backgrounds," based on the values of social justice and "repairing the world" (Healthcare Foundation of New Jersey, "History of the Foundation," [database online] cited 18 September 2001 <www.hfnj.org/history.htm>).

7. Howard Zinn, *The Politics of History* (Urbana: University of Illinois Press, 1990), 104.

8. Lasser was in the 28th Division at the time of the battle (Ernest B. Furgurson, "David Lasser: Struggling to Restore His Good Name," *The Baltimore Sun*, 23 September 1979, K1).

9. Eric Leif Davin, *Pioneers of Wonder: Conversations with the Founders of Science Fiction* (Amherst, N.Y.: Prometheus Books, 1999), 31.

10. David Lasser to Jack Williamson, 22 March 1932, Box 6, Folder 6, t.s., DLP.

11. As of the March 1930 issue of *Science Wonder Stories*, the Associate Science Editors included astronomers Clyde Fisher and Willem J. Luyten, astrophysicist Donald H. Menzel, mathematician James Byrnie Shaw, psychologist Marjorie E. Babcock, entomologist William M. Wheeler, and primatologist Joseph G. Yoshioka. Other editors represented physics, radio, medicine, electrical engineering, chemistry, and botany. One of the science editors, David H. Keller, a psychiatrist who served as the board's representative for medicine, also wrote science fiction (*Science Wonder Stories* 1, no. 10 [March 1930]).

12. See, for example, newsreel coverage of polar explorer Richard Byrd's expeditions in the 1920s and 1930s, Robert Flaherty's ethnographic documentary *Nanook of the North* (1921), the adventure-nature films of Osa and Martin Johnson in the 1930s,

and Merian C. Cooper and Ernest Schoedsack's ethnographic and feature film work in *Grass* (1925) and *King Kong* (1933).

13. Davin, 53.

14. Ibid., 51. David Lasser and David H. Keller, "The Time Projector," *Wonder Stories* 3, no. 2 (July 1931) and *Wonder Stories* 3, no. 3 (August 1931).

15. Only Warren Fitzgerald, president and the lone African American member of the Scienceers, accepted Gernsback's invitation (Allen Glasser, "History of the Scienceers: The First New York City Science Fiction Club, 1929," *First Fandom Magazine* 4 [June 1961]; republished in *Timebinders: Preserving Fannish History* [database online] 19 July 2001 <http://fanac.org/timebinders/scienceers.html>). Frank Winter records that this pioneer of science fiction and the spaceflight movement "dropped out of the AIS within a year" (Frank H. Winter, *Prelude to the Space Age: The Rocket Societies, 1924–1940* [Washington, D.C.: Smithsonian Institution Press, 1983], 73, 146–47). Unfortunately, he does not record the reason for Fitzgerald's departure. Admittedly, extant information on Warren Fitzgerald is minuscule. An exchange of letters between Winter, Lasser, and science-fiction historian Sam Moskowitz establishes his memberships, his race, and his residence in Harlem (Sam Moskowitz to Frank Winter, 22 November 1974; Frank Winter to David Lasser, 14 February 1977, 15 July 1977; David Lasser to Frank Winter, 14 April 1977; Box 1, Folder 4, DLP). Glasser is more detailed, recalling that Fitzgerald was light-skinned, cultured, and older by fifteen years than the rest of the Scienceers. He was also married, and together with his wife graciously welcomed young, white science-fiction fans to their Harlem apartment.

Fitzgerald's brief visibility in the conjoined cultures of science fiction and spaceflight suggests that neither was completely closed to black participation. One wonders, however, what prompted his abrupt disappearance. In the absence of information, I can only speculate that the insecure economic and political status of African Americans in the 1930s forced him to lay aside his avocations. However, during his presidency, the September 1930 issue of the Scienceers's newsletter, *The Planet*, endorsed the idea of "interplanetary travel as a definite possibility in the not too distant future" (quoted in Winter, 147).

16. C. P. Mason, "Interplanetary Society Now Formed," *Wonder Stories* 2, no. 1 (June 1930): 78. Mason would later write fiction for *Wonder Stories* under the pseudonym of Epaminondas T. Snooks ("Traders in Treasures," *Wonder Stories* 5, no. 10 [May 1934]; see also Davin, 33).

17. These sentiments are reiterated in the first typewritten and mimeographed issue of the *Bulletin of the American Interplanetary Society* ("Introductory," *Bulletin of the American Interplanetary Society* 1 [June 1930]: 1, Box 4, Folder 4, t.s., DLP).

18. Davin, 58.

19. Ibid.

20. A Presbyterian minister, settlement-house worker, and ardent pacifist, Norman Thomas ran as Socialist Party candidate for the presidency in six elections. In 1932, at the height of his involvement in presidential politics, he won 884,781 votes. While the two men may not have agreed on American involvement in the Second World War (Thomas was opposed), Lasser approved of Thomas's evolutionary (as opposed to mili-

tant) socialism and followed the antifascist, anticommunist program championed by the Socialist Party leader in the 1940s and early 1950s.

21. Jefferson, 4. Lasser's left-wing sympathies resonated with those of other participants in the science-fiction culture of the early 1930s. Frederick Pohl, Damon Knight, Judith Merril, and James Blish are representative of readers and writers whose intellectual formation included both science fiction and socialism. As the "Futurians"—a loose affiliation of fans in the late 1930s—they were considered "dangerously Red" by their more conservative peers (Jack Williamson, *Wonder's Child: My Life in Science Fiction* [New York: Bluejay Books, 1984], 117–18). Indeed, Pohl was a member of the Young Communist League at a time when American communists defended "jobs, security, democracy and peace" against fascist imperialism. In 1936, the group was committed to the reelection of Franklin Delano Roosevelt playing a less-than-revolutionary role in electoral politics (Frederik Pohl, *The Way the Future Was: A Memoir* [London: Victor Gollancz, 1979], 50).

22. Davin, 57.

23. Jefferson, 5.

24. David Lasser, *The Conquest of Space* (New York: Penguin Press, 1931), 2.

25. Journeys to the Moon have been a feature of Western literature since the second-century publication of Lucian of Samosata's *A True History,* a satire in which the author uses the marvelous travels of his protagonist to engage the follies of his time and place. From this beginning through a line of literary descent that includes Thomas More, Cyrano de Bergerac, and H. G. Wells, Lasser inherits a model of prose fiction that seeks a reformation of the moral and political order. And while his intent is not satiric, his conquest of space is a romantic reform with utopian resonances.

26. This idea would be codified in NASA's 1958 charter as a civilian agency of the U.S. government, which included the declaration, "that activities in space should be devoted to peaceful purposes for the benefit of all mankind" (L. B. Taylor, Jr., *"for all mankind": America's Space Programs of the 1970s and Beyond* [New York: E. P. Dutton, 1974], 4). The phrase has been shortened to a much snappier and often repeated aphorism, "we came in peace for all mankind." But see Amitai Etzioni, who denounces this rhetoric as the "large mountain of space-pushing platitudes" employed by partisans of the American space program (Amitai Etzioni, *The Moon-Doggle: Domestic and International Implications of the Space Race* [Garden City, N.Y.: Doubleday & Co, 1964] 195–96).

27. In his 1897 scientific romance *Two Planets*, the extraterrestrials who need convincing are Martians (Kurd Lasswitz, *Two Planets* [Carbondale: Southern Illinois University Press, 1987]). Lasswitz's novel influenced the space enthusiasts who became the core of von Braun's rocket team in Germany and the United States. For more on Lasswitz, see William B. Fisher, *The Empire Strikes Out: Kurd Lasswitz, Hans Dominik, and the Development of German Science Fiction* (Bowling Green, Oh.: Bowling Green State University Popular Press, 1984).

28. Doris Lessing, *Shikasta: re, colonized planet 5: personal, psychological, historical documents relating to visit by Johor (George Sherban) emissary (grade 9) 87th of the period of the last days* (New York: Knopf, 1979).

29. Lasser, *Conquest of Space*, 137.

30. Albert Einstein, *The Quotable Einstein*, ed. Alice Calaprice (Princeton, N.J.: Princeton University Press, 1996), 148.

31. David Lasser to Arthur C. Clarke, 24 November 1969, Box 1, Folder 13, DLP.

32. "The Forthcoming Annual Meeting," *Astronautics* 4, no. 28 (March 1934): 7 and Davin, 56.

33. David Lasser to G. Edward Pendray, 15 May 1936, Box 1, Folder 4, DLP.

34. David Lasser, President, American Interplanetary Society, to R. H. Goddard, New York, 8 April 1930, Robert H. Goddard, *The Papers of Robert H. Goddard*, Volume II: 1925–1937, ed. Ester C. Goddard and G. Edward Pendray (New York: McGraw-Hill, 1970), 735.

35. R. H. Goddard to David Lasser, 12 April 1930, Worcester, RHG, 735.

36. Carl Sagan, *The Dragons of Eden: Speculations on the Evolution of Human Intelligence* (New York: Ballantine Books, 1978), 88. See also Tom Crouch's detailed account of Goddard's epiphany and its consequences (Tom D. Crouch, *Aiming for the Stars: The Dreamers and Doers of the Space Age* (Washington, D.C.: Smithsonian Institution Press, 1999), 19–20.

37. Carl Sagan, *Cosmos* (New York: Ballantine Books, 1985), 91–92 and Milton Lehman, *Robert H. Goddard: Pioneer of Space Research* (New York: Da Capo Press, 1963), 28. Lowell's early insistence that there was (or had been) intelligent life on Mars made him a necessary but slightly embarrassing ancestor for the generation of planetary scientists that Sagan represents. Astrofuturists and science-fiction writers continue to turn to Lowell's hopeful vision of life on Mars as an important cultural touchstone. Lowell was wrong but in an inspirational way (*Cosmos*, 87–91).

38. Lehman, 23 and R. H. Goddard to H. G. Wells, London, England, Roswell, RHG, 821–23.

39. Lehman, 169.

40. Ibid.

41. R. H. Goddard to David Lasser, 12 April 1930, Worcester, RHG, 735.

42. R. H. Goddard to H. Parrish, 14 July 1930, Worcester, RHG, 755.

43. Crouch, 32.

44. Quoted in "David Lasser, Pioneer Space Man," *The I.U.E. News*, 2 April 1970, 10.

45. "Statement Released by Clark University for Publication in Newspapers of Thursday, July 10, 1930," Worcester, RHG, 752–54.

46. H. Parrish, Office of Ivy Lee to R. H. Goddard, 10 July 1930, New York, RHG, 755.

47. By listing the names of prominent figures in aviation and academic science, including Colonel Charles A. Lindbergh and Dr. R. A. Millikan of the California Institute of Technology, as members of the committee who oversaw Goddard's experiments, the Lee-Clark University statement established the official legitimacy that Gernsback desired but never quite achieved (RHG, 753).

48. David Lasser, "Guggenheim Financial Aid for Goddard Rocket Study Gives New Hope to Man's Efforts to Conquer Gravity," *New York Herald Tribune*, 13 July 1930, IV1.

49. R. H. Goddard to H. Parrish, 14 July 1930, Worcester, RHG, 755.

50. Jefferson, 5.

51. Thomas J. Morrow, "Labor Leader, Federal Aide: 'Radical' Label Haunts RB Man," *Times-Advocate* [Escondido, Calif.], 13 May 1979, A4.

52. Ibid.

53. *Eric Davin v United States Department of Justice, Federal Bureau of Investigation,* No. 94–3590 (3d Cir 1995) (database online) cited 6 August 2001 <http://vls.law.vill.edu/locator/3d/Aug1995/95a1116p.txt>. In *Pioneers of Wonder,* Davin notes that the FBI holds a ten-thousand-page file on the WAA and a smaller but still substantial one-thousand-page brief on Lasser. The Freedom of Information Act has also revealed that the Department of Justice was interested in Lasser's old employer, Hugo Gernsback (Davin, 92–93).

54. The committee would gain more prominence during the Red Scare of the postwar years under Senator Joseph McCarthy (R-Wisconsin) and Richard M. Nixon (R-California) by the shortened form of its name: the House Un-American Activities Committee (HUAC).

55. As part of his work in science fiction, Lasser was briefly involved in the technocracy movement, during its short, newspaper-driven prominence in the early 1930s. In 1932–33, he edited two issues of *Technocracy Review*, a publication that Gernsback sponsored for the organization. Technocracy's insistence that scientists and engineers (technocrats) are better qualified to run the economic and political machinery of the nation than politicians or voters appealed to some members of the early science-fiction community (DLP, Box 5, Fldr 2).

56. Morrow, A4.

57. Jefferson, 6.

58. David Lasser, "Space, Satellites and Survival," *The Trades Unionist*, 31 May 1958, 5.

59. Ibid. The warning Lasser articulates here echoes the stark choice H. G. Wells offered to a previous war-troubled generation in the closing chorus of his 1936 film *Things to Come*. In the 1980s, Carl Sagan would pick up and redeploy this theme in the context of a world heavily militarized by four decades of cold war and nuclear terror (Carl Sagan, *Cosmos* [New York: Ballantine Books, 1985], xviii–xx).

Chapter 2

1. Michael Flynn, *Firestar* (New York: TOR Books, 1996).

2. The Peenemünde engineers had originally named the rocket the A-4 or Aggregate 4. Their numbering system continued that which they had used during the days when they were just an amateur rocket society working at a leased field on the outskirts of Berlin. The Nazi propaganda machine renamed the rocket V-2 for obvious reasons (Richard S. Lewis, *Appointment On the Moon* [New York: Ballantine Books, 1969], 12).

3. Erik Bergaust, *Wernher von Braun* (Washington, D.C.: National Space Institute, 1976), 147.

4. This is a landmark moment in the development of American space capabilities. However, before the end of the Third Reich, General Walter Dornberger had claimed the creation of the spaceship for his own rocket team at Peenemünde (Michael J. Neufeld, *The Rocket and the Reich: Peenemünde and the Coming of the Ballistic Missile Era* [New York: Free Press, 1995], 165). After World War II, rocketry in America is as much a story of technological transfer or appropriation as it is of homegrown invention.

5. Tom Bower, *The Paperclip Conspiracy: The Hunt for the Nazi Scientists* (Boston: Little, Brown, 1987), 125. For more on the von Braun team's involvement in the crimes of the Third Reich, see Linda Hunt, *Secret Agenda: The United States Government, Nazi Scientists, and Project Paperclip, 1945 to 1990* (New York: St. Martin's Press, 1991) and Neufeld.

6. Joseph J. Trento and Susan B. Trento, *Prescription for Disaster: From the Glory of Apollo to the Betrayal of the Shuttle* (New York: Crown Publishers, 1987), 7.

7. Dale Carter, *The Final Frontier: The Rise and Fall of the American Rocket State* (New York: Verso, 1988), 7.

8. Walter A. McDougall, . . . *the Heavens and the Earth: A Political History of the Space Age* (New York: Basic Books, 1985), 229.

9. Arthur C. Clarke, "Space Flight and the Spirit of Man," *Voices from the Sky: Previews of the Coming Space Age* (New York: Harper & Row, 1965), 4.

10. See, for example, Carl Sagan's *The Cosmic Connection: An Extraterrestrial Perspective* (New York: Dell Publishing, 1973) and *Broca's Brain: Reflections on the Romance of Science* (New York: Ballantine Books, 1980).

11. Bergaust, 20.

12. Fredric Jameson, "Progress Versus Utopia; or, Can We Imagine the Future?" *Science-Fiction Studies* 9 (1982): 150–51.

13. For a pioneering academic treatment that argues for science fiction's utility as an anticipatory genre, see J. O. Bailey, *Pilgrims Through Time and Space: Trends and Patterns in Utopian Fiction* (Westport, Conn.: Greenwood Press, 1975 [1947]).

14. Ernst Stuhlinger and Frederick I. Ordway III, *Wernher von Braun: Crusader for Space—A Biographical Memoir* (Malabar, Fla.: Krieger Publishing Company, 1994), 250.

15. Sagan's rhetoric here invokes J. Robert Oppenheimer's remark that many physicists worked on the World War II atomic bomb project because the problem was "technically sweet." The remark was made in the context of Oppenheimer's regret regarding his own participation. The Manhattan Project inaugurated a strong contingent within the American scientific community that questions the militaristic use of science. Its members have created the Pugwash conferences in which scientists discuss the moral and political implications of nuclear weapons; *The Bulletin of Atomic Scientists*, a major antinuclear watchdog publication; and at least one science-fiction novel, Jack McDevitt's *The Hercules Text* (New York: Ace Books, 1986), in which a scientist refuses to pursue the implications of his research because of the cataclysmic dangers posed by its possible application in war. See also Oppenheimer's collection of essays, *Atom and Void: Essays on Science and Community* (Princeton, N.J.: Princeton University Press, 1989).

16. For more on the Americanization of the rocket team, see Michel Bas-Zorhas, *The Hunt for German Scientists* (New York: Hawthorne Books, 1967), 143–44 and Ray

Spangenburg and Diane K. Moser, *Wernher von Braun: Space Visionary and Rocket Engineer* (New York: Facts On File, 1995).

17. According to William Sims Bainbridge's investigation into the class backgrounds of the spaceflight advocates, von Braun was one of only two men who came from the upper class. His biographer, Erik Bergaust, notes that although von Braun's father, Freiherr Magnus von Braun, was a baron of the Prussian Junker aristocracy, this was not common knowledge. Within the American context, such status is generally kept out of public discourse. See William Sims Bainbridge, *The Spaceflight Revolution: A Sociological Study* (Seattle: University of Washington Press, 1976), 37. The British, however, had no such egalitarian pretensions. In the immediate postwar era, the *Journal of the British Interplanetary Society* published a biographical sketch by Willy Ley that makes clear von Braun's connection with German aristocracy. Ley notes that the prewar von Braun was contemptuous of both the Weimar Republic and of the Nazis. These attitudes were typical of his class and formed a plank in "the political platform of the *Deutsche Adels Gesellschaft* (Society of German Nobility)," the party of Magnus von Braun, who served the Weimar Republic as Minister of Agriculture and Education (Willy Ley, "Correspondence: Count von Braun," *Journal of the British Interplanetary Society* 6 [June 1947], 155). David F. Noble argues that von Braun's assimilation into the American mainstream was aided by the assumption of a fundamentalist Christian faith, which also accounts for von Braun's success in making the spaceflight dream consonant with the Bible Belt sensibility of the southern state in which he lived and worked (David F. Noble, *The Religion of Technology: The Divinity of Man and the Spirit of Invention* [New York: Alfred A. Knopf, 1997], 126–29).

18. Frederick I. Ordway III and Mitchell Sharpe, *The Rocket Team* (New York: Thomas Y. Crowell, 1979), 408–9. Adolf K. Thiel, a member of the German rocket team, was one of the fourteen Germans that Allied security classified as "potential or actual threats to the US" because of long-term membership in the Nazi Party and/or membership in the SS or SA. Von Braun was also included on that list (Bower, 237).

19. Stuhlinger and Ordway, 94.

20. See, for example, the scholarship of Dale Carter and Michael J. Neufeld and Tom Lehrer's incisive 1965 satire, "Wernher von Braun," *Too Many Songs by Tom Lehrer* (New York: Pantheon Books, 1981), 124–25.

21. Stuhlinger and Ordway, 251.

22. Spangenburg and Moser, viii.

23. Mike Wright, "The Disney-Von Braun Collaboration and Its Influence on Space Exploration," *Inner Space/Outer Space: Humanities, Technology and the Postmodern World*, ed. Daniel Schenker, Craig Hanks, and Susan Kray (Huntsville, Ala.: Southern Humanities Press, 1993), 153.

24. Michael J. Neufeld, "Weimar Culture and Futuristic Technology: the Rocketry and Spaceflight Fad in Germany, 1923–1933," *Technology and Culture* 31, no. 4 (October 1990): 725–52.

25. Paul Boyer, *By the Bomb's Early Light: American Thought and Culture at the Dawn of the Atomic Age* (New York: Pantheon Books, 1985).

26. Steven Watts, *The Magic Kingdom: Walt Disney and the American Way of Life* (Boston: Houghton Mifflin, 1997), 312.

27. For an incisive account of the Chicago (1933) and New York (1939) fairs, see Robert W. Rydell's valuable *World of Fairs: The Century of Progress Expositions* (Chicago: University of Chicago Press, 1993).

28. Marc Eliot, *Walt Disney: Hollywood's Dark Prince, a Biography* (Secaucus, N.J.: Carol Publishing Group, 1993), 224–25.

29. Watts, 304.

30. Wright, 156.

31. Randy Liebermann, "The *Collier's* and Disney Space Series," *Blueprint for Space: Science Fiction to Science Fact*, ed. Frederick I. Ordway III and Randy Liebermann (Washington, D.C.: Smithsonian Institution Press, 1992), 145. See also Wright, 156.

32. Liebermann, 146. Wright recounts that Ward Kimball, Disney's producer for the Man in Space series, wanted to make this connection as a promotional strategy. Von Braun, fearful of publicity that would derail the political commitment to spaceflight, intervened (Wright, 155–56).

33. Tom D. Crouch, *Aiming for the Stars: The Dreamers and Doers of the Space Age* (Washington, D.C.: Smithsonian Institution Press, 1999), 121.

34. Spangenburg and Moser, 35. Concern for the safety of a valuable engineer, however, prompted officials to block his youthful aspirations in this direction (Neufeld, *Rocket and Reich*, 58).

35. For more on the racism that accompanied the United States's war with Japan, see John W. Dower, *War Without Mercy: Race and Power in the Pacific War* (New York: Pantheon Books, 1986).

36. See the documentary "A Civil Rights Journey," which includes film footage of the time recorded by Huntsville African American physician Sonnie Hereford (Calhoun Community College, "Calhoun News Release," [database online] cited 20 September 2001 <www.calhoun.cc.al.us/Prelations/releases2001/civilrightsjourney.htm>).

37. *Sputnik I,* launched on 4 October 1957, was "the shot heard 'round the world." The Russians quickly followed this success with *Sputnik II,* launched 3 November 1957.

38. Lewis, 58.

39. "Space: Reach for the Stars," *Time,* 17 February 1958, 22.

40. T. Keith Glennan, *The Birth of NASA: The Diary of T. Keith Glennan* (Washington, D.C.: NASA History Office, 1993), 167.

41. Ibid.

42. Ordway and Sharpe, 408–9. Referring to his bibliography on von Braun's work, Mitchell Sharpe notes, "You will quickly see that most of the items are articles and books for the popular press. Von Braun knew where his customers lay: the men in the street and the men in Congress (those who held the NASA purse-strings)." Mitchell R. Sharpe, letter to author, 5 November 1988, Huntsville, Ala.

43. Bergaust, 18.

44. Ibid., 311.

45. "Science fact" is used within the science-fiction community to distinguish actual knowledge from literary speculation.

46. Sagan, *Broca's Brain*, 162–64.

47. Stuhlinger and Ordway, 250–51.

48. Walter McDougall notes that, "Science fiction books and magazines rebounded from the wartime slump (with its paper shortage) to reach a circulation by 1949–53 double the prewar peak and seven times the wartime trough. In 1951 *Life* magazine estimated the science fiction readers in the United States at over 2 million" (100).

49. Ordway and Sharpe, 408.

50. Bergaust, 155–56.

51. Ibid., 156.

52. Wernher von Braun, *The Mars Project* (Urbana: University of Illinois Press, 1962 [1953]), 2.

53. Glennan, 23.

54. Wernher von Braun, "Prelude to Space," *Across the Space Frontier*, ed. Cornelius Ryan (New York: Viking Press, 1952), 50–56.

55. This, of course, is also long before the creation of NASA, with its ostensibly civilian-directed space program, which stabilized the institutional matrix around which a rhetoric of peaceful intent might form. In later years, the peaceful benefits of space exploration would get a more elaborate articulation in the work of von Braun and other astrofuturists, partially as a response to criticisms from the left. At the same time, von Braun would become more explicit about the importance of the high frontier to the security of the free world (Wernher von Braun, *Space Frontier* [Greenwich, Conn.: Fawcett Publications, 1969], 183).

56. Von Braun, *Across the Space Frontier*, 52–53.

57. Ibid., 56.

58. H. Bruce Franklin, *War Stars: The Superweapon and the American Imagination* (New York: Oxford University Press, 1988).

59. Stuhlinger and Ordway, 115. Italics in original.

60. Beryl Williams and Samuel Epstein, *Rocket Pioneers: On the Road to Space* (New York: Julian Messner, 1958), 160. The authors note that Ley was at the "the core of the Society's research program," along with Klaus Riedel, Rudolph Nebel, and von Braun.

61. The meeting occurred in 1930 (Bergaust, 40, Spangenberg and Moser, 18). Oberth, "the Father of Modern Rocketry," is credited with sparking post–World War I interest in rocketry and space flight among Germans (Williams and Epstein, 144; for Oberth's influence on Ley, 117). He also opened a correspondence with Robert H. Goddard prior to the publication of *Die Rakete zu den Planetenräumen*. A brief exchange of information was followed by Goddard's nervous campaign to establish priority for his innovations in liquid-fueled rocketry (RHG, 485–86, 497–98).

62. According to his biography in *Contemporary Authors*, Ley had at least a reading knowledge of eight languages including his own: French, Dutch, Latin, Italian, German, English, Russian, and classical Greek (*Contemporary Authors*, Vol. 9–12: 523).

63. Williams and Epstein, 121–23 and Frank H. Winter, *Prelude to the Space Age: The Rocket Societies, 1924–1940* (Washington, D.C.: Smithsonian Institution Press,

1983), 22. The initial success of the German spaceflight movement in the late 1920s is accounted for by the compensatory narratives it offered of German technological superiority after the national defeat in the late war (Neufeld, *Rocket and Reich*, 8). Peter S. Fisher extends consideration of the racist and nationalist strands of Weimar era *technischer Zukunftsroman* (technological future novel) in *Fantasy and Politics: Visions of the Future in the Weimar Republic* (Madison: University of Wisconsin Press, 1991), 104–56.

64. R. H. Goddard to Edmund Wilson, *The New Yorker*, 10 June 1944, Worcester, The Papers of Robert H. and Ester C. Goddard, Box 13, Special Collections, Robert H. Goddard Library, Clark University, Worcester, Mass. Goddard wrote this letter in response to a review that Wilson had written in *The New Yorker* on Ley's *Rockets: The Future of Travel Beyond the Stratosphere* (New York: Viking, 1944).

65. R. H. Goddard to G. Edward Pendray, 4 September 1944, Worcester, RHG II.

66. Ley attempts to prove this in *Rockets, Missiles, and Space Travel* (the 1957 revision of *Rockets*), by pointing out the limited appeal (though importance) of Goddard's 1920 monograph "A Method of Reaching Extreme Altitudes" in scientific circles, its small circulation in a Europe recovering from the disruption of World War I, and Goddard's refusal to participate in the information network of the early rocket community (Willy Ley, *Rockets, Missiles, and Space Travel* [New York: Viking Press, 1957], 108, 133). He also notes Goddard's tardiness in publishing his findings (145). We should not, of course, entirely discount the possibility that Ley was willing to promote the VfR's precedence in rocketry in the interests of German nationalism.

67. Neufeld, *Rocket and Reich*, 5, 8. Crouch notes that public enthusiasm for spaceflight in Germany during the late 1920s was popularly recognized as a "*raketenrummel*" (rocket craze) (Crouch, 51).

68. Neufeld, *Rocket and Reich*, 24.

69. *Contemporary Authors*, Vol. 9–10, s.v. Ley, Willy (Robert Willey).

70. Neufeld, *Rocket and Reich*, 26.

71. Ibid., 27.

72. Ordway and Sharpe, 104–5.

73. That company included Albert Einstein, Paul Tillich, Kurt Weill, and many of the scientists who became involved in the Manhattan Project (Klaus Wurst and Heinz Moos, *Three Hundred Years of German Immigrants in North American: 1683–1983* [Baltimore, Md.: Heinz Moos Publishing, 1983], 178; Gerald Abraham, *The Oxford Concise History of Music* [Oxford: Oxford University Press, 1979], 823; and Laura Fermi, *Illustrious Immigrants: The Intellectual Migration from Europe 1930–41* [Chicago: University of Chicago Press, 1971]).

74. Frank Winter provides a detailed account of the forces that drove the German rocket enthusiasts apart in the early 1930s. By 1932, the VfR suffered from a series of internal conflicts that occurred between Rudolph Nebel, the de facto president of the society, and the group's board of directors. Nebel was a P. T. Barnum type whose promotional schemes involved promising technological miracles he could not deliver, often leaving prospective investors disappointed. One of his bolder schemes prompted the board to take him to court. The action exacerbated a leadership crisis that the society had been struggling with for some time. Ley, the vice president, had moved out of par-

ticipating in the society's experimental program and into the more rewarding work of popular science (spaceflight) lecturing. The society's president, Winkler, was absent working on a secret project with an industrialist. And von Braun, who was to become one of rocketry's most successful managers, was lured away by the German Army. In other words, it was not simply economics and the intervention of the government and politics that drove the VfR apart, as Ley and other historians of the period would have us believe, but the internal divisions that are inevitable in a small, amateur group (Winter, 44–50). Michael Neufeld records that Nebel was also involved in disputes with Army Ordinance over how rocketry should be developed by the Weimar Republic. There is little doubt that these conflicts hardened the Reichwehr's commitment to keep all rocket work to itself (Neufeld, *Rocket and Reich*, 26–28).

75. Ordway and Sharpe, 103.

76. Williams and Epstein, 169.

77. *Astounding Science Fiction* (ASF) continues as *Analog Science Fiction/ Science Fact*, which remains a popular forum for astrofuturist fact and fiction.

78. Jon Gustafson, "Ley, Willy," *Science Fiction Encyclopedia*, ed. Peter Nicholls (Garden City, N.Y.: Doubleday, 1979), 354.

79. A partial list of those books includes: Chesley Bonestell and Willy Ley, *The Conquest of Space* (1950); Cornelius Ryan, ed., *Across the Space Frontier* (1952); Arthur C. Clarke, *The Exploration of Space* (1951); R. A. Smith and Arthur C. Clarke, *The Exploration of the Moon* (1954); Willy Ley and Wernher von Braun, *The Exploration of Mars* (1956); and Wernher von Braun, *First Men to the Moon* (1960).

80. Ley was undoubtedly aware of the precedent Lasser set with the title in the early 1930s. The traffic between the VfR and the AIS allowed for the sharing of fiction and technical information. Indeed, R. F. Starzl, a science-fiction writer and early AIS member, mailed the first issue of *Science Wonder Stories* to Willy Ley, "thus converting him instantly to science fiction." These exchanges were essential to the imagined community that formed around the wonderful dream. Ley's new *Conquest* can be read as an homage to the Lasser's initial statement. See Eric Leif Davin, *Pioneers of Wonder: Conversations with the Founders of Science Fiction* (Amherst, N.Y.: Prometheus Books, 1999), 33.

81. Quoted in Frederick C. Durant III and Ron Miller, *Worlds Beyond: The Art of Chesley Bonestell*, (Norfolk/Virginia Beach, Va.: Donning/Starblaze, 1983), 8.

82. Lester Del Rey, *The World of Science Fiction: 1926–1976, The History of a Subculture* (New York: Ballantine Books, 1979), 189.

83. The John C. Winston Company published a series of hardbound science-fiction juveniles in the 1950s under the editorial direction of Lester Del Rey. Del Rey's work on the series owed a lot to literary and experimental initiatives of von Braun, Ley, and company.

84. O. B. Hardison, Jr., *Disappearing Through the Skylight: Culture and Technology in the Twentieth Century* (New York: Viking, 1989), 139. See also Thomas Hine, *Populuxe* (New York: Knopf, 1986), 83–90.

85. Michael A. G. Michaud, *Reaching for the High Frontier: The American Pro-Space Movement, 1972–84* (New York: Praeger, 1986), 8.

86. Chesley Bonestell and Willy Ley, *The Conquest of Space* (New York: Viking Press, 1950), 55.

87. Ibid., 56. On Leeuwenhoek's invention of the microscope, see Carl Sagan, *Cosmos* (New York: Ballantine Books, 1980), 117.

88. Bonestell and Ley, 55. Levania is Kepler's name for the Moon. Ley expanded on his systemization of the history of astronomy in his *Watchers of the Skies: An Informal History of Astronomy from Babylon to the Space Age* (New York: Viking Press, 1969 [1963]).

89. Bonestell and Ley, 95.

90. Willy Ley, *Engineers' Dreams* (New York: Viking Press, 1954).

91. While the pulp-fiction and boys' literature of the early twentieth century was dominated by westerns and urban detective stories, stories in which heroic engineering and engineers played a role were also popular. The best of these is the Doc Savage series originally published from 1933 to 1949. Doc Savage is a superhuman scientist who travels the world righting wrongs in the company of "the five greatest brains ever assembled in one group" (Kenneth Robeson, *World's Fair Goblin* [New York: Bantam Books, 1969 (1939)], back cover). One of those brains is an appropriately heroic civil engineer.

92. Further examples can be found in the work of J. D. Bernal, Jacques Ellul, and Freeman Dyson (J. D. Bernal, *The World, the Flesh, and the Devil: An Inquiry Into the Future of the Three Enemies of the Rational Soul* [Bloomington: Indiana University Press, 1969 (1929)]; Jacques Ellul, *The Technological Society* [New York: Vintage Books, 1964]; and Freeman Dyson, *Disturbing the Universe* [New York: Harper Colophon Books, 1981]). We shall see further examples of this obsession with large-scale engineering in astrofuturist proposals in the chapters that follow.

93. Ley, *Rockets, Missiles, and Space Travel*, 331.

94. Ibid.

95. Kenneth McArdle, ed., *A Cavalcade of Collier's* (New York: A. S. Barnes, 1959), xii.

96. Ryan, iv.

97. Ibid.

98. Jeremy Bernstein, "Profiles: Out of the Ego Chamber," *The New Yorker* 45, no. 25, 9 August 1969, 46. A correspondence between Lasser and Clarke followed the publication of the profile and lasted until the former's death. Clarke was happy to show off his copy of Lasser's pioneering book to interested visitors (Arthur C. Clarke, letter to David Lasser, 2 December 1986, Colombo, Sri Lanka, DLP).

99. Sagan, *Broca's Brain*, 172.

Chapter 3

1. Quoted in David Lasser, *The Conquest of Space* (London: Hurst and Blackett, 1930), 39.

2. Dust jacket for Willy Ley's *Rockets, Missiles, and Space Travel* (New York: Viking Press, 1957). This is the "revised and enlarged edition" of *Rockets: The Future of Travel Beyond the Stratosphere* (New York: Viking Press, 1944).

3. My argument runs counter to the dominant thrust of academic criticism of sci-

ence fiction. Darko Suvin, for instance, reads science fiction as satiric commentary on the follies of contemporary life. At its best, he argues, science fiction can be read as experimentation with alternatives to industrial capitalism (Darko Suvin, "Science Fiction and Utopian Fiction: Degrees of Kinship [1974]," *Positions and Presuppositions in Science Fiction* [Kent, Oh.: Kent State University Press, 1988]). But Charles Elkins counters that as popular literature, science fiction reinforces the status quo (Charles Elkins, "An Approach to the Social Functions of American Science Fiction," *Science-Fiction Studies* 4 [November 1977]: 228–32). Although the two possibilities are rarely absolute, in Heinlein's case I find that the emphasis falls on the latter.

4. Martin Green, *The Great American Adventure* (Boston: Beacon Hill Press, 1984).

5. H. Bruce Franklin, *Robert A. Heinlein: America as Science Fiction* (Oxford: Oxford University Press, 1980), 13. For more on the depth of that identification, see the letters Heinlein wrote to John W. Campbell on America's entry into the Second World War (Robert A. Heinlein, *Grumbles From the Grave* [New York: Ballantine Books, 1989], 25–35).

6. Heinlein, *Grumbles*, 3.

7. Malcolm J. Edwards, "Campbell, John W(ood), Jr.," *The Science Fiction Encyclopedia* (SFE), ed. Peter Nicholls (London: Roxby Press, 1979), 100–101.

8. To be sure, science fiction had always included the popularization of science in its raison d'être. When Hugo Gernsback founded his magazines of the 1920s and 1930s, it was with the avowed purpose of using scientific romance and boys' adventure literature to persuade his audience of the wonders of technology. But Campbell, who became the paradigmatic science-fiction editor, had solid formal training in science: he received part of his education at the Massachusetts Institute of Technology and earned a degree in physics from Duke University (Edwards, op. cit.; Heinlein, *Grumbles*, 28). Campbell, therefore, inherited the editorial initiatives that had been pursued by David Lasser while dispensing with the latter's political radicalism.

9. Quoted in Marjorie Mithoff Miller, "The Social Science Fiction of Isaac Asimov," *Isaac Asimov*, ed. Joseph D. Olander and Martin H. Greenberg (New York: Taplinger Publishing, 1977), 14.

10. Judith Merril, "What Do You Mean: Science? Fiction?" *SF: The Other Side of Realism, Essays on Modern Fantasy and Science Fiction*, ed. Thomas D. Clareson (Bowling Green, Oh.: Bowling Green University Popular Press, 1971), 65–67. See also Gary K. Wolfe, *Critical Terms for Science Fiction and Fantasy: A Glossary and Guide to Scholarship* (New York: Greenwood Press, 1986).

11. Franklin, *RAH*, 67. It is apparent in the letters that make up *Grumbles from the Grave* that Heinlein gave a lot of thought to the business of writing. He was very concerned with rates of payment, name prestige, editorial needs or interference, and so forth. He carefully considered the move to the high prestige formats of the mainstream magazines.

12. The struggle over what should and should not be included in a literature for boys and girls was the cause of much tension between Heinlein and his editor at Scribner, Alice Dalgliesh. The letters between Heinlein, his agent, and Dalgliesh provide a fascinating glimpse into the children's book-publishing world. Dalgliesh, the Scribner

editorial board, and the library councils they served sought to influence the manners and morals of their young readers. Heinlein found that he had to satisfy their demands if he wanted access to a lucrative market. His reluctance to do so eventually led to his ouster from Scribner's list in 1959 (Heinlein, *Grumbles*, 47–86).

13. Franklin, *RAH*, 6.

14. Campbell, quoted in Franklin, *RAH*, 27.

15. For Stapledon's "time scales," see Olaf Stapledon, *Last and First Men: A Story of the Near and Far Future* (Los Angeles: Jeremy P. Tarcher, 1988 [1930]), 308–12.

16. Robert Scholes, *Structural Fabulation: An Essay on Fiction of the Future* (Notre Dame, Ind.: University of Notre Dame Press, 1975), 71–72.

17. Robert A. Heinlein, *Revolt in 2100* (New York: Signet Books/New American Library, 1953), 6–7. Over the next decade, Heinlein fine-tuned the future-history chart as events in the real world dated his prophecies. Franklin notes that Heinlein's last revision of his future-history scheme was published in 1967 (Franklin, *RAH*, 28).

18. See, for instance, Heinlein's fourth published story "If This Goes On—," *Astounding Science Fiction* (February/March 1940). The story is reprinted in Robert A. Heinlein, *The Past Through Tomorrow: "Future History" Stories (PTT)* (New York: G. P. Putnam's Sons, 1967), 454–70.

19. Heinlein, *Revolt in 2100*, 7.

20. *The Moon is a Harsh Mistress* (New York: Orb/Tom Doherty Associates, 1997 [1966]); *Between Planets* (New York: Charles Scribner's Sons, 1951); *Red Planet* (New York: Ballantine Books, 1976 [1949]); *Citizen of the Galaxy* (New York: Ace Books, 1957); *The Rolling Stones* (New York: Charles Scribner's Sons, 1952); "Logic of Empire," *PTT*; "Misfit" (1939), *Revolt in 2100*; "Space Jockey" (1947), *The Green Hills of Earth* (New York: Signet/New American Library, 1958); Mark Twain, *Life on the Mississippi* (New York: Bantam Books, 1981 [1896]).

21. Robert A. Heinlein, *Rocket Ship Galileo* (New York: Ace Books, 1947), 24. Paul Boyer makes a detailed and compelling case that atomic triumphalism and fear were dominant sentiments in the immediate postwar era. As editor of *Astounding Science Fiction*, Campbell was one of the experts journalists interviewed regularly for definite statements on the atomic bomb (Paul Boyer, *By the Bombs Early Light: American Thought and Culture at the Dawn of the Atomic Age* [New York: Pantheon Books, 1985], 14, 115–16).

22. It seems that Heinlein was familiar with some aspects of America's early eugenics movement. The premise of "Methuselah's Children" is that late in the nineteenth century, the Howard Foundation was formed with the intention of promoting human longevity. Its method of doing so was no more advanced than that practiced at John Humphrey Noyes' Oneida Colony, but without the religious notion of spiritual perfection: good stock marries good stock until you get a race of extremely intelligent, strong and long-lived, if not immortal, people. Heinlein spins out this idea and its consequences in his utopian novel *Beyond This Horizon* (1948). While he seems to have had some knowledge of bacteriophage biology, "Methuselah's Children" and *Beyond This Horizon* were too early to take advantage of contemporaneous work in DNA.

23. Heinlein, *Red Planet*, 49. The Martian canal controversy was repopularized during the Mariner and Voyager missions of the 1970s and through Carl Sagan's books in the early 1980s. The inhabited Mars thesis persists in science fiction, just as the idea of Venus as the "water planet" persists in popular opinion. Their endurance indicates our widespread faith that other planets will be simply wild variations on terrestrial conditions; indeed, Verne, Wells, and Edgar Rice Burroughs all imagined this to be so. Project Mariner's cameras have shown that there are no canals on Mars, and the Venus probes (both U.S. and Soviet) have proven that the Venusian surface is nothing like a Louisiana bayou. Yet popular culture continues to withstand the assaults of physical knowledge. Larry Niven, for instance, demonstrates great nostalgia for old fictions of Mars in *Rainbow Mars* (New York: Tor Books, 1999).

24. Joseph J. Corn, *The Winged Gospel: America's Romance with Aviation, 1900–1950* (New York: Oxford University Press, 1983). The spaceflight dream, and its attendant cultural apparatus, is in many ways an extraterrestrial analog of the aviation enthusiasm that Corn covers in this valuable cultural history.

25. Heinlein, "Requiem," *PTT*, 197.

26. As a student of U.S. history, Heinlein is not remarkable in his regard for frontiers as the wellspring of American character. In his classic essay "The Significance of the Frontier in American History," Frederick Jackson Turner argued that "American social development has been continually beginning over again on the frontier. This perennial rebirth, this fluidity of American life, this expansion westward with its new opportunities, its continuous touch with the simplicity of primitive society, furnish the forces dominating American character. The true point of view in the history of this nation is not the Atlantic coast, it is the great West" (Frederick J. Turner, *The Significance of the Frontier in American History* [Ann Arbor, Mich.: University Microfilms, 1966 (1894)], 200).

27. Alexei Panshin and Cory Panshin, *The World Beyond the Hill: Science Fiction and the Quest for Transcendence* (Los Angeles: Jeremy P. Tarcher, 1989), 363.

28. Franklin, *RAH*, 21. See also Alexei Panshin and Cory Panshin, *SF in Dimension: A Book of Explorations* (Chicago: Advent Publishers, 1980), 117.

29. Heinlein, "Requiem," in *PTT*, 205. Remember that *Electrical Experimenter* was one of the names that Hugo Gernsback gave to his first magazine, *Modern Electrics* (1908–29). While the magazine consisted largely of popular science articles, it is considered the birthplace of genre science fiction (Malcolm J. Edwards and Frank H. Parnell, "Science and Invention," *SFE*).

30. Jeffrey Richards, "Boys' Own Empire: Feature Films and Imperialism in the 1930s," *Imperialism and Popular Culture*, ed. John M. MacKenzie (Manchester: Manchester University Press, 1986), 147.

31. Heinlein, "The Man Who Sold the Moon," *PTT*, 118.

32. Ibid.

33. George E. Slusser, *Robert A. Heinlein, A Stranger in His Own Land* (San Bernardino, Calif.: Borgo Press, 1977), 4.

34. Andrew Carnegie firmly established this pattern in American business and philanthropy in his famous essay, "Wealth." Carnegie argued that the ability of the

industrialist to create material goods, which produce great wealth, also makes him the best steward of that wealth for the social good. Heinlein echoes Carnegie, which suggests that Harriman's success in "selling" the Moon makes him the best judge of its future development as a human colony (Andrew Carnegie, *The Gospel of Wealth and Other Timely Essays*, ed. Edward C. Kirkland [Cambridge: Belknap Press of the Harvard University Press, 1962 (1900)]).

35. Heinlein, *Galileo*, n.p.

36. A handful of established publishing houses ran science-fiction series for young adults in the 1950s. The John C. Winston Company followed Scribner's success with a line established in 1952. Arthur C. Clarke, Ben Bova, and Lester del Rey all published under the imprint. Del Rey contributed a "fact book on rockets," *Rockets Through Space: The Story of Man's Preparation to Explore the Universe* (Philadelphia: John C. Winston Company, 1957) to the series, as well as several works of fiction (Lester Del Rey, *The World of Science Fiction: The History of Subculture, 1926–1976* [New York: Ballantine Books, 1979], 203–04. See also John Sisson, ed., *Dreams of Space: Space Art in Children's Books 1950's through 1970's* [database online, Science Library, University of California, Irvine, cited 21 June 2001 <http://sun3.lib.uci.edu/~jsisson/john.htm>]).

37. Heinlein, *Galileo*, 19.

38. One of the most famous of these young experimenters was a teenager from North Carolina named Jimmy Blackmon. He was so enthusiastic about designing missiles that he spent two years building a gasoline-fueled rocket, which drew the attention of Wernher von Braun and others. His case was used as an example of the necessity of creating science-education programs in high schools and colleges and a literature that would instruct the next generation of rocket engineers ("A Boy and His Rocket," *Missiles and Rockets* 1 [October 1956]: 43). Also noteworthy is G. Harry Stine, one of the pioneer nonfiction writers in astrofuturism, who worked hard to build up early model rocketry as a business and a hobby in the 1940s and 1950s (G. Harry Stine, Autobiography 76–241, t.s., G. Harry Stine Papers, National Air and Space Museum, Washington, D.C., 6–7). For more on the cultural history of model aviation, see Corn's "Adults and the Winged Superchildren of Tomorrow," *The Winged Gospel*, 113–33.

39. Heinlein, *Grumbles*, 43. *Young Atomic Engineers* was to be the lead book in a series that would have included the titles: *The Young Atomic Engineers on Mars*, or *Secret of the Moon Corridors*, *The Young Atomic Engineers in the Asteroids*, or *The Mystery of the Broken Planet*; and *The Young Atomic Engineers in Business*, or *The Solar System Mining Corporation*. These titles never appeared as Heinlein originally conceived them, but we can see from the subjects he planned to cover that he had an outline for the steady advance of the young atomic engineers out into space.

40. I am reminded of all the boys' adventure series that focused on technical invention, a genre that grew during the great expansion of printing and literacy in the last quarter of the nineteenth century: Frank Reade, Jr., 1876–1913; Tom Swift, 1910–35; Tom Swift, Jr., 1954–71; and, the series for my generation, Danny Dunn, 1956–77 (John Eggeling and Peter Nicholls, "Dime Novels and Juvenile Series," *SFE*, 171–72).

41. Heinlein, *Galileo*, 23. Lionel S. Marks, *Mechanical Engineer's Handbook* (New York: McGraw-Hill, 1926); Charles D. Hodgman and Norbert A. Lange, *Hand-*

book of Chemistry and Physics (Cleveland, Oh.: Chemical Rubber Publishing Company, 1924); Henry DeWolf Smyth, *Atomic Energy for Military Purposes: The Official Report on the Development of the Atomic Bomb Under the Auspices of the United States Government, 1940–1945* (Princeton, N.J.: Princeton University Press, 1945); Arthur Stanley Eddington, *The Nature of the Physical World* (New York: Macmillan Company, 1928).

Marks's handbook is a standard text that has gone through at least ten editions to date as *Marks' Standard Handbook for Mechanical Engineers*. First-edition copies of the first two texts are held in the Harold G. Dick Airship Collection in Special Collections at the Wichita State University Libraries. Dick was a mechanical engineer who spent his early career working on American and German lighter-than-airships for the Goodyear Tire and Rubber Company. Educated at the Massachusetts Institute of Technology and an exact contemporary of Heinlein's (they were both born in 1907), Dick came of age in the same industrial culture that produced early science fiction. It is for and to boys and men such as Dick that Heinlein wrote.

The fiction chosen by Heinlein gives his futurist speculations a cultural context that extends beyond popular literature and science into the more dignified provinces of canonical American and English literature. In "Logic of Empire," his tale of slavery, mutiny, and escape on the planet Venus (the water-logged version so loved by science-fiction writers from the 1920s to the 1950s), Heinlein mentions *Uncle Tom's Cabin, The Grapes of Wrath,* and *Gulliver's Travels.*

42. Heinlein, *Starman Jones* (New York: Ballantine Books, 1988 [1953]), 20. Libraries were important buyers of Heinlein's juvenilia during the 1950s, and the people who influenced library purchases often wielded editorial power over his work. He was also aware that many first-time readers of his fiction, such as myself, most likely would first encounter it on the shelves of libraries rather than in bookstores (Heinlein, *Grumbles,* 69–73). The first Heinlein, in fact the first book of science fiction I remember reading, was a copy of *The Rolling Stones.* I discovered it at the Union Boulevard branch of the St. Louis Public Library in the mid-1960s.

43. Heinlein, *Galileo,* 23. Virginia Heinlein notes that as a boy her husband was an omnivorous reader: "When Robert learned to read, he read everything he could lay his hands on. He did, in fact, read on his way to school, going along the street, up and down curbs, up to the schoolhouse" (Heinlein, *Grumbles,* xi).

44. Heinlein, *Galileo,* 28.

45. British literary studies have long included a vigorous scholarship in the ideology of "new imperialism" during the late nineteenth and early twentieth centuries and its impact on the creation of boys' adventure narratives. Unfortunately, with the important exception of Martin Green, very little scholarship exists on the impact of this literature within the American context. I proceed on the assumption that because of the trans-Atlantic trade in ideas, images, and institutions (e.g., the Boy Scouts) between Britain and the U.S., especially with regard to the education of the young, there is considerable overlap between the two nations. See Patrick A. Dunae, "Boys' Literature and the Idea of Empire, 1870–1914," *Victorian Studies* 24 (autumn 1980): 105–21; Robert H. MacDonald, "Reproducing the Middle-Class Boy: From Purity to Patriotism in the Boys' Magazines, 1892–1914," *Journal of Contemporary History* 24 (1989):

519–39; Richards op.cit.; and Frances M. Mannsaker, "The dog that didn't bark: The Subject Races in Imperial Fiction at the Turn of the Century," *The Black Presence in English Literature*, ed. David Dabydeen (Manchester: Manchester University Press, 1985), 113–34.

46. Franklin, *RAH,* 76.

47. H. Rider Haggard, *Benita: An African Romance* (London: Cassell and Company, 1906) and Patrick Howarth, *Play Up and Play the Game: The Heroes of Popular Fiction* (London: Eyre Methuen, 1973), 112–14, 119.

48. See, for example, the second half of Heinlein's 1964 novel *Farnham's Freehold*, which provides a very nasty portrait of a future in which blacks rule whites (New York: Ace Books, 1987 [1964]).

49. Robert A. Heinlein, *The Star Beast* (New York: Ballantine Books, 1977 [1954]), 95–96.

50. Heinlein had a habit of naming his male characters after respected political leaders of the past—e.g., Woodrow Wilson Smith, a.k.a. Lazarus Long of "Methuselah's Children," and Andrew Jackson Libby, the human calculator of "Misfit." The names signal their bearer's status as representatives of whole cultures or value systems. In the case of "His Excellency the Right Honorable Henry Gladstone Kiku, M.A. (Oxon.,) Litt. D. *honoris causa* (Capetown), O.B.E., Permanent Under Secretary of Spatial Affairs" (*Star Beast*, 27), Heinlein may have had in mind both William Gladstone, the Liberal Prime Minister (1868–70, 1880–85, 1886, 1892–94) who tried to soften Britain's aggressive imperialism and Harry Thuku, a Kenyan nationalist of the Kikuyu people who (with Jomo Kenyatta) began the Kenyan drive for independence from the British in the 1920s. In so doing, he uses the character to blend the best of Western liberalism with the heroic anticolonial resistance that would eventually create an independent Kenya in 1963. Working on *The Star Beast* in the early 1950s, Heinlein was no doubt aware of the Kikuyu-lead Mau-Mau rebellion of 1952, which sped up the dissolution of British dominance in east Africa.

51. Early science-fiction writers commonly depict human racism against extraterrestrials as an instinctual, biological repugnance. For an excellent example of the intense skin-crawling revulsion they imagined, see Jack Williamson's *The Legion of Space* (1947) reprinted in *Three From the Legion* (New York: Pocket Books, 1980). Of course, aliens in science fiction are merely refigurations of the humans we consider "other." Recall that many members of the eugenics movement in England and America argued that their repugnance for nonwhites had a biological basis that could be scientifically proven. For the ways in which issues of race and gender played out in artistic representations on the covers of science-fiction pulps, see Harry Harrison, *Great Balls of Fire* (New York: Grossett & Dunlap, 1977).

52. The final sentence translates roughly as, "—sentence three days bread and water, solution, suspended, reduction one grade, ninety day probation in reference bread and water, solution, only" (Heinlein, *Citizen of the Galaxy*, 186).

53. Heinlein, *Star Beast*, 222–23.

54. In *Starship Troopers*, for example, Heinlein makes explicit the connection between the patriarchal organization of family and the military. In the final pages of the novel, our hero, who has completed his training as a marine, encounters his newly

enlisted father. The difficult relationship that had existed between father and son in civilian life is resolved by their common military service (Robert A. Heinlein, *Starship Troopers* [New York: Putnam, 1959]). The strength of the general cultural desire to exclude women from high office can be measured by comparing Heinlein's military systems with Edward Bellamy's gender-segregated industrial army. Bellamy imagines equality of service in his industrial army of the future. However, no member of the women's auxiliary may be elected to the presidency. That privilege is reserved for men (Edward Bellamy, *Looking Backward, 2000–1887* [New York: Penguin Books, 1982 (1888)]).

55. Heinlein, "Delilah and the Space Rigger," *PTT*, 171.

56. Heinlein, *The Rolling Stones*, 19.

57. Dr. Mader is obviously a thinly disguised reference to anthropologist Dr. Margaret Mead (1901–78).

58. Heinlein, *Citizen*, 92.

59. Ibid.

60. At one point in his correspondence with his agent during the time he was producing the Scribner juveniles, Heinlein calls his young readers, "my boys and girls" (Heinlein, *Grumbles*, 63).

61. Heinlein, *Star Beast*, 163.

62. Heinlein, *Citizen*, 98–101, 124.

63. Heinlein, *Have Space Suit—Will Travel* (New York: Charles Scribner's, 1958), 50.

64. Heinlein, "The Menace from Earth," *PTT*, 341, 344–45. Her mother, by the way, though a "mathematical chemist," is not as bright as the daughter—or so Holly says.

65. Heinlein, *Red Planet*, 151.

66. Heinlein, *Between Planets*, 211.

67. The *Star Trek* franchise reinforces this idea by the convention of awarding its female officers the honorific "sir." This innovation was established in the second *Star Trek* film, *Star trek II: The Wrath of Khan*, dir. Nicholas Meyer, Paramount, 1982.

68. Heinlein, *Star Beast*, 249.

69. Heinlein, *Have Space Suit—Will Travel*, 83.

Chapter 4

1. Peter F. Hamilton, *The Reality Dysfunction, Part 2: Expansion* (New York: Warner Books, 1977), 485.

2. Arthur C. Clarke, *Astounding Days: A Science Fictional Autobiography* (New York: Bantam Books, 1990), 10.

3. Sam Moskowitz, *Seekers Of Tomorrow* (Cleveland, Oh.: The World Publishing Company, 1966), 376.

4. A list of people associated with the BIS in the early years includes Robert Esnault-Pelterie, the French Aviation pioneer; the Count and Countess von Zeppelin, the son and daughter-in-law of the creator of the rigid airship; and the Austrian engineer Friedrich Schniedl, who did pioneering work in rocket mail (Frank H. Winter, *Prelude*

to the Space Age—The Rocket Societies: 1924–1940 [Washington, D.C.: Smithsonian Institution Press, 1983], 89). Another, and more surprising name, is that of George Bernard Shaw.

5. Arthur C. Clarke, "Extraterrestrial Relays: Can Rocket Stations Give World-wide Radio Coverage?" reprinted in *Voices from the Sky: Previews of the Coming Space Age* (New York: Harper & Row, 1965), 233–41.

6. Many of those papers are reprinted in *Ascent to Orbit: A Scientific Autobiography: The Technical Writings of Arthur C. Clarke* (New York: Wiley, 1984).

7. Arthur C. Clarke, *Interplanetary Flight* (New York: Harper & Row, 1951), xi.

8. Arthur C. Clarke, *The Exploration of Space* (New York: Harper & Brothers, 1951).

9. Arthur C. Clarke, "Space Flight and the Spirit of Man," *Voices from the Sky*, 3.

10. Ibid.

11. Arthur C. Clarke, "The Challenge of the Spaceship," *Journal of the British Interplanetary Society* 6, no. 3 (December 1946): 66.

12. Vonda McIntyre echoes this sentiment almost forty years later in *Starfarers*, her feminist revision of the astrofuturist genre (Vonda N. McIntyre, *Starfarers* [New York: Ace Books, 1989]).

13. For a survey of the theme of empire in the popular literature of the late nineteenth and early twentieth centuries in Britain and America, see Martin Green, *Dreams of Adventure, Deeds of Empire* (New York: Basic Books, 1979). My reading of Clarke is informed by Green's valuable analysis of the WASP hero in adventure literature and history.

14. "Man's Empire of Tomorrow" was published in its winter 1938 issue (Moskowitz, 378).

15. Clarke, "Challenge," 72.

16. In a 1961 article, Clarke repeated these words for the American Rocket Society's Space Flight Report to the nation. But in deference to his audience and to the politics of a cold war–inflected space age, he dropped the anti-imperial rhetoric and any hint of criticism of the United States. With the growing importance of the American space program to astrofuturist hopes, even mild criticism might have been inconvenient. The article was later reprinted in *Reader's Digest* (Clarke, "Space Flight and the Spirit of Man," 1–11).

17. Clarke, "Challenge," 77.

18. Clarke, "Space Flight and the Spirit of Man," 8. Clarke cites William James as the originator of the notion that a moral equivalent to war is necessary.

19. Arthur C. Clarke, "Prelude to Space," reprinted in *Prelude to Mars* (New York: Harcourt, Brace & World, 1965), 79. Author's emphasis.

20. Ibid., 81–82. Author's emphasis.

21. The Interplanetary concept, along with supporting arguments, was presented by Clarke during discussions held in 1947 among BIS members. Those discussions occurred during the time Clarke was secretly writing *Prelude to Space* (A. V. Cleaver, "The Interplanetary Project," *Journal of the British Interplanetary Society* 7 [January 1948]: 21–39).

22. Clarke, "Prelude to Space," 18.

23. Clarke inherits this assumption from sources well inside the mainstream of British and American political thought. Both Theodore Roosevelt and Winston Churchill maintained the primacy of white, English-speaking peoples in their speeches and their literary work. Both men were influenced by Francis Galton's eugenicist reading of Darwinian evolution. See Theodore Roosevelt, *Biological Analogies in History* (New York: Oxford University Press, 1910) and Sir Winston Churchill, *A History of English-Speaking Peoples* (New York: Dodd, Mead, 1956–58).

24. In British imperial parlance, the words "black" and the pejorative "nigger" were interchangeable markers for African and Indian subjects. For instance, see its use in the portrayal of India in children's literature in Kathryn Castle, *Britannia's Children: Reading Colonialism Through Children's Books and Magazines* (Manchester: Manchester University Press, 1996), 44.

25. Clarke, "Prelude to Space," 125.

26. The power of this convention to organize popular narratives of the space frontier is represented on the diverse bridge of the Star Trek television show *Enterprise* (2001). Its two people of color, an African American man and Asian American woman, are ensigns. They are brilliant professionals who must learn from their white superiors before they can assume positions of command. Following the legacy of boys' adventure and exploration literature, we are prompted to assume the competence of the white men who command on the space frontier without seeing their education.

27. Clarke, "Prelude to Space," 38.

28. "Boffin," British slang for "scientific expert," as in the character Noddy Boffin from Charles Dickens's 1865 novel, *Our Mutual Friend*.

29. Arthur C. Clarke, *View from Serendip: Speculations on Space, Science and the Sea, Together with Fragments of an Equatorial Autobiography* (New York: Random House, 1977), 12.

30. Arthur C. Clarke, *1984: Spring, A Choice of Futures* (New York: Ballantine Books, 1984), 192.

31. Ibid., 188.

32. Leonard Woolf, *Growing: An Autobiography of the Years 1904–1911* (San Diego: Harcourt, Brace and Jovanovich, 1975), 193–94.

33. Clarke, *1984*, 191.

34. Arthur C. Clarke, *Voices from the Sky: Previews of the Coming Space Age* (New York: Harper & Row, 1965), 137–38. For Clarke's advocacy of and participation in educational satellite programs in India and Sri Lanka, see "Satellites and Saris" and "To the Committee on Space Science" in *The View from Serendip*.

35. Arthur C. Clarke, *Arthur C. Clarke's July 20, 2019: Life in the 21st Century* (New York: Omni/Macmillan Publishing, 1986).

36. The science-fictional sleight of hand that turns the colony into a product of extraterrestrial origin rather than of human design is a generic convenience and, perhaps, a result of Clarke's skepticism that O'Neill's speculative structures are a project for the near future. Clarke mentioned his reservations about the new technological platform introduced by O'Neill in the mid-1970s during a 1975 testimony before the House Committee on Space Science and Applications (Arthur C. Clarke, *The View from Serendip*, 207–8).

37. See Leo Marx's paradigmatic study of that transformation, *Machine in the Garden: Technology and the Pastoral Ideal in America* (New York: Oxford University Press, 1979).

38. When, for example, a woman is promoted to Admiral of the Cylindrical Sea (Clarke, *Rendezvous with Rama* [New York: Harcourt Brace Jovanovich, 1973], 105).

39. By the early 1970s, the Japanese had replaced the Germans in the American popular imagination as the technical wizards of the developed world, so much so that many contemporary Asian characters in popular literature are now machine-like rather than merely inscrutable. As Norton is, however, fully assimilated within a Western future his technical competence cannot be viewed as either threat or condescending stereotype. It is simply part of the education of any competent spaceman.

40. Clarke, *Rama*, 75–76.

41. Two science-fiction anthologies helped define the debate within the science-fiction community during the 1980s and 1990s: *There Will Be War* (New York: Tor Books, 1983), edited by Jerry Pournelle and *There Won't Be War* (New York: Tor Books, 1991), edited by Harry Harrison and Bruce McAllister.

42. Clarke, *Rama*, 75.

43. For more on McIntyre's contribution to astrofuturism, see De Witt Douglas Kilgore, "Changing Regimes: Vonda N. McIntyre's Parodic Astrofuturism," *Science-Fiction Studies* 27, no. 2 (July 2000): 256–77.

44. Steele's cycle of novels chronicling a working-class space future begins with *Orbital Decay* (New York: Ace Books, 1989).

45. Butler's imaginative engagement with the political and physical shape of race, gender, and species in a space future that humanity does not control may be found in the novels *Dawn* (1987), *Adulthood Rites* (1988), and *Imago* (1989). Together these novels are known as the *Xenogenesis Trilogy*.

46. Lee is an MIT graduate and a space-systems engineer who worked on the Viking program and was chief engineer of Project Galileo. On learning that Lee greatly admired *Rendezvous with Rama*, Clarke flabbergasted him with the suggestion that they work together on a sequel. With Lee writing and Clarke editing, they undertook a three-novel partnership that took five years to complete (Gentry Lee, "Happy Birthday, Arthur," *Space.com*, 15 December 2000, cited 17 October 2001 <http://www.space.com/opinionscolumns/gentrylee/gentry_lee_001215.html>).

47. Arthur C. Clarke and Gentry Lee, *Rama II* (New York: Bantam Books, 1990), 10.

48. Before the 1970s, the narrative centrality of white men held true even in books written by women. See, for example, Leigh Brackett's far future series collected in *The Book of Skaith: the Adventures of Eric John Stark* (Garden City, N.Y.: Doubleday, 1976).

49. Arthur C. Clarke and Gentry Lee, *The Garden of Rama* (New York: Bantam Books, 1991), 427.

50. Arthur C. Clarke, *The Fountains of Paradise* (New York: Harcourt Brace Jovanovich, 1978).

51. This, of course, flies in the face of the strong mystical strains that exist in Western culture. One of the most fascinating aspects of Anglo-American popular culture in the nineteenth and twentieth centuries is its periodic return to a chivalrous and

fantastic medievalism. The work of Sir Walter Scott, the utopianism of William Morris, the recent rise of various new age witcheries, the popularity of the contemporary urban fantasy novel, and the television show "Beauty and the Beast" (1987–90) are all aspects of the phenomenon. There are always those who persist in the belief that there is more in the world that can be accounted for by the standards of enlightened rationalism. In American popular culture, the medieval, broadly speaking, has become the repository for all that is not rational in the West. For an excellent account of how a brand of medievalism operates in contemporary media culture, see Henry Jenkins's chapter on *Beauty and the Beast* in his *Textual Poachers: Television Fans and Participatory Culture* (London: Routledge, 1992).

52. Arthur C. Clarke and Gentry Lee, *The Garden of Rama* (New York: Bantam Books, 1991), 33.

53. Ibid., 141. Clarke and Lee's liberalism allows them to assume (as a conservative such as Pournelle cannot) that someone such as Nicole des Jardins could serve to bridge the gap between groups of people—that is, that blacks and women can assimilate into the privileged space of white, male, Western knowledge.

54. Clarke and Lee, *Garden of Rama*, 219–20.

55. See Chapter five in this book.

56. Clarke and Lee, *Garden of Rama*, 143–44.

57. Ibid., 175.

58. See Philip K. Dick, *Do Androids Dream of Electric Sheep?* (New York: Ballantine Books, 1982 [1968]), the motion picture made from the novel, *Blade Runner* (dir. Ridley Scott, 1982), and Marge Piercy, *He, She and It* (New York: Alfred A. Knopf, 1991).

59. Clarke and Lee, *Garden of Rama*, 302.

60. Ellipsis in original text.

61. Arthur C. Clarke, *Imperial Earth* (New York: Bantam Books, 1976), 117.

62. Ibid.

63. Harriet Beecher Stowe, *Uncle Tom's Cabin* (New York: W. W. Norton, 1994 [1852]), 376.

Chapter 5

1. Quoted in George Dyson, *Project Orion: The True Story of the Atomic Spaceship* (New York: Henry Holt, 2002), 186–87.

2. By "economic movement," I do not mean economic expansion, but the opportunity for radically changing relations of production.

3. Charles Elkins notices this trend in science fiction in an important essay published in *Science-Fiction Studies* (Charles Elkins, "An Approach to the Social Functions of American Science Fiction," *Science-Fiction Studies* 4 [November 1977]: 228–32). Mack Reynolds is a significant exception to this rule. In a series he started in the early 1960s called the "North Africa Trilogy," he imagined a future in which representatives of the peoples of the African diaspora return to the continent and, with the help of native Africans, build a nation that successfully challenges the colonial domination of the

West (Mack Reynolds, *Black Man's Burden, Border, Breed nor Birth,* and *The Best Ye Breed* [New York: Ace Books, 1961, 1962, and 1978]).

4. Frederick I. Ordway III and Mitchell Sharpe, *The Rocket Team* (New York: Thomas Y. Crowell, 1979), 455.

5. See Camille Bacon-Smith, *Science Fiction Culture* (Philadelphia: University of Pennsylvania Press, 2000). Bacon-Smith's ethnography is particularly informative about the transformative effect that feminist women had on the genre.

6. Carole S. Briggs, *Women in Space: Reaching the Last Frontier* (Minneapolis: Lerner Publications Company, 1988), 21–22. See also Khephra Burns and William Miles, *Black Stars in Orbit: NASA's African American Astronauts* (San Diego: Gulliver Books/Harcourt, Brace, and Company, 1995) and Elwood Exley, Jr., "The New Astronaut Breed," *Space World* (November 1981), 18–21.

7. Peter Nicholls, "Politics" and Brian Stableford, "Social Darwinism," (SFE), 467–69, 553–54. Gregory E. Rutledge notes that according to critic David G. Hartwell, Campbell expressed a "white supremacist bent" in *Astounding Stories* (Gregory E. Rutledge, "Futurist Fiction and Fantasy: The *Racial* Establishment," *Callalloo* 24, no. 1 [2001]: 241–42).

8. The first full Earth picture was taken by an ATS satellite in November 1967 (Stewart Brand, ed., *The Last Whole Earth Catalog: Access to Tools* [Menlo Park, Calif.: Portola Institute, 1971] and Frank White, *The Overview Effect: Space Exploration and Human Evolution* [Boston: Houghton-Mifflin, 1987]).

9. R. Buckminster Fuller, *Critical Path* (New York: St. Martin's Press, 1981), 55.

10. *Big Blue Marble* is a children's educational program that aired on PBS from 1974 to 1983. It closely followed the political and ethical perspectives of the internationalism suggested by the various full Earth photographs taken during the 1960s space program.

11. Michael A. G. Michaud, *Reaching for the High Frontier: The American Prospace Movement, 1972–84* (New York: Praeger, 1986) 42.

12. Donella H. Meadows, Dennis L. Meadows, Jørgen Randers, and William W. Behrens, III, *The Limits to Growth: A Report for the Club of Rome's Project on the Predicament of Mankind* (New York: Universe Books, 1972). Some members of the original MIT team refined and extended their analysis in the early 1990s. See Donella Meadows, Dennis L. Meadows, and Jørgen Randers, *Beyond the Limits: Confronting Global Collapse, Envisioning a Sustainable Future* (Mills, Vt.: Chelsea Green Publications, 1992).

13. Meadows, *Limits to Growth,* 183.

14. Ben Bova, "The Role of Science Fiction," *Science Fiction, Today and Tomorrow,* ed. Reginald Bretnor (Baltimore, Md.: Penguin Books, 1974), 4.

15. Meadows, *Limits to Growth,* 171.

16. See, for example, the articles comprising *Models of Doom: A Critique of the Limits to Growth,* ed. H. S. D. Cole, Christopher Freeman, Marie Jahoda, and K. L. R. Pavitt (New York: Universe Books, 1973).

17. Carl Sagan's expression of liberal, even leftist views, in his scientific work, popular science, and science fiction has raised many hackles on the right. "Radical Saganism" is used by critics to describe his support for the robotic exploration of space

(as opposed to manned exploration), his notion that science might not be the exclusive property of Western culture, his opposition to nuclear weapons and militarism, and his novelistic presentation of racial others and white women rising to Nobel-class levels in international science. For a representative hostile critique of his 1985 novel *Contact*, see Daniel Seligman, "Saganism," *Fortune*, 25 November 1985, 152. Janet Morris's disgust with Sagan's work on nuclear-winter scenarios seems to have as much to do with finding grounds for continuing to write postholocaust stories as any real concern with the validity of his science. See her "Introduction," *Afterwar* (New York: Baen Books, 1985), 7.

18. Bova, "The Role of Science Fiction," 4.

19. Robert Fishman, *Bourgeois Utopias: The Rise and Fall of Suburbia* (New York: Basic Books, 1987), x.

20. Gerard K. O'Neill, *The High Frontier: Human Colonies in Space* (New York: Bantam Books, 1978), 276.

21. Ibid., 278.

22. In *Science in American Society*, George Daniels describes how important finding a social mission was to the professionalization of American science in the nineteenth and twentieth centuries. Arguments for its moral significance, material utility, and centrality to social and political reform influenced American notions of its value as a cultural project (George Daniels, *Science in American Society: A Social History* [New York: Alfred A. Knopf, 1971]).

23. Bergaust describes the "joke" during his discussion of the *Physics Today* paper that introduced O'Neill's concepts to the scientific community (Erik Bergaust, *Wernher von Braun* [Washington, D.C.: National Space Institute, 1976], 538–39).

24. O'Neill, *High Frontier*, 279.

25. See, for example, Todd Gitlin, *The Sixties: Years of Hope, Days of Rage* (New York: Bantam Books, 1987), 429–30.

26. Brand, *The Last Whole Earth Catalog*. The catalog uses Earth and Moon pictures taken during various Apollo missions to signal a new sense of the physical environment and to foster the creation of appropriate communities. It directly acknowledges the utility of science and technology to utopian plans and communitarian adventures.

27. O'Neill, *High Frontier*, 284.

28. Ibid., 292.

29. According to an O'Neill presentation to members of Congress, NASA and the NSF contributed $40,000 to the development of space colonization in 1975 (Dr. Gerard K. O'Neill. "Space Colonization and Energy Supply to the Earth: Testimony of Dr. Gerard K. O'Neill Before the Sub-committee on Space Science and Applications of the Committee on Science and Technology, United States House of Representatives, July 23, 1975," *Space Colonies*, ed. Steward Brand [San Francisco: Waller Press/Penguin, 1977], 18). NASA also supported a study of the idea by contributing $100,000 at its NASA/Ames research seminar during summer 1975 (Brand, 26).

30. O'Neill, *High Frontier*, 300.

31. Michaud, 87–88.

32. Art Kleiner and Stewart Brand, *News That Was News: 1974–1984* (San Francisco: North Point Press, 1986), xii.

33. Ibid., xi.

34. Brand, *Space Colonies*, 6.

35. Ibid., 34. Despite his sympathy with flower children, Mumford's relationship with Brand and the Whole Earth movement was a bit testy. In response to an invitation to Whole Earth's tenth-anniversary celebration, he wrote, "Thank you! But to escape the Whole Earth Jamboree I'd buy a one-way ticket on a spaceship to Saturn" (Art Kleiner, "Appendix: A History of CoEvolution Quarterly," in Kleiner and Brand, 333).

36. Brand, *Space Colonies*, 36.

37. Ibid., 40.

38. Freeman Dyson has suggested that we might detect evidence of extraterrestrial civilizations by looking for the tremendous infrared sources that would result from a highly advanced technical civilization's efficient use of its sun's energy. Dyson assumes that the evolution of a civilization can be measured by its ability to divert environmental resources for its own ends. According to his typology, the Dyson sphere would be characteristic of a type II civilization, and complete control of resources on a galaxy-wide level would indicate a type III civilization. Humanity is at somewhere less than a type I stage, as we do not yet control efficiently the resources available on this planet and certainly not to any single benign purpose (Freeman Dyson, *Disturbing the Universe* [New York: Harper Colophon Books, 1981], 212).

39. O'Neill, "The High Frontier," in Brand, *Space Colonies*, 8.

40. During a conference, the idea seemed so good that a participant who had just that morning been in a gas line gleefully remarked, "We can put the Middle East out of business!" (O'Neill, "The High Frontier," in Brand, *Space Colonies*, 18). O'Neill, of course, took a more moderate view. However, the comment does undermine his promise that access to space resources will automatically improve human relations.

41. O'Neill, *High Frontier*, 183.

42. Paul R. Ehrlich, *The Population Bomb* (New York: Ballantine Books, 1978). See also *The Silent Explosion* by Indiana University English professor Philip Appleman, with a foreword by the eminent naturalist and science writer Julian Huxley (Philip Appleman, *The Silent Explosion* [Boston: Beacon Press, 1966]).

43. O'Neill, *High Frontier*, 260–61.

44. Ibid., 234.

45. Stewart Brand, "Is the Surface of a Planet Really the Right Place for an Expanding Technological Civilization?: Interviewing Gerard O'Neill," in Brand, *Space Colonies*, 28.

46. Carl Sagan, "Comments on O'Neill's Space Colonies," in Brand, *Space Colonies*, 42.

47. Carl Sagan, *Broca's Brain: Reflections on the Romance of Science* (New York: Ballantine Books, 1980 [1978]), 44.

48. O'Neill, *High Frontier*, 234.

49. Wendell Berry, "Comments on O'Neill's Space Colonies," in Brand, *Space Colonies*, 36.

50. Allen M. Steele, *Clarke County, Space* (New York: Ace Books, 1990), 91. The term "biosphere" indicates an enclosed, self-sustaining environment. The most com-

plete biosphere known is that in which we live. See Dorian Sagan, *Biospheres: Metamorphosis of Planet Earth* (New York: Bantam Books, 1990).

51. Fishman, 129.

52. O'Neill, *High Frontier*, 273.

53. For a good evaluation of Patrick Geddes' ideas, see Rosalind Williams, "Lewis Mumford as a Historian of Technology in *Technics and Civilization*," *Lewis Mumford: Public Intellectual*, ed. Thomas P. Hughes and Agatha C. Hughes Oxford: Oxford University Press, 1990).

54. O'Neill, *High Frontier*, 84–85.

55. Current work in the creation of biospheres suggests that because of the complexity of the ecosystem in which we live, it will not be as easy to craft a space colony to environmental order. For example, we might be constrained by the need to replicate the rain forests and deserts required for a self-maintaining, recycling environment. Much of the raw material—insects, bacteria, and so forth—would have to be imported from wherever they occur on the Earth.

56. K. Eric Drexler and T. A. Heppenheimer joined O'Neill's space-colony and space manufacturing movement as students in the 1970s and went on to become important public advocates for the physicist's technological proposals. Drexler is now better known for his work in the new science of nanotechnology. In his several popular technical books on the subject, he articulates an expansive futurism that enumerates the prospects and dangers of molecular engineering. See T. A. Heppenheimer, *Colonies in Space* (New York: Warner Books, 1977) and Drexler and Heppenheimer, "On the Feasibility of Small Power Satellites," *Journal of Energy* 1 (May-June 1977): 200.

57. For Carl Sagan's interest, see his comments in Brand's space-colony debate (Brand, *Space Colonies*, 42). Freeman Dyson is, as of this writing, president of the Space Studies Institute Board of Directors.

58. Gerard K. O'Neill, *2081: A Hopeful View of the Human Future* (New York: Simon and Schuster, 1981), 265–66.

59. O'Neill, *High Frontier*, 234.

60. O'Neill, *2081*, 105.

61. O'Neill, *High Frontier*, 237.

62. O'Neill, *2081*, 105.

63. David M. Potter, *People of Plenty: Economic Abundance and the American Character* (Chicago: University of Chicago Press, 1954).

64. O'Neill follows astrofuturist and science-fiction convention by naming his fictional ship after a notable member of the spaceflight community, engineer and science writer Dandridge M. Cole.

65. O'Neill patterns the *Cole*'s amenities after those on a first-class ocean liner. In his explanatory notes for Rawson's account, he notes that one of the benefits of space travel will be that "it will restore the elbowroom, the leisure, and the time for human interaction that the older generation tells us was so wonderful about the age of ocean liners" (O'Neill, *2081*, 122).

66. Joseph J. Corn and Brian Horrigan, *Yesterday's Tomorrows: Past Visions of the American Future* (New York: Summit Books, 1984).

67. For example, the twentieth-century image of the future as cities built around the automobile found expression in the work of designers such as Norman Bel Geddes. See, for instance, his "Futurama" exhibit for the General Motors pavilion at the 1939 New York World's Fair. Since O'Neill was born in Brooklyn, New York, in 1927, it is very likely that he, like so many other children of his generation, was exposed to the industrial futurism Bel Geddes mounted in nearby Flushing. There can be little doubt that the earthbound forecasts of the 1930s and 1940s had a great influence on O'Neill's futurism of the 1970s and 1980s. Even Bel Geddes's attempt to promote industrial design as a profession with a public service mission beyond the needs of its clients has its resonances in O'Neill's own ideals for space science and engineering (Arthur J. Pulos, *American Design Ethic: A History of Industrial Design* [Cambridge, Mass.: MIT Press, 1986], 352).

68. Paul and Percival Goodman, *Communitas: Ways of Livelihood and Means of Life* (New York: Vintage Books, 1960 [1947]), 125–52.

69. Paolo Soleri, *Arcology: The City in the Image of Man* (Cambridge, Mass.: MIT Press, 1969).

70. O'Neill, *High Frontier*, 234.

71. O'Neill, *2081*, 117.

72. See William S. Kowinski, *The Malling of America: An Inside Look at the Great Consumer Paradise* (New York: Morrow, 1985) and Michael Sorkin, ed., *Variations on a Theme Park: The New American City and the End of Public Space* (New york: Hill and Wang, 1994 [1992]).

73. O'Neill, *2081*, 205.

Chapter 6

1. Quoted in Daniel S. Goldin, "Statement of Daniel S. Goldin, Administrator National Aeronautics and Space Administration before the Subcommittee on Space, Committee on Science, House of Representatives," 1 October 1998 (database online) cited 30 June 2002 <http://legislative.nasa.gov/hearings/gold10-1.html>.

2. Ben Bova, *The High Road* (New York: Pocket Books, 1983), 218.

3. Ibid., 29.

4. Ben Bova, "President's Message," *Space Advocate*, October 1987, A8.

5. Ben Bova, *Starpeace: Assured Survival* (New York: Tor/Tom Doherty Associates, 1986 [1984]), 44.

6. John Clute, "Haldeman, Joe (William)," SFE, 269 and Brian Aldiss with David Wingrove, *Trillion Year Spree: The History of Science Fiction* (New York: Atheneum, 1986), 370–71.

7. *Contemporary Authors*, New Revision Series, Volume 11, s.v. "Bova, Ben(jamin William)," by Thomas Wiloch and Jean W. Ross.

8. Michael A. G. Michaud, *Reaching for the High Frontier: The American Prospace Movement* (New York: Praeger, 1986), 49 and Erik Bergaust, *Wernher von Braun* (Washington, D.C.: National Space Institute, 1976), 526–29.

9. Bova, "President's Message," *Space Advocate*, January 1988, 8 and "President's Message," *Space Advocate*, August 1988, 7.

10. Michaud, 53.

11. The term "managerial liberal" is used by Todd Gitlin in his excellent history *The Sixties* as a description of John F. Kennedy and the type of men he gathered around him (Todd Gitlin, *The Sixties: Years of Hope, Days of Rage* [New York: Bantam Books, 1987]).

12. Bova, "Society Pages," *Space World*, December 1986, 40.

13. In the parlance of the 1960s, "commitment" was opposed to alienation. It was an indicator of whether or not the individual believed that he or she could change the world or help change it. Those who were committed believed they could; those who were not, did not. The equivalent term for the 1980s (at least in the African American community) is "down," as in: "Are you down for the cause?" 1960s equivalent: "Are you committed to the cause?"

14 Bova, "President's Message," *Space Advocate*, January 1988, 8.

15. Bova, "Insight," *Space World*, February 1986, 40 and "Society Pages," *Space World*, December 1986, 40.

16. Bova, "Society Pages," *Space World*, December 1986, 40. See also "President's Message," *Space Advocate*, April 1988, 8.

17. A number of factions split off from the NSS to form independent organizations. For instance, Bruce Murray and Carl Sagan founded The Planetary Society because of their dissatisfaction with the way that the NSS's inability to meet the needs of scientists (Michaud, 51).

18. Bova, "President's Message," *Space Advocate*, July 1988, 6.

19. Bova, "President's Message," *Space Advocate*, October 1987, A8.

20. Bova, "Society Pages," *Space World*, January 1987, 40. OMB is the Office of Management and Budget of the U.S. government's Executive Branch. Another acronym—not so flattering—is TOMB.

21. Bova, *The High Road*.

22. This identification of an antitechnology bias in the left comes in the main from radical opposition to military technology and the often cruel dislocations occasioned by large-scale industrial capitalism. To say that the left, however, is inherently Luddite is reductive. Appropriate technology, virtual reality, biospheres, and personal computers are all technologies whose initial champions came from the left. Their advocates hoped they would trigger changes leading to an equitable political and economic order.

23. Bova, *The High Road*, 41.

24. Ibid., 40.

25. Thomas Hine, *Populuxe* (New York: Alfred A. Knopf, 1986), 38.

26. Bova, *The High Road*, 40.

27. Print Project, *The Techno/Peasant Survival Manual* (New York: Bantam Books, 1980), 1–5.

28. Bova, *The High Road*, 44.

29. In the 1980s, science-fiction writers such as William Gibson and Bruce Sterling produced futures in which earthly wealth is held by powerful individuals who

direct vast corporations from their orbital havens. In these futures, wealth does not "trickle-down" from space either to the First or Third Worlds. Rather, the world becomes a ghetto in which the poor, the unlucky, and their predators compete to survive. This view of the future became a fixture in the strand of science fiction called "cyberpunk," whose authors represented an insurgency within the science-fiction community (William Gibson, *Neuromancer* [New York: Ace Books, 1984] and Bruce Sterling, ed., *Mirrorshades: the Cyberpunk Anthology* [New York: Ace Books, 1986]).

30. Ben Bova, *The Kinsman Saga* (New York: Tor/Tom Doherty Associates, 1988), v.

31. For the space future as a paradise of millionaires, see James P. Hogan, *Voyage From Yesteryear* (Garden City, N.Y.: Nelson Doubleday, 1982).

32. Knowledge of the history of African Americans in the military would justify his paranoia. See Bernard C. Nalty, *Strength for the Fight: A History of Black Americans in the Military* (New York: Free Press, 1986).

33. Bova, *Kinsman Saga*, 26.

34. In *The Kinsman Saga*, an African American is indeed elected president of the United States. A Roxbury politician, his politics and personality seem somewhat akin to Ronald Reagan's.

35. Ben Bova, *Star Peace: Assured Survival* (New York: Tor Books, 1986).

36. Bova, *Kinsman Saga*, 260–61.

37. The shade of George Washington is twice invoked to authorize Chet Kinsman as a revolutionary hero (Bova, *Kinsman Saga*, 534, 538).

38. Ben Bova, *Kinsman Saga*, 402–4, 386–88, 356–58.

39. R. Buckminster Fuller, *Utopia or Oblivion: the Prospects for Humanity* (New York: Bantam Books, 1969).

40. This nostalgia for the road not taken in the American space program is also apparent in Stephen Baxter's late 1990s novels giving Apollo-program technology a role beyond the Earth-Moon space race (Stephen Baxter, *Titan* [New York: Harper Prism, 1998] and *Voyage* [New York: Harper Prism, 1997]).

41. The failure of the Mars Polar Lander in December 1999 forced NASA and the Jet Propulsion Laboratory to reevaluate the merits of the "cheaper, faster, better" policy ("NASA to Re-evaluate Entire Mars Program," *Exploring Mars: In-depth Reports*, CNN.com, December 1999, cited 15 February 2002 <http://www.cnn.com/1999/TECH/space/12/07/mars.review/>).

42. See Robert Zubrin, *The Case for Mars: The Plan to Settle the Red Planet and Why We Must* (New York: Free Press, 1996), with a foreword by Arthur C. Clarke.

43. Ibid., xxi–xvii.

44. It is possible to read this Martian future as multiracial/cultural/national rather than one that privileges the Navaho. The point here is that the directive vision is supplied by a Navaho who embraces his heritage and imagines a future in which it thrives.

45. Stuart Udall, *The Quiet Crisis* (New York: Holt, Rinehart and Winston, 1963). The book includes an introduction by John F. Kennedy.

46. Jay McDonald, "Men on Mars, Women on Venus: Interview with Ben Bova," *BookPage: First Person* (June 1999), cited 19 April 2000 <http: www.bookpage.com/9906bp/ben_bova.html>.

47. Ibid.

48. Bova, *Mars* (New York: Bantam Books, 1993), 103–4.

49. Al thinks of himself as a Navaho but acts like an Anglo businessman. In the second Mars novel, he becomes a spirit guide to his grandson. The relationship between Jamie and Al is similar in function to that between Nicole des Jardins and her mother in *The Garden of Rama*.

50. When Al Waterman witnesses Jamie's moment, he exclaims, "The boy did it!" as though Jamie carried out a plan to make a political statement (Bova, *Mars*, 20). Although this lone moment introduces ambiguity, it is not sufficient to sustain an alternate reading of Bova's character.

51. George Lipsitz coins "possessive investment" to describe the material interest that whites have in a system that distributes goods and attributes along racial lines (George Lipsitz, *The Possessive Investment in Whiteness: How White People Profit from Identity Politics* [Philadelphia: Temple University Press, 1998]).

52. Bova, *Mars*, 281.

53. Ben Bova, *Return to Mars* (New York: Avon Books, 1999), 375. A space-tourism industry already exists and it is championed by entrepreneurs, not astrofuturists. See Jim Kingdon's "Space Tourism" web page, cited 10 June 2002 <www.panix.com /~kingdon/space/tourism.html>, and the Space Policy Institute website at George Washington University, cited 10 June 2002 <www.gwu.edu/~spi>.

54. Bova, *The High Road*, 213.

55. Ray Bradbury entertains this possibility for African Americans in two of his classic Mars short stories, "Way in the Middle of the Air" in *The Martian Chronicles* (New York: Bantam Books, 1987 [1950]) and "The Other Foot" in *The Illustrated Man* (New York: Bantam Books, 1969 [1951]).

56. I use "brotherhood" intentionally here. Absent from this chapter, because of limited space, is a reading of the troubling gender politics of *Return to Mars*. If included, it would question the validity of a symbolic racial resolution cemented by male camaraderie. Bova's hopes for a racial brotherhood of "alpha males" (313) requires that women validate the masculine desires that remain at the heart of Bova's space-future vision. Although women are present in the Mars project as fully accredited professionals, their sexuality must be policed and contained lest it provoke fraternal competition injurious to the enterprise.

Chapter 7

1. Michel Foucault, "Of Other Spaces: Utopias and Heterotopias," *Rethinking Architecture: A Reader in Cultural Theory*, ed. Neil Leach (London: Routledge, 1997), 356.

2. Raymond Williams, *Problems in Materialism and Culture: Selected Essays* (London: Verso, 1980), 203.

3. Ibid.

4. George Lipsitz, *The Possessive Investment in Whiteness: How White People Profit From Identity Politics* (Philadelphia: Temple University Press, 1998), 3.

5. Ibid., 22.

6. Tyson notes that there are four thousand astrophysicists in the nation (Neil de Grasse Tyson, *The Sky Is Not the Limit: Adventures of an Urban Astrophysicist* [New York: Doubleday, 2000], 124).

7. Ibid., 114.

8. Jeffrey Allen Tucker, "Studying the Works of Samuel R. Delany," *Wired for Books* (database online) cited 25 April 2002 <http://wiredforbooks.rog/scifi/delany.htm>.

9. Tyson, 12–14, 49.

10. Tyson writes, "I never told him this, but at every stage of my scientific career that followed, I have modelled my encounters with students after my first encounter with Carl" (28–29).

11. He notes, for instance, that freedoms allowed in one state may be denied in another. His account of Midwestern radio stations censoring "crap" from a Paul Simon song only hints at the violence often occasioned in the name of public morality and traditional inequalities (19–20).

12. During *Apollo* 11's flight to the Moon, the Southern Christian Leadership Conference (SCLC) demonstrated against the spending priorities that made it possible. They argued that humanity's first steps on the Moon "sharply contrasted with the failure of the United States to make a bold move to rectify chronic poverty" (Thomas R. Peake, *Keeping the Dream Alive: A History of the Southern Christian Leadership Conference from King to the Nineteen-Eighties* [New York: Peter Lang, 1987], 264).

13. Space scientists such as Carl Sagan and Bruce Murray, cofounders of the Planetary Society, were dismayed by the low priority of science at NASA during the 1970s. They preferred an exploration of space that did not rely exclusively on the vast systems required to sustain human life beyond Earth's atmosphere and prioritized science over flags and footprints (Bruce Murray, *Journey into Space: The First Thirty Years of Space Exploration* [New York: W. W. Norton, 1989], 21).

14. Foucault, 350–56.

15. Quoted in Edward W. Soja, *Thirdspace: Journeys to Los Angeles and Other Real-And-Imagined Places* (Cambridge, Mass.: Blackwell Publishers, 1996), 151.

16. Cornel West, "The Dilemma of the Black Intellectual," *Breaking Bread*, ed. bell hooks and Cornel West (Boston: South End Press, 1991), 143 and quoted in Soja, 153.

17. Allen Steele, *Orbital Decay* (New York: Ace Books, 1989), 236.

18. Norman Mailer, *Of a Fire on the Moon* (New York: Plume Books/New American Library, 1982) and Tom Wolfe, *The Right Stuff* (New York: Bantam Books, 1980). Mailer is particularly interested in the racial politics of the space program (Mailer, 134–39).

19. Steele, *Orbital Decay*, 277. Theoretical physicist Freeman Dyson, current president of the Space Studies Institute's Board of Directors, has argued that space should be colonized for the sake of the common man (Kenneth Brower, *The Starship and the Canoe* [New York: Holt, Rinehart and Winston, 1978], 242).

20. See, for example, Chris Claremont's work on Marvel Comics's "X-Men" (Kim Thompson, "Interview with Chris Claremont," *The Comics Journal*, August 1992, 71–87).

21. For excellent accounts of the creation of the technotopian spaces created in the world's fairs of the late nineteenth and early twentieth centuries, see Alan Trachtenberg, *The Incorporation of America: Culture and Society in the Gilded Age* (New York: Hill and Wang, 1982), 208–34 and Robert W. Rydell, *World of Fairs: The Century-of-Progress Expositions* (Chicago: University of Chicago Press, 1993).

22. For instance, in *Clarke County, Space,* Jenny Schor steps out of her husband's shadow to become the New Ark community's political leader and in *Lunar Descent,* Butch Peterson, the African American lunar geologist, does not give up her career to follow her man back to Earth (Allen Steele, *Clarke County, Space* [New York: Ace Books, 1990] and *Lunar Descent* [New York: Ace Books, 1991]).

23. The inclusion of minority actors within Steele's progressive space future does not extend to the inclusion of minority communities. The isolated characters function as representatives of difference within a plural community, in which class is the only significant source of conflict.

24. Steele, *Clarke County, Space,* 91.

25. For an explication of Vonda N. McIntyre's parodic astrofuturism, see my article, "Changing Regimes: Vonda N. McIntyre's Parodic Astrofuturism," *Science Fiction Studies* 27 (2000): 256–77.

26. The tradition of representation that I am addressing here is related only tangentially to the work produced by the black science-fiction and fantasy writers (e.g., Samuel R. Delany, Octavia E. Butler, Charles Saunders, and Stephen Barnes) working in the same period. As the writer who has insisted upon the paradigmatic and deciding presence of black female characters in science fiction, Butler is undoubtedly an important influence for McIntyre (see Butler's *Dawn* [1987], *Wild Seed* [1980], *Parable of the Sower* [1993], and *Parable of the Talents* [1998]). But influential as these writers have been in redefining the social and literary landscape of science fiction, they do not directly engage the astrofuturist project that orients McIntyre's work.

27. See, for instance, the admirable Dr. Nicole des Jardins in Arthur C. Clarke and Gentry Lee's *The Garden of Rama* (1991) and the brilliant and amoral terrorist Skida Thibodeau in Jerry Pournelle and S. M. Stirling's *Go Tell the Spartans* (1991).

28. Arthur C. Clarke's *Childhood's End* (1953) exemplifies this habit. In it, a black man, Jan Rodricks, eventually represents common humanity. When the human race evolves beyond earthly existence, he remains behind to witness the apotheosis. Rodricks is an emblem of Clarke's hope that the future will bring a final solution to the problem of race. But racism no longer exists in the future of this novel, only because racialized figures are left behind as the species evolves (Arthur C. Clarke, *Childhood's End* [New York: Harcourt, Brace and World, 1953], 213–14).

29. Thulani Davis makes this point in "The Future May Be Bleak, But It's Not Black."

30. See, for example, Nicole Des Jardins's saintly demeanor and philosophy in Clarke and Lee, *The Garden of Rama.*

31. Donna Haraway, *Primate Visions: Gender, Race and Nature in the World of Modern Science* (New York: Routledge, 1989), 28.

32. The persistence of this astrofuturist trope is evident in the Heinleinesque young adult novels recently published by Charles Sheffield, *The Billion Dollar Boy*

(New York: Tor Books, 1997) and James P. Hogan, *Outward Bound* (New York: Tor Books, 1999).

33. Vivian Sobchack, "The Virginity of Astronauts: Sex and the Science Film," *Alien Zone: Culture Theory and Contemporary Science Fiction Cinema*, ed. Annette Kuhn (New York: Verso, 1990), 103–15.

34. McIntyre's invention tropes Heinlein's reconfigured family structures on the high frontier: see the "line-marriages" of *The Moon Is a Harsh Mistress* (1966) and the "patrilocal matriarchy" of the Free Traders in *Citizen of the Galaxy* (1957). In *Aliens and Others*, Wolmark notes that McIntyre experimented with this as a challenge to Starfleet's patriarchal norms in *The Entropy Effect*, a *Star Trek* novel (Jenny Wolmark, *Aliens and Others: Science Fiction, Feminism and Postmodernism* [Iowa City: University of Iowa, 1994], 70–71). See also Diane S. Wood, "Family Ties in the Novels of Vonda N. McIntyre," *Extrapolation: A Journal of Science Fiction and Fantasy* 29, no. 2 (summer 1988): 112–27.

35. McIntyre, *Starfarers* (New York: Ace Books, 1989), 63.

36. Readers familiar with McIntyre's work will recognize Merit as a reworking of Merideth, an ungendered character in *Dreamsnake* (1978). According to Carolyn Wendell, Merideth is a feminist construct that makes gender "less important than one's personality and capabilities" (Carolyn Wendell, "Responsible Rebellion in Vonda N. McIntyre's *Fireflood, Dreamsnake,* and *Exile Waiting,*" *Critical Encounters II*, ed. Tom Staicar [New York: Ungar, 1977], 126).

37. In *Schismatrix*, space-faring humanity has transformed itself into posthuman factions: the genetically engineered Shapers and the cybernetically enhanced Mechanists. Conventional human differences have been superseded by increasingly powerful technological interventions into the very structure of biological life (Bruce Sterling, *Schismatrix* [New York: Ace Books, 1986]).

38. "Interview: Kim Stanley Robinson Answers Your Questions," *Science Fiction Weekly* 23, no. 2 (17 June 1996) (database online) cited 16 April 2002 <*http://www. scifi.com/sfw/issue23/interview.html*>.

39. Bud Foote, "A Conversation with Kim Stanley Robinson," *Science-Fiction Studies* 21 (1994): 56.

40. Kim Stanley Robinson with David Seed, "The Mars Trilogy: An Interview," *Foundation* 68 (autumn 1996): 77.

41. Robert Markey, Harrison Higgs, Michelle Kendrick, Helen Burgess, ed., "Interviews: Kim Stanley Robinson," *Red Planet: Scientific and Cultural Encounters with Mars* (Philadelphia: University of Pennsylvania Press, 2001), slide 6 of 10.

42. Dave Slusher, "Kim Stanley Robinson Interview," *Reality Break: A Talk Show of Fantastic Literature* (database online) cited 16 April 2002. <*http://realitybreak.sff.net/ archive/robinson.http*>. Robinson is a social ecologist influenced by the land ethic of Aldo Leopold and sympathetic to Murray Bookchin's social anarchism.

43. In his interview for *Science Fiction Weekly*, Robinson notes that he is "not a fan of the coherent future history that overarches several different books."

44. Kim Stanley Robinson, "Introduction," *Future Primitives: The New Ecotopias*, ed. Kim Stanley Robinson (New York: Tor Books, 1994), 11.

45. Emerson's poem commemorates the battles of Lexington and Concord in

1775: "Here once the embattled farmers stood / And fired the shot heard round the world" (Ralph Waldo Emerson, "Hymn: Sung at the Completion of the Concord Monument, April 19, 1836," *Collected Poems and Translations* [New York: The Library of America, 1994], 125).

46. Robinson, *Blue Mars* (New York: Bantam Books, 1997), 743.

47. Gerard Piel, *The Acceleration of History* (New York: Alfred A. Knopf, 1972), 40–41.

48. This is the kind of endlessly processional space future that H. G. Wells heralds in his 1936 film *Things to Come*. Robinson accepts the challenge implicit in the British socialist tradition that inspired Wells's literary utopian inventions. Raymond Williams, another important figure in that tradition, is also influential in Robinson's theory of a history that moves through a series of hegemonic blocs.

49. Robinson, *Blue Mars*, 744. Author's emphasis.

50. Robinson, *Future Primitives*, 9–10.

51. Ibid.

52. Foote, 55.

Index

Abernathy, Ralph D., 225

ABMA. *See* Alabama Ballistic Missile Agency

Across the Space Frontier, 67–68, 77

Adams, Brooks, 178

aerospace industry, 188, 189, 191, 192, 197, 212; history of, 6–7, 62, 72, 202

Africa, 137, 183, 184; images of Africans, 13, 100–103, 133–38, 139, 271 n.3

African Americans, 13, 16, 28, 37, 61; and criticism of space program, 198; images of, 139, 206–9; and science, 223–26; as writers, 243 n.31, 250 n.15, 281 n.26. *See also names of individuals*

AIAA. *See* American Institute of Aeronautics and Astronautics

Air Wonder Stories, 33, 34, 43

AIS. *See* American Interplanetary Society

Alabama Ballistic Missile Agency, 60

Aldiss, Brian W., 9

Alger, Horatio, 93, 195

alterity, 172, 176, 179, 181, 183, 185, 223, 233

Alvarez, Luis, 113

American Institute of Aeronautics and Astronautics, 161. *See also* American Interplanetary Society

American Interplanetary Society, 31, 35, 41–42, 161, 259 n.80; goal of, 32–33; and Goddard, 44; and Heinlein, 97; and Lasser, 43, 45. *See also* American Institute of Aeronautics and Astronautics; American Rocket Society

American Rocket Society, 31, 42, 59, 71, 76, 92. *See also* American Interplanetary Society

American Security Union, 45–46

Analog Science Fiction/Science Fact, 186, 189, 190

Annual Symposium on Space Travel, 76–77

Apollo program, 278 n.40, 280 n.12; aftermath of, 151, 156, 186, 189, 218; and

Clarke, 112, 127; and Heinlein, 93; and "Spaceship Earth," 153–54; and von Braun, 52

Archigram Group, 180

Argosy, 87

Armstrong, Neil, 202

Asian Americans, 24. *See also* Takei, George

Asians, East, image of, 130, 139

Asians, South, image of, 122–23, 130

Asimov, Isaac, 19, 83, 86, 87, 131

Astounding Science Fiction, 71–72, 86–87, 88, 91, 92, 153

astrofuturism: aerospace industry and, 72, 82, 115, 152; American experiment and, 51; class and, 132, 255 n.17; conventions of, 2–4, 65, 69, 83–84, 88, 178, 212, 218; definition of, 2, 4; development of, 31, 78–81, 109, 111, 148, 152, 156, 222; as discursive practice, 30, 221; as education, 64–65; as escape, 1, 143, 213; ethical promise of, 39; feminism, 230–33; first generation, 2, 51, 74, 91, 98, 127–28, 144, 151–52, 229; impact of, 29–30; imperialism and, 11, 98–99, 221; irony of vision, 51–52; and loss of faith, 112; military in, 187; origins of, 1, 3; as political struggle, 153; politics of, 3–5, 9, 28, 132, 159, 167, 200, 221, 227–28; posthumanism and, 233; race and, 8–11, 144, 203, 212–13, 223, 231–33; science and, 5–6, 82–83, 202; science fiction and, 59, 64–65, 76, 82–83; second generation, 78, 150–51, 159, 161, 174, 186; as "sense of wonder," 83; suburban ideals, 156; third generation, 226–27, 234, 238; utopianism and, 115, 138, 234, 237

astronautics, 63, 95, 114, 116

astronomy, 74–75, 115

atomic bomb, 58, 73, 118, 254 n.15, 262 n.21

Avco-Everett Research Laboaratory, 189

Acknowledgments

Although this book has a single author, it was not written in isolation. I am grateful to John L. Thomas, Joan Richards, Charles Nichols, and Robert Scholes, all of Brown University, for their early encouragement of my investigations into the cultural intersections of literature and science. My work has also been informed by a myriad of wide-ranging conversations over the years with several friends and colleagues: Davida K. Craig, Harry McKinley Williams, Yardena Rand, Joseph L. Brown, Patrick McNally and Madeleine Cody.

I am grateful for the kind and enthusiastic support that Daniel Horowitz, director of Smith's American Studies Program, has provided over the years. The tremendous personal and professional debts that I owe to Josephine D. Lee, Kevin Kinneavy, Leyla Ezdinli, and Ranu Samantrai date from our years in Northampton, Massachusetts. These words are only a small token of my esteem for their company and conduct.

At Washington University, St. Louis, I benefited from the sanity and solid judgment of my senior colleagues Garland E. Allen and Richard G. Fox. I am grateful to colleagues at Indiana University for valuable and defining exchanges too numerous to list here. I thank Joan Pong Linton, Nicholas M. Williams, Scott Russell Sanders, Patrick Brantlinger, Steven M. Watt, Paul Zietlow, and Albert Wertheim for providing support and good cheer when and where it mattered. Finally, sincere thanks are due to my editor, Peter Agree, for championing this project over many years.

My list of acknowledgments would not be complete without due recognition of the family that has made both me and my work possible. This book is dedicated to my grandfather, Cecil Douglass Bell, who stands for the extended family that he and my grandmother anchored in St. Louis during the second half of the last century. They laid the moral foundation that I hope this book represents. Their daughter, Yetta B. Kilgore, ignited the intellectual curiosity that has defined my life. To my father, De Witt Kilgore, Jr., I owe two parts of my name and an appreciation for the value of my commitments. It is to Ranu Samantrai that I owe the frame of my life and whatever grace my work has attained. Without her brilliant commentary and fearless editing, my future would not be written.

Portions of two chapters have been published previously, in substantially different form. An early version of Chapter 2 appeared as "Engineer's Dreams: Wernher von Braun, Willy Ley, and Astrofuturism in the 1950s," in *Canadian Review of American Studies* 27, no. 2 (1997): 103–31, and Chapter 7 contains a section of "Changing Regimes: Vonda N. McIntyre's Parodic Astrofuturism," *Science-Fiction Studies* 27, no. 2 (July 2000): 256–77. My thanks to these publications and their editors for permission to reprint.

CPSIA information can be obtained at www.ICGtesting.com
Printed in the USA
240398LV00001B/31/A